C0-ATI-876

CLEARING THE AIR

The Rise and Fall of Smoking
in the Workplace

Gregory Wood

ILR PRESS

AN IMPRINT OF

CORNELL UNIVERSITY PRESS   **ITHACA AND LONDON**

Copyright © 2016 by Cornell University

All rights reserved. Except for brief quotations in a review, this book, or parts thereof, must not be reproduced in any form without permission in writing from the publisher. For information, address Cornell University Press, Sage House, 512 East State Street, Ithaca, New York 14850.

First published 2016 by Cornell University Press
Printed in the United States of America

Library of Congress Cataloging-in-Publication Data

Names: Wood, Gregory, 1973– author.
Title: Clearing the air : the rise and fall of smoking in the workplace / Gregory Wood.
Description: Ithaca : ILR Press, an imprint of Cornell University Press, 2016. | Includes bibliographical references and index.
Identifiers: LCCN 2016012389 | ISBN 9781501704826 (cloth : alk. paper)
Subjects: LCSH: Smoking in the workplace—United States—History—20th century. | Antismoking movement—United States—History—20th century. | Smoking—Social aspects—United States—History—20th century.
Classification: LCC HF5549.5.S55 W66 2016 | DDC 331.25/6—dc23
LC record available at http://lccn.loc.gov/2016012389

Cornell University Press strives to use environmentally responsible suppliers and materials to the fullest extent possible in the publishing of its books. Such materials include vegetable-based, low-VOC inks and acid-free papers that are recycled, totally chlorine-free, or partly composed of nonwood fibers. For further information, visit our website at www.cornellpress.cornell.edu.

Contents

Acknowledgments

Many individuals made contributions that helped me complete this book. In particular, I warmly thank the members of the DC Working-Class History Seminar, whose enthusiastic responses to an early draft of chapter 4 encouraged me to think more deeply about space, power, and the body in the social and cultural history of the workplace, and I also thank the members of the Faculty Seminar in the Department of History at West Virginia University, who helped me to see greater nuance in my work on the 1987 US Gypsum smoking ban. I also am grateful to the anonymous reviewers for the *Journal of Social History* and *Labor: Studies in Working-Class History of the Americas*, and their respective editors, Peter Stearns and Leon Fink, for their probing and supportive comments on significant portions of chapters 2 and 3. Over the past few years, I have presented several papers at conferences and other events based on this research; I especially thank the audience members and commentators at the Rush Holt History Conference at West Virginia University (especially Elizabeth Fones-Wolf and Ken Fones-Wolf), the Pennsylvania History Conference, the Labor Studies Program at Michigan State University (especially John Beck), and the North American Labor History Conference at Wayne State University (especially Michael Goldfield) for their helpful insights related to various sections of the manuscript.

For their help with many of the sources used in *Clearing the Air*, I sincerely thank Jane Ingold and Richard Hart of Penn State Erie's Lilley Library, as well as the staff members of the Walter P. Reuther Library at Wayne State University, Wayne State's Purdy Kresge Library, WVU's Downtown Campus Library, and the Ort Library at Frostburg State University. I am also grateful to the librarians at the Legacy Tobacco Documents Library at the University of California, San Francisco, for their prompt replies to my queries about several sources.

At ILR Press of Cornell University Press, I warmly thank Frances Benson for her early support for the project and for her help throughout the lengthy process of publishing the book. I am also indebted to Emily Powers, Sara Ferguson, and Drew Bryan for their expert assistance with the manuscript. Finally, I thank the anonymous reviewers at ILR Press for their illuminating readings of the entire project.

My colleagues and friends at Frostburg State University, the University of Pittsburgh, Northern Michigan University, Wayne State University, and elsewhere sustained me with their interest in my "smoking book." For their support, friendship, advice, and assistance throughout the writing process, I thank Alem Abbay, Bob Archibald, Paul Charney, Bill Childs, Jorge Chinea, Maureen Connelly, José Cuello, Chet DeFonso, Sarah Deprey-Severence, Nick Demichele, Katie Dignan, Elizabeth Faue, Elizabeth Fones-Wolf, Ken Fones-Wolf, Mark Gallagher, Maureen Greenwald, Steve Hartlaub, Cindy Herzog, Brian Ingrassia, Erica Kennedy, Steve Kennedy, Aiden Krautner, John Lombardi, Melanie Lombardi, Russ Magnaghi, Jean-Marie Makang, Elly McConnell, Adam Mertz, Steve Meyer, Marc Michael, Bob Moore, Richard Oestreicher, Mary Jane O'Rourke, Jody Pifer, Kathy Powell, MaryJo Price, John Raucci, Elesha Ruminski, Todd Anthony Rosa, Kara Rogers Thomas, Maria Luisa Sanchez, Daniel Silver, Lisa Simpson, Steve Simpson, Jessica Smith, Jason Tebbe, Jason Thomas, Glenn Thompson, Ahmad Tootoonchi, Nazanin Tootoonchi, Harley Wade, Dan Weir, and Shari Whalen. For help formatting digital images, I owe many thanks to Jared Ritchey of Allegany College of Maryland in nearby Cumberland.

Much of chapter 2 appeared in earlier form as "'Habits of Employees': Smoking, Spies, and Shopfloor Culture at Hammermill Paper Company," *Journal of Social History* 45:1 (2011): 84–107, published by Oxford University Press. A large part of chapter 3 appeared as "'The Justice of a Rule That Forbids the Men Smoking on Their Jobs': Workers, Managers, and Cigarettes in World War II America," *Labor: Studies in Working-Class History of the Americas* 13:1 (2016): 11–39, reprinted by permission of the publisher, Duke University Press.

Finally, my immediate and extended family generously supported me during research trips, gave me time to write, and nudged me away from my laptop from time to time in order to do other things. I owe many thanks to my parents, James and Janis Wood, who let me stay with them over the course of several lengthy research trips to Detroit. Most importantly, I lovingly thank my spouse, Mihaela Wood, and my son, John Michael Wood, for so nicely distracting me with a dizzying multitude of Little League games, soccer practices, road trips to see the Baltimore Orioles, Washington Nationals, and the Pittsburgh Pirates, and visits to JM's beloved National Aquarium. Thank you so much for your endless love and support! This book is dedicated to you both.

NICOTINE AND WORKING-CLASS HISTORY

> Servers and dishwashers leave their cigarettes burning at all times, like votive candles, so they don't have to waste time lighting up again when they dash back here for a puff. Almost everyone smokes as if their pulmonary well-being depended on it—the multinational mélange of cooks; the dishwashers, who are all Czechs here; the servers, who are American natives—creating an atmosphere where oxygen is only an occasional pollutant.
>
> Barbara Ehrenreich, in *Nickel and Dimed: On (Not) Getting By in America* (2001)

"Almost everyone smokes," Barbara Ehrenreich observed soon after immersing herself in the labor of waitressing. She began her undercover exploration of working conditions and social class after the demise of Aid to Families with Dependent Children (AFDC) in a Key West restaurant she called "Jerry's," where she noticed that many of her coworkers persistently smoked cigarettes whenever the opportunity presented itself during their busy shifts. (Employees were forbidden to smoke in sight of customers.) Despite their personal financial difficulties and general lack of access to health care, cooks, waitresses, and dishwashers never seemed to be without a cigarette at the ready. They indulged their unhealthful habit even though they had the most urgent reasons not to smoke: these workers of the postwelfare economy could ill afford the health problems and economic pressures that addictions to nicotine created. As Ehrenreich surmised, the demands of work relentlessly required these servers, cooks, and dishwashers to "serve the people," and to do so for very little reward. But smoking was personal, pleasurable, and social—and thus subversive: in this context, smoking constituted a quiet mutiny against the many demands of their work. Workers filled the airspace of the tiny break room and bathroom with the grungy smoke of burning tobacco, and they left ashy remains that told of smokers' refusal to surrender all of themselves to their jobs.[1]

This book examines cigarette smoking's importance to the social and cultural history of labor and the workplace in the twentieth-century United States and the impact of nicotine addiction on the politics of worker resistance, workplace management, occupational health, vice, moral reform, grassroots activism, and the labor movement. It highlights the frequent (and not so well-known) intersections and tensions among addiction, labor, the body, and space in working-class history. At the same time, the many experiences, social relations, demands, and disputes that accompanied cigarette smoking in the workplace shaped the histories of tobacco and tobacco control in the twentieth century.[2]

Working People and Nicotine Addiction

Addiction is a topic that is not well-understood in histories of labor, despite its regular presence in twentieth-century workplaces. For example, in films that examine working-class lives in depth, such as Barbara Kopple's documentary *Harlan County USA* (1976) or Mike Nichols' docudrama *Silkwood* (1983), workers' addictions to nicotine were presented as commonplace and understood to be interwoven with work. Historians of working people, on the other hand, have only skirted the edges of addiction history. Working-class experiences with addiction are introduced in some historians' discussions of working-class alcohol consumption, especially in the nineteenth century, and in urban histories that examine narcotics.[3] Looking further ahead in time, some historians of labor in the twentieth-century auto industry have noted the presence of alcohol on the assembly line. Furthermore, in *Rivethead: Tales from the Assembly Line* (1991), former Flint autoworker Ben Hamper discusses coworkers who not only drank regularly but explored other drugs such as marijuana and cocaine. Despite the presence of drug use (and even outright abuse) on the job, labor and working-class historians do not suggest that addiction was a day-to-day concern of workers or managers.[4]

The wide extent of cigarette smoking and nicotine addiction among working people throughout much of the twentieth century, however, points to the greater importance of experiences with addiction in US working-class history. Over the course of the twentieth century, the tobacco industry flooded the market with nicotine-rich products: the Venners cigarette rolling machine of the British American Tobacco company cranked out 480 cigarettes every minute in 1899; the Standard Triumph machine produced 700 per minute in 1924; the Molins Mark VI machine spewed 1,600 cigarettes every minute in 1955; and the Molins Mark 9 machine yielded 5,000 cigarettes every minute in 1976.[5] The bonds of dependence between legions of working-class smokers and the mountains of cigarettes in the marketplace brought many workers into conflict with employers in twentieth-century workplaces, as the demands of nicotine addiction regularly drew workers away from assiduous attention to their jobs, causing frustration among managers who viewed worker-smokers' habits and desires as impediments to diligent labor. Employers' opposition to smoking (in addition to actors in government, the medical profession, social reform, and grassroots political activism) greatly shaped antismoking politics in twentieth-century America.[6]

What is nicotine? The substance is a stimulant found in tobacco leaf; when burned, this "naturally occurring colorless liquid" turns brown and "takes on the odor of tobacco when exposed to air."[7] Nicotine is but one of more than four thousand known chemicals in tobacco smoke. This alkaloid acts directly on the brain, stimulating reward pathways that yield elevated levels of pleasure-producing dopamine. In addition, nicotine produces a "kick," the result of its stimulating effect on the adrenal glands and subsequent release of epinephrine. Infusions of the drug into the body spike the production of glucose, and it elevates blood pressure, heart rate, and respiration. The drug is absorbed in two ways: through the skin surfaces in the mouth or nose, or through inhalation. When tobacco users inhale smoke, it takes only seven seconds to feel the stimulating effects, as levels of nicotine peak quickly in the bloodstream.[8] By contrast, it can take fourteen seconds for other drugs in the bloodstream to reach the brain, even when injected with a syringe. Almost all the nicotine in a single puff (around 92 percent) is absorbed.[9]

The tobacco cigarette is an efficient "nicotine delivery system."[10] Levels of nicotine in the body decrease within a matter of minutes, however, which forces addicted users to consume frequent doses of the drug, most often through the smoking of more and more of these nicotine-rich cigarettes. A smoker usually puffs ten times on a single cigarette over a time frame of nearly five minutes. For those who smoke a pack and a half of cigarettes per day, these small devices deliver around three hundred hits of nicotine to the brain every twenty-four hours.[11] Recurring use can lead to addiction. Over time, the smoker's brain and central nervous system come to depend on the regular presence of the drug in order to operate normally, despite the destructive health effects that are produced by exposure to tobacco. While not every tobacco user becomes addicted to nicotine or experiences dependence in the same way, 70 percent of regular smokers, according to a 2013 Gallup Poll, self-identify as "addicted."[12]

What withdrawal symptoms follow the absence of nicotine in the smoker's body? As the body struggles to adjust, withdrawal produces nausea, irritability, depression, difficulty concentrating, restlessness, headaches, sleep disturbances, and increased appetite.[13] Relapse among quitters is common, in part because of the acuity of withdrawal symptoms. Observers of smoking practices have long recorded the pains of withdrawal. For instance, the *New York Times* observed in 1885 that the "cigarette may be laid aside" by habitual users, "but the depressing or nauseating effect increases for some time."[14] A 1910 report in the *Chicago Daily Tribune* cautioned readers of the "disastrous effect" of cigarettes: withdrawal caused "sickness" that showed how "tremendously the system accustoms itself to a stimulant."[15]

Addiction to drugs (nicotine included) engenders new forms of emotional and physical labor that demand continual attention. As observers noted at the turn of the twentieth century, for example, cigarettes dangerously transformed constant users into insidious "fiends." In an article about "ruin and death in the wake of the cigarette habit," adventure story author Henry Oyen noted that cigarettes make "a man a slave to the habit, make a 'fiend' of him."[16] Addiction to nicotine forced dependent users into the perpetual routine of feeding their habit the tobacco it demanded. As a traveling circus troupe made its way to Indiana in 1905 in the aftermath of the state's new ban on smoking and cigarette sales, the visiting workers recoiled from the state government's intent to interdict their tobacco habit. Their spokesman, "Chief Iron Bird," drafted a letter to the governor to register the workers' opposition to the law. "There was consternation in the camp," he wrote of his coworkers, and the avid smokers in the circus vowed to forfeit their jobs in order to maintain their cigarette habit. "So desperate are some of them for their cigarets [sic] that they threaten to jump their contracts and go to other states where they can be free to smoke anything they please," Chief Iron Bird wrote. Indiana's governor, James Frank Hanly, never responded.[17] Another man in Indiana reportedly stockpiled packs of cigarettes as the 1905 law took effect. Scared and surrounded in his room by "coffin nails," he supposedly "smoked self to death."[18]

Nicotine addiction was ordinary and pervasive throughout the "cigarette century." By 1920, the per capita annual smoking rate in the United States equaled almost 700 cigarettes; by 1940, it was 1,900; in 1965, it was more than 4,300.[19] In 1965, almost half (43 percent) of all US adults smoked. While smokers' ranks declined in the 1970s, 1980s, and 1990s, nearly 26 percent of adults still smoked regularly in 2000.[20] As historian Robert N. Proctor explains in *Golden Holocaust: Origins of the Cigarette Catastrophe and the Case for Abolition* (2011), six trillion cigarettes are still consumed every year. If placed end to end, this line of cigarettes would reach 300 million miles. Worldwide, that amounts to 30,000 miles of cigarettes smoked every hour, 24 hours per day.[21] For much of the twentieth century the poisonous plumes of smoke from "coffin nails" saturated many workplaces, but also homes, planes, cars, elevators, college classrooms, city sidewalks, sports arenas, bars, and restaurants.

Smokers' Work Cultures

As cigarette smoking and subsequent nicotine addiction became significant components of many working-class lives in the twentieth century, smokers in a multitude of workplaces shaped, established, and defended the work cultures that sustained their need to use nicotine regularly during the workday. These developments at times accommodated or challenged employers' rules that limited or even banned working-class smoking practices outright. Worker demands for the right to smoke, and their abilities to cultivate spaces and times (sometimes clandestinely) for smoking, underpinned a new dimension of shop floor politics in the cigarette century. As more and more workers smoked cigarettes, they pressed for new privileges and for adjustments of formal and informal rules that would both permit smoking and allow productive work to happen. Smokers in factories and offices often revised daily managers' commands as they rejected regimented labor and rules in favor of more latitude on the job: the decision to interrupt work for occasional (or regular) cigarettes; the ability to smoke while on break near work areas; the ability to smoke and work at the same time; and the ability to limit management's authority over workers' bodies. Smoking was something personal amid places of work governed by employers, even if workers' most common vice was hazardous. In other words, the expansion of nicotine addiction over the first half of the century, its dogged persistence later, and the work cultures that surrounded workers' smoking habits were wellsprings of working-class resistance to many of the demands of modern work: to work at efficient paces, to adhere to work processes laid out by management, to mind all rules in the workplace, to observe the ordering of time, and to stay close to the job, etc.[22]

The history of smokers' practices in twentieth-century workplaces illustrates the ongoing importance of work culture in examinations of labor-management relations; at the same time, smokers' work cultures add some new dimensions to the conversation. Historians such as Susan Porter Benson and Barbara Melosh defined work culture as "the ideology and practice with which workers stake out a relatively autonomous sphere of action on the job" and a "realm of informal, customary values and rules [that] mediates the formal authority structure of the workplace."[23] "Work culture is very much an in-between ground," Susan Porter Benson wrote. "[I]t is neither a rubber stamp version of management policy nor is it a direct outcome of the personal . . . characteristics of the workers. It is the product of these forces as they interact in the workplace and result in collectively formed assumptions and behavior."[24] Smokers' work cultures fit within these definitions, as cigarette users tried to develop and maintain spaces, times, and privileges that would ensure regular access to nicotine, an agenda that often fostered a critical reading of employer power.[25] While discussions of on-the-job skills and dissenting views within specific occupations have usually driven historians' examinations of work culture, the history of smoking in US workplaces highlights the broad interplay and impact of addiction, the body, space, labor, and power in many workers' lives.

Lastly, the topic of smokers' work cultures in the twentieth century expands chronologically the conversation among labor historians about the topic of work culture, a field that is mostly grounded in the long nineteenth century and the early-to-mid twentieth.[26] The rise and fall of smoking in workplaces extends this familiar topic appreciably forward in time, adding to the limited body of work that explores more recent periods.[27] Working-class smokers struggled to sustain work cultures throughout the twentieth century, as this book will show, but these smokers' struggles often became untenable in the 1970s, 1980s, and 1990s. In particular, nonsmokers in US workplaces forcefully pressed from below for revisions to smoking norms and on-the-job rules against the backdrop of compelling reports by physicians and government officials (such as 1964 report of the US Surgeon General's Advisory Committee on Smoking and Health) that tobacco smoke caused chronic illnesses such as heart disease, cancer, and emphysema. At the same time, unions that protected smokers' privileges declined in power. Throughout the twentieth century, the ebb and flow of developments such as Progressive Era reform, urban Victorians' antivice politics, the growth of industrial unions during the 1930s and 1940s, changing medical knowledge of tobacco's health risks in the 1960s through the 1990s, and weakening union power in the final third of the twentieth century greatly shaped the privileges (and the limitations) that undergirded smokers' work cultures.

The Chapters

The swift expansion of cigarette smoking at the turn of the twentieth century coincided (and collided) with the Victorian-era moral reform concerns of many native-born Americans and with the hopes of employers to strengthen their authority over labor processes, worker behavior, uses of space, and the arrangement of time on the job. Moral reform crusaders, city dwellers, and industrial employers spoke about cigarettes as an insidious and rising threat to the morals and virtue of boys and young males and to upward economic mobility. Chapter 1 examines the importance of class, manhood, and youth in turn-of-the-century conversations about cigarettes, when moral reform crusaders such as Lucy Page Gaston of Illinois viewed "coffin nails" as a sure path to physical and emotional doom. Reformers warned that smoking stunted the potential of young working-class males for growth to respectable and healthy manhood and crushed their chances of adult success as workers. The wrecked lives of young smokers, according to reformers, were prima facie evidence of the corrosive and harmful impact of cigarettes on modern society. At the same time, the relationship between cigarettes and urban fires suggested the growing presence of smoking at work, as dropped cigarettes and matches ignited deadly fires such as the Newark Factory Fire (1910) and the Triangle Shirtwaist Fire (1911).

Chapter 2 explores early-twentieth-century employers' opposition to smoking in the workplace, focusing on a case study of smoking practices and shop floor disputes at the Hammermill Paper Company in Erie, Pennsylvania, during the long, hot summer of 1915. Uniquely detailed reports of working conditions and workers' behaviors in this large mass-production factory, written by a pair of curious labor spies, documented nicely the ongoing efforts of many workers to circumvent the company's prohibition of smoking. In response to the refusal of management to allow smoking, workers improvised an assortment of surreptitious strategies that would allow them to smoke at work and enjoy time away from their jobs. As the Hammermill case illustrates, the wide extent of worker subversion made the no-smoking rule a dead letter, much to the constant frustration of management and the spies themselves.

If smoking was so opposed by employers in the early twentieth century, why did cigarettes become accepted fixtures in the workplace later on? Chapter 3 explains that World War II was a major historical moment when cigarettes became respectable in American culture and soon became permissible in the industrial workplace. Wartime popular culture connected smoking to military service and support for soldiers' sacrifices, making the cigarette an acceptable and respectable symbol of patriotic expression. At the same time, workers pressed employers for the right to smoke on the job, and smoking disputes played a significant role in several strikes in the automobile-turned-defense plants of Michigan. By 1950, many major employers such as General Motors and the Ford Motor Company had rescinded their bans on smoking.

The remaining chapters examine the demise of smokers' work cultures in the second half of the twentieth century, utilizing extensively the online Legacy Tobacco Documents Library at the University of California, San Francisco, a colossal archive of more than fourteen million digitized documents related to tobacco industry practices in the twentieth century. While many of these sources relate to advertising, manufacturing, research, and health issues, there is a host of news clippings, press releases, lobbyist reports, copies of government reports, and letters from smokers that cover other topics. Among these sources is a treasure trove of documents on smoking disputes in workplaces during the 1970s, 1980s, and 1990s. The archive began in 1994 when Stanton Glantz, a professor of medicine at the University of California, San Francisco, received several thousand documents in the mail from an anonymous industry whistleblower. Throughout the 1990s, the archive received additional collections of documents from state attorneys general as well as tobacco company releases of documents to the public as a result of the industry's violations of the Racketeer Influenced and Corrupt Organizations Act (RICO) in the *US vs. Philip Morris, et al.* case. As part of the federal lawsuit, the tobacco industry was obligated to disclose all documents related to smoking and health in light of its proven history of efforts to mislead the public about the dangers of its products.[28] Used extensively by the historian of science Robert N. Proctor in *Golden Holocaust*, these abundant and rich sources had not yet been investigated by labor and working-class historians.

Chapter 4 examines how the prevalence of smoking in postwar indoor workplaces gave rise to mounting opposition from nonsmoking workers in the 1970s and 1980s. Nonsmokers in postwar offices, for instance, recoiled from their colleagues' continual spewing of toxic and irritating secondhand smoke, lobbying managers and government officials for new restrictions on smoking. The most determined and energized nonsmokers took disinterested employers to court and built nonsmoker advocacy groups from below that lobbied for a clearing of the air at work. Much to their frustration, though, nonsmoking workers faced active opposition from working-class smokers, and managers often did not want to provoke smokers' opposition by revoking their privileges, even as medical knowledge about the health risks of smoking (and secondhand smoke) became abundantly clear in the 1970s through the 1990s.

By the 1980s and 1990s, smokers' work cultures groaned under the weight of increasing pressure from employers and the state, as concerns about public health, health care costs, and worker productivity led to a new ouster of tobacco use in the workplace. Smokers struggled to adapt to their banishment by relocating to outdoor spaces they would claim as new sanctuaries, as chapter 5 shows, while at the same time lodging complaints with interested tobacco lobbyists in Washington, DC, about those employer actions that had triggered their exile from indoor spaces of work. Some employers took their new prohibitions of smoking to the fullest extent possible by requiring workers to quit smoking altogether, a development that highlighted the limited means at smokers' disposal for responding to the demise of their rights and privileges in the workplace amid the ebbing strength of organized labor.

Chapter 6 examines the relationship of the labor movement to the decline of smokers' work cultures from the 1970s to the 1990s. As newspaper articles, letters to lobbyists, and published National Labor Relations Board decisions illustrate, the demise of smoking at work often intersected with the efforts of many employers to roll back the power of organized labor. Employers sometimes used no-smoking rules to discipline workers, committeemen, and union organizers for unwanted efforts to shape managerial policy making. Unions often fought for working-class smokers and their vanishing privileges, as the increasing marginalization of smoking and smokers seemed to portend the overall demise of labor's power in the late twentieth century. The NLRB discovered in numerous cases brought by workers and unions that employers tried to sidestep collective bargaining by abruptly creating new no-smoking rules and using smoking restrictions to harass union supporters. The conclusion of the book explores the persistence of addiction to nicotine at the turn of the twenty-first century. While quitting smoking is the new normal among tobacco users, there are many "holdouts," frequent relapses, aborted quit attempts, and harm-reducing electronic cigarettes that allow nicotine addiction to endure.

This examination of the history of smoking at work is not intended to valorize tobacco use nor to support a libertarian argument for an unencumbered right to enjoy tobacco products. Instead, this is a social and cultural history of smoking and nicotine addiction as contested issues in the everyday politics of workplaces, and of how these issues greatly shaped the lives of many workers, even as this habit destroyed health and cut short millions of lives. 400,000 people die every year as a result of smoking-related illnesses in the United States.[29] Many smokers wisely continue to work at quitting, and by doing so they take a positive step toward living healthier lives. This history of smoking in workplaces, however, should be recognized as another major byproduct of damaging and long-lasting addictions to nicotine: workers' frequent and persistent demands to smoke precipitated daily conflicts over the rights of workers. Secondhand smoke certainly dulled and poisoned the air of many factories and offices with its gray haze, but smoking controversies made clear the struggles among workers and managers to determine the content and limits of the other's power.

1

REFORMERS, EMPLOYERS, AND THE DANGERS OF WORKING-CLASS SMOKING

Once you start, it's hard to stop.

—kidshealth.org

For children in Chicago, the summer of 1900 began with a busy day of outdoor activities on 15 June, organized for them by the Cook County Anti-Cigarette League. The boy members of the league attended the field day "en masse," according to a visiting reporter for the *New York Times*. Just as the fifty-yard dash was set to begin, a bedraggled "street urchin" elbowed his way through the crowd, clenching a lit cigarette between his teeth. Speaking to F. A. Doty, the assistant superintendent of the Cook County Anti-Cigarette League and the referee of the race, he tersely asked, "Wot's dis?" Doty answered the newcomer with an invitation to participate in the race, telling the boy, "Just to show people why you cannot win because you smoke cigarettes, I will let you enter." The "stunted" boy apparently accepted the challenge, tossed his cigarette away, and lined up with the other boys of the under-fifteen age group. Surprising everyone, the street urchin "cigarette fiend" won the race and took with him a trophy for his efforts.[1] In his own way, the boy challenged the growing movement to curtail cigarette smoking in America, running against then-prevalent assumptions about the ineptitude, dullness, and weakness of smokers. And as this anecdote suggests, attention centered on working-class children as the embodied objects of reform. The Cook County Anti-Cigarette League worried not about adults' smoking; they focused on boys' habits.

Throughout the Progressive Era, reformers' and judges' assertions that tobacco was a physically, mentally, and morally dangerous drug clashed with working people's desires to satisfy their addictions, habits, and tastes by smoking cigarettes. Working-class people's inclinations and actions rested at the heart of antismoking politics during the early twentieth century. In addition, the Progressives who attacked smoking not only wanted to reform working-class behavior, but they also seemed to want to transform their own sensory experiences of urban life. The omnipresent smells and sights of cigarette smoke surely offended and even overwhelmed the respectability of their senses, and antismoking politics provided middle-class men and women with a way to temper the physical presence and environmental influence of the urban working class. One city dweller and "AN ADMIRER OF JUSTICE," for example, wrote to the *New York Times* in 1903 to ask whether or not nonsmokers of the big city had "the right to breathe fresh air." She or he wrote, "Do smokers ever realize the annoyance and positive injury that they cause to those who have that right?" The user of "nasty stinking tobacco" ruined the environment, "defil[ing] himself and the air around him."[2] To improve the smells and sights produced by the working class, reformers focused on modifying the actions and attitudes of boys, the immediate future of upright working-class manhood. The pervasive stench of cigarettes signaled to Progressives the problem of boys' diminishing health, a real threat to the development of respectable working-class manhood in boys. Could boys who smoked develop the fully formed bodies of adult men? Could they complete the productive labors that were necessary for working-class men in industrial America? Would those boys who smoked habitually descend into crime, depravity, and stupidity? As Progressive reformers' observations and reactions led them to believe again and again, nicotine fueled the absence of decency, the prevalence of criminality, and the economic failures they associated with working-class culture.

Social and cultural historians' extensive research into the Progressive Era certainly shows us a great deal regarding middle-class anxieties about working-class culture and morality, but the topic of reformers' reactions to smoking opens up new dimensions of Progressives' worries about their own surroundings, views of social class, and what urban "reform" meant.[3] Their comments about working-class smokers at the turn of the twentieth century provide us with telling insights regarding their views of urban space, class, and gender, environmental stimuli, personal and public health, and their senses of sight and smell.

This chapter identifies the three fundamentals of antismoking politics at the turn of the twentieth century: (1) Progressives' concerns about the damaging relationship between smoking and the bad health and behavior of working-class children (specifically boys and adolescents); (2) employers' and reformers' concerns about young males' cigarette smoking as a destroyer of respectable working-class manhood, as tobacco use undermined their health, morals, and abilities and rendered them supposedly imbecilic, unreliable, immoral, and unemployable; and (3) the close relationship between smoking and the very real danger of fire in

FIGURE 1.1   "Boy with a cigarette during the 1904 Stockyards Strike." (1904) *Chicago Daily News* negatives collection, Chicago History Museum, http://hdl. loc.gov/loc.ndlpcoop/ichicdn.n001019. Courtesy of the Library of Congress.

turn-of-the-twentieth-century urban life, specifically conversations during these years about working-class smokers as deadly sources of factory fires. Overall, the subjects of working-class culture and conduct proved to be central concerns of the men and women who forged antismoking politics in the early twentieth century.

Working-Class Boys and the Making of Antismoking Politics

Victorian moral reformers, Progressives, and other middle-class men and women in the largest American cities at the turn of the twentieth century saw, heard, and smelled much that surely offended their senses and notions of respectability and proper decorum: overflowing garbage bins, noisy immigrant hucksters, dank and overcrowded tenement dwellings, unkempt people, alleys, and streets, unfamiliar languages spoken and shouted in the streets, noisy trains and loud factory whistles, and the odors of unfamiliar cooking.[4] Among the many smells and sights of the city, smoking loomed large in middle-class city dwellers' uneasiness about urban life. Restaurant customers in New York City during the 1910s complained often of the "sickening fumes of tobacco puffed" by legions of cigarette smokers, while members of the Non-Smokers Protective League lamented in 1913 that smoking permeated "almost all public places" and was "generally offensive."[5] In addition to their apparent concerns about the urban environment, middle-class urbanites worried that cigarette smoking was dingy evidence of working-class immorality, physical decay, and mental weakness. In particular, reformers and other urban middle-class residents who condemned cigarettes worried that smoking ruined the potential for respectable manhood in working-class boys and adolescents, as the cigarette purportedly pulled them downward into the physical and moral filth of the city. As the worried automobile magnate Henry Ford proclaimed in his treatise *The Case against the Little White Slaver* (1916), "the American boy of today" is "the man of tomorrow." The future of manhood was at stake, he claimed, as young boys turned more and more toward the cigarette.[6] In response, Ford hoped to reshape boys' behaviors and morals with the same strictness that guided the work of his industrial Sociological Department: the institution inside Ford Motor Company plants that policed the personal and professional conduct of adult Ford workers.[7]

Working-class boy smokers were a ubiquitous presence in cities at the turn of the century, much to the dismay of their worried social betters and elders. For example, in Brooklyn, the school board in 1894 begged local police to arrest boys under the age of sixteen they found smoking, as well as the area sellers who sold them "nauseating and filthy cigarettes." Brooklyn residents complained of the "customary" practice of high school students to "take possession" of elevated train cars, where they "smoke[d] cigarettes openly and defiantly" during their after-school commutes. Urging the police to act, Brooklyn's school board members recoiled from what they claimed to be the "alarming extent to which the pernicious and injurious habit of cigarette smoking has spread among schoolboys." Even when sellers did not provide cigarettes to child consumers, the board complained that boys found individuals who were older than the age of sixteen to buy them.[8] Middle-class residents of Los Angeles during the 1890s worried often about the general presence of boy smokers in the city. A visitor from Stockton walked down a main street one evening in 1891 and observed a group of boys smoking on a corner adjacent to a saloon. The visitor moved in closer to watch and listen. "They seemed a good deal animated and were very earnestly discussing some weighty problem of mutual interest," the observer wrote. The observer spoke to these boys, who were between eight and twelve years old, but was quickly sickened by their rough talk and chain smoking. The hour was 10 p.m. In the dark, the boys smoked foul cigarette stubs they culled from the street. As the observer spoke to them, the boys denounced parental authority, complaining of "apron strings" at home and bragging of the freedom found in the streets. "What will be the future of this republic," the observer lamented, "if its boys are to grow up robbed of their manhood, brains and morality by this cigarette iniquity?" The observer complained there seemed to be "three sexes": men, women, and "dudes." While real men and women were respectable nonsmokers, the "dude" was a lowly working-class male of the city who was "useful" only as "demonstration of the fact that an animal can live on smoke and without brains."[9] Another observer of urban life in Los Angeles noted that if an individual stood at the busy corner of Kearny and Market Streets, that person would witness not just one newspaper boy chain smoking, but "a score of others like him."[10] Working-class boys proved to be major producers of smelly and filthy urban cigarette smoke at the turn of the twentieth century.

As boys smoked their way into the new century, opponents of smoking often framed their views of boy smokers and nonsmokers within a dichotomy of effeminacy versus manliness. William McKeever, a professor of philosophy at

FIGURE 1.2 "11:00 A.M. Monday, May 9th, 1910. Newsies at Skeeter's Branch, Jefferson near Franklin. They were all smoking. Location: St. Louis, Missouri." Photograph by Lewis Hine. LOT 7480, v. 2, no. 1384 [P&P] LC-H51-1384. Courtesy Library of Congress.

the Kansas State Agricultural College, took it upon himself to survey the physical characteristics of 2,500 boy smokers in schools, and what he found suggested that smoking put boys on a definite path to delicateness. He characterized the boy smokers he observed as "sallow," "squeaky voiced," "sickly," and "puny," pitiable specimens of manhood in formation.[11] In contrast, observers assigned the most positive attributes to those boys who were dedicated nonsmokers. Virginia Steel of New York City praised a ten-year-old boy of a Lower East Side neighborhood who organized his own version of an anticigarette club. As the "president" of this apparently "sizeable" club, he set up his office on the basement steps of his tenement building, complete with an overturned ash barrel that he used as a chair. Praising his earnestness and rigorousness (the young president fined club members one and two cents for rule violations such as relapsing into the habit or picking up cigarette butts in the street), Steel lauded the young boy as the "most manly, bright little commander" of his organization.[12] In 1916, concerned physician D. H. Kress visited a Detroit school and examined twenty-six boys between the ages of twelve and sixteen. Only two of the boys had never smoked cigarettes, and, according to Kress, they "were, in all respects, the best developed boys in the room." In his analyses of the boys' traits, Kress praised the nonsmokers as "the best developed in every way." They showed the most potential as future men, especially when compared to the sickly and poor-performing boys who smoked. Henry Ford preached to young boys that the competitive world of the 1910s "needs men" who possessed "initiative and vigor"; but the boy who smoked stupidly rendered himself physically, mentally, and morally inadequate for the demands of modern manhood. The famous Detroit Tiger, Ty Cobb, concurred with Ford. "No boy," he said, "who hopes to be successful in any line can afford to contract a habit that is detrimental to his physical and moral development."[13]

As tobacco smoke saturated the lungs of working-class boys, one observer claimed that cigarettes produced "curious" physical deformities in their fragile young bodies, marked proof of the ruined potential for manhood. A report in the *Los Angeles Times* claimed that constant cigarette smoking led to the eruption of strange and unsightly spots all over the bodies of two working-class boys, "giving them the appearance of leopards." The boys' addictions to nicotine were so great they even had to smoke several cigarettes after retiring to their beds at night. As they were "spotted all over their bodies," the youths looked less like upright boys on the path to manhood and more like animals.[14]

Frequent discussions of early deaths due to chronic cigarette smoking underlined observers' anxieties about the physical vulnerability of boys and adolescents. For instance, William F. Lewis of Brooklyn, New York, died in 1893 as a result of what his doctor believed was "cigarette poisoning." A pair of friends brought home the limp "Young Lewis," who appeared to be intoxicated. His parents carried him into the kitchen of their home, where they tried to revive him. They failed. The parents quickly called a local doctor who rushed to the house, but he too failed to bring back their comatose son. He died around 9 p.m. that night. William F. Lewis reportedly smoked heavily, consuming between ten and twelve packages of cigarettes every day, leading the doctor and the aggrieved parents to conclude that his chronic smoking habit surely killed him.[15] In Pasadena, California, a twenty-three-year-old male purportedly died as a result of his own "[e]xcessive cigarette smoking." He smoked as many as fifty cigarettes every day according to the mention of his death in the pages of the *Los Angeles Times*. As he declined rapidly, the unnamed young man supposedly lived out his last days as an "imbecile" at a hospital. "If a man wishes to commit suicide," the press opined, "the revolver or strychnine would seem to be preferable to the cigarette."[16] Boys and young adults would never have the chance to become real men when excessive smoking and addiction destroyed their lives.

Concerned public officials viewed smoking not only as a sure path to an early death for young males, but also to working-class criminality. At the 1899

FIGURE 1.3 "11:00 A.M. Monday May 9th, 1910. Newsies at Skeeter's Branch, Jefferson near Franklin. They were all smoking. Location: St. Louis, Missouri." Photograph by Lewis Hine. LOT 7480, v. 2, no. 1383 [P&P]. Courtesy Library of Congress.

National Conference of Charities and Correction meeting in Cincinnati, George Torrance, who ran the Illinois State Reformatory, lectured on the topic of "The Relation of the Cigarette to Crime." As he reviewed the records of his charges, he concluded "I am sure cigarettes are destroying and making criminals of more of them than the saloons." Torrance found that 92 percent of the boys in the Illinois State Reformatory were, in his words, "cigarette fiends" when they were jailed. He estimated that fifty-eight of the sixty-three boys of twelve years of age smoked cigarettes, and seventy-three of the eighty-two boys at the age of fourteen did the same. Of the eighty-two boys who were fifteen years old, he said that seventy-three smoked cigarettes. In his view, smoking did not merely coincide with criminal deeds; rather, cigarettes fueled their wrongdoing.[17]

Readers likely agreed when they read about the later deeds of ten-year-old "Little" Eddie Luke of Brooklyn, New York. The young truant, habitual cigarette smoker, and frequent talker during study hours wielded a "fancied grievance" with his teacher, Edna Campbell. Luke had a long history of run-ins with authorities at school as a result of his many infractions of the rules and was thought to be "practically incorrigible." After Miss Campbell rebuked him for misbehaving in the hallway while waiting to meet (yet again) the principal, Luke supposedly planned, as he put, to "get hunk" (get even) with the teacher by starting a fire in her classroom. He thought of the matches he carried in his pocket. Moving quietly, he snuck into the room and opened Campbell's supply closet, where papers and other "rubbish" were stored, and scattered a large pile of papers on the floor. Luke started a "bonfire" in the classroom, aided no doubt by the three matches he applied in order to start the blaze. As the fire quickly began to create enormous flames, the fire starter fled the building and ran down the street. Edna Campbell returned to her classroom to see the entire room consumed by flames. While Campbell, the principal, and other teachers rushed to put out the fire, others evacuated the entire student body of 1,500. As the teachers and the principal discussed who might be guilty of starting the "bonfire," they saw dropped matches and immediately thought of their resident troublemaker, Eddie Luke. Soon apprehended by police and charged with arson, the ten-year-old fire bug admitted to starting the blaze but claimed he only wanted to "scare the life out of" Campbell, not burn down the school or hurt anyone inside. Eddie's mother tried to defend her son by claiming that he was "not so bad a boy as the teachers say."[18] Smoking featured prominently as one his appalling behaviors, making him a very bad boy and very much distanced from respectable manhood.

In 1900, during the trial of accused teenage murderer John Garrabrant of Jersey City, New Jersey, testifying police and physicians disagreed as to whether or not cigarette smoking could actually drive a boy to commit criminal acts. His defense lawyer argued in court that Garrabrant was surely "a moral degenerate of the most pronounced type," as he reportedly smoked as many as 150 cigarettes per day since he was a mere five years old. As a result of so much smoking, he was surely suffering from acute "nicotine poisoning," which undoubtedly affected "his entire system, including his brain," and drove him to kill another teenage boy with a high-powered sling shot. The boy's mother remarked that he had both smoked and read "trashy novels" since his earliest years; as a result, he long exhibited intense "destructive qualities." Doctors concurred that Garrabrant was surely the moral degenerate claimed by the lawyer for the defense, Alexander Simpson. The chief of police in Jersey City, however, disagreed with the views of the medical professionals. In his estimation, there was an unmistakable coincidence that criminals (both adults and boys) "habitually smoked," but he would "not attribute their criminal habits to the use of tobacco."[19]

Discussions of boy smokers' criminal activity coincided with frequent assertions that chronic smoking brought young males to insanity. In upstate New York, twenty-year-old Peter S. McMahon smoked so many cigarettes for so long that he made himself "crazed," according to the brief wire story that was printed in the *Los Angeles Times*. Five days before Christmas in 1897, he committed suicide by shooting himself in the chest as he stood alone in front of a mirror. In Minnesota during the early twentieth century, a successful young doctor smoked "incessantly." As he smoked cigarettes throughout his youth and into early adulthood, he began to make mistakes in his delicate labors as a surgeon. His mind collapsed ("the young doctor went to pieces") after he lost a patient on the operating table. It was only then understood how much his cigarette habit had destroyed his mental acuity and stability. "He was a wreck in mind as well as in body," an author cautioned, "and ended his days in a maniac's cell."[20]

If cigarettes drove young working-class boys to depravity and even madness, the sights and smells of smoking pushed other individuals to the opposite extreme: to zealous moral reform crusades that were intended to rescue urban boys from the pitfalls of the cigarette habit. Born in 1860 to a Midwestern family that was long-dedicated to reform causes such as abolitionism and temperance, Lucy Page Gaston of Illinois would make antismoking politics the foundational cause in her lifelong work on behalf of moral reform. As accounts of her early years in Illinois illustrate, the sights and smells of boy smokers frustrated and even sickened her. Teaching school at the age of sixteen in 1876, she was quickly "appalled" by the sight of "surly, shuffling boys" who were poor-performing students and no-accounts elsewhere. On the streets of Lacon, Illinois, where she lived, she must have loathed the sights and smells of the boy smokers who "loitered on street corners" every day after school. Struggling to live a life that was free of these disgusting habits, she relocated to Harvey, Illinois, during the 1890s, a town that completely prohibited tobacco as well as alcohol and gambling; it was

FIGURE 1.4   "Portrait of Lucy Page Gaston outside the First District Police Court in Chicago, Illinois. Perry Rathbun, a boy detective who worked with anti-cigarette groups, is standing to the side. Ms. Gaston was involved in the Anti-Cigarette League." (1904) *Chicago Daily News* negatives collection, Chicago History Museum, http://hdl.loc.gov/loc.ndlpcoop/ichicdn.n001988. Courtesy of the Library of Congress.

a veritable paradise of purity. (That is, until liquor began to make inroads in the town during the latter part of the decade.) Here she began to take up the cause of rescuing boys from their "coffin nails." She launched the Anti-Cigarette League in 1899 and published a magazine called *The Boy*, a periodical that showed her predominant concern for working-class boys' apparent predilection toward smoking cigarettes. Quoting her colleague and donor David Starr Jordan, president of Stanford University, Gaston said, "Cigarette-smoking boys are like wormy apples; they drop long before the harvest time."[21]

The experience of relocating to Chicago at the turn of the twentieth century surely intensified her disgust and aversion to the sights and smells of smoking. In Chicago, she would have seen more boys smoking on many more corners and streets throughout a much larger cityscape than what she would have known in the sleepy rural hamlet of Lacon, Illinois. In the mean streets of Chicago, she once again observed (and likely smelled) streetwise boys growing up too fast, smoking cigarettes in defiance of their elders. As she took in these repulsive sensations of the Chicago streets, she suggested these boy smokers were actually losing their morals, "offering burnt incense to Satan" with every puff. She also read the tragic newspaper accounts in Chicago papers that detailed supposed cases of insanity and criminality among boys that were brought about by the awful seductions of the cigarette. Gaston claimed that she even watched a boy smoker fall down in the street, convulsing uncontrollably. A policeman pointed out to her that the boy's yellowed fingers were a sure sign that the cigarette habit brought him to this lowly state.[22] Witnessing an urban crisis of out-of-control boy smoking, Gaston would struggle to situate her brand of moral righteousness and prohibition at the intersection of vulnerable boyhood and the cigarette.

Lucy Page Gaston's efforts to push working-class boys away from cigarettes relied not only on moral suasion, but also on the creation of social and political spaces that were intended to fortify boy nonsmokers in the face of the temptations, addictions, and poisons found in turn-of-the-twentieth-century urban America. By 1900, her Anti-Cigarette League chapters, established first in Chicago and then later in other cities such as New York and Boston, brought boys into the center of Progressive Era moral reform. Led and organized by adult men and women of white Anglo-Saxon Protestant backgrounds, the leagues organized "mass meetings" and athletic events for boys, especially in Chicago, where the group first started. Gaston and her colleagues in the Anti-Cigarette League urged boys to embrace moral reform activism. In Boston, a group of young boys enjoyed a free dinner at a local hall where they listened to an address by Colonel James H. Davidson, the national president of the league, who traveled from Chicago to visit them. Perhaps encouraged by the adults present, the boys in attendance formed their own branch of the Anti-Cigarette League. The adults urged them to take their tobacco-free passion to the wider city that lay beyond their meeting space. A program of "missionary work" in area business establishments, where the boys of the Boston league could reach out to wayward young males (e.g., messenger boys at work) on behalf of the anticigarette cause, was necessary.[23]

Gaston often enlisted her nonsmoking boys in choreographed spectacles of antismoking vitriol, injecting performance into the realm of moral reform. In 1902 at the Women's Temple in Chicago, she held a pageant for boys that combined music, marching, theater, and biblical symbols in a dramatic protest against cigarettes. Boys sang songs and marched in unison throughout the hall. "Hurrah! Hurrah!" the assembly sang loudly, "The cigarette, you know. Hurrah! Hurrah! The cigarette must go!" One boy from Hyde Park, devilishly dressed in red tights, hooves, and horns, used a pitchfork to stir a cauldron filled with cigarettes. For the dramatic climax, the cigarettes were ignited and soon tobacco smoke filled the hall. The smoke caused considerable discomfort among the children at the event, as many of them sneezed, coughed, and rubbed their eyes. Later, Gaston explained that she deliberately intended "to make things smell bad."[24] What better way to drive boys away from cigarettes than to make them sick?

Nonsmoking boys mattered more to Lucy Page Gaston than just as components of her agitprop. She relied on them as collaborators in her war against smoking. Gaston employed boys as spies (she called them "detectives") for the Anti-Cigarette League, battling to bring punishments to those storekeepers who sold cigarettes to youths. Following Gaston's directions, boy detectives tried to buy cigarettes at numerous stores, gathering intelligence that would be relayed to Gaston. While sometimes criticized for "corrupting" boys by using them to infiltrate the "meanest and most contemptible industry conceivable," Gaston made no apologies for her tactics. In this war for the bodies, minds, and souls of urban boys, the ends justified the means. "This is the only way to get evidence," she claimed. One "boy detective" employed by Gaston was Perry Rathbun, who in 1904 posed for a photograph with his boss outside the First District Police Court in Chicago. Another Gaston "protégé" and "sleuth," thirteen-year-old Stanley Kurkzisci, appeared in a Chicago court in 1904 to testify against eight merchants who illegally sold him tobacco. "He wears knee trousers, a mop of curly hair, and an abiding smile," the press said of the boy's appearance. On the street, however, Kurkzisci "wore the disguise of a small and tearful boy."[25] As Gaston relied on boys to gather intelligence, she faced real trouble on at least one occasion when Chicago courts accused her of illegally exploiting these boys as child labor, as she kept them out of school for the purpose of spying.[26]

Lucy Page Gaston, however, did not sit idly by while her boy detectives patrolled the streets on her behalf. She sought out and received police powers from the city of Chicago in 1911, a designation that allowed her to personally make arrests of boy smokers and prosecute other wrongful offenders. Sworn in as a "special policeman" by the chief of police, John McWeeny, Gaston could now wield state powers directly on behalf of her moral suasion efforts. "It has come to pass," the press opined, "that the small Chicago boy who would enjoy his cigarette must sneak up an alley, hide in a basement, and puff furtively." There was a new sheriff in town, and arrests began right away as she ventured into the smoke-filled streets. Working-class boy smoker Joseph Pfeiffer may have been Gaston's first arrest. The arrest of the boy, who worked to support his widowed mother, stoked sustained opposition from his mother, his employer, and even members of the Anti-Cigarette League. The widowed mother visited the office of the league, where she urged them to drop the case against her son. She claimed that "it would be cruel" to punish the boy since he might lose his job if he had to miss any work. Pfeiffer's unnamed employer phoned the Anti-Cigarette League himself, asking them to abandon the case since the hard-working boy promised that he would not smoke cigarettes ever again. Furthermore, officials of the league announced they would drop the case if the Chicago juvenile courts wanted to drop the charge. Lucy Page Gaston, however, was adamant: Since the law had been broken, the boy must stand trial. She wrote to the Anti-Cigarette League with her objection, and the members sided with their leader. "We had decided to let the matter drop," league officer Kathryn Staley Sears said, "[b]ut we received Miss Gaston's letter, and the case must be tried." A writer for the *Chicago Daily Tribune* complained that Gaston "did not like to see her first arrest go for nothing."[27]

In addition to legal coercion, Gaston explored the use of various "cures" to wrench addicted boys (and others) away from the clutches of the cigarette. In the streets, she was known to press boys she caught smoking to take up a fruit-only diet that she claimed would get them over the habit in two or three days. Gaston surely imagined that nutritious fruits would restore the health of the lowly cigarette fiend; she may have also understood that the fruit's acidity would have likely given the cigarettes a very poor taste. Also, Gaston claimed that smokers could wean themselves from the little white slaver by chewing on the root of gentian flowers, another organic product that yielded similar results.[28] In 1913, she opened a free cigarette "cure" clinic at the Women's Temple in Chicago, inviting addicted boy smokers and anyone else who wanted help to receive treatment for their habit. As a litany of patients came and went, Dr. D. H. Kress swabbed their mouths and throats with Gaston's "new wash" of silver nitrate. When combined with cigarette smoke, the solution produced severe nausea. By pushing smokers to the verge of vomiting, the chemical concoction was "guaranteed to 'cure' them of the naughty cigarette habit." According to the *Chicago Daily Tribune*, a man brought his four-year-old nephew to receive the miracle treatment. "This boy smokes from fifteen to twenty cigarets a day," the uncle reported. "Is your wash good for children?" The doctor said the solution was not safe for infants, but speculated that a diluted version of the formula would be safe enough. At the same time, a concerned mother brought in her fifteen-year-old son. He had to be "persuaded" to accept the treatment. Another boy of fifteen arrived for a second treatment, finding hope that he could quit as a result of the first go-round, which he believed had helped him to lower his intake of cigarettes from thirty each day to four. He speculated that in three more days he would finally be "free" of smoking for good. Other visitors to the clinic included messenger boys, real estate men, clerks, "the idly curious," and working women in the chorus.[29] The "new wash" solution at Gaston's clinic was certainly hokum, since a topical liquid could never undo the personal and emotional habits and likely physical addiction produced by the chronic intake of nicotine.[30] Gaston's foray into medicine, however, can be read as part of her strenuous effort to abruptly halt boys' downward trajectory into addiction and depravity and away from adult health and manhood.

Did boys ever resist Lucy Page Gaston's tough love and strong-arm tactics? Very few examples of disapproval among working-class boys can be found, which is surprising since so many boys smoked cigarettes at the turn of the twentieth century and Gaston seemed to frequently observe and interact with them. During a visit to Boston in 1905, Gaston lectured to a group of young newspaper boys who congregated on Newspaper Row. As she criticized the cigarette and harangued the boys of its dangers, at least three of the boys started smoking in front of her. A reporter asked one what he thought of Gaston's speech, and he replied that she said, "Aw, de nicotine is bad for de troat and lungs." The boy continued, "But as for me I smoke cigars." The reporter asked if he might consider attending a meeting of the Anti-Cigarette League? The boy answered smartly, "Naw, it's bad fer de troat."[31] In other settings, young males' frustrations with the moralizing of their social betters also episodically emerged. In a Harlem court, the local magistrate heard the assault case of teenager John Ryan and twenty-six-year-old Patrick Ahearn after the pair had a supposed altercation with a thirty-eight-year-old African American man in 1903. As he reviewed the case, the magistrate queried the two young males about whether or not they smoked. Patrick Ahearn, the older man, spoke up and said that he did. As the magistrate launched into a "lecture" on cigarettes (possibly warning them that tobacco was a dangerous gateway drug to alcohol or even opium), Ahearn stopped him short. "It's none of your business whether we smoke cigarettes or smoke dope," he said with an edge in his voice. "You are here to judge us, not to ask us what we smoke. That's none of your business." The stunned magistrate was speechless. He ordered that the pair of young males would remain in custody.[32] Nonetheless, Ahearn refused to listen to the high-minded moralizing of the magistrate. He did so even though his case was still very much in the hands of the court. Some young males had no patience for such preachy talk.

Antismoking politics during the Progressive Era stemmed from prevalent worries among middle-class men and women that the cigarette would undermine working-class boys' chances to reach manhood and, as we will see in the next section, respectable working-class status. Smoking was thought to be nothing less than a social evil unto itself, a powerful source of emotional, mental, and physical ruination for vulnerable young boys. Urban newspapers of the Progressive Era documented numerous cases of working-class boy smokers who supposedly succumbed to horrific criminal impulses, debilitating mental illness, and even early, tragic, and painful deaths. In the cause of antismoking, class, gender, and age intersected in upper-class men and women's understandings of who needed urgent help in the turn-of-the-twentieth-century city, as well as how best to give

aid. And reformers' sensory experiences of the city around 1900 fueled their feelings of disgust, as individuals such as Lucy Page Gaston targeted cigarettes for
their many moral, medical, and environmental offenses.

Boy Smokers, Work, and Manhood

Employers were key contributors to the antismoking politics of the Progressive
Era. As they responded to the queries of antismoking reformers, early-twentieth-
century employers reinforced reformers' warnings that cigarettes would undermine boys' later manhood, as boys would likely confront workplaces that
discriminated against smokers seeking work. Cigarettes destroyed a boy's fragile health and moral code precisely at the moment he was only just beginning
to transition to manhood. Like Progressive reformers who opposed cigarette
smoking in young boys and adolescents, employers too wanted to engineer better working men from the material of working-class boys. Their disapproval of
tobacco echoed the warnings of moral, physical, and mental damages envisioned
by reformers, but employers' disdain for smoking also stemmed from their concern for effective work and obedient workers. Reformers and employers deployed
the themes of wrecked careers and ruined manhood to argue against cigarettes.
They told boys that smoking would surely destroy their opportunities to follow
the essential path of respectable work to the attainment of manhood. Cigarettes
would destroy their bodies, minds, and morals and would guarantee life-long
failure. And employers too would cause further tragedy, as more and more managers simply refused to employ cigarette fiends.

Reformers and employers insisted that the hard-working path to respectable
manhood was littered with the wreckage of "the little white slaver," citing the
ruined careers of smokers as evidence that smoking would erode their abilities
to become real men. Auto tycoon and cigarette opponent Henry Ford reprinted
the sad story of a big-city newspaper writer (and heavy smoker) in his antismoking treatise *The Case against the Little White Slaver*. Author Len G. Shaw met two
young newspapermen in Michigan—the first a political writer from the big city,
the second a small-town cub reporter—during a political campaign. "Both were
splendid specimens of manhood, clean-cut, alert, immaculately attired—men
who would attract attention in a crowd," he wrote of this meeting. As they sat in
their chairs, the political writer produced a pack of cigarettes and offered them
to his companions. "They were declined with thanks," but the big-city political
writer laughed. "Ha," he said, "you have no small vices, eh?" The cub reporter
looked at him gravely. "I am not sure that is such a small vice," he said. Throughout the night, the political writer smoked a pack and a half of cigarettes. As Shaw

reflected on the man's subsequent downward spiral through life, he claimed to have met him several times in the years that followed. The cub reporter became a successful journalist, while the big-city political writer descended into sickening addiction and decay. He lost his respectable job and became a casual laborer, laboring in Georgia as a peach picker and working on docks as a lumber shover. When Shaw met him, he noted the yellowness of the man's fingers and the rasp of his breathing. He was a ruined man, with his "coat of grime," darkened face, "withered limbs," and hands that "were dark as those of an African." Smoking apparently pulled the once-successful man away from his career and downward into blackness, Africanness, and the loss of manhood. "I have seen men in the throes of delirium tremens, screeching for help at the top of their voices, while hospital attendants fought to restrain them," Shaw wrote. "I never saw so horrible a spectacle as was represented by this one-time Beau Brummel, who had forfeited every claim to consideration, and sunk to unbelievable depths—victim of the Little White Slaver."[33]

Reformers argued that nicotine addiction led young boys to make poor decisions that threatened opportunities to secure manhood through respectable employment. In "tobacco-hating" Utah of the early twentieth century, reformer Frederick James Pack relayed the story a young "boy" in Salt Lake City in his early twenties whose dedication to cigarettes caused him to turn down a golden opportunity to advance himself in the working world of men. The boy's father lamented that he had struggled for several years to find a good job that would support him as an adult. As the father told a friend about his son's troubles, the friend asked if they had heard of a program offered by the Consolidated Wagon and Machine Company in Salt Lake City. The company offered boys the opportunity to study salesmanship and business practices while earning a small allowance of $20 every month. At the end of the course, the young men would be hired by the company on a permanent basis. The father was elated, as were his wife and son. As they looked at the requirements, however, the boy's enthusiasm faded. The company prohibited users of tobacco from enrolling in the program. Suddenly the boy complained that the program was not "so attractive after all," that it was "really not just what he wanted." With that, the "boy's opportunity" that had "at last arrived" was now gone forever. The boy drifted back to his usual routine of looking for lesser jobs where "the requirements were not so rigid and the work more congenial."[34]

Reformers, schoolteachers, and employers cautioned working-class boys and adolescents that cigarette smoking would surely ruin their chances of attaining respectable jobs in an early-twentieth-century labor market that discriminated more and more against smokers. "Cigarette smoking can be of no advantage to a boy in his life's work," Henrietta Amelia Mirick wrote in her 1901 *Oral Lesson*

Book in Hygiene for Primary Teachers, "and may seriously interfere with his business chances." She urged schoolteachers who worked regularly with young boys to remind them continuously that "[m]any business men will not employ boys who smoke," insisting to her readers that the number of US firms that discriminated against smokers is "yearly increasing." The Oregon State Department of Education concurred in 1915 when they told of reformers' efforts to remind working-class boys that "many large business concerns are refusing to employ cigarette smokers." The Department of Education lamented how working-class boys failed to realize how even their first cigarette put them on a path to ruination, as "the habit" wrecked precious chances.

Reformers' antismoking treatises of the early 1900s catalogued an extensive selection of companies' policies that discriminated against boy smokers, as authors tried to overwhelm readers with employers' widespread hostility to tobacco use. Henry Ford's *The Case against the Little White Slaver* and Frederick James Pack's *Tobacco and Human Efficiency* (1918) cautioned working-class boys and parents that employers consistently denied boys entry to employment as a result of nicotine addiction and the physical, mental, and moral conditions that in their view resulted. The JC Ayer Company, for example, a chemical manufacturing firm, issued a statement to employees that read: "Believing that smoking cigarettes is injurious to both mind and body, thereby unfitting young men for their best work, therefore, after this date we will not employ any young man under twenty-one years of age who smokes cigarettes." JC Ayer managers included a rationale in their report to Frederick James Pack. In their view, only nonsmokers possessed the quickness of mind and body that was necessary for success. At the Irving-Pitt Manufacturing Company, managers reported bluntly, "We certainly discriminate against employees, particularly young men and boys, addicted to the use of cigarettes . . . we prefer to avoid employing them on general principles."[35] In Ford's censure of smoking, he cited the Cadillac Motor Car Company's policy not to employ boys who smoke, where managers insisted that "[c]igarette smoking is acquiring a hold on a great many boys in our community." The managers of the Burroughs Adding Machine Company pointed to smoking as evidence of hidden criminal tendencies among boys. Even if a boy would not lie about business, managers complained they still lied to parents about "the fact that they are smoking cigarettes." Boys who smoked hid their cigarettes, tried to conceal their habit, and stayed away from home to smoke. "They try," managers told Henry Ford, "in every way to conceal the truth."[36]

Fragments of available evidence suggest that working-class boys struggled to negotiate the tightening of employer opposition to smoking at the turn of the twentieth century. Some boys embraced the politics of antismoking to make claims of their own respectability, challenging the negative connotations of working-class boyhood that rested at the heart of antismoking reform. Still other boys voiced angry criticism of employers who prohibited smoking; these boys embraced their cigarette habit and tried to overturn the actions of managers who would ban the practice, as well as employers' insistence that boys must seek nonsmoking respectability.

Some messenger boys struggled to make antismoking politics work for them in their relationships with employers. In 1894, seventeen-year-old Charles Warren of New York, who worked for the Postal Telegraph Company, organized a reform movement among messenger boys that called for the abolition of smoking among the members of their trade. As the *New York Times* pointed out, messenger boys were "admittedly in need of reformation in several directions," which perhaps led Warren to the cause of antismoking. He apparently wanted to improve the image of messenger boys like himself by removing smoking as one of the negative activities that observers connected to his work. With the help of other adolescents, Warren tried to build a disciplined organization. Anticipating the later work of Lucy Page Gaston, he called his group of nonsmokers the "Anti-Cigarette League" and required members to sign a no-smoking pledge. Those boys who failed to abstain and broke the rules had to pay a five-cent fine.[37]

A later group of messenger boys rejected antismoking politics outright and demanded an end to the ban at the firm where they worked. A group of fifteen messenger boys in 1905 threatened to strike against the Maritime Exchange office of New York City, where the superintendent prohibited both smoking and the reading of popular dime novels among the boys in his employ. Led by a young Irish American working boy known as Mickey Aiker, the group of boys demanded the reduction of their working time by one hour each day, a fifty-cent raise in their weekly pay, permission to smoke cigarettes ("Dey wont let us smoke."), and permission to read their beloved novels. Aiker, a charismatic and influential leader among his peer group, organized the group of fourteen would-be strikers himself, and the boys sealed their loyalty to one another by burning their left arms with the "stump" of a cigarette in a "dark alley." After the boys presented their demands to the superintendent at the Maritime Exchange, the boss coolly delayed them by asking the boys to run a few errands while he considered how to address their grievances. When the messenger boys under Aiker's command returned, the superintendent told them they would be terminated the next morning if they did not arrive to work as scheduled. (As the superintendent spoke to the boys, he was simultaneously writing a "boys wanted" ad to be printed in the newspaper, according to the *Times*.) When dawn arrived the next day, only two boys actually walked off the job; Mickey Aiker was not among them. It was "Tug" O'Neil and "Mucker" Murtha who carried out the threat to strike. The fates of the fifteen working-class boys are not known; the superintendent probably quickly broke the two-man strike by bringing in new boys through the publication of the "boys wanted" notice.[38]

The extent of discrimination in workplaces widened during the Progressive Era, as employers envisioned the boundaries of the employable in terms that went beyond race, gender, ethnicity, and age. The smoking of cigarettes, too, informed managers' views of who was (and was not) an acceptable worker. In this framework of increasing discrimination against young smokers, reformers and employers cautioned boys that smoking jeopardized their chances to achieve manhood through employment. Going further, early-twentieth-century employers' disapproval of boy smokers not only legitimized discrimination against those young workers; managers' disdain for smokers extended to all job-seeking members of the working class.

Workplace Fires and Antismoking Politics

The deadly reality of frequent industrial fires, often caused by worker cigarettes and matches, lent substantial credibility and urgency to antismoking politics during the 1900s and 1910s. Reform-minded fire officials in New York City, for example, launched new efforts to regulate worker conduct in the wake of the disastrous Triangle Shirtwaist Fire of March 1911, and they identified worker-smokers as predominant sources of fire danger. Working-class adults and children certainly brought their cigarettes to work with them, as numerous examples of workplace fires illustrated. By the 1910s, the concept of "reform" in New York City industries hinged not only on justice for clothing trade workers and better fire codes and enforcement; "reform" was also very much rooted in an urgent war against working-class smoking. New fire inspectors employed by the city of New York pursued smokers throughout the factories, battling to separate working people from their perilous cigarettes. Horrible workplace fires such as the Triangle fire, often caused by workers' discarded cigarettes, reinforced the reasoning behind smoking prohibitions in the workplace. In New York, local government (rather than employers themselves) occupied the most important role in the enforcement of the bans.

The Triangle Shirtwaist Fire was one of the most horrifying disasters in the history of American industry, as 146 immigrant workers in New York City, most of them young women, died as a result of a rapidly spreading fire in a barricaded women's clothing factory. A carelessly discarded cigarette caused the blaze. This manmade crisis disrupted fundamental assumptions about labor relations and managerial authority in New York industry. The crisis disrupted the lives of hundreds of families, as loved ones were forced to confront the deaths of wives, sisters, mothers, and friends. In addition, the city of New York and the United States as a whole read journalists' accounts and court testimonies with horror. The fallout from the fire briefly created new social and political openings into which spilled public outcry, shock, calls for justice, and demands for reform. The outrage that followed the fire questioned employer management of sweatshops and other factories and led to an examination of the rights of working people within these spaces of industry, which contributed to the growing strength of the International Ladies' Garment Workers' Union (ILGWU) and the Women's Trade Union League (WTUL), legitimized ILGWU and WTUL demands for improved working conditions in New York industry, and led to greater public scrutiny of labor practices in Progressive Era factories.[39] But public anxieties regarding the sources of fire in urban space—especially cigarette smoking—also led to new scrutiny of worker behavior. As "fire prevention" quickly dominated the debates that followed the fire, a new regime of rules and regulations, sustained by expanding state powers, rapidly emerged. In particular, local authorities in New York City, especially the New York Fire Department and its new Fire Inspection Bureau, hurriedly mobilized to crack down on smoking in workplaces. Throughout the 1910s, fire inspectors went undercover to investigate tobacco use in New York's factories, issuing fines, arresting smokers, and jailing workers (and managers) for fire code violations. Following the Triangle fire, inspectors not only attacked the hazard of fire; their actions imposed new restrictions on workers' needs to smoke. While industrial safety become a matter of public concern during the Progressive Era, the new regime of fire safety rules enforced standards that curtailed personal privileges, especially working people's needs and desires to satisfy their nicotine cravings with cigarette breaks.

Writing in 1962, Leon Stein, who edited the ILGWU's *Justice*, described the Triangle fire as a "holocaust."[40] During the late afternoon of Saturday, 25 March 1911, around 4:40 p.m., as the six hundred working women and one hundred men of the Triangle Waist Company in the Asch Building near Washington Square waited for their shift to finally end and for the weekend to begin, a haphazardly discarded cigarette ignited a fire in a scrap bin filled with hundreds of pounds of cloth. The man responsible for the fire may have been cloth cutter Isidore Abramowitz or one of the men who worked near him, as the fire originated in the cloth bin at his cutting table. As David Von Drehle points out, the cloth cutters at Triangle often smoked at their tables, where they sneaked puffs of cigarettes and camouflaged the smoke by exhaling through their coat lapels. The men who smoked did so clandestinely, since the Triangle owners—Isaac Harris and Max Blanck—forbade smoking and posted no-smoking signs in Yiddish, Italian, and English. Ignoring the rule, the cloth cutters not only smoked at their workstations, but also in the stairwells of the ten-story building. The men were not, as a rule, careful with their cigarettes. As was the case on 25 March, their discarded cigarettes even found their way into the bins of cloth under the cutting tables.[41]

Fueled by a workroom that was full of cloth and cotton fibers, the fire spread rapidly from the eighth floor to the two floors above. Smoke and flames billowed from the windows. By 4:45, the first fire alarm had been sounded from the street, and more than thirty-five of New York City's firefighting "apparatuses" (most of them drawn by horses) soon arrived on the scene. Firefighters and bystanders could only look on helplessly as the horror unfolded above. Barricaded by locked doors from stairwells inside and blinded by smoke and fire, the trapped workers, most of them young women, began to jump from the windows of the Triangle shop. Some managed to climb out onto ledges, only to fall or jump when flames came too close. Using tarps and blankets, New Yorkers on the street tried to catch the jumpers, but almost all of them fell through. Their bodies crashed to the sidewalk or fell through large glass plates that covered the building's basement. Women fell into the elevator shaft as they tried to find ways to escape the flames. Fire hoses could not reach the upper floors, and the blaze continued to burn uncontrollably. By the morning of the next day, Sunday, 26 March, the extent of the death and devastation was clear: 146 workers died as a result of the fire. Trauma followed as distraught family members, friends, and frightened onlookers visited the makeshift morgue at the Twenty-Sixth Street pier to identify the dead. Overwhelmed by the charred, crushed remains of so many dead, authorities lined up the bodies in rows and asked shocked families to locate their loved ones.[42]

The Triangle crisis exposed the inner dangers and imbalanced power relations of New York's loft factories and tenement shops. In these spaces, male foremen commanded groups of women workers to work at fast paces over long hours for little money.[43] The factories were dangerous, often situated on the locked upper floors of buildings that lacked fire escapes, coordinated evacuation plans, and travelable stairwells. Published in 1912, the New York Factory Investigating Commission's *Preliminary Report* concluded that a lit cigarette, dropped on a "pile of cuttings," ignited the fire. The *Preliminary Report*'s discussions of industrial fire hazards and the issue of smoking emphasized the importance of "Prevention of Fire" as the way industry would preclude further disasters. In particular, the commission criticized management's inattention to safety. "An ounce of prevention," the commission warned, "is worth a pound of cure," and factory owners and managers had not behaved wisely. Managers of tenement shops ran their businesses without consideration for removing "rubbish," keeping the floors clear of unused cloth, or storing wasted cloth in "fireproof" receptacles.

In addition, managers and business owners failed to maintain adequate fire escapes and stairwells or to impose and enforce no-smoking rules, which were essential to preventing fires in cramped (and often wooden) tenements. For example, investigators visited a cigar factory in New York, where they spoke with a foreman about the shop rules that supposedly banned smoking. The foreman flatly told the investigators that his shop "prohibited" tobacco use, but he "was busily engaged in smoking his own cigar."[44] Managers were hypocrites. An angry letter to the *New York Times* condemned the "unnecessary peril of promiscuous smoking," a "careless" act that had triggered the Triangle fire and other industrial fires in the New York area.[45]

As the *Preliminary Report* indicated, "prevention of fire" (the commission's first recommendation) depended on successfully banning cigarette smoking. "Smoking in a factory is a constant menace to all employed therein," investigators concluded. To accomplish this important goal, the commission laid out a program that would quietly enlarge the role of local government as a regulatory body in industry and empower it with the authority to educate managers and workers about the danger of fire, inspect factory sites, and punish managers and workers for violations of fire codes and no-smoking regulations. The disruption of industrial practice caused by the Triangle Shirtwaist Fire and its aftermath created this new space. The New York Factory Investigating Commission inserted state and local government into this space and began to impose revisions to the industrial order. They demanded that managers create safer factories. Bosses would now be responsible for mandatory scheduled fire drills (overseen by the fire department), eliminating smoking, posting signs "on every floor" of their shops in multiple languages to communicate new no-smoking rules, creating safe stairwells and fire escapes, maintaining cleaner workplaces, securing exposed gas jets and sources of flame, and keeping doorways and exits "clear and unobstructed."[46] "Fire prevention" indirectly meant better treatment of workers: by creating safer spaces, the local and state governments of New York hoped to better secure the basic safety of human life on the job, establish a degree of government oversight, and foster a new ethos that stressed management's accountability to the state.

Even as the New York Factory Investigating Commission indicated that managers were to blame for dangerous conditions found in industry, the New York City fire department's subsequent focus on cigarette smoking as a key source of industrial danger brought considerable scrutiny to bear on working-class behavior. After 1911, inspectors fined and even arrested foremen and factory owners who were caught smoking; the war on smokers quickly eroded workers' immediate post-Triangle status as victims of sweatshop injustice. The prevalence of worker-smokers on the shop floor during the 1910s ensured that inspectors would view working people themselves as a key threat to industrial safety.

The 1911 Triangle fire was not a singular event, but rather part of a broader pattern of industrial fires and explosions in turn-of-the-twentieth-century New York. Workplaces burned throughout the nineteenth century and well into the twentieth, as wooden buildings, fuel oils, chemicals, paper, cloth, dropped cigarettes, heating elements, lanterns, and discarded matches frequently collided, combusted, and caused immense destruction. A survey of New York newspapers yields numerous references to fires and explosions in area workplaces—many started by dropped cigarettes and matches—that led to extensive damage and loss of life. In 1890, for example, an errand boy in Brooklyn dropped his cigarette on some discarded cotton cloth in a tailor's shop. The rapidly spreading fire destroyed much of the tailor's stock (worth about $4,500) and damaged parts of the building.[47] Later in 1901, a worker's dropped cigarette or match caused a fire in a paper factory that consumed the entire building. In fact, it was the fourth time that unlucky five-floor building had been "destroyed" by fire over the previous eight years. The following year a young woman who danced with the "Merry Maidens" burlesque show at Miner's Eighth Avenue Theatre carelessly "threw" a smoldering cigarette onto a bundle of papers in the dressing room, causing a fire that destroyed the building. The four-alarm fire burned so hot that the iron fire escapes melted, according to the write-up that appeared in the press, and a fireman named Thomas Flaherty fractured both of his legs after he fell through the burning roof onto the floor beneath. Damage estimates put the total loss at $200,000.[48]

In early November 1909, a working man accidentally dropped a cigarette down an elevator shaft at a comb-making celluloid factory in Brooklyn, igniting a blaze that killed nine and injured seven. The fire eerily prefigured the horrors of the deadliest fires of the 1910s, as the factory had iron bars on the windows that prevented workers from getting out of the building and no fire escapes that led to the street. According to survivors' accounts, workers heard a bellowing "Whoof!" sound that rumbled from below, followed quickly by fire that shot up the elevator shaft and exploded onto the floors where men worked, rupturing the windows. The sudden blast seemed to lift floors up for a moment and drop them again. The workmen, mostly Italians, stampeded as they struggled to get out of the burning building. The coroner who later inspected the wreckage was "indignant" when he saw that the factory had barricaded windows and no fire escapes.[49]

The deadliest Progressive Era fires in the New York area occurred between 1910 and 1913. On 26 November 1910, a fire in a four-story factory in Newark, New Jersey, killed at least twenty-five women and injured forty more. The fire began on the third floor, which housed a small lamp factory, and consumed the entire building within ten minutes. The floors of the factory in the fifty-year old wooden building were reportedly saturated with oil, and according to

speculation in the papers, "a careless dropping" of a match or cigarette possibly ignited the fire.[50] As the flames surged through the factory's two stairwells
and exploded from the windows, the women workers of the fourth-floor Wolf
Muslin Undergarment Company were trapped behind a locked door. Eyewit-
nesses described horrifying scenes: blinded women who leaped from the windows of the fourth-floor "furnace" and crashed on the spikes of an iron fence
below; women clinging to the sides of the building with their dresses on fire; and
women who held hands and leaped from the fourth floor to the street below,
only to crash through the firemen's nets. As the fire raged, the floors of the building quickly collapsed, crushing and burning those below who could not escape.
Two nearby hospitals filled quickly with wounded survivors and dying victims,
and family members thronged the hallways looking for sisters and daughters,
reportedly impeding the harried work of doctors and nurses. The New York Times
reported that "it was impossible to restrain them."[51] As night fell, the ruins of the
factory still smoldered, and firemen's efforts to search for bodies had to wait since
the embers still burned.[52]

As Newark reeled from the nightmare of 26 November, the vice president of
the Wolf Muslin Company, Irving Wolf, placed blame for the deaths with fore-
woman Anna Haag. He claimed that she neglected orders to coordinate fire drills
and leave doors unlocked. (Haag died as a result of her wounds—broken bones
and multiple lacerations—incurred during her escape.[53]) Following a July 1913
industrial fire in Binghamton, New York, where fifty women died, a letter to the
New York Times described cigarettes as portable sources of doom, death, and
destruction that had to be banished from all industrial settings. "We shall always
have these fire horrors," the writer noted, "as long as we have the smoke habit
which allows mankind to carry lighted fire brands into all the nooks and corners
of buildings."[54]

Passed in response to the widespread outrage that followed the tragedy at the
Triangle Waist Company, the Hoey Law of 1911 reorganized the New York Fire
Department into two branches: a division that fought fires (known as the Bureau
of Fire Extinguishment) and the new Bureau of Fire Prevention. The Bureau of
Fire Prevention made the new war against factory smoking and cigarette smokers
its core mission. As the New York Times reported in January 1912, Joseph Johnson, the new fire commissioner, was "empowered to deal with those who throw
matches, cigar and cigarette stubs heedlessly in a manner calculated to deter them
effectually from repetition of the offense and keep many other players with fire
from like heedlessness."[55] For members of the bureau, their assignment was of
utmost importance: the city of New York seemed to be menaced by "fire bugs."
In 1911 alone, the "careless" use of cigarettes, cigars, and matches accounted for
3,332 fires in New York City.[56]

Under Joseph Johnson's aggressive leadership, the Bureau of Fire Prevention fought fire danger on multiple fronts. In its first full year, 1912, the Fire Prevention Bureau ordered the installation of 128 fire extinguisher systems in factories that did not have such "protection," completed a staggering 132,601 inspections of worksites, posted more than 100,000 signs that prohibited smoking in workplaces, distributed 50,000 more signs to homeowners to warn against fire hazards in kitchens, and issued more than 18,000 citations.[57] Pursuing its work with deliberate speed and swiftness, the bureau hoped to establish itself as a key defender of public safety; at the same time, by fighting and preventing New York's fires, they wanted to establish a new regulatory order in industry.

To stop industrial smoking at the source—workers on factory floors—the Bureau of Fire Prevention deployed new fire inspectors to find and punish those men and women, both managers and workers, who smoked on the job. Smokers were regarded as dangerous elements of industrial life that had to be rooted out. Under New York's public nuisance laws, offenders could be fined or jailed for any offense that "annoys, injures, or endangers . . . the health or safety of any considerable number of persons." Attorneys advised bureau chief Joseph Johnson that he could use these laws to prosecute workplace smokers, particularly in settings that dealt with flammable materials. Smokers' actions, he would argue, constituted a threat to "the order and economy of the State."[58] Armed with this legal authority, the bureau could intervene directly and forcefully in factories, disciplining those managers and workers who violated the public trust.

Workers and managers would now have to work while looking over their shoulders for fire inspectors. If they dared to smoke indoors, they ran the risk of arrest, fines, and even imprisonment. The basic rules of the Progressive Era workplace had not changed as a result of the Triangle Shirtwaist Fire, even if factory spaces featured new sprinklers, covered trash receptacles, better fire alarms, and new fire drill requirements and prohibited the employment of children under the age of fourteen.[59] Managers still commanded the labors and work routines of the men and women who served as their employees. But working people and even members of management faced new challenges. Newspaper accounts in the *New York Times*, for instance, detailed fire inspector sweeps of workplaces that led to, in some cases, dozens of arrests for smoking. The New York City fire chief, Edward F. Croker, remarked during the New York State Factory Investigating Commission hearings in 1911 that it was "almost impossible" to stop working people from smoking. It was, he argued, regarded by working-class men and women as a "tonic" that helped them to cope with their work.[60] The Fire Inspection Bureau, however, persistently tried to use legal sanction and the power of the state to punish workers for the continued use of their "tonic."

Newspaper reports of worker-smoker arrests first appeared in February 1913. Interestingly, these early reports did not discuss the problem of smoking in textile factories or tenement sweatshops. Rather, the New York Times reported first on fire inspectors who went undercover ("out of uniform") to wage a sweeping campaign against smoking in New York auto garages, where in the month of February 1913 alone there were "several large fires" allegedly "started by careless smokers." Over a two-week period, undercover firemen secretly reported on the extent of smoking in various garages and ascertained the names of the supposedly guilty parties. Their work resulted in the arrest of twelve chauffeurs for violations of public nuisance laws. Despite the scope of the crackdown, the outcome was anticlimactic. Tried in Special Sessions, only one of the accused smokers received a $20 fine.[61]

The majority of fire inspectors' efforts centered on factories, even though the auto garage crackdown piqued the interest of the New York Times. Fire Inspection Bureau chief Joseph Johnson told the newspaper that he had "another squad of inspectors at work to stop smoking in factories."[62] A young woman, Sarah W. H. Christopher, led the group. Johnson appointed Christopher because she was a woman: there were more than 150 textile shops in the city that employed fifteen thousand women. She could (and did) disguise herself as an "operative" to infiltrate the sweatshops populated by women, searching exhaustively for smokers and fire hazards. During her first days with the bureau, Christopher sought permission to enter New York's clothing manufactories only to be refused by managers. But she returned in disguise as an "operative," secured jobs with various companies, and "obtain[ed] such information as she desired."[63]

Sarah Christopher proved to be the most successful and aggressive fire inspector in the Fire Inspection Bureau, making hundreds of arrests during her eight-month stint as an employee of the Fire Department. In January 1913, for example, three months into her service, she "caused" sixty arrests of smoking workers and foremen; in February, she put fifty-three others in jail. Christopher's tally of arrests continued to grow, and the legend of her exploits frequently appeared in the newspapers. In one instance, as Christopher toured a factory with the owner, she spotted a working man smoking a cigarette "down the length of a rather long room." She pounced, moving quickly the length of the factory hallway, cluttered with boxes and tables, to apprehend her target. The offender "choked on a mouthful of criticism" as the young woman "seize[d] the man by the collar and arrest[ed] him in the name of the law."[64] On another occasion, while inspecting fire escapes in a tenement factory, Christopher peered into a dark stairwell and noticed the tip of a "lighted cigarette" bouncing up the stairs. Once again, she "bounded" after the "man . . . at the other end" of the cigarette and quickly caught him and tore "the shirt off his back" in the process of making the arrest.[65]

Christopher was proud of the fact that she was equally tough on managers *and* workers. As a result of her February 1913 arrests alone, Christopher brought in thirteen factory owners, eleven superintendents, and twenty-nine employees. Her supervisor, Joseph Johnson, noted, "We are holding the proprietors responsible now for violations of our smoking order."[66] Sarah W. H. Christopher worked for the Fire Inspection Bureau until her civil service contract ended in May 1913. She helped to convict nearly four hundred factory "proprietors and employees" for smoking during the eight months of her service.[67]

The war on smokers lumbered on even after Sarah Christopher's departure. As Justice Zeller of the Special Sessions court remarked, "it is the intention of this court to make an example of men who persist in violating the law. There is not going to be another Triangle Shirt Waist Co. fire if this court can help it."[68] In early August 1913, the *Times* reported on the arrests of forty worker-smokers who had been cited for public nuisance violations. The lives of more than two thousand individuals, the bureau inspectors claimed, had been jeopardized by the dangerous actions of the forty accused smokers. Three of men cited were factory owners, but the rest of the accused were employees, specifically working-class men.[69]

While "fire prevention" propelled New York City's war on industrial smokers, the vigorous efforts of local officials introduced new and sustained burdens in working-class life, such as bans of the right to smoke during what were long shifts on the job, surveillance and prosecution by (often disguised) fire inspectors, hefty monetary penalties for wrongdoing, and jail terms if an individual could not (or would not) pay the fines. The war on smoking gave working people something new to worry about when they reported to work. Newspaper accounts of the Fire Inspection Bureau's war on smoking during the 1910s offer some clues as to how working-class New Yorkers improvised responses to these new burdens. As factory inspectors swept into workplaces to make arrests, some workers claimed they were only "holding" the cigarette for another individual who had just run away. Others claimed that the clouds of smoke that surrounded them stemmed from nearby gas irons, pipes, or machinery and not from recently smoked cigarettes or cigars. In one case, an accused worker-smoker claimed he was only cleaning the pipe he was holding, not smoking it, as the arresting fire inspector accused.[70]

The Triangle fire changed the daily lives of working-class smokers in ways that were burdensome and enduring. Smoking at work now brought working people under the punitive scrutiny of the state, as authorities made smoking the principal target of their war against industrial danger. In 1917, for example, fire inspectors arrested Samuel Gilbert, who worked at a shoe factory on Long Island. Found guilty of "smoking in the factory," Gilbert was sentenced by the magistrate at the Long Island City Police Court to a $20 fine or two days in jail. The worker was defiant, saying he was "unwilling to pay the fine." As Gilbert was readied for transport to jail to serve a two-day sentence, he asked the judge if he could serve his time on Saturday and Sunday so that he would not miss work. "I have to work today," he told the judge, and "You see, I be nothing out and you be nothing out." The judge refused and Gilbert went to jail. The man wryly claimed that "the Magistrate did not know a good bargain when he heard it."[71] The *New York Times* reported the incident as a joke, but Gilbert's struggle in court suggests the extent to which smoking prohibitions could disrupt workers' lives. For his defiance of the court-ordered fine, which he may not have been able to pay, Samuel Gilbert lost a day of work and possibly more as a result of his two-day jail sentence. The war on smoking *did* take prisoners.

The war on smoking also unfolded in New York's commuter spaces. Subways and surface trains increasingly became sites where local authorities scrutinized and policed smoker activity every day. The *New York Times* noted that the number of police citations issued for smoking on trains had jumped from 127 in 1911 to more than 226 for January and February 1912 alone.[72] In these antismoking dragnets of public spaces, police frequently penalized working-class individuals. On the Brooklyn Bridge, a pair of "printers' devils" had been "nabbed" as they smoked. Feeling arbitrarily harassed by the police, the printers "decided to stay around and see that others were served as they had been, that the rich men's finest leaf, if lighted, should be penalized as well as the little home-made cigarette of the impecunious." They noisily called for nearby policemen to act as other city dwellers boarded the train with lit cigarettes.[73] During the same day, policemen issued a citation to an African American man for smoking a cigarette on a train who coolly remarked, "One cigarette—one summons." After receiving the citation, he "serenely finished his smoke." In response, members of the Health Squad later explained to police that "each subsequent puff" should be treated as "a fresh offense."[74] By 1913–1914, tobacco stores in New York featured signs in their windows that proclaimed "Smokers, Assert Your Rights!" but a United Cigar Stores petition to the Public Service Commission that one of every five subway cars should be a smoking car, which received seventy thousand signatures, was quashed by a commission resolution to uphold smoking bans on the trains.[75]

For working men and women in Progressive Era New York, improving safety measures and the added scrutiny of industrial practices in industry came at a price. The city's war on smoking emerged from the smoldering ashes of the Triangle Shirtwaist Fire and led to new scrutiny of shop floor behavior that would have greatly affected the everyday work experiences of working-class men and women. As local government mobilized to fight smoking in factories in order to create safer workplaces and ultimately a safer city, worker-smokers came to be regarded as major sources of industrial peril. Loud complaints about "careless" smokers were broad enough to encompass managers and workers, but working people lost their status as sufferers of shop floor injustice and became targets of Fire Inspection Bureau sweeps and arrests. The Triangle Shirtwaist Fire of 1911 created a political space where numerous "reforms" could be envisioned and implemented during the Progressive Era, but the state's actions during the crisis engendered new burdens for working-class men and women that would continue for years: worker-smoker arrests in New York continued into 1920s, 1930s, and 1940s. The Triangle crisis created a moment where witnesses could press for change, but the consequences of the state's actions were varied, multi-dimensional, and unexpected. Subtly, the war on smoking transformed labor relations in New York, adding layers of workplace surveillance that condemned worker-smokers' behaviors and addictions to nicotine.

Despite the efforts of concerned moral reformers and employers, "the little white slaver" continued to expand in popularity throughout the early twenti-eth century. In 1916, US tobacco companies produced an estimated 25 billion cigarettes; by 1943, the number had increased to 255 billion.[76] Cigarette smoke continued to envelope the streets of major cities, inundate the lungs of many working-class boys and adults, and drift into the workplace. Addictive ciga-rette smoke even directly entered the airways of some of the most prominent citizens and allies of the anticigarette cause. In 1911, Elizabeth White of the Anti-Cigarette League charged into the Boston office of Governor Eugene N. Foss (a vice president of the league), hoping to urge the governor to involve himself more directly in the work of the busy League. As White flew into Foss's office, the governor hastily dropped his lit cigarette into the ashtray on his desk. A pack of cigarettes was in plain sight. Not realizing at first what Governor Foss was doing, White praised him for "investigating these terrible things yourself." Still not realizing that the governor was actually smoking a cigarette White mused, "Can you believe it? Some men of prominence have actually declined to help me—even said they smoked the filthy things themselves. Can you believe it?" The governor responded, "Madam, I can. In fact, I smoke them myself and that's my favorite brand you've got your hand on." The *New York Times* jokingly speculated that Elizabeth White's next act of business would surely be to eject Governor Foss from his high-profile post as vice president of the Anti-Cigarette League.[77] Despite the moralizing of the Anti-Cigarette League and the impas-sioned appeals of prominent citizens such as Henry Ford, the popularity of ciga-rette smoking continued to grow throughout the early decades of the twentieth century. In this particular incident, "the little white slaver" apparently claimed one of the league's most visible and prominent leaders, its vice president for the state of Massachusetts, Governor Eugene N. Foss.

During the Progressive Era, moral reformers and industrial employers forged a powerful antismoking culture that was intended to sweeten the air of the city, uplift the morals, abilities, and potential of working-class boys, and better regulate the impact of working people on the urban environment. In addition to moral, gender, and sensorial arguments against smoking, prevalent urban worries about the reality of fire dangers led to aggressive state policing of worker smoking. As the antismoking politics of the Progressive Era illustrates, social class and the workplace were central concerns of those reformers and employers who so staunchly opposed cigarette smoking. Moreover, the bodies and morals of working-class boys became central sites in middle-class crusades against the sinister cigarette.

The power and influence of antismoking politics could be readily felt in the workplace, yet the shop floor emerged as a key site of worker resistance to no-smoking rules and the power of the employers that instituted them. Facing long hours on the job, workers would push again and again for the ability and the time to smoke cigarettes at work. Just as working-class boys sometimes did in their own work sites, adult worker-smokers of the 1900s and 1910s often rejected outright the tedious and frustrating bans of smoking that were now so central to manager policies at work.

2

SMOKING BANS AND SHOP FLOOR RESISTANCE DURING THE EARLY TWENTIETH CENTURY

Nicotine is an addictive drug. It causes changes in the brain that make people want to use it more.

—American Heart Association

As expanding numbers of men and women smoked cigarettes during the early 1900s and became addicted to nicotine, they needed to consume more cigarettes more frequently. They would smoke at home, on the train, in restaurants, at work, on sidewalks, and even in elevators. According to the *New York Times*, in 1908 alone Americans consumed an estimated 5.5 billion cigarettes, which equaled 2,500 for "each man and each boy" in the country over the course of the year, an overall increase of 250 million cigarettes since 1907. (The paper wrongly assumed that all smokers were men.[1]) The typical smoker, the paper claimed, consumed as many as forty cigarettes per day.[2] Widening addiction during the early twentieth century facilitated a bottom-up challenge to the socially and culturally conservative Victorian rule makers of American society. Between 1893 and 1909, state governments in Washington, North Dakota, Wisconsin, Iowa, Tennessee, Kansas, South Dakota, Indiana, Oklahoma, and Minnesota banned the sale of cigarettes, while a broad cross-section of employers both large and small discriminated against smokers.[3] "Men with yellow forefingers and thumbs," the *New York Times* noted in 1909, "became more and more conscious of the fact that in job hunting they carried a handicap."[4] Despite their opposition, employers would not be able to stem the rising tide of addiction to nicotine nor the impact of smoking on working-class life. As their businesses grew and increasing numbers of workers walked through the factory gates, adult smokers brought their addictions and habits (and stained fingers) with them to work every day. Many working people became worker-smokers in the early 1900s, and their habits and addictions to nicotine would ignite struggles over workers' shop floor rights and the ability of employers to set rules, establish discipline, and monitor behavior. Workers needed to dampen their hunger for nicotine with frequent, and often clandestine, breaks from work, typically in defiance of "no-smoking" rules, employer designations for the uses of factory space, and bosses' demands for continuous production.[5]

This chapter revisits the shop floor in American labor history, terrain that is well-worn by social historians of the working class. Beginning in the 1960s and 1970s, historians of labor wrote about new generations of industrial workers who struggled with changing work processes and the degradation of work as a result of industrialization and mechanization, which resulted in worker resistance on the shop floor and sometimes broader forms of collective protests such as strikes and unionization.[6] Still other historians of labor, influenced by scholarship in women's history and African American history, have shown how workplaces have been key sites of struggle over racial, gender, and ethnic identities, boundaries, and entitlements. Workers, both skilled and unskilled, have historically defined their occupations along these lines, and thus work cultures typically affirm these boundaries. Work culture provides a basis for criticism of management,[7] but the gendered and racialized foundations of many work cultures ensure they are often just as parochial and conservative, hostile to newcomers and outsiders.[8]

The subject of cigarette smoking leads us to new paths and footprints in the familiar terrain that is the factory floor. Throughout the nineteenth century, alcohol consumption intoxicated much of American society and the industrial working class, fostering oppositional work cultures among men that belied employer, reformer, and craft union demands for steady work and respectable temperance.[9] In the early twentieth century, cigarettes added a new dimension to drug use in the workplace. The convergence of intensifying tobacco addiction and the rise of mass production labor during the 1910s transformed work cultures and shop floor relations. Struggles over cigarette smoking on the shop floor heightened labor-management conflict in the workplaces of modern industry, as smoking created new reasons for workers to oppose management's rules and industrial work discipline and paved the way for new forms of worker collectivity. The pangs of nicotine addiction compelled workers to reclaim time from employers to satisfy their cravings, and smoking created informal social networks that nurtured conversations among workers about workplace policies and management's shortcomings.[10] Lastly, worker-smokers pursued wide, sometimes secretive patterns of movement that encompassed familiar and forbidden areas of factory space—and led them to claim many of these prohibited spaces as their own—as they sought out sanctuaries where they could smoke without being detected. If a depressant (alcohol) dominated working-class culture during the nineteenth century, cigarettes introduced a stimulant (nicotine) to the working class during the early twentieth. As cigarette smoking became a central part of working-class culture, workers' desire for nicotine would challenge, and even begin to trans-form, the space, motion, and time discipline of modern industrial capitalism.

This chapter begins with an examination of early-twentieth-century employ-ers' views of adult smokers' purported tendencies and liabilities in the workplace and with policies that discriminated against smokers at the point of hire and on the shop floor. The bulk of the chapter explores the surprising intensity of working-class resistance to smoking prohibitions on the industrial shop floor, using a uniquely detailed case study of labor-management relations in one Pro-gressive Era factory to highlight the intensity of workers' evasions and opposi-tion to smoking bans. The connections between smoking and the shop floor are not easily studied in a consistent fashion for the early twentieth century, as refer-ences to smoking in mass-production factories and other workplaces are scatter-shot. A specific set of surviving records from the Hammermill Paper Company, a paper manufacturer once based in Erie, Pennsylvania, however, provide a valuable opportunity to explore the impact of cigarette consumption on labor relations during the era of mass production, as two nosy factory spies probed and docu-mented worker actions and attitudes during the summer months of 1915. The spies discovered a factory-wide work culture rooted in the addictive pleasure of cigarette smoke, and the discovery worried them. Working-class smokers moved about the factory in ways that made surveillance difficult, while at the same time they disregarded their work and ignored many rules pertaining to managerial con-trol of time and space.

Employer Discrimination against Adult Smokers, 1900–1918

The Hammermill Paper Company was one among the many industrial firms of the early twentieth century that prohibited smoking among workers. Employers, in industry but also in other areas of the economy, insisted throughout the 1900s, 1910s, and beyond that worker-smokers were sources of low-quality work, inef-ficiency, liability, and subversion. During the early twentieth century, newspapers and reformers' antismoking treatises referenced smoking bans in numerous areas of the economy, such as railroad operations, where "it is the general practice to forbid smoking of any kind while on duty"; carpentry, where contractors "will not employ even moderate drinkers and forbid smoking upon the job"; and the auto industry, where at Cadillac and the Ford Motor Company the manage-ment "allow no cigarette smoking about the plant." Going further, numerous early-twentieth-century workers in manufacturing, public school teaching, sales, and retail confronted smoking bans.[11]

The expansion of employer discrimination against adult smokers coincided with the nadir of workers' and organized labor's power during the early twentieth century. Between the years of the Haymarket bombing (1886), the failed strikes at Homestead (1892) and Pullman (1894), and the onset of CIO unionism (1935), union representation and membership throughout the United States remained ephemeral or outright unattainable for the vast majority of working people, especially those who were regarded as unskilled. Of 15.9 million workers in US industry in 1900, for example, only 2 million of them were in a union in 1904, a number that showed a hefty 400 percent increase since 1896. Despite this spurt of growth at the turn of the twentieth century, only 12 percent of US workers belonged to a union in 1904.[12] While major strikes, organizing efforts, and periods of union growth did occur during these years, these actions did not produce an enduring industrial union presence that could significantly counter the expansion of employer control of work during the early twentieth century. For instance, the 1909 "uprising" of immigrant women garment workers in New York City, the 1913 coal strike in southern Colorado, and the nationwide steel strike of 1919 produced moments of hope that unskilled working people might secure greater control over the conditions of their labor, but employer violence and continued state cooperation in the breaking of strikes ruined these opportunities to bring democracy to the shop floors of the East and Midwest and the coal tipples of the West.[13]

Amid such limited avenues for formal worker protest, employers of the 1900s and 1910s were able to forge and institutionalize a powerful culture of hostility to working-class smoking, framing cigarettes as a dangerous threat to the functioning of productive labor, a menace to employers' control of the workplace, and a source of worker dishonesty in the factory. The open shop proved to be an enabler of both antiunionism and antismoking politics.

Managers of the early 1900s and 1910s worried that cigarette smoke sickened and slowed those men who labored in their operations, creating widespread inefficiency. In Chicago, for instance, the *Chicago Daily Tribune* noted in April 1900 that numerous places of business in the city banned cigarette smoking largely because "the habit is incompatible with efficient service." In a city that imagined itself as the most dynamic and expansive commercial hub of the US economy, employers surely would be quick to condemn the cigarette habit that drew adult workers away from their posts. Employers reported of their objection to cigarettes "that physically they affect the employee so that he cannot give the best service to the employer." In these years after the Pullman boycott, managers throughout Chicago were able to demand (and receive) the cooperation of workers in their intensifying demands for efficiency. Cigarettes would have to be jettisoned in the service of employers' rising expectations. Employers such as the inventor Thomas Edison, who operated electrical products factories in West

Orange, New Jersey, that employed 6,700 workers, believed that cigarette papers (not the tobacco itself) contained so many poisons that they wrought "havoc with a man's mental activity." Edison lamented, "His mind becomes clouded." As a result, men who smoked became the dumbest and least capable workers. In 1914, Edison banned smoking in his plants, posting signs that read: "Cigarettes NOT TOLERATED. They Dull the Brain." Employers insisted that non-smokers were simply the better brand of worker for modern industry. At Cadillac in Detroit, managers claimed that men who abstained from cigarettes (and the saloon) "make better automobiles."[14] Employers' claims of a connection between smoking and poor work performance and inefficiency greatly legitimized anti-smoking policies. If a factory were to function properly, its workers must be smoke-free.

Employers of the early twentieth century complained that cigarette smoking not only produced sluggish adult workers but left enduring physical imprints on

FIGURE 2.1 "Anti-smoking sign in Zion City." (1912) Founded in 1901, Zion City is directly north of Chicago on the coast of Lake Michigan. *Chicago Daily News* negatives collection, Chicago History Museum, http://hdl.loc.gov/loc. ndlpcoop/ichicdn.n058627. Courtesy of the Library of Congress.

the body that rendered worker-smokers unattractive and offensive to the senses of customers and nonsmoking coworkers. In a *Chicago Daily Tribune* overview of cigarette bans and anticigarette group activities in Chicago retail, the unnamed writer pointed out that the "smell of nicotine" that emanates from the breath of worker-smokers "is annoying" to customers as well as to other employees of the firm who "are not users."[15] Another *Tribune* article in 1912 narrated the troubles of a smoker ("Mr. Smith") seeking a sales position at a manufacturing firm in Chicago. At the start of his interview, the "expert salesman" Mr. Smith lit a cigarette as the conversation began with his would-be boss, "Mr. Manufacturer." The job seeker assumed there would be no problem since the manager smoked a cigarette of his own. After remarking on the applicant's fine taste in "good cigarettes," Mr. Manufacturer said, "I'll drop you a line alright" about the position. Smith did not get the job. Angry about not being hired, the "expert salesman" returned to demand a reason. Mr. Manufacturer received him kindly but explained that "it was the cigarettes" that ruined his application. While the boss smoked cigarettes himself, he made no apologies for the fact that he would not hire smokers for his sales force. "I know many of this concern's customers who take a violent dislike to them, but I don't see these people," he said. "If you should go into one of my customers' stores and offer him a cigarette, even if he were smoking one himself, he would have you down as a man who was weak as himself." In other words, the sight and smell of cigarettes in the realm of business could jeopardize company sales, as customers made arbitrary judgments about the personal qualities of the salesman. "This is a new era of selling," Mr. Manufacturer explained. Smokers could never serve as effective company representatives. Of cigarette smokers he said, "They can't shine in the world of big business anymore."[16]

Much to workers' frustration, managers' actions toward the adult smokers in their employ could be arbitrary and unpredictable. In 1908, for example, the Pittsburg Railways Company quietly broadened the scope of the firm's ban on smoking to include conduct while off duty. An unknowing conductor returned to work after a layoff only to discover that he had been fired for "smoking a cigarette while he was enjoying leisure time." Another off-duty worker visited the Pittsburg Railways car barns to collect his pay, walking into the workspace "smoking a cigarette." He was fired. In Chicago, "AE" was dismissed in 1905 after he left his desk one too many times to smoke. The clerk was a purported "cigarette fiend" whose addiction led him to take a break every hour to satisfy his cravings. Apparently, he had done so for quite some time and was never warned that he was jeopardizing his job. "One day the boss found him," the *Daily Tribune* wrote of the man, "and he learned that bosses can do things that mere employes [*sic*] cannot do," for although the boss was himself smoking, he fired AE.[17]

Some industrial managers of the early twentieth century readily pointed to cigarettes as a source of danger on the job, subtly using smoking to point to worker error as the overriding source of workplace accidents. In St. Louis, the superintendent of a local streetcar company claimed that men who smoked cigarettes were just as dangerous on the job as those who drank alcohol. Due to smokers' addictions to nicotine, they possessed jangled nerves that were "apt to give way at any moment." The superintendent even insisted that he worried more about smokers than drinkers on his streetcars. "If I find a car running badly," he said, "I immediately begin to investigate to find if the man smokes cigarettes." According to the superintendent, nine of ten cases of poor performance resulted from tobacco use.[18] In Chicago, the Rock Island Railroad banned smoking in 1900 on the basis of managers' belief that smokers were "listless" and "careless" as a result of their all-consuming addictions to nicotine. Smokers were thought to be irresponsible, lazy, and dopey, "of no account." To be a trainman, workers needed to possess both a clear head and strong body. In fact, the Rock Island Railroad no longer considered the application of any man who smoked.[19] Employers on the rails condemned smoking as a guarantor of poor and unsafe performance.

Employers of the early 1900s also feared that cigarette smoking clouded and stained the morals of their working-class employees. In his *The Case against the Little White Slaver*, published in 1916, auto magnate Henry Ford claimed that cigarette smokers were "loose in their morals" and "very apt to be untruthful," which were the central reasons why his Ford Motor Company refused to employ them. Ford lifted his words from the Cadillac Motor Company smoking ban, where managers boasted of a totally smoke-free factory: "We allow no cigarette smoking about the plant; in fact, will not hire men who we know use cigarettes. . . . It is our desire to weed it entirely out of the factory."[20] A business manager in Chicago claimed in 1905 that workers' addictions to nicotine brought about moral and physical ruin: "there is something in cigaret smoking which saps a man's character and manhood the same time as it is sapping his health, and long before he is 'all in' as to his body he is a wreck in character. He is dishonest, unself-respecting, and this is the end of any man." In particular, the Chicago employer viewed the working-class smoker as a "slave to the habit," which retarded the worker's self-respect, decency, and ambition over time.[21] Men in moral decline presumably scared managers, as these individuals would be more likely to disobey orders, question management's authority, and possibly commit acts of thievery and deceit. Cigarettes could thereby undermine the business foundations of managerial authority and productive labor from within.

Prohibitions against smokers were so widespread that newspapers of the early 1900s thought it unusual when employers voiced no apprehension about smoking or if they even proclaimed a preference for those who contented themselves with cigarettes or cigars on the job. R. F. Haegelin of Franklin MacVeagh & Co. in Chicago remarked that he did not find fault with smoking among the men in his sales force. "I presume that some cigaret smokers are poor and some very good salesmen," Haegelin said. He noted that "a genuine cigaret fiend" would probably struggle in his role as a salesman, but there was no urgent reason to otherwise deny employment to a smoker. An employer from outside New York City boasted of his outright preference for smokers. He claimed that working men completed their tasks more quickly and with greater care when they were allowed to smoke. "Mind, I do not find any fault with the non-smoker—on the contrary I admire the man who does not use the weed," the man remarked. "But when it comes down to real old hard work I will take the smoker every time when I want my job done quickly." The man's preference for smokers was so unusual that his business contacts in New York City "gave a laugh" when he told them "smokers preferred."[22]

The potentially vast scope of employer smoking bans and manager discrimination against smokers in industrial regions is subtly underlined by commuter reactions to the city of Chicago's ban of smoking on its elevated trains during the 1918 influenza pandemic. In October 1918, the city health commissioner of Chicago, John Dill, announced that smoking would be banned on elevated trains in order to minimize the aggressive spread of the flu. (Blowing secondhand smoke into the air would spread germs.) "Darn the flu!" the editors of the *Chicago Daily Tribune* complained, adopting the opinion of many readers. "Bid farewell, devotees of nicotine, to that long cherished after breakfast cigar or cigaret on the way downtown."[23] The announcement stoked significant opposition among Chicago smokers, who depended on the train as a place and time to smoke their cigarettes and cigars before venturing into places of work, where apparently no one could smoke. Some worker-smokers sent a petition to the mayor of Chicago, William Hale Thompson, to voice their anger. "The petition makes the point," the *Tribune* noted, "that to thousands of workers the sole opportunity in each day for indulgence in cigar, pipe, or cigaret is afforded in the ride to and from employment."[24] Smokers' protests might have influenced policy makers' views of the ban, as the city council overturned it in 1919.[25]

Despite widespread smoking bans at work during the early twentieth century, adult smokers could still be seen in many workspaces throughout the US economy. In 1900, a Chinese American laundry worker found himself charged with "talking disrespectfully" to a customer when he "disdainfully" flicked ashes from his cigarette onto the angry customer's laundry. In February 1906, immigrant working men who had been contracted to shovel snow smoked cigars and cigarettes as they worked in the chilly New York City streets. In 1909, nervous

FIGURE 2.2   "Smoker (train car) on the Chicago and Oak Park elevated line with people sitting on benches on either side of the car facing inward." (1909) *Chicago Daily News* negatives collection, Chicago History Museum, http://hdl. loc.gov/loc.ndlpcoop/ichicdn.n007938. Courtesy of the Library of Congress.

strikebreakers in McKees Rocks outside of Pittsburgh smoked cigarettes at the Pressed Steel Car Company, where managers punished them by imprisoning the rule breakers inside a railcar-turned-jail cell.[26] And despite the ban on smoking at the Hammermill Paper Company in Erie, Pennsylvania, workers there smoked cigarettes in blatant defiance of management, much to the vexation of the labor spies who were hired to watch and document their every move.

The Decision to Hire Spies at Hammermill

Historians can only speculate why Ernst Behrend, owner and president of the Hammermill Paper Company, decided to hire a pair of professional spies to prowl around his mill in 1915. No letter, memo, or document housed in the Hammermill archive at Penn State Erie specifically explains his reasons. But based on the language of the spies' reports, recent events inside Hammermill, patterns of labor unrest in the Progressive Era paper industry, and broader insurgencies of labor in the 1900s and 1910s, it is possible to gain a fuller understanding of the likely concerns regarding the political and personal habits of the working class that surely shaped Behrend's decision.[27]

HAMMERMILL PLANT *in* 1899
TAKEN FROM THE BEHREND RESIDENCE
House under construction at left is Sulphite Mill superintendent's home

FIGURE 2.3   Hammermill Paper Company Collection, Accession 1994.1, Behrend College Archives, University Libraries, Pennsylvania State University.

Behrend did not intend at the outset for the labor spies to specifically root out smoking. He was undoubtedly most concerned about precluding labor unrest. During the early 1910s, there had been significant conflicts between Hammermill managers and working men and women in various departments over wages and hours. For example, Behrend was aggravated by a sudden March 1913 strike of the Polish men in the wood room over wages. The strike turned violent, as Polish strikers "intimidate[d]" and "interfere[d]" with workers who wanted to stay on the job. Two men were reportedly injured during the picketing. Behrend complained that the local police "sympathize[d]" with the Poles, and the local government was afraid to intervene for fear of losing worker votes in upcoming elections.[28] To break the strike, Behrend used his state-given "right to arrest" and hired two "special detectives" from the renowned William J. Burns' National Detective Agency to help re-establish control over the factory grounds.[29] Management slowly undermined the strike with the introduction of strikebreakers, though Behrend complained about the poor quality of their work.[30] Exactly one year later, Behrend received a petition from fifty-seven women in the finishing room, presumably about low wages. In a letter to an associate in Germany, Behrend complained that Erie "has been overrun by professional labor agitators," which has created "warlike and riotous" labor conditions in his mill and other factories.[31]

For Behrend, the wood room strike and even the finishing workers' petition surely reflected what he must have seen as ominous developments in the early-twentieth-century paper industry and labor relations writ large over the previous handful of years. In August 1908 and March 1910, for instance, the *New York Times* reported on sudden surges of labor unrest in the paper mills of New England and New York. In 1908, the trouble began in New York State when the International Paper Company (the "Paper Trust") announced a 10 percent wage cut, prompting locals of the International Brotherhood of Paper Makers to call for a strike. Initially, 2,000 workers walked off the job, but the strike quickly spread from the unionized mills to the independents. The number of strikers grew from 2,200 in August to more than 7,000 by late September. In October 1908, however, the strike ended when workers abruptly gave up and accepted a 5 percent wage cut. If Behrend or his executives read the *New York Times* or corresponded with managers at the striking paper companies, they would have been alarmed by the impact of the union's strike call on the mills of New York and on those of Maine, Vermont, and New Hampshire. During the strike, the production of paper in the embattled mills of the East slowed to a trickle, as manufacturers could only run machines with occasional strikebreakers or, as the *New York Times* euphemistically noted, "any one the company could find competent."[32] Their concerns would have been reinforced by future paper mill strikes at International Paper facilities in New York during 1910, when 5,700 men walked off the job at twenty-five different factories. As a result of the 1910 strikes at International Paper, the men secured the abolition of Sunday work, a wage increase, and an eight-hour day maximum for machine workers.[33] The outcome of these strikes would have certainly given Behrend reason for concern.

Closer to home, Progressive Era strike violence in the nearby cities of Cleveland, Buffalo, and Pittsburgh surely caused additional worry for the Erie-based management of Hammermill. In the spring of 1909, for example, seamen "of all classes" who worked for various Great Lakes shipping companies launched a massive strike against the nonunion Lake Carriers' Association that idled more than twelve thousand workers throughout the region. The *New York Times* dubbed it "the great struggle."[34] Worker rebellion on the waters and shores of the Great Lakes rocked port cities throughout the region.[35] Riots and assaults occurred on the docks in Milwaukee, Chicago, Cleveland, and even Erie itself. On the Cleveland waterfront, only one hundred miles west of Erie, "there were several riots" as strikers threw stones at the boats; private guards from the Erie Railroad police opened fire, injuring one man. On the Erie docks, a nonunion watchman on a boat from Cleveland was shot "during a wrangle" between strikers and nonunion workers.[36] This "great struggle" for the unionization of the Lakes Carriers' ships, and the Great Lakes region as a whole, surely forced Ernst Behrend and Hammermill managers to confront the immediate possibility that labor unrest on the shores of the Great Lakes would eventually find its way into the lakefront facilities of Hammermill, as it actually did in 1913.

In the Great Lakes and Northeast regions that surrounded Erie, the labor insurgencies of the Progressive Era often looked like social revolution from below. On 14 July 1909, only a few weeks after the Great Lakes seamen struck, immigrant workers and their families at the Pressed Steel Car Company in McKees Rocks, Pennsylvania, near Pittsburgh went on strike to protest low pay and the lack of fixed wages. Managers there rebuffed riveters' petitions for a set wage, which led to the strike call. "Then the men in various departments became interested," the *New York Times* noted, "and although there is no union in the plant, practically all formed a mutual agreement to strike."[37] More than 3,500 men walked off the job.[38]

Violence erupted in McKees Rocks throughout July and August and lasted until 8 September, when the strike ended. Strikebreakers, police, state troops, and company guards battled against thousands of angry working men and women in the streets of the town. Class struggle became class warfare in western Pennsylvania. Five hundred women attacked the company-owned restaurant, where they reportedly threw "small bombs" at state troops. Striking men shot and seriously wounded a company doctor, and six strikebreakers were poisoned.[39] Nine men died and "scores" more were wounded in the fifty-five-day Pressed Steel strike.[40] The anger did not dissipate, and a second violent strike erupted in April 1910.[41] The press's discussions of the violence in McKees Rocks surely worried newspaper readers in Pittsburgh, Erie, and beyond.

The various strikes demonstrated the possibilities for militant labor unrest among local and regional workers and the potential for violence those struggles could entail. Behrend wanted to maintain a stable operating basis for his business by preventing unionization and strikes, and he sought to preclude the labor unrest and unionization that erupted in the region. (The later Mine Wars of the early 1910s, which occurred in the nearby state of West Virginia and states in the West, might have reinforced Behrend's worries about the explosiveness of labor relations in early-twentieth-century America.[42]) Certainly, Behrend imagined that labor spies would provide him with crucial firsthand intelligence that would help him maintain control over the present and future of his paper mill.

The Arrival of the Labor Spies

Was Ernst Behrend new to the business of spying? Maybe, since he secured the services of a noted industrial spying firm that specialized in the task. He apparently wanted the job done right. Probably in the spring or early summer of 1915, he made arrangements with Howard W. Russell, owner of the Manufacturers and Merchants Inspection Bureau, a family-owned and family-operated company based in Milwaukee, that specialized in "systematic surveillance" and "espionage work in factories," to secure the services of two agents.[43] Behrend possibly first learned of the company's services as a result of Russell's marketing efforts: unsolicited letters, sent directly to owners of industrial firms, describing how his "trained representatives" could help employers efficiently and effectively preclude any troubles with labor.[44] In a note Russell sent to Behrend, the letterhead assured him:

> We . . . Observe What is Not for the Eyes of the Boss . . . Insure You Against Loss, Trouble and Worry . . . Take Charge of Strikes and Labor Troubles . . . Furnish Union Reports . . . Disclose Collusion/Expose Theft and Graft . . . Ascertain Habits of Employees . . . Stop Vitiation of Employees by Agitators . . . Discourage Idleness . . . Report All Irregularities . . . Investigate Salesmen, Purchasing Agents, and Department Heads.[45]

The Manufacturers and Merchants Inspection Bureau promised to help Behrend extend managerial authority into the most mysterious and distant depths of his business: the dingy shop floor areas populated by working-class men and women. Bureau investigators boldly promised to unearth "what is not for the eyes of the boss," that is, the attitudes and behaviors of unskilled laborers and the insidious actions of union organizers (labeled by Howard W. Russell as "agitators, chronic kickers, [and] dishonest or disloyal employees"), as well as possible wrongdoing by white-collar workers and department-level managers.

The pair of spies sent by the bureau, known only as "FP" and "HC," arrived in Erie at different times during the summer of 1915. FP arrived in town on 22 June, HC in August. According to FP's first report, he traveled by train from an unspecified destination (probably Milwaukee) to the city of Chicago, where he boarded a second train bound for Erie. He rode on the Lake Shore & Michigan Southern Railway and spent a comfortable night in a sleeper. FP arrived in Erie at 5:05 a.m. and journeyed by streetcar to the Hammermill plant, where he turned up at 8:15. He met with Ernst Behrend (whom he referred to as "the Client"). Behrend explained to FP what he wanted, but the spy did not disclose the details: "Briefly, the Client told me about what information he desired, and he laid special stress on what he *did not* [*sic*] want; that is, anything that I know nothing about." Following this short conversation, a member of the Hammermill management took FP on a tour of the mill. He was instructed that he would begin work the next day as a sulphite weigher. FP never spoke again with "the Client." He secured a room at a boarding house ("Bergenkamp's home") on 708 Payne Avenue in Erie. The next day, on 23 June, he began his intelligence gathering.[46]

HC's early August journey to Erie, Pennsylvania, closely resembled FP's itinerary. Like FP, HC traveled by train to Chicago, where he boarded another that took him east to Erie. HC's writings proved to be less descriptive than those of his colleague. He did not provide many additional details about his trip or arrival in town except to note that he was an hour late as a result of a flood in downtown Erie. Company records and the spies' reports fail to specifically explain why the Manufacturers and Merchants Inspection Bureau sent a second spy to Hammermill so long after FP's arrival, but it was standard practice in the labor spy industry to deploy at least two spies to the site under surveillance.[47] Russell and Behrend surely expected that the spies, working in different departments at different times, would provide the most comprehensive view possible of worker attitudes and actions in the factory. HC received specific instructions to "apply" for work in the paper machine rooms. HC did not discuss any meeting with "the Client," but he did meet a man named Nesbitt, who was a factory superintendent. HC finally found a position in the finishing room on 6 August, where women workers counted paper sheets and men worked as pilers, stacking paper bundles.[48] He began there, in the department where the workers' petition of 1914 originated.

The spies' first duty was to file daily reports (five to eight pages long, on average) that explained in detail any problems they noticed in the locations where they worked. The content of these reports suggests that the agents interpreted this aspect of their work to mean any waste or ruining of materials or other deficiencies in the production process and ineffective supervision of workers and the physical condition of the factory floor and external grounds (cleanliness, organization, etc.). Their second and more important responsibility was to name names: troublemakers, loafers, complainers, "kickers," and unionists. On HC's first day of work, for example, he noted several incidents in his five-page report to managers. He spoke with new coworker John Gode, a paper piler, who complained that workers in the finishing room never received full pay for full-time work. Gode went on to angrily describe Hammermill "as 'cheap' a 'dump' that he had ever worked in."[49] HC talked about other coworkers in the paper piling section who "make a practice of bothering the girls." This flirting, he wrote, prevented the women in the finishing room from completing their work and led the men to "neglect their own duties."[50] The spies, however, routinely went beyond their orders to simply report. They offered frequent suggestions to managers

about how to effectively manage worker behaviors. HC specifically blamed working men's flirting on "lax" supervision. A firmer hand would be needed to rein
in these rollicking, oversexed men, and "I would therefore suggest that the Client
'brush up' the foreman on this."[51]

These reports provide a detailed and intimate look at the workings of shop
floor culture inside Hammermill. The spies entered the factory looking for signs
of social revolution, but they found scant evidence of the deep-seated discontent
that fueled upheavals like the coal miner strikes of the early 1910s. Rather, the
spies discovered an overwhelming degree of everyday rebelliousness: men who
frequently did not show up to work or only chased women when they did; workers who took hour-long breaks in the bathroom; conversations about baseball
or buying tickets for prohibited baseball pools; "booze fighters" who reported to
work smelling of whiskey; men who slept on the job and only woke up to lazily
urinate behind a machine; and, most frequently, workers who left their jobs
to smoke cigarettes and pipes and to chew tobacco.[52] As they discovered, these
transgressions seemed to transform the factory from a site of coordinated and
controlled mass production to a leisure site dominated by smokers, drinkers,
baseball fans, flirts, and seekers of sleep. The spies' reports indicated, however,
that smoking was very much a foundation of workers' everyday rebellions. It
was the overriding reason why working men abandoned their machines, lingered in the factory bathrooms, and gathered to talk (and complain) with their
coworkers.

While industrial employers used spies as part of their effort to undermine
unionization, the writings of factory spies, where available, provide useful information about social relations and working-class culture in early-twentieth-
century industry.[53] The production of spy reports are testimony to employers'
growing power in the early 1900s, but the content of the reports at Hammermill
indicated that workers were establishing significant limits on employer power
and imposing their own interpretations of rules and privileges.

Smoking and the (Ab)uses of Space

Paper manufacturing at the Hammermill factory was heavily mechanized by the
1910s, and as a result, the machines did not require workers' constant attention.[54] While autoworkers, for example, often complained about the physical-
ity, repetitiveness, and discipline that accompanied the transition to mechanized
labor during the 1910s, 1920s, and early 1930s, the workers at Hammermill took
advantage of casual management and largely mechanized work processes and
often left the machines unattended to take smoke breaks.[55]

As of the summer of 1915, however, managers at Hammermill strictly forbade smoking on factory grounds, and the physical spaces of the factory were covered with "no smoking" signs. The no-smoking rule was a key policy. After all, burning ash, lit cigarettes, and careless individuals in a factory filled with paper, wood, and chemicals were costly and even deadly problems to be avoided at all costs. But Hammermill managers' hopes for the no-smoking rule, as the spies' writings suggest, were more than just an effort to prevent fire. They stressed the assertion of management's power over labor. The factory walls bore physical reminders of managers' desire to establish control by imposing specific behavioral rules. In August 1915, HC referenced "the signs that are posted throughout the shop prohibiting smoking."[56] But laborers blatantly disregarded the message. "[R]egardless of the signs," HC often saw men smoking throughout the factory, "in total disregard" of management's no-smoking rule.[57]

While Behrend surely worried about the possibilities of accidental fire, he was probably more concerned about getting factory hands to *do their work*. The men at Hammermill were expected to remain at their posts for their entire eleven-to-thirteen-hour shift, except for the half-hour lunch or dinner break at the midway point. Workers' smoking habits, however, facilitated patterns of movement that constantly took them away from their jobs. First, men enjoyed cigarettes in areas that were close to their machines, where they could quickly enjoy a smoke and get back to work. The huge paper machines, for instance, housed in the largest rooms of the factory, provided the men with some concealment close to their posts. Both spies occasionally noticed workers hiding behind machines to smoke. In the cavernous paper machine rooms, HC watched a man smoking a pipe, and twice in July, FP noticed a clique of three men "smoking behind the machines."[58] Because managers were a constant presence in the main rooms of the paper mill, the men who smoked there had to be very careful. "There was a good deal of smoking being carried on around the mill today," FP wrote in September. "This morning . . . three of the beater helpers were down in the save-all room smoking, while the save-all man was on watch, so as to warn the men behind the machines if anyone in authority came in."[59]

The need to smoke in secret encouraged the men to move away from their assigned places, and the pleasures of smoking, sociability, and a desire for a break in the routine, accompanied by the need to avoid the watchful eyes of management, brought men to forbidden and out-of-the-way areas of the mill, which they claimed for themselves.

The factory bathrooms provided a secure place where the men could get away from the machines and smoke with a modicum of security. Since the restrooms were regarded as an "untidy" and "very unclean place," managers spent no time there.[60] There were a pair of dingy toilets, and the men would sit, read, talk, chew, and smoke at all hours of the day or night.[61] HC and FP sternly disapproved of workers' uses of the lavatory space. FP described the grimy lavatories as a "'hang out' for loafers and those who desire to smoke while on duty."[62] HC visited the bathroom one afternoon and witnessed "quite a filthy sight": used plugs of chewing tobacco and tobacco spit "all over the floor." The lavatories were workers' spaces, and they marked their claims with spit and ash. (While the company did employ a man to clean the bathrooms, he was often found elsewhere—in the machine room, smoking.[63]) Everyday, FP and HC witnessed a steady stream of workers who came to the bathroom to smoke and chew. They came from all over the factory: beater room workers, paper truckers, and paper-making machine workers, both both native- and foreign-born. FP and HC worried about the lavatory as an isolated space that encouraged the men to avoid work, indulge in filthy vices, and defy managerial authority. The spies urged managers to tighten their grip over the factory by acquiring control over workers' conduct in the lavatories and the physical state of the rooms themselves. FP noted that "it is very necessary for the Company to adopt new rules or enforce the old ones in respect to the lavatories."[64]

The spies frequently connected immigrant workers to the subversion and seediness they saw in the lavatories. Their apprehensions about "workers' control" of the bathrooms veered from questions of class into an uneasiness about the immigrant element of the workforce at Hammermill. As the spies' reports suggested, the immigrants' "foreign" languages, accompanied by their social and occupational separateness from native-born American laborers, made them a mysterious and suspicious group. The spies were careful to point out immigrant workers' actions to management, which were often connected to discussions of smoking in the grungy lavatories. On 10 July, FP visited the lavatory and reported that he "found four men up here—all foreigners—two of whom were smoking, while others were reading foreign papers." Two weeks later, he "found two men—both strangers to me—sitting on the seats, carrying on a jolly foreign conversation."[65] FP suggested that immigrant men's smoking habits led to behavior that was possibly devious. During an afternoon in August, he visited the bathroom, as he did on most days to track workers' movements, and he "could smell cigarette smoke in here but could not see anyone smoking, as the two foreigners who were on the seats probably ducked the smokes when they heard someone approaching."[66]

While smoking fostered sociability among the men and thus a basis for group cohesiveness, smoking practices typically reinforced ethnic boundaries, as men smoked among those of their own ethnic group. Discussions of smoking pointed to subtle, though very real, immigrant/native-born divisions among the men. As HC looked for a quiet place to eat lunch one afternoon in September, he happened upon a group of "four foreigners" smoking in the storeroom, and on another occasion he saw a cohort of "four foreigners" who punched the time clock and then walked back outside to smoke cigarettes on company time.[67] FP wrote in July about "a number of men, most of whom belonged to the foreign element, out on the platform smoking."[68] During one of his many conversations with other Hammermill workers, FP spoke with a native-born worker-smoker, Bob Smith, who told him that he was not worried about being caught because management, in his opinion, only cared about immigrant smoking. "They don't care if they see us 'white' men smoking," Smith told FP, "but they only restrict the foreign element from doing so."[69]

The spies' reports did not reference the particular groups of immigrants they observed in the paper mill. Two sources suggest, however, that these foreign-born workers were Polish: Ernst Behrend's correspondence of 1913 regarding the Polish-led wood room strike and US census data from the period.[70] Behrend may have asked the spies to carefully watch the troublesome cohort of Polish men in the mill to learn whatever they could about their attitudes and behavior. As suggested by US census numbers, the 1910s were a period of considerable change in the composition of Erie's immigrant residents. For the census year 1910, Germans (5,603), Russians (2,273), Italians (1,307), and Irish (1,122) were the four most numerous foreign-born populations in the city. The total foreign-born population in Erie was 14,963, or 22.5 percent of the total (66,525).[71] According to the 1920 census reports, however, the number of Polish immigrants had surged toward the top of the list of foreign-born populations, and the number of Italian immigrants had overtaken the Russians. Not reported at all in Erie's data for 1910 was the number of Polish newcomers in the city, 3,090 in 1920. Writing in 1915, it is probable that FP and HC were referring to working-class men of this rapidly expanding group of immigrants, the Poles, or possibly the growing number of Italian newcomers, who likely sought job opportunities at Hammermill. In the 1920 US census reports, Germans (3,645), Poles (3,090), Italians (2,382), and Russians (1,731) were the four most numerous immigrant groups in the city of Erie.[72]

The loading docks and railway cars that carried raw materials in and manufactured paper away from the factory were another popular location where worker-smokers enjoyed their habit. The spies reported seeing many men in these areas throughout the day. In August, FP watched fifteen men smoking cigarettes on their lunch hour at one of the factory's loading platforms, and on another occasion he witnessed a group of "at least" twenty doing the same.[73] Many of the men who used the rear areas as smoking spaces believed it was acceptable to smoke in these locations because they were closer to the outdoors, even though Hammermill managers forbade *any* smoking on factory grounds, both inside and out. FP wrote in July, "Time after time I saw men leaving the mill with a cigarette some place in sight on their person, on their way to the rear platform to smoke. Some of these men go in the box cars." These worker-smokers asserted a moral economy of space: officially, managers controlled the production spaces inside, but laborers were determined to reserve certain spaces for their own non-work uses.[74] "I have talked with quite a few of the men about the mill, about the smoking question," FP wrote, "and they apparently do not feel any responsibility when smoking, nor fear of penalty for doing so."[75]

Still, the traffic in and out of the loading areas made them spaces where security was not certain. The spies' reports indicated that many men took precautions to avoid detection when smoking in the loading areas. The empty boxcars provided the best cover for the men to smoke in relative secret. "Most of these men go into empty box cars," FP observed, "where they cannot be seen, to smoke."[76] "Cover" was important.[77] On his first day of work in June, FP spoke with a foreman named Fromm, who told him that men who worked on the wet machines often left their jobs to "smoke and chat" either in the empty boxcars outside or down by the lake.[78] On the loading dock, there was a large pile of sulphite materials that allowed the men to reach the tall ceilings above. There, the men had access to a small crawl space where they could sleep, hide, and smoke in a completely out-of-the-way location: "During the course of the night, I discovered a sort of a hole on the top of the . . . pile on the platform. The men . . . go up there and lie down. At times they also smoke while up there, for it is an out of the way place and also entirely out of sight."[79] Another man who worked on the second floor of the factory thought it best to crawl out of a window and onto the roof of the platform, where he could smoke in complete privacy during the warm summer months.[80]

As the summer of 1915 reached its zenith, the men took full advantage of the warm weather to move further and further away from the points of production inside the factory to the open spaces outside, including the banks of nearby Lake Erie. As FP indicated, the men "go down on the lake bank, as a rule, to smoke and chat."[81] Since the bathrooms were usually kept in poor condition, used more for smoking and chewing than for other bodily needs, workers preferred to relieve themselves at the lakeshore. "Time after time," FP wrote, "I saw men go out to the lake-bank to have a passage. They would usually roll a cigarette before starting out, and then as they smoked, they would take their time while about their mission." During late June and early July, FP spent several days working on the night shift, where he noted the wide extent of nighttime smoking near the lake. On a night without any breeze, the spy claimed he could "smell the obnoxious odor" of cigarette smoke (and other pungent odors) hanging over the factory site near the lake. In fact, the smell may have been more powerful than usual during these summer days for FP, as he was "unfortunate enough" to step in an unseen lump of human "refuse" near the lake bank.[82]

Despite the popularity of the lake bank as a smoking site, the area was by no means free of company surveillance. While in the presence of spies (unbeknownst to laborers themselves), worker-smokers worried that managers might catch them using tobacco near the lakeshore. Outside and inside the plant, they took precautions to avoid detection. There were piles of stock and other equipment kept outside between the factory buildings and the lakeshore, and the men would position themselves between the lake and the stockpiles, thus shielding themselves from managers' prying eyes. "There are several places, I understand, that they go to down here," FP noted, "but most of them are in the habit of going down to sit behind a pile of lumber."[83] Management did not move quickly to stop the surreptitious practice, as FP found more of the same later in the week. On 1 and 2 July, FP noted the actions of repeat offenders: "During the night, smoking was again a common sight around the outside of the Mill. At one time, I went down on the Lake-bank with one of the truckers, who took me to the place where the men go to 'kill' a half-hour or so while smoking. This place is behind the pile of barrel-heads and staves, facing the Lake."[84]

The centers of managerial authority—offices—actually provided the safest locations for smoking. Various skilled workers, such as the head beater room workers, and other low-level supervisors, worked in small, enclosed shop floor office spaces; here they coordinated the work of the various factory departments. Inside these offices, skilled workers and supervisors occupied a personal space that was not easily transgressed or watched by other workers or managers. (At the same time, managers stayed inside their offices so much that it surely impeded their ability to assert their authority over workers' actions in the shop.) As suggested by the spies' writings, the factory floor offices did not have windows, so when their occupants closed the doors, they were alone and could not be seen. Here the spies' efforts fell far short of their own expectations, much to their dismay. FP described how he literally sniffed around managers' doors to detect the use of tobacco. In August, FP noted that he "smelt smoke of a cigarette in the office," but he could not be sure if the night superintendent, Charles Sherrei, had been smoking or if someone else nearby was guilty of the offense.[85]

Worker-smokers had to carefully navigate the varying extent of employer authority over factory spaces. To satisfy their addictions to nicotine, men needed to create a series of clandestine strategies that would afford them opportunities to smoke and to construct a complex and dynamic geography of smoking sites on the factory grounds. Many men blatantly ignored management's ban of smoking, using tobacco whenever and wherever they could. "I wish to report that the men openly smoke, going to and from work, on the company's grounds," FP called out to managers.[86] Could they be stopped?

Workers and Managers on the Move

The Manufacturers and Merchants Inspection Bureau's spies were not the only company agents who monitored worker actions at Hammermill. To restrict working men's on-the-job movements, management deployed mobile agents—watchmen—who moved about the factory grounds to interdict worker movement. But in particular, the watchmen closely pursued worker-smokers, whose addictions to nicotine led them to pursue wide, undercover patterns of motion. As the spy reports showed, managers relied on the watchmen as a mobile but direct extension of their authority.

The spy reports of 1915 describe a continuous game of cat-and-mouse between worker-smokers and the probing eyes of the watchmen. Working men demonstrated a fluid, constantly changing strategy of preserving access to multiple smoking sites, and their strategies varied in response to managers' efforts to police factory space. For example, smokers avoided locations where the watchman might be working in a given moment, shifting quickly to other spaces. In July, FP lamented that while a watchman was typically on the job, he could not cover every location at once: "The watchman was on the job, yesterday noon, and there was little smoking going on here, but as he was any place about, this noon, the men seemed to take advantage of the fact, for at 12:15 pm, I counted eight fellows smoking on the platform, while five went down to the bank for the purpose of smoking." The men, he noted, took "advantage" of his location by shifting their smoking sites. Since the watchman was not in the vicinity of the platform, this place quickly became a destination for smokers.[87]

The spies viewed smokers' efforts to dodge the watchmen as evidence that working-class men were shifty and untrustworthy and needed to be managed with a firm hand. FP learned a lot about the men's strategies for evading the watchmen, and he warned management that their shrewdness had been underrated. He noted that management "can readily see that even though only common laborers, they are clever enough to 'get around' the rules of the Company, as placed before them, by such 'tricks' as keeping close tab on the watchman."[88] Unskilled factory hands, he suggested, were not supposed to be capable of such intelligent strategizing, but to his dismay they were. FP was alarmed to learn that men had carefully studied the watchmen's movements, tracking the timing and patterns of their whereabouts: "I asked one of them if he were not afraid that the watchman would catch them out here. In reply, he said, 'We still have plenty of time, as the watchman does not get around until 8:05 pm—that is, five minutes after each hour.'"[89] If they could "get around" managers' rules this way, what else could they accomplish? Strikes? Unionization?

What happened to those men who were caught by the watchmen? Very little, according to the men who spoke with FP. Theoretically, the watchman could fire any man who broke company rules, including the "no smoking" rule. But as the spy reports suggest, nobody lost his job. FP heard a story from a worker-smoker who told him about a close call with the watchman after he had been caught down by the lake bank while smoking with another man. "The watchman bawled them out for it," FP noted with satisfaction, "and said that if he ever caught them out there again he would report them."[90] (Strangely, given his disdain for those who flagrantly broke the rules, FP thought the man only deserved a warning, possibly because he was out of doors and not inside the mill.) After the "bawled out" incident, the spy noted with pleasure that the ranks of worker-smokers who wasted time at the lake appeared to be "getting thinner." FP took this as evidence that assertive and vigilant watchmen could curb worker smoking and movement, restoring management control. "I think if the watchman will only open his eyes and look around," FP told his superiors, "and report those whom he catches I am quite certain that these men who hang out" could be stopped.[91]

Despite the presence of the watchmen around the factory, the men continued to assert their own uses of space and to move about the factory according to their own designs. FP occasionally heard workers who questioned the extent of the watchmen's powers. "Why be afraid of the watchman?" a man quipped to FP on the night shift in July. "He could not have all of us fired." As he spoke, roughly a dozen workers smoked with him in an empty boxcar. Another man remarked that he did not care if the watchman fired him for smoking because "he was not stuck on his job."[92] FP was not surprised to see and hear the men openly defying and questioning management. "All of these men are common laborers," the spy noted, "and there are few, if any of them, who seem to be satisfied with their work."[93]

Even as the watchman relentlessly pursued smokers, workers could feel some measure of security around other managers, as many foremen themselves were heavy smokers. Around some foremen, workers could finally stop running and enjoy their tobacco in peace. These managers' actions worried the spies; instead of enforcing the no-smoking rule, managers themselves flagrantly broke it, and smoking appeared to break down the social division between labor and management. The prevalence of worker autonomy and assertiveness in the factory, and the breakdown of managerial authority, could be seen in the wide circles of worker movement and clouds of tobacco smoke (exhaled by labor and management alike) that hung in the bathrooms, the loading docks, and the lakeshore.

Night superintendent Charles Sherrei was a subject of particular concern to FP. Sherrei frequently smoked with the men, breaking down the social divisions between management and labor while at the same time violating the company rules he was expected to uphold. FP often devoted many lines in his reports to Sherrei's lackadaisical behavior. "I found Charles Sherrei sitting in front of the small electric supply house with two of the men from the engine room," FP wrote on 12 July. "I cannot say how long before this he had been there, but when I went up to him and asked a question, I observed that all three were comfortably seated on the steps and undoubtedly had been smoking, as I could detect the odor of cigarettes."[94] Here was a member of management breaking down crucial class boundaries by cultivating social relationships with members of the suspect working class and casually sharing their vice of choice. FP went so far as to suggest that Sherrei no longer had the ability to appropriately manage the men. The spy observed, "Sherrei came up on the platform from the direction of the lake. He saw me smoking, but did not say anything. The fellow with whom I had been talking 'ducked' his cigarette when he saw Charlie, but I purposely let him see me smoking to see if he would say anything to me because of it and he did not. The other fellow went upstairs, but I talked with Charlie out here for fully ten minutes."[95] Sherrei was not an effective source of class discipline.

At Hammermill, struggles over the use of cigarettes, uses of space, and the right of workers to control their own freedom of movement propelled conflict between labor and management, and management deployed watchmen (and spies) as part of a concerted effort to interrupt workers' mobility. When working men smoked on the job, they challenged the spatial order of the factory, using rooms, loading docks, and lake banks for uses that management had not sanctioned. Moreover, they asserted personal interpretations of freedom of movement that violated managers' insistence that they remain on the job.

Management, however, sent mixed messages to workers. Supervisors were not always averse to sharing cigarettes and conversations with laborers, which broke down class divisions that governed production and social relations in the factory. And as FP suggested, management lacked a clear-cut strategy for re-establishing discipline. On one hand, they used watchmen to interrupt worker movement and tobacco use; on the other, shop floor managers seemed to sanction worker actions by participating in the smoking culture themselves.

Smoking, Conversation, and Shop Floor Culture

Like smoking, conversation was a foundation of shop floor culture. The spoken word injected sociability and recreation into the workday and provided a basis for collectivity and political expression.[96] When workers smoked, it was often more than a solitary exercise. The men at Hammermill used their stolen cigarette breaks to break away from the mass-production regimen, and these breaks assumed collective dimensions. Conversations flowed among the workers during these interludes, on topics ranging from the recreational to the political. Words, as well as smoke, blew through the air in the workrooms, the loading docks, the lake bank, the shop floor offices, and the dank restrooms.

As men smoked, conversations with others added to the pleasure of their time away from work and to the lengths of the breaks they took. The men at Hammermill did not, by and large, leave their posts to quickly smoke a cigarette and rush back, although some men did exactly that when they needed to satisfy their cravings. Rather, the men typically smoked several cigarettes during these breaks, spending as long as thirty minutes or even an hour chatting with coworkers. Both of the company's spies, FP and HC, inserted themselves into workers' conversations whenever they could, monitoring the idle chatter for signs of union sentiment, the presence of clandestine union organizers, worker complaints about long hours and low wages, inclinations to strike, and general complaints directed against management. Most often, however, the men discussed topics that had nothing to do with the company; they often talked about baseball, "booze" parties, and weekend plans.

Still, men's conversations over cigarettes, pipes, and cigars sometimes veered into direct criticisms of management. The spies carefully documented workers' conversations that featured complaints about managers and company policies. On Labor Day 1915, for instance, FP joined a conversation among an angry group of smokers who had gathered in a boxcar near the loading platform. There, he heard "several sarcastic remarks" about the company's disregarding the holiday and making the men show up for work. "The Hammermill," a bitter man noted, "was the only whistle that blew in Erie today." Since the Hammermill Paper Company was a firm operated by a German family—and the controversial Great War had only recently begun—the men were quick to criticize the company's supposed disregard for its mostly American workers. One of the men complained to FP that the company "did not even have an American flag hanging out on the flag pole."[97] Because Hammermill operated on lengthy eleven- and thirteen-hour shifts, the long hours aroused the ire of many men. FP asked a man who worked in the beater room if he planned to take a week off during the remaining days of summer. The man told the spy that he was, in fact, planning to take a permanent leave of absence; he wanted out. For him, "it would be good bye to the Hammermill," FP noted, "as he was getting sick and tired of working." The spy was quick to point out to his supervisors that the worker had been trying to spread his views on the hours question among other workers. "He is a strong eight hour man," FP warned, "and has talked to the men on this subject several times."[98]

As the men smoked and talked, they tried to guard against disclosing information among those they believed could be informers. On one occasion, when a group of men spent more than forty minutes smoking at the lake bank, FP coolly listened as men warned against being too friendly with a suspicious beater room worker named Mann. Mann, the men believed, was a company informant, passing along information to bosses in exchange for an alleged "confidential pay envelope" that allowed him to take extended, lavish vacations.[99] The available evidence does not explain why the men so distrusted him; perhaps rumors circulated that Behrend hired men to spy on his factory. Perhaps Mann enjoyed close personal relationships with individual managers, which his coworkers evidently disapproved of and resented. Perhaps someone saw him carrying or pocketing a bloated envelope of money. Perhaps his apparent movements in the factory, which may have carried him away from the grime of the beater room to the cleaner offices of management, led the men to believe he was a stooge. Or their unease and suspicions may have been the result of the widespread knowledge during the Progressive Era that management in industries from automobile manufacturing to steel to paper typically deployed spies and strikebreakers in their efforts to undermine unionization, break strikes, and gain control over the shop floor.[100] At Hammermill, at least some of the men suspected that managers would use these tactics against *them*.

The men were suspicious of snitches in the ranks, but they never caught on that FP and HC were company spies; their true identities were never discovered. FP was able to successfully use the workers' smoking culture to gain admittance to their social circles and secure their confidence. FP's most significant discovery, as a result of his many conversations with workers, was the presence of a unionist in the factory, a man the spy believed was an experienced organizer of paper workers. Behrend's evident concern for the growth of a union movement inside his factory surely motivated him to hire FP and HC. In his report, dated 5 August, FP recalled with pride his discovery of a "union man." He met the fidgety, inquisitive man in one of the large machine rooms as the suspicious newcomer was in the process of asking about job openings. FP described how he coolly observed the visitor's mannerisms, claiming the newcomer "appeared to be a little above the average workman." Quickly, the energetic spy engaged the man in conversation and soon gathered enough information to conclude that he was a certainly a professional "agitator." FP wrote, "After talking to him for some time, I came to the conclusion that he was a pretty clever fellow, as he showed more intelligence than the average workman." The spy "closely" questioned him, learning he had worked at paper mills in Rhinelander, Wisconsin; Kalamazoo, Michigan; and Watertown, New York. The spy quickly made correlations between these disparate locations, noting "these places are having, or have recently had strike trouble." (Watertown paper workers joined the strikes of the independent mills in 1910.[101]) During the course of their exchange, FP was somehow able to look at an envelope in the man's coat pocket that featured a Kalamazoo address. A manager interrupted the conversation by notifying the newcomer there were no jobs at the moment but that he should check in again later. Later in the afternoon, the suspicious man returned, this time not looking for a job. He wanted to speak again with FP. During this second conversation, the spy concluded the fellow was certainly a unionist "through and through." The man criticized the Hammermill men for working their eleven- and thirteen-hour shifts while other paper mills featured eight-hour shifts. But the alleged union man soon left the factory and never returned, at least during the remainder of FP's time with the company.[102]

Smoking facilitated ongoing, sporadic dialogues about tensions between management and labor. For spies like FP, the wide extent of workers' conversations on the shop floor was the very premise of the intelligence-gathering enterprise. In exchanges with workers, the spies mined the men's words for fragments of evidence about negative feelings toward management and the potential for insurgencies from below (or from the outside). Among the men, conversation was a major facet of their shop floor culture, a way they literally asserted a voice and cultivated a degree of autonomy on what was supposed to be management's terrain. As they smoked together, they frequently talked: to complain, to relax, to socialize. By doing so, they reclaimed time off the clock and defied management demands for dependable, constant work. Cigarette smoking not only threatened to burn paper; smoking facilitated workers' pursuit of autonomy and on some occasions engendered discussions that rumbled with discontent.

As FP maneuvered himself into these conversations, he became a contributor to the smoking culture he condemned. To blend into this shop floor culture of smoke and talk, FP himself began smoking cigarettes, possibly as a way to gather even more information; after only a few weeks in Erie, his daily reports began to disclose that he too was consuming tobacco on a daily basis. On 22 July, as FP walked outside the factory toward the lakeshore, he met an acquaintance along the way who reminded him "to be careful about smoking down at the lake-bank." Three days later, on 25 July, he spoke with a beater room worker who was trying to roll a fresh cigarette. "I . . . offered him a cigarette," FP wrote, "already made up, which I had." He continued, "I also asked if it would be alright to smoke in here." The man noted he would "rather go outside." They left together, cigarettes in hand.[103]

FP could have been playing the part of a smoker as a way to gain their acceptance, or to show his superiors he would go as far as was necessary to gain needed information. It is possible, however, that as he smoked he became quietly dependent on nicotine. FP never made remarks that suggested a yearning for cigarettes, but he was smoking enough that it had become part of his daily routine, perhaps even a habit. The spy could not insulate himself from the shop floor culture he was sent in to dissect; cigarettes and smoke—integral components of that culture—permeated the factory environment and now his lungs. Ironically, by smoking cigarettes he added to the culture of smoking in the factory, a personal and social practice that had so irritated managers.

Changing the Rules

Based on available evidence, workers secured the right to smoke at Hammermill, at least informally. While managers posted no-smoking signs, employed watchmen to police worker movements, and even hired spies to monitor workers' habits and politics, surviving letters and documents do not indicate that management was so committed to stopping workers from lighting up. The issue of smoking on the shop floor is absent in future company correspondence, memos, and other texts. FP even alluded to managers' inaction on 2 August:

> I have noticed that there has been little, if anything, done to stop the men from smoking, and I would suggest that if there is nothing going to be done in the way of stopping the men from smoking in the mill, or about it, that I be notified, so that it will not be necessary for me to report this any longer.[104]

The spy was frustrated. FP suggested that managers had asked him to assess the extent of cigarette smoking among the men, and the spy assumed, based on the orders of his superiors, that managers were committed to fighting the practice. FP's remarks indicated, however, that managers failed to act (and possibly did not care to act). On the issue of tobacco use, management relented. By August, they were giving up the effort to eliminate smoking and tacitly accepting workers' right to smoke. Presumably, workers continued to smoke on what was supposed to be the company's time and in spaces that management had sanctioned only for work uses. So as the end of September approached, FP and HC boarded trains out of Erie, ending their time at Hammermill after finding almost none of the labor militancy and revolutionary sentiment that managers so feared, and aggravated by Behrend's choice to pay no heed to the more significant problem of everyday rebelliousness. Perhaps the contracted duration of the spies' stay in Erie had been fulfilled and they had to move on to their next assignment, or perhaps the Hammermill president, now satisfied that his paper mill would not become the next McKees Rocks or Ludlow, chose not to renew his arrangement with the Manufacturers and Merchants Inspection Bureau.

Maybe the spies simply walked away from the job. Their reports offered no clues. FP ended his last dispatch: "I left the mill after registering out my time at 6:03 p.m. and discontinued for the day."[105]

Life and labor would go on at Hammermill, but workers' daily disregard of the no-smoking rule in the 1910s had begun to redraw key boundaries and rules within the factory. As management withdrew from the fight over tobacco, workers won small privileges that now informed daily life in the factory: opportunities to stop work, even briefly, for smoking breaks; an excuse to leave their machines and move about the factory; and opportunities for sociability on the job.

During the late 1910s, Ernst Behrend probably imagined his relaxing attitude on the smoking issue as a trade-off: cigarettes and breaks in exchange for worker cooperation in other matters such as hours, wages, and labor peace. But labor problems still plagued Hammermill. For instance, in 1918 the men of the beater room walked off the job and demanded a wage increase. Initially, management refused to talk, claiming the men had violated the foundation of Hammermill paternalism when they brusquely went on strike: that workers "teach, don't boss" in their dealings with management.[106] Behrend was stern. He launched the new company newsletter, the *Hammermill Bond*, to communicate his refusal to negotiate. The walkout ended quickly, though, and Behrend ultimately agreed to bargain with a committee over wages.

"Life has not been monotonous here lately," Behrend wrote to a colleague in June 1918, as he reported on the frequency of talks with the pushy men of the beater room. Hearing of events that spring, his friend replied, "I did not know they [the beater men] were again dissatisfied."[107] Behrend believed he treated his factory hands well; after all, he had relented on the unpopular no-smoking rule. Perhaps because of earlier generosity, Behrend viewed the strike of 1918 as a vulgar display of ingratitude.

Smoking was a vital component of the shop floor culture that nurtured the everyday forms of collectivity seen at Hammermill. By smoking, workers, both as individuals and in groups, had to engage in a daily, ongoing struggle against company rules and the agents of management. Perhaps the easing of the no-smoking rule in 1915, resulting as it did from widespread noncooperation, emboldened the men to press for further changes. As the beater room walkout of 1918 showed, men had won earlier small victories in the workplace and they were determined to push for a few more.

Even as worker-smokers at Hammermill appeared to overturn the company ban on smoking by their persistent defiance, smoking prohibitions remained a fixture of the workday elsewhere throughout the Progressive Era and beyond. By 1937, members of the National Industrial Conference Board would conclude that "relatively few" of the 865 factories surveyed (employing more than 1.5 million people) permitted smoking.[108] Mexican American workers in Chicago told sociologist Paul S. Taylor that working in a factory meant "No Smoking all over the place." Apparently, managers stringently upheld these policies in their plants, and one worker remarked that he did not envy the men in meatpacking and steel even if they had regular work. The man noted, "I like a little liberty."[109] There were several cases brought before the new National Labor Relations Board between 1935 and 1940 that highlighted managers' commitment to no-smoking rules, as well as workers' struggles with this prohibition from above.[110]

Labor and the workplace were important components of antismoking politics, and industrial employers pushed forward an antismoking culture that judged workers' behavior harshly. For employers, smoking appeared to threaten their control, as adult smokers' habits supposedly worsened their physical performance, mental acuity, and moral codes. Managers struggled to maintain their command of the workplace at a moment when widening nicotine addiction drew more and more workers away from their posts for surreptitious cigarette breaks. At Hammermill, smoking was so prevalent that managers could not stop it. Despite widespread bans on smoking that were management policy in much of industry during the early twentieth century, it is likely that the intensity of nicotine addiction continued to draw men away from their assignments, even at risk to their jobs.

During the 1920s and 1930s, the conversation about working-class smoking in the factory quieted to less than a whisper; reports in newspapers nearly cease after 1918. By then, smoking bans had become commonplace in industry, and workers' everyday forms of resistance behind factory walls probably escaped the notice of most writers and journalists. But intense controversies over smoking would resume during World War II, as workers confronted long-established bans on smoking at work while a growing acceptance (and even celebration) of smoking in wartime culture arose.

3

WORKERS, MANAGEMENT, AND THE RIGHT TO SMOKE DURING WORLD WAR II

**So why haven't you quit? Why hasn't everyone?
Because smoking feels good.**

—Martin Downs in the *New York Times*

United Automobile Worker (UAW) Local 600 member and Ford River Rouge worker Dan Campbell was a happy man in the early summer of 1945. He had recently become a father. Jubilant after the birth of his child, he sent over an assortment of cigarettes and cigars to the members of the Local 600 executive board for them to enjoy during their early June meeting. As members gathered at the UAW hall in Dearborn for the meeting, some of them surely partook of the free smokes.[1] Not only was there a joyous event to celebrate, but the union meeting itself presented an occasion and a space where autoworkers *could* smoke. In contrast, smoking had for years been forbidden at their place of work, the nearby Ford River Rouge plant. For example, when the journalist and author John Gunther visited the Rouge, he immediately noticed the company's hostility to smoking. As he rode in a company car toward Dearborn, the chauffer "refused a cigarette" when Gunther offered him one. When the visiting writer offhandedly asked him why he was worried about smoking in the car, the driver explained that even though they were still miles from the factory, "there were spotters everywhere." If the man were seen smoking by these company agents, "he'd be fired."[2]

The workers and local union leaders at the Rouge factory complex in Dearborn, Michigan, would have been all too aware of the contradiction between long-standing prohibitions of smoking in industrial workplaces such as the Rouge and the ubiquitous smoking of cigarettes going on in working-class life outside. Despite the moralizing and prohibition campaigns of Victorian reformers at the turn of the twentieth century, dependence on nicotine became widely shared among many Americans as the twentieth century unfolded. In 1880, adults consumed an average of fifty cigarettes per year in the United States, which increased to five hundred in 1920, a thousand in 1930, and two thousand in 1940. By 1950, US smokers consumed an estimated 1.5 billion pounds of tobacco in their cigarettes, a hefty increase from 250 million pounds in 1880.[3] For workers during World War II, smoking bans at work increasingly constituted an anachronistic, taxing, and frustrating rule that coldly stood between them and their much-craved and much-desired cigarettes.

During World War II, working-class addictions to nicotine and industrial workers' demands for the right to smoke fueled wartime labor militancy to a surprising degree. During these years there were several instances of worker strikes in defense industries in opposition to employer smoking bans, fueled not only by the pressing reality of worker-smokers' addiction to nicotine, but also by a wartime popular culture that celebrated smoking as a respectable activity. Heroic soldiers and sailors smoked to relieve the stresses of war; patriotic men and women organized bundles of cigarette cartons to mail overseas; and Hollywood filmmakers celebrated smoking as the epitome of cool. Wartime labor militancy against smoking bans surely stemmed, in part, from glaring contradictions in workers' lives: wartime culture celebrated smoking while Victorian employers strictly forbade it. As a result, working-class Americans insisted more and more that cigarette smoking should be allowed in the day-to-day spaces and routines of work. At the same time, wartime smoking strikes partly enabled the legitimization of smoking in American culture on a scale that had not existed previously. As John Gunther observed when he visited the Rouge a second time in 1945, the rule against smoking appeared to be relaxing a bit, at least in the executive offices at the Ford Motor Company. In his meetings with Ford leaders at the Rouge, they invited him to smoke if he wished.[4] To some small extent, smokers in 1945 had finally begun to breach the antismoking fortress that was the Ford River Rouge plant of the early- to mid-twentieth century.

The years of World War II hastened public acceptance of cigarette smoking in ways that World War I could not. While the federal government certainly encouraged widespread nicotine addiction by giving free cigarettes to thousands upon thousands of soldiers in both wars, thereby legitimizing the mass consumption of nicotine, World War II featured much larger numbers of smokers throughout US society, a growing and militant labor movement that empowered working people to challenge employers' rules in the workplace, and a wartime popular culture in the United States that celebrated smoking as respectable, commonplace, and uniquely patriotic. For smokers, the World War II era produced particularly frustrating contradictions in working people's daily lives. More and more people smoked cigarettes in the midst of a wartime culture that celebrated smoking, yet major industrial employers continued to stringently ban the practice. World War II–era smokers had heightened expectations of the right to smoke, at work and else-where in their daily lives. By the 1940s, workplace smoking rules had become exasperating Victorian relics in a very modern world.

While World War II broadened the respectability of cigarette smoking to an extent not before seen in American culture, the outcome of workers' struggles was never inevitable. The resistance of employers and concerned judges to work-ers' pushes for change from below was substantial. For managers and judges, smoking cigarettes at work remained a significant threat to labor discipline and proper morality, a danger made all the more urgent by employers' and judges' expectations that workers must facilitate industrial production in support of the war effort.

Wartime Morality and Worker-Smokers in the Courts

Throughout the interwar period, press reports of fines and penalties for worker-smokers disappeared from city newspapers. Occasionally, newspapers reported on sporadic efforts to push smokers out of subways and elevated train stations and cars, but the press conversation about workers asserting the right to smoke on the job quieted down after the Progressive Era. The onset of World War II, however, led to a renewed and intensified debate in the United States about smoking at work, as views of industrial production as a necessary path-way to victory seemed to be threatened by the working class's apparent desire to smoke on the docks, in factories, and in the shops that manufactured and moved the materiel needed for war. Wartime worries led to a new wartime morality, a development that was especially apparent in the industrial port city of New York. In the New York City area, judges and employers moved sternly against worker-smokers, asserting not smoking as a marker of proper wartime conduct. Workers faced renewed policing of their actions and the cumbersome fines and suspensions from work that resulted. The wartime working class struggled to continue smoking while serving industry and the nation, caught between their addiction to tobacco and judges' and employers' strict interpretations of proper wartime working-class behavior.

The February 1942 fire that destroyed the *Normandie* (a luxury ocean liner in the process of conversion to service as a troopship) served as a major catalyst for World War II anxieties in New York about workers handling flammable materi-als (such as matches and cigarettes) on the job. *Life* magazine reported that the ship "mysteriously caught fire," but government investigations concluded that sparks from a welder's torch ignited a nearby burlap-covered life preserver and other fabrics nearby.[5] The catastrophic blaze that resulted lasted for three hours and killed two men, and the ship capsized and lay on its side at its dock on the Hudson River. News of the fire and the aftermath roared across the headlines of the New York papers. In court soon after, judges "decided to make an example of carelessness" in cases where workers were caught smoking in defense industries. In Brooklyn, for instance, Magistrate Charles Solomon doubled the fines of accused worker-smokers in his courtroom (from the usual $5 to $10) during the week that followed the *Normandie* debacle. "He said that carelessness on the part of workers was, in effect, potential sabotage," the *New York Times* reported. The "reason for the stiff fines was the carelessness exhibited by the workers."[6] A dropped cigarette or match could produce another *Normandie*-sized fire in some other defense-related workplace, a prospect that judges urgently wanted to prevent. Workers would have to adopt their viewpoint or face legal sanction. Attorney Edward Thompson, who prosecuted workplace smoking cases in New York City–area courts, noted that "what happened on the *Normandie* should not be allowed to occur again either on ships or in defense plants."[7] According to Thompson's estimates for 1940 and 1941, there were a thousand more factory fires in 1941 than in 1940, and a third of the 1941 fires were attributed to workers' mistakes with cigarettes.[8]

Comments they made to the press suggest that judges and magistrates hoped to engender a new morality for wartime, especially among the working class. They imagined that the foundations for proper wartime patriotism were equality of sacrifice on the battlefront and home front and the achievement of safety in defense-related industries. Authority figures invoked these themes in several smoking cases that appeared on their dockets. At the end of February 1942, Magistrate Jenkin R. Hockert of Queens, New York, harshly rebuked eleven accused smokers who claimed they acted appropriately because they chose to smoke in the factory bathrooms at the Brewster Aeronautical Corporation's factory, where the tiled surfaces guaranteed a space that was free of fire hazards. The magistrate insisted that the smokers behaved like spoiled children, oblivious to the struggles of soldiers in combat and of their duty to support the troops. "General MacArthur and his men work long hours too and I'll bet they don't have much time to slip off for a cigarette," the magistrate chastised. "Most of them [workers]," he continued, "are young and have probably been deferred from military service because they are working at defense contracts. They are earning much more than our soldiers. They should realize that they are supposed to be working for our country's best interest. This plant has much paint and other inflammable material. One misdirected cigarette may cause a fire that might ruin just the number of planes needed to turn the tide of an important battle."[9] Judges and magistrates used heated language and real force to push forward the new antismoking crusade. "This is a genuine evil," Brooklyn magistrate Charles Solomon told accused smokers. "We are at war and you people must realize that we must not have fires in defense factories. I for one will give straight prison sentences to any offender who deserves them."[10] In other words, smoking equaled deadly subversion.

New York City's antismoking crusade during World War II mirrored the pattern of authorities' responses that first emerged during the Progressive Era in the wake of the 1911 Triangle Shirtwaist Fire. The nightmare of that fire stoked a stern reaction from local authorities, as the new Fire Inspection Bureau deployed inspectors to root out smokers in the workplace. The 1942 *Normandie* blaze produced a similar pattern: publicized dangers of smoking that led to a crackdown in workplaces and in the courts. During World War II, fire inspectors once again pursued their quarry in shops, in factories, and on the docks, looking to snuff out lit cigarettes before they could spark much larger fires.

The New York City docks proved to be the most accessible sites for wartime fire inspectors to nab worker-smokers. Reports of fines issued in these workplaces appeared most frequently in the press. Since the docks were heavily trafficked and not obscured from view by factory walls, worker-smokers proved vulnerable as they loaded and unloaded ships and took breaks close to their posts, which were in plain sight. In one instance, three longshoremen and a seaman were fined $50 each for smoking at Pier F at Exchange Place. As the judge determined their guilt, he told the men they would be jailed for thirty days if they did not pay the fines.[11] Inspectors fined truck driver Frank Juliano the sum of $1 for smoking at Pier 86 on the North River. Since he had to work, the court allowed his spouse to attend the hearing instead. The judge ordered the woman to pay the fine and "explained the importance of the law" to her and the court.[12] In October 1942, magistrate Anna M. Kross of the Essex Market Court issued much heavier fines to six working men "found guilty of smoking" on two different piers of the East River. Their supervisor, John T. Ryan of the Central Vermont Railroad where the men worked, spoke on their behalf at the hearing. The railroad superintendent insisted that "it is a hardship for a man to refrain from smoking for eight hours," an assertion that brought a "sharp rebuke" from the magistrate. "It's just too bad that the smokers must endure such a hardship as you claim," Kross told the railroad operator. "Smoking in defense factories and on our piers is pure sabotage. It is endangering life and property, the latter running into many millions of dollars." Issuing fines to the six men that ranged from $25 to $50, Kross rationalized her ruling by invoking the sacrifices of soldiers in the crucible of combat. "To overlook these violations would be failing in our duty to the men we have sent to battle," she noted.[13] Worker-smokers would have to endure the hardships of cold turkey on the job and fines in court.

There were one hundred inspectors searching for smokers in New York City's factories, probing for lit cigarettes behind industrial walls and factory doors.[14] They found many offenders. Inspectors caught Hyman Seigel of Brooklyn smoking a pipe in a factory where workers were engaged in war-related production. Though he was up one floor from the actual work, he was nonetheless issued the heavy fine of $50. In court, Seigel tried to argue that he only "sucked" on a pipe because he was too ill to chew gum or eat candy at work. But the judge would not be swayed. "I'm sorry," he said. "I cannot fine you less than $50. You look sick and I know you are sick, but the law says I must fine you or send you to jail for thirty days." Because Seigel was unable to pay, his friends in the courtroom raised the money for him.[15] In a more urgent case, where a working man had been found smoking a cigarette in a five-floor chemical factory, the magistrate ordered Ludwig Hirschman of Brooklyn to jail for five days. Speaking "sharply" to the accused, the magistrate said that "[t]he inspector did you a favor serving a summons. . . . He saved your life and the lives of other workers in the building." Hirschman pleaded guilty, but received no mercy from the court.[16] Magistrates reserved their harshest treatment for repeat offenders. For example, Magistrate Joseph DeAndrea gave three-time offender Jacob Wiener of the Bronx, caught smoking on the job at a factory where workers manufactured US Army uniforms, the choice of a $150 fine or sixty days in jail. Unable to pay, Wiener went to jail for nearly two months.[17] In the same court session, DeAndrea issued fines to seventeen more workers from four other New York City–area defense factories. Clearly frustrated by the long line of worker-smokers in his courtroom, the magistrate issued a request to the fire department "to bring the 'bosses' of plants before him" because "he believed operators of war-goods factories should make additional efforts to prevent smoking."[18] Smoking on the job was out of control, and more needed to be done to curb workers' behavior.

Corruption and abuse by local officials existed in the system of smoking inspections. For example, fire commissioner Patrick Walsh "received complaints" from workers regarding Bureau of Fire Prevention inspectors who tried to "shake down" smokers at a factory on Broadway where army coats were made. In July 1943, police arrested inspector Harold J. Macaulay of the Bureau of Fire Prevention for an incident at the Broadway plant. Employee Gabriel Visconi charged that Macaulay caught him lighting a cigarette, but the inspector offered "not to serve a summons on him if he would hand over $10." A policewoman in the factory saw the men shake hands and witnessed a $10 bill fall to the floor. Macaulay insisted he never touched any money or asked Visconi for a bribe. Nonetheless, the magistrate of the Bowery Court arraigned him on extortion charges.[19]

As New York City–area officials cracked down on wartime smoking at work, some worker-smokers resisted the movement to push smoking out of defense plants. For instance, fire inspectors noted that at several factories the no-smoking signs were missing or had been obviously torn down.[20] Resistance was also vocal. Caught smoking at Pier 95 on the North River in May 1942, worker George Bertie must have spoken harshly to police officers, as he received a charge of "disorderly conduct at the time of the arrest." The magistrate gave him five days in jail for the incident.[21]

New York unions also intervened on behalf of worker-smokers in the local criminal justice system. On the New York City subway, for example, workers on the train lines resented the practices of authorities who issued hefty three-day suspensions for smoking on the job, while passengers who were caught smoking only received small fines of $1 to $2. In February 1944, the Transport Workers Union of the CIO, the Civil Service Forum, and the American Federation of Municipal Transit Workers of the AFL issued a joint protest statement to the Board of Transportation in New York City. The organizations pointed out that the suspensions of New York's subway employees for smoking cost them between $15 and $24 in lost wages, a serious imbalance when compared to the low fines for passengers. A spokesman for the Board of Transportation made no apologies for the practice, noting that the "trial of a 'fair number' of employes [sic]" was central to the board's deliberate "campaign" to "stop smoking on the city's system."[22]

The onset of war and the 1942 *Normandie* fire intensified concerns about working-class smoking in New York. Since authorities viewed industrial production as an important pathway to victory, judges demanded that the working class submit fully to the war effort as productive and disciplined citizens who put country first. Judges insisted that smoking was a menace to the war effort, as the portable fires smokers held in their hands could all too easily trigger disastrous conflagrations. Nonsmoking was to be a pillar of wartime patriotism and civic duty.

Cigarettes, Soldiers, and Workers

While anxious judges in New York condemned smoking, cigarette manufacturers, popular magazines, and working men and women created a wartime culture of tobacco use that framed the issues of patriotism and smoking very differently. In pitches to consumers, tobacco companies and magazine advertisers embedded the smoking of cigarettes not in the realm of dangerous or reckless behavior but in the celebration of soldiers, wartime workers, and their service, and ads depicted upstanding (and smoking) soldiers and defense industry workers. At the same time, working people embedded smoking in their own patriotic sensibilities. They collected cartons of cigarettes for care packages that were sent overseas to military personnel, delivered free cigarettes to troops who guarded defense plants, and donated cigarettes to wounded warriors in veterans' hospitals. From above and below, cigarettes became an emblem of patriotic expression. Lastly, wartime films played a significant role in shaping the legitimacy of smoking in American culture. In many films of the war years, smoking cigarettes was the vice of choice among the period's famed celluloid icons.[23]

Cigarette companies connected the smoking of their products to the celebrated ideal of service to the military and to soldiers' and sailors' understandable pursuit of personal comforts (such as a fresh cigarette while walking along with a romantic partner). Tobacco ads during World War II presented images of male as well as female smokers in uniform, and they presented smoking as an undeniably upright and decent activity. Advertisements in *Life* magazine in 1942 and 1943 for Philip Morris and Fleetwood Imperials cigarettes, for instance, depicted soldiers in dress uniforms coolly smoking, smiling, and walking arm-in-arm with their equally happy significant others. Other ads transported readers away from home-front romance and leisure to the job sites of war, such as naval warships and airfields. In one example, Regent cigarette advertisements showed both a younger sailor and an older officer smiling as they enjoyed a smoke on the deck of their ship.[24]

Images of and references to smoking as a way for soldiers to cope with the anxieties and stresses of war powerfully underlined the integration of smoking and the wartime values of patriotism and service to the nation. Magazine readers observed images of lit cigarettes as a vital source of consolation amid the strains of warfare and separation from home. In a 1942 *Life* magazine ad for Chesterfield cigarettes, a fighter pilot remarks that "a good cigarette is mighty comforting to have along." A 1943 Camel advertisement more directly referenced smoking as a necessary comfort for battle-weary troops. "I say that a pack of Camels is a lot of company," a soldier says. "Because when I can lean back and light up a Camel, everything's okay." Camel made repeated claims of its popularity in the armed forces. "With men in the Army, Navy, Marines, and Coast Guard," the company claimed, "the favorite cigarette is Camel." Advertisers so frequently connected smoking to the experience of military service that, as historian John C. Burnham writes, cigarettes became "an undefinable American something that was even an aspect of what servicemen in World War II were fighting for."[25]

Cigarette companies, however, not only marketed their wares to men; they also eagerly courted women as key consumers of tobacco products. Companies

FIGURE 3.1 Liggett & Myers' Chesterfield brand advertisement, 1943.
Courtesy Stanford Research Into the Impact of Tobacco Advertising.

such as Camel and Chesterfield imagined women as important embodiments of the new smoking chic during World War II, as advertisements connected happy young women, cigarettes, and wartime service, both in and out of uniform. The Camel firm, for example, used parachutist Adeline Gray's test of a new nylon chute design for the military as a way to vividly highlight the keen sense

FIGURE 3.2   R. J. Reynolds Tobacco Company's Camel Brand advertisement, 1943. Courtesy Stanford Research Into the Impact of Tobacco Advertising.

of adventure women brought to military service, a trait that was thought to be reflected in their choice of cigarette.

Chesterfield presented smoking as evidence of women's wartime assertions of equality with men, including in the context of service in uniform. One advertisement for the brand showed actress Joan Bennett (who starred in the film

FIGURE 3.3 Parachutist Adeline Gray in Camel advertisement, 1943.
Courtesy Stanford Research Into the Impact of Tobacco Advertising.

Twin Beds) in her American Women's Voluntary Services uniform, lighting her cigarette with a coy and contented smile. "His Cigarette and Mine," she says to the consumer. "It's Chesterfield."

Clothed in blue-collar overalls rather than a uniform, Rosie the Riveter contentedly worked on behalf of the war effort with a lit cigarette dangling from her

FIGURE 3.4   Hollywood star Joan Bennett in Chesterfield advertisement, 1942. Courtesy Stanford Research Into the Impact of Tobacco Advertising.

FIGURE 3.5   Chesterfield advertisement, 1943. Courtesy Stanford Research Into the Impact of Tobacco Advertising.

lips, as various wartime Chesterfield advertisements indicated. After all, "When you're doing a bang-up job you want a bang-up smoke."[26]

In addition to print advertising, music and film gave smoking further respectability and considerable panache in wartime culture. Tobacco companies positioned themselves as the underwriters of major swing bands, radio programs, and concerts, for example. R. J. Reynolds Tobacco sponsored Benny Goodman, while Liggett & Myers worked with Glenn Miller and his band. On the radio, Kool cigarettes sponsored Tommy Dorsey programs on the NBC network, and Lucky Strikes of the American Tobacco Company (who famously went "green" when World War II began) endorsed the "Your Hit Parade" radio program.[27] Early in the war, in movie theaters from coast to coast, audiences took in the iconic Humphrey Bogart ("Rick Blaine") in *Casablanca* (1942), who coolly smoked his way from anger to loving-while-letting-go of his great love, Ingrid Bergman ("Ilsa Lund"). In wartime Hollywood film, smoking became "one of the basic features of the suave American man," an idealized expression of adult masculinity. Smoking was an activity that appeared on the screen as a key feature of the "heroic male lead," made popular by Bogart's stylish and commanding performance, with a lit cigarette almost always in hand.[28]

The currents of acceptance and celebration of smoking in wartime popular culture were not confined to the two-dimensional realms of magazines and film. Working men and women themselves actively participated in shaping the respectability of wartime smoking and contributed to the interrelationships between smoking, patriotism, and public acceptance of the smoking habit. In union halls and even in factories, workers in industry devoted considerable time and effort to collecting cigarette cartons for special care packages that would be donated to military personnel, and the rank-and-file of local unions often did the same for those members that were in the service. At the UAW Local 600 meeting hall, a member of the union snapped a picture that appeared in a May 1944 edition of *Ford Facts*: a shot of seven men and women from the Ford River Rouge plant arranging cigarette cartons, shown on a table piled high, for a mailing overseas. "Thanks to these volunteers," the caption read, "the servicemen from that department will have smokes." As the paper remarked, the men and women donated their own time to organize, wrap, address, and "mail cigarettes to their servicemen."[29] The UAW reminded working men and women that sending cigarettes in bulk cartons to their fighting men in Europe or the Pacific was a thoughtful way to give them much-needed support. "The ideal package for a soldier to receive in his mail," one article noted, "is ten inches long, three inches wide and two inches deep. He knows without opening it that it contains 'the soldier's best friend,' the cigaret [*sic*]. It is a remarkably thoughtful gift." Every time a soldier smoked one of the cigarettes he received from friends at home, "he thinks of the sender."[30] Gifts of tobacco were thus an important way to support the troops.

Working men and women subtly defied factory prohibitions of smoking to deliver free cartons of cigarettes to the soldiers who were typically stationed at their workplaces as part of the conversion to defense production during the war. Coordinated by the members of union locals, working men and women conspicuously carried these cartons of cigarettes into the shop, delivering them personally and publicly to the servicemen. In December 1943, UAW Local 600 recording secretary Shelton Tappes detailed Brother Grant's update of "arrangements made for the distribution of cigarettes to the service men stationed at the Rouge." He asked how the executive board wanted the cartons handed out to the soldiers. Tappes noted that the executive board's belief was that "three young ladies be chosen." Brother Paul Good quickly said that he knew three women in the tire plant with "the prime requisites for this assignment." This cheeky motion was "Supported and CARRIED."[31]

Union locals also organized cigarettes for delivery to their members who were confined to veterans' hospitals as a result of their war wounds. In October 1945, for instance, Brother Near of UAW Local 600 requested funds to purchase twenty-five cartons of cigarettes every two weeks for this purpose. The executive board supported and carried the motion without question.[32]

Working men and women thus actively helped shape the acceptability of smoking in wartime culture, collecting cartons of free cigarettes for distribution to military personnel and veterans in the name of patriotic service. This activity occurred beyond, but also within, the boundaries maintained by their employers in the factories where they worked. These boundaries delineated an outside world where smoking was commonplace from the factory itself, where smoking bans threatened worker-smokers with tough consequences for their habit. The patriotic organization of cigarette deliveries for soldiers allowed workers to affirm the importance and acceptability of smoking in working-class life and subtly question the bans sustained by employers.

As workers participated in a patriotic culture that embraced cigarettes as one of its important features, they surely noted the evident contradiction between the respectability of smoking in much of wartime culture and employers' continued opposition to smoking on the job.

Smoking Bans in Wartime Industrial Workplaces

The practice of creating cigarette care packages for soldiers fighting overseas and distributing cigarette cartons to soldiers who were stationed at the defense factories where they worked stood in stark contrast to the smoking bans that existed in mass-production industries, especially the automobile industry. Throughout the Progressive Era, the interwar period, and World War II, major employers such as the Ford Motor Company, General Motors, Fisher Body, Cadillac, Briggs, and the Chrysler Corporation all enforced smoking bans. With workers, these bans were unpopular and barely tolerated, if at all. Even a single puff on a cigarette in the washroom could lead to a one-day suspension (as was the case at Chrysler) or even prompt dismissal from employment (Ford). During the years of World War II, as smoking became a visible, popular, and respectable feature of wartime culture at home and abroad, many workers concluded that no-smoking rules were onerous anachronisms that should no longer shape the daily experience of work.

As World War II began, legions of new defense workers in Detroit and Flint factories observed industrial landscapes marked by conspicuous signs and policies that reminded them not to smoke. The no-smoking rules of peacetime continued into the defense era, and industrial workers encountered managers that meticulously enforced the no-smoking policies that were enshrined in print. For instance, an "old-timer" who worked in Flint complained of "Notices plastered everywhere 'NO SMOKING'" in local factories during the war. The fact that he could not smoke at all—especially since all the floors in his workplace were cement—"don't make sense."[33] At Briggs in Detroit, personnel managers observed that the company's long-standing no-smoking prohibitions were likely to blame for a wartime problem of absenteeism, that it was "the reason that so many employees are absent from jobs and are in the crowded restrooms."[34] At the River Rouge plant, Ford's decades-old no-smoking policy was so unpopular that it was listed as one of the grievances during the April 1941 effort to unionize. In addition to pervasive opposition to the Ford spy system and the vicious antiunionism of the Service Department, striking workers at the Ford Motor Company complained they had no access to lunchrooms, "no time allowed for toilet needs," and "no smoking or chewing anyplace in the plant."[35]

The pangs of nicotine addiction and the need to smoke at work put working men's jobs in real jeopardy, as antismoking surveillance loomed large in the auto factories. At Briggs in 1942, members of the UAW local there observed, "Smoking has caused a number of discharges particularly among skilled workers," men whose important jobs did not afford them opportunities to sneak away to the bathrooms where they might smoke in secret. They were easily caught since they often tried to smoke at their work stations.[36] At Ford's Rouge plant, Harry Bennett's plainclothes servicemen enforced the company's no-smoking policy. Veteran autoworker and longtime member of UAW Local 600 Archie Acciacca recalled of daily life at the Rouge: "They [the Ford Service Department] were rough. . . . Oh yes, their job was just walking around in plain clothes; you didn't know who they were. They watched. If a guy was loafing a little bit, they thought, or goofing off or stalling. And they'd go to the toilets and check the toilets. If they see somebody staying too long, or smoking (you couldn't smoke in those days), they were turned in. They had the authority to fire."[37] At the Ford Motor Company, security personnel could dismiss workers for *any* reason. Workers undertook great risk if they dared to smoke in the lavatories, the only spaces at the Rouge that, in theory, offered workers anything remotely private. Antismoking measures overlapped with the company's practice of using fear and coercion as management tools. In March 1944, Ford labor relations officers fired two working men who were caught smoking in the Rouge aircraft plant. Apparently given a warning for an earlier offense, they were swiftly discharged for the second. The pair of smokers were former Marines and discharged veterans of the Pacific War. On this occasion, the routine dismissal of two smokers sparked what Ford managers and the local press labeled a "riot," as angry coworkers stormed the offices of the Service Department (the "labor-relations office"), destroyed files, broke windows, and beat up a guard. The incident reportedly went on for two hours. Afterward, leaders of Local 600 sympathetically noted, "These men who have come through the horrors of battle with shattered nerves need a cigarette once in a while!"[38]

The October 1942 smoker "sit-in" incident at the Chrysler Jefferson Avenue assembly plant in Detroit was probably the largest incident of industrial managers punishing workers for smoking on the job in violation of company regulations. Chrysler management had forbidden smoking in their plants since 1917. Penalties for worker-smokers were compounding, meaning they became more punitive for each offense. For the first incident, the offender would be sent home for one day; for the second, the worker would be kept away for two days; for the third, three days. The fourth violation led to the termination of the smoker's employment. The rule was supposed to apply to both labor and management, covering both the shop floor areas and the glass-enclosed offices throughout the Jefferson Avenue facility.[39]

Problems between workers and managers over the issue of smoking had intensified significantly throughout the summer and early fall of 1942, as the matter of the unpopular no-smoking rule had been slowly working its way through grievance channels at the factory. As suggested in UAW press accounts, even workers who were caught only "sneaking a puff or two" faced the full measure of punishment.[40] Although workers had been commanded by their union stewards not to strike over the matter, workers on the shop floor forced the issue themselves. When management issued one-day suspensions for smoking on the job to three men at Chrysler's Jefferson Avenue plant, their coworkers quickly formulated a challenge to management: they told the penalized smokers to report for work the next day as if nothing happened, and if managers tried to force them to leave, then "everybody in the plant would start smoking." When the suspended men arrived the next day, hundreds of workers lit cigarettes and proceeded to smoke. All of these "smoke-iners" were reportedly sent home by the company and issued slips that catalogued their suspensions. According to the union, the number of penalized workers at Chrysler was an astounding 2,500.[41]

FIGURE 3.6   "Detroit, Michigan. Assembly of Rolls Royce engines at the Packard motor car company. Workmen smoking cigarettes in an aisle during a five minute recess." (1943) Farm Security Administration-Office of War Information Photograph Collection, Library of Congress, LC-USW3-012897-C [P&P] LOT 99. Courtesy of the Library of Congress.

As workers at Chrysler launched their effort against shop floor penalties for smoking, the local press wrongly labeled the incident a walkout, a wildcat strike that was deliberately intended to bring wartime production to a standstill. As the *Detroit News* editorialized, "It is another stoppage of war work for trivial cause [*sic*] that risks, at some later time, loss of a battle and the lives of many American fighting men."[42] Jack Zeller of UAW Local 7 responded that the press accounts of the Chrysler workers' actions were blatant "lies." While in his statements to the press he tried to distance his union from any association with the controversial wartime trend of unplanned strikes, he nonetheless upheld the workers' basic assertion that no-smoking rules at work were a daily injustice. The workers *did* smoke, he said, and the managers were guilty of petty harassment for punishing them.[43]

Much to workers' frustration, managers could often be seen smoking in their offices and even as they walked through the shop floor areas of several Detroit and Flint factories. At Dodge Main in Hamtramck, workers reported how several foremen often "[kept] the home fires burning [i.e., smoking cigarettes and cigars] every day at lunch time."[44] Autoworker A. J. Cobb of Dodge Main spoke at length about the feelings of injustice workers experienced when they saw managers smoking:

> Boy, oh boy, I have met up with some goofy situations, but the one in our Department regarding smoking is the goofiest yet. For the information of anyone interested I will try to explain in a lucid manner. They say we are not allowed to smoke on the job, it's against the rules. That is alright, and we are not going off the deep end and strike about it or anything like that, but will someone please tell us the justice of a rule that forbids the men smoking on their jobs where the real work is being done, but allows all the office force to smoke in the office and also permits the Supervision to parade down the aisles with their cigars in their mouths, puffing away for all the men at their machines to see?[45]

While A. J. Cobb thought that walking off the job was too drastic at that moment, it is easy to see how managers' actions intensely irritated the workers at Dodge Main. "I realize the company thinks no one has an iota of brains that has to really work for a living," Cobb quipped, "but won't someone please take pity on us, in our dumb state, real or fancied, and tell us why a cigarette will start a fire and a cigar won't? This situation is unfair."[46] At the Chrysler Jefferson Avenue plant, Jack Zeller of UAW Local 7 pointed out that "supervisors of departments sit in glass enclosed offices and smoke all of the time."[47] "If bosses are allowed to smoke," he said, "the employes [sic] should be allowed a few drags in the washrooms."[48] After a Buick worker noticed inspectors looking for cigarette smokers on the shop floor at the plant where he worked, he complained to the union newspaper. "PS," the worker wrote, "Plant Portion Commandos made two raids in our plant on 14 September. They had better raid the front offices. As long as the privileged big shots are allowed to smoke in their offices, so will we."[49]

As discussions of suspensions and dismissals for smoking illustrate, the issue of cigarette smoking sharpened class lines and intensified class conflicts during World War II. Workers demanded a revised understanding of what constituted acceptable behavior on the job. For workers, the issue of what constituted "vice" would have to be rethought. Workers insisted that cigarette smoking no longer constituted a behavior that should be subject to arbitrary regulation from above.

Smoking and Labor Militancy: General Motors

In the long history of workplace smoking during the twentieth century, the World War II era presents conspicuous anomalies. Frequent strikes related to smoking bans occurred during these years, events that had possibly never occurred in US factories in the years before the war and would never appear again in the decades that followed. Between 1941 and 1945, workers' demands for the right to smoke at work gave rise to numerous strikes against long-standing employer policies that prohibited smoking. Since the early twentieth century, smoking bans constituted an ordinary and regular feature of management authority on the shop floor; they were a method of discipline intended to regulate and reshape behavior that was deemed an impediment to industrial efficiency. But industrial workers never mobilized themselves in strike actions against these rules until World War II. As workers struck against employers and policies that stood between them and their cigarettes, they assailed the age-old Victorian opposition to smoking at work and broadened the acceptability of smoking in American culture. At the same time, worker frustration over smoking very much contributed to the broader labor upheavals of the war years and impacted workers' relationships to new unions and to the state.

The increasing number of working hours during the early 1940s likely played a role in the intensification of conflicts over smoking during World War II, as workers now spent significantly more time in the factory. During the Great Depression, the realities of widespread unemployment and underemployment decreased the number of hours spent in the workplace. There were far fewer encounters between working-class smokers and no-smoking policies, which might have muted frustrations and complaints about the unpopularity of the bans. Between 1938 and 1941, however, US workers' hours on the job began to expand, increasing by 15 percent.[50]

The explosive growth of industrial unionism during the mid- to late 1930s and early 1940s was the likely the second reason why conflicts over smoking escalated during World War II. As union representation became more commonplace, industrial workers were empowered to press for changes in the rules and conditions of their work, as contracts codified work rules, collective bargaining provided opportunities to press for rule changes, and union organizers and militant shop stewards proved to be effective allies of workers seeking a "new deal" with management.[51] With a growing union movement behind them, industrial workers surely felt empowered to confront matters that were not always addressed by the processes of collective bargaining or grievance procedures during these early years of the Committee for Industrial Organization (CIO), such as the behaviors of unpopular foremen and managers and unpopular day-to-day work rules such as no-smoking policies. In addition, even in areas of the economy that lay beyond the scope of union organizing campaigns, the growth of industrial unionism during the Great Depression and World War II emboldened even the most marginal of workers to press for changes in their workplaces, as they saw shop floor democracy expanding throughout much of the economy.[52] Between 1933 and 1937, five million workers joined a union in the United States; by October 1937, the CIO could boast of two million members, six thousand local unions, and three thousand different agreements with employers. More than 400,000 participated in sit-down strikes that year.[53] By the early 1940s, unionization was widespread in the mass-production steel, auto, electrical, meatpacking, and rubber industries, as well as trucking, railroads, shipping, municipal transit, and commercial construction. The labor movement represented nine million workers in 1941 and by 1945 would gain six million more.[54]

The worker militancy that began in the 1930s escalated during World War II. Workers in industry and elsewhere struck their employers not only for union recognition during the 1940s, but also over other issues such as racial and gender tensions, forced overtime, and frustration with the "no-strike" pledge. The number of strikes in the United States shot up from 2,508 in 1940 to 4,288 in 1941. While the number declined to 2,968 in 1942, it would grow dramatically once again to 3,752 in 1943, 4,956 in 1944, and 4,750 in 1945. Among those strikes that occurred in industry during the war, many of them were concentrated in the automobile and aircraft manufacturing industries. In 1941, an estimated 39 percent of strikes in industry were found in these areas, followed by 50.5 percent and 75.9 percent in the final years of the war.[55]

The CIO's official commitment to the no-strike pledge did not easily translate into practice, as the various smoking strikes of World War II illustrated. But in their newspapers, union locals typically expressed a faithfulness to labor peace, even if the reality on the ground was often different and the shop floor situation was not always under their control. For instance, John W. Anderson, a leader of the UAW local at the Detroit Fisher body plant (Local 15), wrote, "In order to reaffirm the determination of the CIO and its members to render every aid to push the productive efforts of our country to the utmost limits to produce the guns, planes and cannons needed for victory over the fascist enemy . . . the single goal of production for victory." Labor's "goal" for the war, he wrote, was "To out-produce the slave labor of Hitler, to assure adequate equipment for our armed forces and for those of our allies to achieve complete victory over fascism." He concluded, "Hitlerism must be smashed."[56] At the national level, the head of the Congress of Industrial Organizations, Philip Murray, told a meeting of the House Naval Affairs Committee in 1942 that the government could expect organized labor to put away its strike weapon for the duration of the war. William Green of the AFL concurred. He praised local unions for doing everything in their power to get striking workers back to work immediately.[57]

On the ground, however, local unions and shop stewards were much more closely connected to the militancy of workers and invested in the outcome of shop floor conflicts. For example, the personnel director at Briggs, F. H. Taylor, complained to Walter Reuther in a letter that "the minority group of Union leaders continued their controls over production" throughout the war years in his plants. This, coupled with "steadily increasing evidence of growing lack of discipline on the part of employees generally," created an impossible situation for management. Strikes erupted at Briggs throughout World War II: eight work stoppages at the Briggs Mack Avenue plant in 1941, eight in 1942, and 113 in 1944. Looking back to the prewar year of 1939 and the early to mid-1940s, Taylor saw continuity between the labor militancy of the Great Depression and World War II, noting that "unauthorized stoppages had become so prevalent not only in our Company but throughout the automobile industry generally."[58] Throughout the United States, in 1942 there were 2,970 strikes and 3,572 the following year. Strikes throughout 1942 led to the loss of 4 million work days; 13.5 million in 1943; and 9 million in 1944.[59] The UAW, however, complained that supervisors at Briggs, for instance, were guilty of trying to provoke strikes by harassing union stewards; managers fired them "for the flimsiest excuses" and tried to instigate walkouts in order to embarrass the union. The UAW's response was to remind workers that "sporadic walkouts" were too risky to be of use to workers and the union, but they quietly left the door open for other, more significant (planned?) strike actions.[60]

Despite the CIO's worries about the efficacy of wartime strikes, the unpopularity of no-smoking rules and the power politics that enabled these prohibitions (in an era when smoking enjoyed considerable legitimacy in wartime culture) influenced several noteworthy strikes against employer policies. Most of these strikes (but not all) erupted in Detroit and Flint, the gilded hearts of mass-production industry. These strikes both reflected and propelled the growing legitimacy of smoking in American culture. At the same time, worker demands for the right to smoke were an important component of workers' conflicts with employers during the war, and they brought them into a closer working relationship with the growing CIO labor movement. Workers' vocal and sometimes forceful demands for smoking privileges forced local unions to respond to their constituents' desires, keeping these growing unions very much grounded in the shop floor during this period of significant institutionalization.[61]

The July 1942 strike at the new Fisher Body tank manufacturing plant in Grand Blanc, Michigan, near the capital of the GM empire in Flint, illustrates how worker-smokers' cravings for cigarettes could fuel militant action, as dependencies on nicotine brought workers into conflict with employer smoking policies. The longest and most publicized of the smoking strikes during World War II, the Grand Blanc case nicely highlights the interplay of workers, managers, state and federal governments, and organized labor at an early moment in the war. At the time, workers did not feel the full weight of labor and the state's wartime disapproval of worker militancy, and management at Fisher Body/GM seemed to worry that workers might somehow push forward a new transformative agenda in the factory, something not unlike what GM confronted in 1937.

Just as they had often done during the Depression, skilled workers led the workers' push against company policies at Fisher Body.[62] The tank plant in Grand Blanc was a new facility, specifically constructed to address wartime needs for armaments production. (Sherman tanks rolled off the assembly lines there.) It was not even a month old when trouble began. The plant was also not unionized, though the UAW-CIO *and* the UAW-AFL claimed many members among its workers. Most of the skilled and unskilled workers at Grand Blanc, as UAW regional chief Carl Swanson pointed out, transferred to the new plant from other unionized GM factories, especially Fisher Body No. 1, "where they were members of the UAW (CIO)."[63] As GM imported unionized workers into their nonunion shop at Grand Blanc, they also imposed their long-standing no-smoking rule, a policy they believed, in the words of Fisher Body general manager E. F. Fisher, guaranteed "safety, maximum production, and reasonable efficiency."[64] According to the *Detroit News*, the workers at Grand Blanc quickly accumulated a list of twenty complaints in this new open-shop operation, especially opposition to the smoking ban.[65] Skilled welders at the plant pressed the matter over the company's "refusal" to allow a pair of five-minute breaks for smoking during every shift. On 30 June, Fisher Body managers issued formal warnings to forty worker-smokers for their coordinated violation of the company's ban on smoking. Carl Swanson of the UAW reported that the conflicts over the ban had been "the last straw" in the growing list of workers' complaints.[66] On 15 June, the welders tested management's resolve again: they walked away from their machines and stepped outside the factory to smoke. As the men returned after several minutes, managers suspended each of them for three days.[67] Soon after, an estimated 80 percent of the plant's workforce walked out on strike, forming picket lines ("a score of pickets," according to the *Detroit Free Press*) outside the factory.[68] GM officials feigned outrage, claiming they had had been "willing to discuss the smoking ban," but "had not been approached."[69]

As the strike unfolded, the workers of the UAW-CIO maneuvered quickly to align themselves with the workforce at Grand Blanc. Speaking to strikers, the press, and management at Fisher Body, the UAW "offered its services in settling the dispute," citing their long-standing connections to the Fisher Body No. 1 workers who staffed many of the positions in the plant and those "from other GM divisions" who also worked there.[70] In addition to the sizeable CIO presence among the workers at Grand Blanc, labor organizer Kenneth Wells, who worked for the UAW-AFL, boasted of "a considerable number of members in the plant."[71]

Despite the presence of the AFL, the UAW-CIO dominated the union presence during the Grand Blanc tank strike. During the first forty-eight hours of picketing, members of UAW Local 581 (Fisher Body No. 1) held a closed-door meeting with "all tank plant workers," but what "transpired at the meeting was not revealed." GM officials complained that the workers and the union behaved haphazardly and without a discernible purpose, and "thus far no local to bargain with management had been organized among the men employed at the tank plant."[72]

Mediators from the federal and state governments moved swiftly to broker a resolution to the strike, in the process giving legitimacy to the UAW-CIO's effort to assert its presence. While the press announced that the Federal Labor Relations Board conciliator S. W. Duncan was due to head to Flint after conferring with GM officials, the State Labor Mediation Board in Michigan took the lead on the third day of the strike to lay the foundations for a solution. Paul R. Ricketts of the State Labor Mediation Board reported that a proposal had been forwarded to the UAW-CIO and the AFL for their approval, an agreement he said they quickly accepted. The terms were not revealed, but an article in the *Detroit Free Press* featured the subheading "Lack of Grievance Committee Blamed for Tie-Up of Vital War Materiel Plant."[73] Bernard H. Sweeney of GM was reportedly "considering" Ricketts' proposal. At the same time, Carl Swanson of the UAW conferred with a committee of the strikers, led by Joseph Beebe (their "chairman") and Russell Howell, the secretary of the workers' group, to "gather material to be used in a petition to the National Labor Relations Board for an election in the plant."[74]

As the fourth day of the strike loomed, there was still no resolution in sight. The managements of GM and Fisher Body did not give their assent to the State Labor Mediation Board's proposed solution, turning instead to the press in an effort to mobilize public opinion against the strikers at Grand Blanc and the CIO unionists who wanted to organize the new factory. E. F. Fisher, the general manager of the Fisher Body division, released a return-to-work plea to the press, calling the strike a "national disgrace." Suggesting that the long duration of the strike promised to jeopardize the combat readiness and safety of the men at war, he cautioned, "Are we going to miss the boat?" He praised the minority of men and women who stayed at their jobs, "those who have the courage of their convictions, believing that it is more important to build combat vehicles than it is to demand smoking privileges and who have continued to work." On the other hand, Fisher criticized "those who have hesitated or refused to go through the picket lines—and to that small group of you who have been doing the picketing and promoting the strike."[75] As strikers picketed at Fisher Body's Grand Blanc plant and other workers simultaneously struck a local Detroit-area railroad company, the *Detroit Free Press* editorial page erupted with fury. "Every moment lost on Detroit's war production lines is a gain for the enemy," editors wrote, "and the news columns today are witness to the number of man-hours lost because of the operations of roving gangs." They continued, "There is no room in Detroit, there is no room in an America at war, for the type of hoodlum unionists who ran amok."[76] A UAW member at Buick reported that "some radio squeals" accused the strikers at Grand Blanc of "helping Hitler, etc., for the sake of a smoke." He went on to say that the voices on the radio probably knew nothing about defense work, combat, or the pleasures offered by "two drags at a cigarette" after such important work.[77]

As the impasse neared one full week in length, Michigan state officials grew more and more impatient. But GM management's resistance to any negotiated solution prevented the auto company from benefiting in some way from the state's frustrations with the strike. On July 21, the governor of Michigan, Van Wagoner, issued angry words that put the company and the strikers on notice. The federal government or his office, he said, "would act within 24 hours" to force the resolution of the "labor dispute" at the Fisher Body tank plant. "This is a serious situation," the governor said, "and any further delay will cause a dangerous disruption of production. . . . I don't know what procedure we will take, but something will have to be done quickly." At the same time, "an agent of the State" conferred with the strikers "in the hope of bringing about speedy resumption of production."[78] At the same time, GM officials claimed they would not negotiate over the smoking issue until the strikers "return to work."[79] Throughout the strike trouble at Grand Blanc, workers and union organizers cooperated with state inquiries and gave their cooperation to the state's proposed compromises, perhaps finding no reason to interrupt GM's self-imposed isolation from the negotiations and hostile stands in the press. GM's defiance forced the state to push harder for a compromise solution to the problem. When GM dug in and prolonged the strike as a result, the state did not lend the company any significant support.

The strike ended abruptly after an entire week of picketing, and the men quickly returned to work. Federal War Labor Board mediator Tilford Dandlay settled the strike when he "arranged the agreement" with representatives of the UAW-CIO, the UAW-AFL, and GM. Strikers accepted the two unions as their bargaining agents in the short term, now claiming the smoking ban "was only one factor in the dispute." Their "major objective," according to the press, was to ensure the unionization of the tank plant and the establishment of a functioning grievance procedure. The agreement itself did not reference any specific grievances, only that a NLRB election would be "held as quickly as possible" to determine whether the CIO or the AFL would become the workers' bargaining agent at Grand Blanc. In the interim, temporary "grievance machinery" would be established at Fisher Body's tank plant, which would give workers the right to send their unaddressed complaints to the federal War Labor Board for a hearing. The War Labor Board and the various parties involved, however, failed to address the hated smoking ban that started the strike. It would be "left for negotiation" at a later date.[80]

Left for negotiation. . . . After the conclusion of the strike, the conversation about smoking in the tank plant at Grand Blanc disappeared from area newspapers and union materials. While the smoking issue was not formally resolved, workers probably believed the strike served their overall purpose of gaining greater influence over the conditions of work. The prospect of formalized union representation and the establishment of a working grievance procedure would give them some leverage and influence in their relations with management. Also, the workers at Grand Blanc most likely saw the strike's outcomes as reasonable pathways to resolving the smoking grievance that led to the strike. With the aid of union representation, collective bargaining, and grievance mechanisms, workers surely believed the smoking issue would ultimately be resolved in their favor.

The attitude of the federal government toward wartime strikes grew significantly more adversarial during the first half of 1943, especially among conservative members of Congress. In June 1943, Congress passed the Wartime Labor Disputes Act (known as the Smith-Connally Act) in an effort to curb worker militancy in defense-related industries. This draconian legislation gave the president of the United States the authority to take control of industries "threatened" by strikes, established "criminal penalties" for those workers who struck against enterprises that were under government management, gave the National War Labor Board (NWLB) the power to subpoena individuals to appear at hearings, made all NWLB strike decisions "final and binding," and mandated a National Labor Relations Board (NLRB) election before any strike could be called and a thirty-day "cooling off" period before any strike action could occur. Congress passed the law over a presidential veto.[81] Although the Smith-Connally Act was a blow to the labor movement and its strike weapon, especially John L. Lewis's United Mine Workers, who presented the most significant and controversial challenges to the wartime no-strike pledge, the act failed to end strike activity. Indeed, there were an estimated 377 "wildcat" strikes in 1943–1944.[82]

While the Smith-Connally Act aimed to curb workers' militancy on the shop floor and slow down the pace of their challenges to employers and the wartime state, the law actually created some spaces where frustrated workers could pursue other (though certainly limited) avenues of resistance besides a strike. Early on, the controversial law created media spectacles out of shop floor disputes, giving workers new opportunities to articulate their grievances and goals before the larger public. An early test case of the Smith-Connally Act occurred in Flint at Chevrolet, a contentious site long characterized by a militant rank and file that could boast of their close connection to the successful GM sit-down strike of 1936–1937.[83] (Working men in Flint once smoked cigarettes in the occupied factories during the sit-down strike.[84]) Throughout the war years, numerous grievances led Chevrolet workers to demand the authority to strike in 1943: the "revocation of smoking privileges which had been in effect for years" in one work department; management's refusal to increase workers' pay rates according to contract obligations; and poor working conditions for women.[85] Frustrated smokers were near the forefront of the gathering storm in the plant in 1943.

The prominence of the smoking grievance at Chevrolet stemmed from a surprising reality about working-class smoking during World War II: there were miniscule pockets of acceptable smoking activity scattered through various parts of the auto industry, most likely secured by workers themselves on an informal basis. Despite GM's prohibition of smoking in all of its factories, the *Detroit News* briefly referenced the Chevrolet work department's "smoking privileges" that had existed "for years." Management's rescission of this informal right to smoke engendered considerable anger among the workers in this unnamed department and among the broader workforce. Beyond Flint, there were other tiny oases of smoking privileges in the industry, such as the example of the Buckeye Bumper Company factory in Springfield, Ohio. At the "small operation" of the Buckeye Bumper Company, UAW members mentioned restrooms where managers permitted employees to "lounge and smoke." In this well-trafficked space, members of UAW Local 465 maintained their bulletin board and a wall desk.[86] But because of the overall prohibitions against smoking throughout the auto industry during the war, these legitimate smoking spaces would have been unusual. The most common smoking areas would have been clandestine ones, but because of their illegitimacy and necessary secrecy, they would not have been betrayed by workers in print.

The "cooling off" period mandated by the Smith-Connally Act actually provided the frustrated workers at Chevrolet with the means to maintain the *threat* of a strike, and the NLRB-coordinated vote about whether or not to strike gave definite form to the power that could be wielded by the angry plant workforce. On voting day at Chevrolet, in an election coordinated by Thomas H. McKeon of the NLRB in Detroit, workers voted for a strike by a four-to-one margin (8,099 to 2,070). The federal government used the wording of the question on the ballot as a final opportunity to influence workers' actions. The printed question was, "Do you wish to permit an interruption of war production in wartime as a result of this dispute?" In other words, are smoking privileges, women's working conditions, and squabbles about pay rates worth the injury to the war effort? Most workers answered yes.

The union leaders of UAW Local 659 made a point of standing shoulder-to-shoulder with the rank and file, citing their local's opposition to the no-strike pledge and their determination to secure the blessing of the UAW's leadership to strike to remedy their grievances. For example, Terrell Thompson, the president of the local, "said he would seek authorization" from the UAW hierarchy, and, the *Detroit News* suggested, he would have to follow them all the way to the CIO convention in Philadelphia to speak to them. Local union leaders at Chevrolet aligned themselves closely with rank-and-file members when they told their delegates to the UAW convention in Buffalo to "vote against a renewal of the no-strike pledge." Also, the local's leadership declared their support of the rank and file when they filed an intention-to-strike notice earlier in September and presented the "accumulation of petty grievances," presumably to representatives of the NLRB or the NWLB.[87]

The strike probably never occurred, though, as the Detroit news dailies and the UAW newspapers did not report on any further developments at Chevrolet in late 1943. At the same time, in the weeks that followed, the city newspapers reported on other, smaller strikes at locations such as the Ford Rouge plant and at General Motors in Saginaw.[88] The silence that followed the early November 1943 announcement of Chevrolet workers' support for a strike suggests that management yielded concessions to the workers or that GM management threatened to fire any strikers.

Smoking and Labor Militancy: Ford

Wartime strikes over smoking privileges also reached southward from Flint to Dearborn and Detroit, where the Ford Motor Company operated the massive Rouge complex as well as its older Highland Park plant on Woodward Avenue in Detroit. There was extensive strike activity at the Ford factories during World War II. Between the signing of the UAW contract in June 1941 and the conclusion of the war in August 1945, there were an estimated 773 strikes at the Ford plants, an estimated 250 wildcat strikes in 1943 alone, equaling nearly one job action every forty-eight hours. In fact, the Ford Motor Company experienced the most strikes of any of the major automakers during the war years.[89]

Day-to-day conflicts over workers' asserting the right to smoke could be found at the center of several of these wartime strikes at Ford. That working men were willing to risk their jobs and confront the possibility of Ford's repression underlines the importance of cigarette smoking and nicotine in the daily lives of industrial workers. They insisted that smoking and cigarette breaks were necessary, desired, and acceptable features of the workday. Furthermore, these wartime struggles over smoking privileges intersected (sometimes explosively) with broader struggles during these years over the rights and restrictions of managers, workers, and the UAW.

The 30 December 30 1941 strike of Ford Rouge tool-and-die men against no-smoking rules and the lack of break time was one of the more widely publicized incidents at the company during the war. Here, we see once again the prominence of skilled workers in CIO-era shop floor militancy during the 1930s and 1940s. Angered by the lack of five-minute rest periods, opportunities to wash up, and crackdowns by management on smoking in the tool-and-die room, the tool men reportedly launched the "spontaneous" protest; nearly a thousand men were involved. Harry Bennett, the notorious head of the Service Department, complained, "The men . . . attempted to operate their machines with cigars, cigarettes, and pipes and we can't have anything like that." The strike ended twenty-four hours later, but the terms of the arrangement between management and the tool-and-die workers were not disclosed. The press, however, claimed the "dispute" had been "settled"—"including smoking."[90] *Ford Facts* (Local 600's newspaper) offered an additional fragment of insight into the strike. While the reported majority of the tool men walked off the job, at least one man remained. When the foreman told the stubborn individual to "go home," he responded defiantly. "Listen buddy," he said. "I've got a brother at Pearl Harbor and I figure him and the guys with him need this stuff. If the company don't want to pay me for it, then I'm donating my services to the US government."[91] To him, petty conflicts over smoking need not occur. He was likely frustrated with both management, which enforced unpopular and trivial policies, and with his fellow men in the tool room, whose protests against company rules detracted from the man's hope of giving aid to his embattled brother and other military personnel overseas.

The no-smoking policy at the Ford Motor Company gave managers a convenient means to strike back against UAW functionaries who served as committeemen. In late January 1944, Ford managers at the Highland Park plant in Detroit called a union committeeman who had been "caught smoking" in a "restricted" section of the factory into the labor relations office for a formal reprimand. Smoking cigarettes, however, was not the primary complaint of management: the committeeman had earlier refused to accept a particular work assignment, and the no-smoking rule gave managers further justification to put the man on notice. When other UAW committeemen of Local 400 joined the accused in the labor relations office, managers refused to talk with the group. Soon after, as many as 5,600 Ford workers struck the Highland Park factory and the nearby Standard Tube Plant, led out of the shop by the committeemen of Local 400.[92]

At Highland Park, the months of December 1943 and January 1944 had been a period of particularly tense relations between working men and management over the issue of smoking. On 29 December, Martin Glaberman reported, "Employees accompanied fellow-worker to labor relations office for smoking," and a "dispute" of unknown duration ensued.[93] For workers at Highland Park, the punishment of two worker-smokers only four weeks apart (one of whom was apparently a respected committeeman) might have caused workers to feel that they were on the receiving end of an arbitrary management crackdown on smokers and unionists. On 15 February, the Local 400 president Ben Garrison published an editorial in the UAW paper that called on Henry Ford to do whatever he could to reverse the "virtual reign of distrust" that "enveloped the atmosphere" of the Highland Park factory. In particular, Garrison cautioned the company's owner to look carefully at the actions of his labor relations office (once known as the Service Department), who he insisted were ultimately to blame for the "unhealthy condition" of worker-manager relations at the factory and were responsible for workers "being constantly provoked."[94] Overall, there had been numerous shop floor conflicts and disputes at Highland Park since the earliest months of the war. In August 1942, for example, the Local 400 edition of the UAW newspaper carried an editorial complaining that wartime strikes at Highland Park "have been prompted by the indifference and actions on the part of management." The unnamed writer claimed in the editorial, "I hold and contend [that] under these circumstances, management is, to say the least, equally (if not more) guilty of being the instigators."[95]

Tensions and disputes continued at both Ford plants, however. The March 1944 "riot" that resulted from the dismissals of the two war veterans for smoking led to a subsequent strike by workers at the Rouge, probably the largest attempted at Ford Motor Company during World War II. But the motivation for, and scope of, this particular strike led the local and international leadership of the UAW to turn fully away from the politics of shop floor militants and forcibly reassert control over the restless rank and file.

After the worker invasion of the personnel office, managers fired or suspended twenty participants, including eleven union committeemen, who, as Nelson Lichtenstein points out, were actually "tangential" to the incident (*Ford Facts* indicated the committeemen had been fired[96]). As militants inside the Rouge planned for a plant-wide strike in protest, led by worker Lawrence Yost, the leadership of Local 600 was initially sympathetic to the punished men. Joseph Twyman, president of Local 600, described the incident as workers' "spontaneous reaction" against "dictatorial treatment."[97]

The UAW international leadership, however, immediately condemned the explosive job actions at the Rouge. Seeing the office invasion as a repudiation of the union commitment to the no-strike pledge (and the authority of the union's leaders who embraced it), UAW president R. J. Thomas stated his unequivocal approval of Ford managers' punishments. "Our union," Thomas said to the *Detroit Free Press*, "cannot and will not tolerate rowdyism as a means of adjusting its problems."[98]

On the night of 14 March, militants launched the strike, demanding the reinstatement of the ex-Marine smokers, the office invaders, and the committeemen. Shop floor militants from the aircraft plant (where Yost worked) tried to shut down the entire Rouge facility with barricades of cars and picket lines of strikers, a redeployment of tactics used in the 1941 strike to unionize the Ford Motor Company. "Thousands" answered the call to strike, but the international union and even the typically left-leaning UAW Local 600 undercut the strikers by condemning their actions.[99] Closing ranks to protect their leadership of the union and to minimize public criticism, the high- and low-level leadership of the UAW at Ford reported they would not interfere with managers' punishment of the strikers, sacrificing the militants to management. Over time, 121 men were fired or suspended for their involvement.[100] Resistance to no-smoking rules, however, did not end with the unraveling of the strike and the punishment of those involved; incidents continued to stir up the Rouge. In December 1944, management caught two men smoking, and, as Martin Glaberman later wrote, "fellow-employees accompanied them to labor-relations office in sympathy."[101]

While the most publicized wartime strikes against smoking bans occurred in the arsenal of democracy in Michigan, there were job actions in other locations. For instance, as the American Viscose Corporation pushed forward the construction of new additions to their new Front Royal, Virginia, plant in June 1944, employees of the Rust Engineering Company, contracted to work on the construction, "staged a walkout" in opposition to the American Viscose ban on smoking. The strike began on a Thursday and lasted through the weekend. According to commonwealth attorney John Downing, between 2,100 and 2,200 men, "affiliated with various craft unions," participated in the "unofficial strike." Worried about worker mischief in the streets, Downing ordered the closing of a nearby liquor store ("a precautionary measure") until the strike concluded. The walkout ended when American Viscose management quickly agreed to "relax the non-smoking rule in certain construction areas." Since the contracted men worked outdoors outside the factory, they were permitted to smoke.[102]

From Flint to Detroit and even southward to Virginia, conflicts between workers and managers over smoking fueled several significant strikes during World War II. Smokers were pushed to the forefront of broader conflicts over the unionization of the shop floor, the no-strike pledge, and the relationship of the state to workers and new unions. The workers' need to smoke very much informed and intersected with their politics.

At the same time, wartime strikes over workplace smoking created a frame-work where working-class smokers could press for the legitimacy and respect-ability of their habit. Throughout the war years, workers (in word and deed) insisted that smoking was not detrimental to industrial production; rather, they saw smoking as one of their day-to-day rights in the shop, a personal choice that should be allowable even in these spaces that were officially governed by fore-men, managers, and employers. Workers insisted that smoking was no longer an activity within the purview of controlling and puritanical managers. World War II strikers in industry played a significant role in dismantling the Victorian culture of smoking bans in the workplace and helped to foster the acceptability of smoking in wartime and postwar American culture.

The cessation of hostilities in 1945 did not bring an end to the cycle of rebellion against industrial smoking bans, as workers on at least one other occasion in the immediate postwar period struck to protest the firing of a man for smoking. The *Baltimore Sun* printed a story from the newswire that other major newspapers such as the *New York Times* and the *Chicago Daily Tribune* entirely ignored: The management of Dorsey Trailers Inc. in Elba, Alabama, "fired a worker for smok-ing in violation of a plant rule" in May 1946, prompting the members of the UAW local to "walk out in protest." Management retaliated by announcing a shutdown of the entire plant for two weeks, throwing out the entire workforce and forc-ing them to deal with a severe "wage loss" as a result. The company leadership, though, backed away from the strike-busting shutdown scheme after only four days. The National Labor Relations Board later ruled that Dorsey managers acted illegally when they closed down the plant, calling the shutdown a case of "ille-gal discrimination" against workers for "concerted union activity." In 1948, the NLRB ordered Dorsey Trailers Inc. to pay their workers for the wages they lost.[103]

Stories of strikes over smoking bans disappeared from newspapers after the 1946 Elba incident. This makes sense, since reasons for workers to complain about smoking prohibitions were quickly disappearing from industrial shop floors by then. In the spring and summer of 1945, at the behest of the National War Labor Board, General Motors and UAW local unions began negotiations over new smoking rules. As a result, GM workers in 1945 were now able to smoke during break times at work and in various locations such as washrooms, work rooms, factory lobbies, and lunchrooms.[104] The Ford Motor Company soon fol-lowed suit. Henry Ford II, the new president of the Ford Motor Company as of 1945, announced in October 1947 that his firm was now abandoning the no-smoking rule that had been his "tobacco-hating" grandfather's policy for the past thirty-four years. Ford did not fearlessly break with the past, however. The company's president told the press that the new policy was instituted on a "trial basis," and if the "privilege" were "abused" the ban would be reintroduced by management. But beginning on 15 November, blue- and white-collar workers on the factory floors and in company offices could smoke.[105] By the 1980s, auto-worker and gonzo journalist Ben Hamper would write of an autoworker's life that was very much defined by the use of cigarettes (and other drugs) in the factory. Even as a young boy, he visited his chain-smoking father on the assembly lines at GM in Flint and noticed that smoking was a regular feature of mass-production labor. "We stood there for forty minutes or so, a miniature lifetime, and the pattern never changed," Hamper later wrote of the visit. "Car, windshield. Car, windshield . . . Cigarette to cigarette."[106]

By 1950, the "triumph of the cigarette" in American culture was assured. At midcentury, Americans smoked a staggering 350 billion cigarettes every year.[107] In 1945, Emily Post noted the general "custom of smoking in nearly all places at nearly all hours and by nearly all people," making it necessary for her readers to accept without comment the practice of smoking at parties and dinners and when traveling by bus or train.[108] A significant part of the growing respectability of smoking was the long-standing shop floor struggles between working people and employers over day-to-day privileges in the shop, struggles that reached a crescendo during the 1940s. Strikes against smoking bans during World War II surely helped to pry open the industrial workplace to smokers, guaranteeing that cigarette smoke would ultimately pervade more and more spaces in the postwar United States. The prevalence of cigarettes in post–World War II America not only resulted from the cultural power of corporate advertising and influence, but also very much from the bottom up from worker-smokers' aggressive pursuit of their habit in their places of work.

These struggles against smoking bans likely resulted from the contradiction between a wartime popular culture that embraced smoking as respectable and patriotic, and zealous judges and widespread company prohibitions that severely penalized worker-smokers for their desires to smoke cigarettes. At the same time, the large growth of the CIO labor movement during the 1930s and 1940s surely emboldened workers to challenge employers over the day-to-day grievances they confronted in the factory. These clashes fueled not only the legitimization of smoking in the industrial workplace but also played a noteworthy role in wartime struggles over the extent of union power and the influence of the state in labor relations.

But how long would the "triumph of the cigarette" last?

4

ANTISMOKING POLITICS IN POSTWAR WORKPLACES

You don't have to be a smoker for smoking to harm you.

—National Institutes of Health (NIH)

By 1976, a clerk named Vivian Cannon, who worked for the US Department of Health and Human Services at the Atlanta branch office, could no longer tolerate the constant presence of cigarette smoke in her office. She filed a grievance with her employer—a division of the federal government that watched out for Americans' health—that demanded the banning of smoking from her area. "I think I have a right to clean air," Cannon insisted, "but it seems that smokers have all the rights, and think that they have the right to pollute the air."[1] While smoking was commonplace, acceptable, and often tolerated in the years that followed World War II, the smoking consensus began to fall apart during the 1960s and especially in the 1970s because of powerful new medical knowledge about the dangers of tobacco and the efforts of nonsmoking workers to combat the toxic smoke in the air. Like many other staffers of the 1970s, Vivian Cannon demanded that management foster better indoor air quality and safeguard the health and comfort of nonsmokers. Cannon's grievance briefly reveals increasingly hostile attitudes about smoking in postwar American culture. More and more nonsmoking workers—particularly in offices—became vocal about their opposition to smoking and were determined to press for changes in the rules that underpinned worker-smokers' seemingly unquestioned right to smoke.

As this chapter illustrates, white-collar workplaces became a wellspring of antismoking sentiment. The emergence of worker criticism of smoking, the rise of antismoking activism, and the appearance of legal challenges to smoking privileges stemmed from specific contexts in the postwar years. The expansion of white-collar employment and the spatial features of many postwar office workplaces intensified workers' experiences with secondhand smoke, which led to a growing chorus of opposition to smoking in the 1960s, 1970s, and 1980s.

Smoking was not only a major public health issue; it was also a central issue in labor-management relations. Growing controversies over smoking at work fostered new divisions among workers that earlier in the twentieth century were either muted or entirely absent. At the same time, frustrated nonsmoking workers directly engaged management in business and government workplaces to press for changes in smoking rules. These struggles over tobacco use led to sustained conflicts between labor and management, and among office workers themselves, over the extent of worker influence and managerial power on white-collar shop floors.

Until recently, histories of office workers usually focused on the years between the Gilded Age and the Great Depression.[2] This chapter illustrates several new dimensions in the social and cultural history of the white-collar workplace. It broadens the field chronologically to encompass a significant portion of the post–World War II decades and thematically to highlight the importance of smoking as a source of conflict among office workers and managers. It also shows how the postwar experience of white-collar labor contributed to the rise of antismoking activism and legal action against tobacco. At the same time, historians of tobacco use focus on struggles over smoking in the areas of government, public policy, and the media, highlighting corporate wrongdoing and improving medical knowledge as the central themes in tobacco's postwar history.[3] This chapter more fully historicizes struggles over smoking by demonstrating the significance of post–World War II white-collar workplaces as sites that gave rise to antismoking politics and the importance of white-collar workers to the new movement against tobacco use.

Smoke, Health, and Space in Postwar Offices

Nonsmoking white-collar workers often lamented the wide-ranging acceptance of smoking in the United States. For one small group of frustrated government workers in Pennsylvania, for instance, the evidence of Americans' illogical approval of smoking was all around them. As they looked around the office, they saw dusty ashtrays overflowing with cigarette butts that were splayed out all over the desks. Carol Klauber and her nonsmoking colleagues who worked at a government office in Mechanicsburg, Pennsylvania, noticed cigarette burns on desk blotters throughout the room and "the unpleasant scene" of so many secretaries and staffers talking and typing with lit cigarettes dangling from their mouths. "Everything else must go by rules and regulations, yet because you are a non-smoker you have no rights," they complained. "You must sit in these terrible conditions with burny eyes, ears, nose and throat; coughing and gagging until you end up the day with a headache or a sick stomach because you are forced to put up with some elses [*sic*] *habit*." Lowell Thomas, who worked for State Farm Insurance in Maryland during the 1960s and 1970s, recalled how the desks were engineered with a built-in ashtray in the top-left corner.[4] Desks covered with grungy ashtrays, the sight of secretaries smoking while working, burn marks on desk blotters, and workstations with built-in ashtrays can be read as physical evidence of the "triumph of the cigarette" at the middle point of the twentieth century. As the historian Allan M. Brandt observes, smoking rose to "cultural dominance" after World War II, graced with a new, "almost universal acceptance and appeal."[5] The postwar decades were surely the bedrock of what Brandt calls "the cigarette century."

Why did opposition to smoking shift from the reformers, employers, and judges of the early twentieth century to workers themselves after World War II? Why did the voices of nonsmoking workers—silent or unnoticed in the first half of the twentieth century—emerge so powerfully in the 1970s and 1980s? The interaction of cigarette smoke and postwar workspaces played a significant role in the creation of bottom-up tobacco-control politics. The nonsmokers who so vigorously opposed smoking at work in the post–World War II years were members of the white-collar working class, laborers with the pen, paper, file, typewriter, and, later, computer, who opposed smoking and employer policies that seemed to protect their smoking coworkers at the expense of everyone's health and comfort.

The interactions of secondhand smoke (also called "sidestream" or "environmental tobacco smoke") with nonsmokers' eyes, noses, and airways, and the growing pre-eminence of postwar office environments in America, produced powerful opposition among nonsmokers to the ubiquity of smoking at work in postwar America. While workers had smoked cigarettes on the job throughout the early- to mid-twentieth century, the changing settings of labor in the post–World War II years led to more and more antismoking sentiment among nonsmoking workers. In contrast to the grimy and open industrial spaces of automobile manufacturing plants, where workers thought smoking was entirely acceptable, more and more Americans worked in in white-collar office settings after World War II. While manufacturing employment began to decline after 1960 (from 27 percent to 15 percent of the US workforce in 2000), the number of workers in finance, insurance, real estate, business services, and professional services significantly increased. Professional services workers' ranks expanded from 10 percent of the American workforce in 1960 to 26 percent in 2000, while workers in the other occupations—finance, insurance, etc.—increased from 5 to 13 percent during the same period.[6]

Compared to the large mass-production auto factories of Detroit, Flint, and Dearborn, white-collar offices presented a very different geography of work: more compact rooms with lower ceilings, inconsistent or inadequate ventilation; carpets, seats, and wall surfaces that absorbed and retained the tar found in tobacco smoke; workspaces with less obvious grit and grime; and tailored men and women who often wore pressed slacks, skirts, ties, blouses, ironed shirts, and high-heeled shoes to work. While blue- and white-collar workers could both be seen smoking on the job, nonsmokers likely experienced sidestream smoke in the compact white-collar milieu more intensely than did their blue-collar counterparts on the assembly lines at Ford, Chrysler, or General Motors. Roughly half of white-collar workers regularly smoked during the early 1970s alone.[7] As we will see, almost all nonsmoker opposition to workplace smoking emerged from office workspaces in the 1970s, 1980s, and 1990s.

Of course, not every office was the same, but by the 1960s there were three predominant types of white-collar workspace arrangements: the open-plan office, the combo-office, and the individual office (i.e., private office). Individual offices (occupied by a single person) afforded the most privacy and the least exposure to outside disturbances. Most white-collar workers, however, did not execute their labors in individual offices because their spot in the company hierarchy determined whether or not they could have their own office.[8] Most white-collar laborers after the late 1960s worked in open-plan or combo-office settings. In the open-plan and combo-office arrangements, staffers usually worked in large rooms with numerous individual desks and workstations (and later cubicles). To facilitate communication among workers, promote identification with the group, and create "flexible" space, employers and designers in the late postwar years cast aside the permanent barriers of walls and doors. In the combo-office style, however, managers and executives occupied the smattering of individual offices that remained among the wide-open terrain occupied by the rank and file.[9]

The open-plan office's emphasis on free-flowing communication, movement, and interaction produced a day-to-day work environment characterized by significant noise, frequent interruptions, a lack of privacy, and constantly close quarters. The potential for elbow room was limited. Postwar offices further limited worker access to space since employers and the designers of open-plan offices typically underestimated or even ignored storage needs, guaranteeing that files and boxes competed with their laboring handlers for space. Not only did white-collar workers experience a barrage of sounds, sights, and bodies in the open-plan environment, but they also often worked in rooms with poor air flow. Later designers of the early twenty-first century referred to these open-plan offices as "dead-air cul-de-sacs."[10] While people and noise moved freely about the open-plan office, the air did not. As more and more workers could smoke without employer sanction in the post–World War II years, the transition to these "dead-air cul-de-sacs" as the principal settings of labor guaranteed that many nonsmokers would be exposed to gathering plumes of cigarette smoke. Murky clouds of smoke lingered constantly in the dead air of the postwar office, and frustrated nonsmoking office workers of the 1970s and later played a major role in forcing employers, local and state politicians, judges, and doctors to question the acceptability of smoking in postwar American culture. The interplay of space, environment, and labor played a significant role in the rise of postwar antismoking sentiment.

Nonsmokers recoiled from the smoke that saturated their office workplaces. They commonly spoke of frequent eye irritation, offensive smells, nagging headaches, and labored breathing, among other problems. Nonsmoker opposition began with the immediate ills caused by sidestream smoke. "I am too miserable right now," wrote Walter W. Heinze to his local Shrewsbury, New Jersey, newspaper in 1977. "My eyes burn. I have trouble breathing and find it difficult to speak." His immediate suffering with sidestream smoke was so severe that he was "not concerned about ill effects years later," such as heart disease. Anti-smoking organizations such as the Group Against Smoking Pollution (GASP) and Action on Smoking and Health (ASH) received numerous complaints from nonsmokers during the 1970s about the day-to-day suffering caused by the smoky haze they worked in. The New Jersey GASP chapter, for example, received firsthand testimonies in the mail and in conversation that cigarette smoke "made sick" many nonsmokers in offices. Working people complained of headaches, sore throats, burning eyes, breathing discomfort, coughing, respiratory infections, sneezing, and nausea.[11] An optometrist noted in 1978 that many contact lens wearers who passed through his office complained of itching, burning, and tearing of the eyes as a result of their daily exposure to cigarette smoke at work. Lorraine Van Buren, who worked at the Michigan Department of Education during the early 1970s, missed fifty days of work and incurred $3,000 in medical bills for health troubles brought about by exposure to tobacco smoke in her office. "I swelled up and my breathing was cut off," she wrote of the incident that incapacitated her and forced her into treatment. Working in a windowless office where clouds of smoke lingered, Van Buren suffered from swelling and irritation that hurt her eyes, caused nagging headaches, triggered acute sinus pain, and hampered her breathing.[12]

Tobacco—whether smoked, chewed, or sniffed (known as "snuff")—is extremely injurious to delicate human tissues. Cigarettes and cigarette smoke contain at least four thousand chemicals, including cyanide, arsenic, ammonia, vinyl chloride, lead, benzene, formaldehyde, butane, nitrogen dioxide, sulfur dioxide, and carbon monoxide; at least sixty substances in cigarettes have been identified by researchers as carcinogens. While tobacco smoke itself is not an allergen, it is a severe irritant. (Cigarette smoke, however, contains particulate matter that functions as a "platform" for allergens.) Mainstream and sidestream smoke will cause respiratory problems that look exactly like an allergic reaction. One such condition is vasomotor rhinitis, a condition characterized by irritated nasal passages, an inflamed respiratory tract, and continued soreness of the eyes. Nonsmokers with asthma suffer greatly from tobacco smoke as a trigger of asthma attacks and other breathing complications.[13] For instance, coworkers' daily smoking habits greatly exacerbated US government worker Irene Parodi's chronic asthma during the late 1970s and early 1980s. She sued the federal government (her employer) after she had to leave her job, and in 1984, after a five-year battle in the courts, she won an out-of-court settlement of $50,000 in damages and monthly disability payments of $500.[14] During the 1970s, the AMA estimated there were thirty-four million adults in the United States who struggled with allergy symptoms as a result of exposure to sidestream smoke.[15]

In the close quarters of the postwar office, smokers *and* nonsmokers confronted a laundry list of both short-term and long-term health problems. In addition to respiratory illnesses, health problems included heart disease and cancer. Those who smoke cigarettes are two to four times as likely to develop heart disease compared to nonsmokers, and they face double the risk of stroke. Secondhand smoke also significantly increases the likelihood of heart problems among the nonsmoking population. For nonsmokers regularly exposed to environmental tobacco smoke, they face a 25 to 30 percent greater risk of heart disease. In addition, the Centers for Disease Control and Prevention (CDC) concludes that sidestream smoke significantly increases nonsmokers' chances of suffering a heart attack.[16] The office was a major site of exposure. During the 1980s, the Environmental Protection Agency (EPA) estimated that men and women ingested 467,000 tons of burnt tobacco in indoor spaces every year, an amount equal to six hundred billion cigarettes, four billion cigars, and eleven billion bowls of pipe tobacco. Nonsmokers who worked with cigarette smokers in close quarters became unwilling "passive" smokers as they inhaled an amount of sidestream smoke that equaled more than eleven cigarettes per day.[17] A 1985 cartoon in the *New York Times* called attention to the problem of environmental tobacco smoke in the office. This illustration depicted a bevy of smokers in an open-plan office filled with cubicles and numerous plumes of rising cigarette smoke creating black indoor smog. As the human smokestacks fired and spewed their exhaust, scattered nonsmokers can be seen with respirators, plugged noses, sore eyes, and even handkerchiefs held over the mouth. No one could escape the smoke.[18]

Smoking causes cancer, but sidestream smoke, too, leads to cancer in nonsmokers. Since smoking was so widespread at work, journalist Toni Wood pointed out in 1981 that nonsmokers in the office often need only look beyond their own workstations to see a smoker lighting up "at the next desk." Any lit cigarette could possibly burn for ten to twelve minutes, filling the smoker's (and the nonsmoker's) space with environmental tobacco smoke. In this kind of smoke-saturated environment, nonsmokers would be "envelop[ed]" by smoke. The American Lung Association stated in the early 1980s that sidestream smoke was actually *more* toxic than mainstream smoke, as sidestream smoke contained twice the tar and nicotine, five times as much carbon monoxide, fifty times as much ammonia, and three to four times the amount of benzpyrene (a carcinogen).[19] Medical data shows that a nonsmoker who lives with a smoker has a 20 to 30 percent higher chance of developing cancer in her or his lifetime. Roughly five thousand nonsmokers die every year as a result of lung cancer believed to be caused by environmental tobacco smoke, and there may be links between sidestream smoke and an increased risk of breast cancer, nasal sinus cavity cancer, and throat cancer.[20]

Serious awareness about the deadliness of smoking emerged and became increasingly common knowledge in the late 1950s and early to mid-1960s. A key 1957 report of the Study Group on Smoking and Health, a public-private research group convened by the National Cancer Institute, the National Heart Institute, the American Cancer Society, and the American Heart Association, concluded that the "sum total of scientific evidence establishes beyond reasonable doubt that cigarette smoking is a causative factor in the rapidly increasing incidence of human epidermoid carcinoma of the lung."[21] Three years later, in 1960, the American Cancer Society ended its silence on smoking that had prevailed through the 1950s and insisted that it was "beyond any reasonable doubt" that smoking was "the major cause of lung cancer and ought to be addressed as such."[22] A 1962 article in the *New England Journal of Medicine* detailed a study that found the significant presence of cancer cells in the lungs of deceased heavy smokers that had died of other causes. Scientists dubbed these abnormalities "preinvasive" tumors.[23] Most influentially, however, the lengthy 1964 report of the Surgeon General's Advisory Committee on Smoking and Health highlighted, with compelling and detailed scientific and medical research data, the very real connection between cigarettes and cancer. The findings of the surgeon general's experts led many nonsmokers and even some smokers to condemn tobacco use and initiated a sustained process of medical investigation into the health risks that accompanied cigarettes and other tobacco products.[24] The forceful conclusion of the 1964 report—that there are definite causal links between tobacco use and cancer—provided nonsmokers with strong medical evidence and the moral authority to challenge tacit public acceptance of smoking. As nonsmoker Carol Klauber and the eight other men and women who signed their names to a lengthy

FIGURE 4.1   American Cancer Society public service announcement, dated 1964. Courtesy Stanford Research into the Impact of Tobacco Advertising.

letter to a local newspaper in Mechanicsburg, Pennsylvania, angrily proclaimed, "A PERSON MUST BREATHE TO WORK, BUT MUST A PERSON SMOKE TO BREATHE? Where is the non-smokers right [*sic*]—WE ARE THE ONES DYING ON THE JOB!"[25] By 1964, there was no denying what scientists were discovering about the connections between tobacco use and cancer.

Office spaces of the 1970s, 1980s, and 1990s guaranteed a groundswell of worker opposition to smoking. Their typically poor ventilation and compression of workers into "open" (but concentrated) spaces of labor, as well as many work-ers' choice to smoke at work, intensified the experiences of nonsmokers with sidestream smoke. Throughout these years of growing scrutiny of tobacco, smok-ers, nonsmokers, and employers struggled to negotiate the boundaries of smok-ers' and nonsmokers' rights in the close quarters of the office. As Lou Cenci of the National Interagency Council on Smoking and Health observed in 1981, "I don't think there is a more volatile issue in the workplace."[26] Nonsmokers literally wanted to clear the air. They challenged employer policies that accepted smoking, and they confronted smokers' behaviors and assumptions about the acceptability of their habit, citing new medical knowledge to undermine "the triumph of the cigarette" that made their workdays, restaurant visits, plane rides, and even trips to the local grocery store so uncomfortable and unhealthful.

Negotiating Smoke, Space, and Power: Segregation Schemes

In addition to public health concerns, troubled relations between smokers and nonsmokers produced the growing movement against the cigarette. Amidst the orderly rows of desks in open-plan offices, tensions simmered. Nonsmokers' complaints about cigarette smoke in their work environments highlighted the personal pain and suffering experienced by many as a result of the sidestream smoke that saturated the workplace. While scientific investigation and expand-ing medical knowledge certainly exposed the serious harm done by smokers to themselves, nonsmokers' criticisms of smokers' behavior broadened the conver-sation about smoking to the issue of whether or not smokers should have the right not only to hurt themselves but everyone else in the immediate area, includ-ing those who did not smoke.

Smoking cigarettes divided the postwar white-collar workforce, and that trend intensified in the years after the 1964 surgeon general's report. Nonsmok-ers often viewed smokers not as coworkers but as dangerous polluters: their side-stream smoke, after all, caused serious illness, discomfort, and ultimately death for both smokers *and* nonsmokers. While historians of the United States after 1945 rightly highlight race and gender as salient dividers of postwar workers, smoking created surprising and significant fissures among workers that defied any resolution.[27] Moreover, smoking mattered greatly within the frameworks of white-collar work, as managers' feelings about smoking greatly shaped the expe-riences and privileges of workers.

In white-collar offices, nonsmokers struggled to protect themselves from the smoke-saturated air spaces they regularly worked in, and many nonsmokers became increasingly frustrated as a result of their limited abilities to change the atmosphere of their immediate surroundings. Despite the medical validity and growing understanding of the dangers of sidestream smoke, smoking did not disappear from the workplace; it remained a widespread practice in the late postwar years. The result was ongoing conflicts over who had the right to control the airspace at work: smokers who needed tobacco, or nonsmokers who needed clean air? Could managers and workers resolve the competing demands of smokers and nonsmokers? Could these conflicts be negotiated in such a way that both sides could be fairly accommodated?

Considerable animosity among smokers and nonsmokers can be found in offices, as nonsmokers often found they could not escape the constant presence of sidestream smoke. Throughout the early to mid-1970s, Donna M. Shimp of the New Jersey Bell Telephone Company, for instance, struggled to avoid cigarette smoke without having to quit her job. While she previously smoked during the 1960s, she later began to experience a series of health troubles as a result of her exposure to sidestream smoke at work, including a corneal abrasion, frequent headaches, and vomiting. Although she complained to her employer about the smoky environment found in the smallish New Jersey Bell offices, managers were not willing to prohibit smoking in these workspaces to accommodate her. When New Jersey Bell managers closed Shimp's branch office and required employees to transfer to other locales, they warned her that she would find smoke-heavy airspace in both of the locations offered to her. At her new job in Bridgeton, there were thirteen workers in the office and seven of them were smokers. Her health troubles intensified when she could not get away from their frequent smoking. She began missing work and tried wearing a respirator, and her cornea abrasion problem returned. The company provided her with an allergist to help treat her symptoms, but after the doctor visited the office he concluded that "it was a disgrace for any employee to have to work in such an atmosphere." She would spend a lot of time away from work, and management regarded her as an "absence problem." Shimp demanded that supervisors turn on the ventilator fan that could pull smoke out of the room, but her coworkers complained since it caused the office to become too cold during the winter. Her frustrations continued to the point that she decided to sue New Jersey Bell.[28] In Florida, Sandra Louise Cahill was a dispatcher for the Fort Lauderdale Fire Department who worked in a twenty-foot by thirtyfoot office with several smokers. Like Donna Shimp, she experienced health complications as a result of daily exposure to sidestream smoke; Cahill's troubles included breathing difficulties and recurring nausea. Over a two-year period, Cahill wrote letters to the city asking that smoking be banned and requested several transfers, which were all denied. As a result of her increasing absences from work, the city administration fired her in 1978.

"Sandra Louise Cahill went to bat against the system," her local newspaper, the *Fort Lauderdale News*, reported. "The system won." Cahill appealed to the city for reinstatement, but her request was denied by a panel of administrators.[29]

"The system" also caused great frustration for nonsmoker Bob Fox, who worked for the Boeing Company in Seattle. In 1980, he lamented to a local newspaper that "he's been moved six times and can't get away from the smoke." In the office where he worked, there was simply no avoiding the clouds of cigarette smoke that hovered throughout the room; he tried and repeatedly failed.[30] Also in 1980, readers of the *St. Louis Post-Dispatch* saw the strange picture of Paul E. Smith, a forty-nine-year-old engineer at the Western Electric Company office in Ballwin, Missouri. Every day he wore to work a cumbersome ventilator mask that completely covered his head; at the same time, a long and bulky hose extended downward to the filtration device he wore on his belt. For Smith, such a device was entirely necessary, as it was the only way he could protect himself from the cigarettes, cigars, and pipes that so sickened him. In the open-plan office of nearly sixty people where he worked, managers moved him to new desks several times as he tried to escape the high volume of smoke. Smith "complain[ed]" to managers on many occasions about having to work near smokers, but "the problem" of bad air quality "persisted" even after supervisors relocated him to the most distant areas of the room. Eventually, management stopped trying to solve the problem by moving him to other spaces. Ultimately given the choice of transferring to a lower-paying job in another locale or wearing a ventilation mask, Smith grudgingly chose the latter. The first mask provided to him did not fit, so managers gave him a second. Since so many of the staffers at Western Electric smoked and would chafe at any actions that would limit their habit, management did not want to take them on in order to clear the air. In fact, an earlier no-smoking policy had been overturned by the nicotine-dependent and very vocal "rank and file." Several nonsmoking coworkers, however, voiced their support of Paul Smith's complaints. "The air where we work is sometimes so bad you have to force yourself to breathe," one coworker said of the offices at Western Electric.[31]

Beyond the white-collar workplace, nonsmokers in customer service fields habitually confronted smokers when they worked. In restaurants, for example, smokers presumed they had the right to smoke before, during, and after their meals. They expressed an assumed right to space, guaranteed, no doubt, by their payments for goods and services rendered. When a young Kristen Iverson started her first summer job as a truck stop waitress in suburban Denver during the early 1970s, her workplace was "dim and smoky all day long." Every day she had to contend with customers' constant smoking at the crowded counter and with coworkers who always smoked their own cigarettes "in the back." Even when

Iverson's mother visited her at work, she chain-smoked cigarette after cigarette the entire time.[32] Grocery store clerks sometimes complained of smokers who passed through their check-out lines with lit cigarettes in hand. "It's unbearable," a Miami-area clerk remarked in 1974. "Whew, I just can't take it." Some even smoked cigars. Smokers responded to these complaints with the claim that smoking in grocery stores was necessary since it took so long to complete their shopping. Smokers thought it was reasonable to smoke in the store—especially as they were preparing to pay for their items and depart.[33]

Some new state laws that emerged in the 1970s, however, armed nonsmoking service workers with the legal authority to limit the presence of smoking in their airspace. In the months that followed the passing of the Minnesota Clean Indoor Air Act of 1975, a journalist described a tense exchange between smokers and a busy server in an airport coffee shop. As a husband-and-wife pair of smokers entered the restaurant, the woman leaned over the (nonsmoking) counter, with lit cigarette in hand, to get the attention of the server. The writer was dismayed to see the woman's lack of regard for the fact that "there was no ashtray to catch" the falling cigarette ashes. "I'm sorry," the waitress responded, "but could you please sit at one of the smoking counters—there's plenty of room." The woman and her husband ignored the waitress's request and began ordering breakfast. "That's all right, we're already settled here," the woman told her, calling out an order for two cups of coffee, French toast, and orange juice. When the waitress told the couple that it was Minnesota's new law that limited smoking, the man and woman erupted in frustration. "Oh please don't give me that," the woman grumbled. "It's just disgusting, depriving people of their rights like that; I'll be glad to get back to Philadelphia." The couple brusquely stalked out of the nearly empty restaurant in a huff. (The journalist wryly noted that the man and woman walked past "about 50 available smoking seats" as they marched away.) Though she lost a paying customer, the server was unapologetic about trying to enforce the limitation of smoking in her workspace. "Of course, no one ever gets fined, but I have to mention it sometimes to get people to listen," she told the writer.[34]

These growing divides between smokers and nonsmokers in postwar workplaces can be further seen in the proliferation of desk signs and lapel buttons on the furniture and bodies of nonsmoking workers. Unsure about how to best protect nonsmokers' health and to mitigate nonsmokers' complaints about the smoky airspace at work without banning smoking entirely, numerous companies such as IBM allowed workers to claim their immediate workspace as a nonsmoking space and to delineate their airspace as nonsmoking with small desktop signs (e.g., "No Smoking Please"). IBM staffer Rose Fletcher can be seen in a 1982 picture working at a desk that featured a no-smoking sign situated prominently in the upper left corner. As coworkers passed her area, they would have surely noticed the sign right away, as it sat on the very edge of the desk facing the walk-way. The prevalence of these desk signs can even be noticed in some popular films of the 1980s, such as the fast-paced buddy action film *Lethal Weapon 2*, a blockbuster sequel that featured a chain-smoking cop on the trail of diplo-matically immune South African drug dealers, or the uproariously dark comedy *9 to 5*, where three frustrated and embattled working women at a large corporate office struggle to outwit and outlast their "sexist egotistical lying hypocritical bigot" of a boss.[35] Nonsmoking men, women, and even teens expressed opposi-tion to smoking and fashioned identities as nonsmokers by wearing buttons that read "Thank you for not smoking," "No smoking," and "Cancer cures smoking." The buttons were a new political statement in the contested airspaces of the 1970s and 1980s and were often a sign of personal anger. "We have politely surrendered our rights to health, telling smokers we didn't mind if they lit up," Kathleen Mar-quardt of Milwaukee lamented. "They [smokers] rarely ask; they assume their privilege. But we can no longer afford to be so tractable. We have to start telling people when their smoke bothers us."[36] Nonsmokers hoped the clear messages emblazoned on desk signs and lapel buttons would help constrain the geography of smoking at work and create new smoke-free spaces that were to be guaranteed by warning away presumptuous smokers.

Even as they rightly hoped to create work environments that better guaran-teed health, nonsmokers' expressions of their demands contributed to the divi-sions between workers along the lines of smoking vs. nonsmoking. Throughout the 1970s and 1980s, nonsmokers' repeated calls for their separation from smok-ers heralded that segregation would likely become a significant part of workers' and employers' efforts to accommodate the conflicting demands of nonsmokers and smokers. Calls for the segregation of smokers and nonsmokers were often bottom-up demands, forcefully voiced by nonsmokers themselves. At the North-western National Life Insurance Company offices in Minneapolis, for instance, executive Carl Nerison noted how he wanted to urge top management at the firm to segregate smokers to "some room in the basement." There, they could work and smoke without affecting anyone else. Nerison imagined a wholesale purge of smokers from the usual work areas of the building. He wanted them sent into isolation in the distant basement, an underground site of physical low-ness that was far removed from the customarily productive spaces on the floors above.[37] When moved, smokers complained of their consignment to "little tiny smoking room[s]," hidden away in the bowels of the workplace, writing to the Tobacco Institute to voice their displeasure and frustration.[38] But in offices where smoking was so controversial, managers could quickly impose a resolution by deferring to calls for segregation. As Richard Reid of Control Data Corporation in Minneapolis told a visiting reporter, management deferred to nonsmokers' requests for segregated spaces for themselves, showing off various work rooms that nonsmokers claimed as their own. Reid believed that Control Data was able to minimize conflicts between smokers and nonsmokers by making it possible for nonsmoking workers to create a more pleasant and desirable environment for themselves.[39]

In practice, the segregation of smokers from nonsmokers proved to be an often inconvenient and ineffective solution to the problem of smoky airspace. While workers could be arranged in new combinations in open-plan offices, for example, smoke still traveled across increased distances and attempts at separation, and it continued to bother nonsmokers, even as many office workers and managers accepted separation as perhaps the only way to accommodate both groups. Large companies and institutions with large spaces to work with had the most resources for pursuing separation schemes as a solution to workplace smoking issues; smaller offices confronted severe space limitations that complicated or undermined such efforts. For example, Marie Lee and Judith Caron, one a nonsmoker and the other a smoker, worked in an open-plan workspace at the Massachusetts Department of Public Welfare with thirty-five other coworkers. In 1983, Lee sued Caron for her smoking, claiming that the smoke caused her "general malaise" and "discomfort." As they grappled with the battle raging in the office, managers could not envision a solution that would please both women. Since the office was a "single room," it was "questionable whether the two can be sufficiently separated to provide adequately for the comforts of both."[40]

The segregation of smokers and nonsmokers proved to be complicated to achieve and difficult to sustain. During the 1970s and early 1980s, the top managers at IBM encouraged lower-level management to think in democratic and equitable ways about how to accommodate the conflicting expectations of their 200,000 workers. (Nearly two-thirds did not smoke.) The result was a complex balancing act of fairly managing nonsmoker demands for smoke-free airspace and smokers' insistence upon their customary smoking privileges. IBM policy ensured the continuation of smoking (and surely some nonsmokers' frustrations) in many of the work areas and common areas found in company offices, despite managers' claim of "sensitivity to the needs of the non-smoker."[41]

In 1982, the IBM senior advisor for health and care planning, Cole Mandelblit, told the American Lung Association that his company worked hard to address fully the nonsmoker's demand for fresh air. His company offered "guidance" (rather than commands) to supervisors about setting aside areas in cafeterias and other shared spaces to accommodate smokers and nonsmokers as situations demanded, as well as a training program that taught managers how to adjudicate smoking disputes among staff members. The most compact spaces at IBM—shuttle buses, copy rooms, elevators—were designated nonsmoking.

Elsewhere, however, managers needed to respond carefully to local circumstances in order to accommodate both groups. In conference rooms, supervisors needed to carefully assess ventilation capabilities; staffers could smoke in a conference room if the ventilation was thought to be sufficient, but the meeting room would be labeled nonsmoking if managers found it lacking.[42]

While Mandelblit's policy statements present a well-ordered, thorough, and equitable system, real work situations must have tested this fragile arrangement. Even if conference rooms featured ample ventilation, if some of those present smoked during a long meeting then nonsmokers might smell and breathe at least some smoke. How did nonsmokers respond? What happened to pre-existing arrangements if, due to new hires, retirements, or transfers, the number of smokers or nonsmokers increased? What if some smokers gave up their habit? Could new arrangements be continually developed that would satisfy everyone? Complaints continued to surface during the 1980s. In 1984, for example, four IBM staffers at a Florida office unsuccessfully sued the company for not guaranteeing reasonable safety in the workplace with a total smoking ban, citing their discomforting and unhealthful experiences with secondhand smoke that included "permanent and irreversible lung damage." After failing to build a class action case, they ultimately dropped their lawsuit.[43] IBM continued its "permissive" policies toward smokers and nonsmokers in its many offices nationwide. Mendelblit imagined that workers themselves would resolve disputes as they arose. He referenced the individual "no smoking" desk signs that IBM made available to nonsmokers. Nonsmokers themselves could create nonsmoking spaces in their vicinity, but "the problem," he noted, was "what to do if there are three or four desks in an area where some people are smokers and some are not." In these cases, problems typically resulted despite the good intentions of managers to accommodate everyone. "We certainly don't have 100 percent success," Mandelblit admitted, "but we work pretty hard at it."[44]

A handful of other institutions adopted similar segregation plans. The Department of Health and Human Services office in Washington State banned smoking outright in its classrooms, elevators, and auditoriums, but they carried the policy further than IBM by forbidding all smoking in its conference rooms. The Washington State office, however, segregated smokers and nonsmokers to completely separate work areas in the building. In this highly segregated arrangement, the two groups would presumably no longer bother the other ever again. The Department of Health and Human Services, however, established another key policy that suggests a great deal about the likely imperfections of segregation: The bureau took on the responsibility of guaranteeing that every nonsmoker who wanted complete relief from sidestream smoke could have his or her own smoke-free work area, especially those workers with "an especially severe reaction to smoke." The institution of this policy subtly points to the difficulties of trying to allow smoking to continue by separating smokers from nonsmokers. Despite the segregation policy of the Washington State Department of Health and Human Services, the air was not smoke-free. Those staffers with a "severe reaction" to smoke could retreat to fully separated workspaces, but it must not have been feasible to guarantee the right to private space to every nonsmoker since the amount of such spaces would ultimately be limited by the amount of working space available. In other words, there was only so far that nonsmoking workers could run to get away from cigarette smoke, whether at a state office or elsewhere. In fact, so rare were these guarantees of "overhauled seating" that one journalist noted they occur "[m]uch less often."[45] Only a fraction of companies could fully separate smokers and nonsmokers. By 1983, only fifty companies had instituted separation policies to manage the demands of both camps.[46]

Nonsmokers were critical of segregation schemes that failed to eliminate the presence of cigarette smoke. Despite the creation of separated areas and separated rooms for smoking and nonsmoking personnel, sidestream smoke was not always so easily contained. If smoking was especially prevalent, the imperfections of segregation schemes would have been all the more apparent. Office worker Ron Fontaine of New Hampshire criticized his employer's policy of permitting smoking only in "designated areas." Despite the containment effort, Fontaine could still see and smell the sidestream smoke that bled beyond the "designated areas." He complained, "The smoke in a smoke-filled room has only one place to go and that is throughout the entire building."[47]

Machine-Mediated Airspace: Possibilities and Problems

Since segregated spaces could not fully protect nonsmokers from expansive clouds of tobacco smoke or preclude conflicts between smokers and nonsmokers, workers and employers frequently turned to technology in their effort to mute the tensions between smokers and nonsmokers. After the 1960s, workers and employers explored and experimented with building ventilation systems, fans, and smokeless ashtrays in their efforts to break up the dull haze of cigarette smoke that lurked in many offices. But even as technology could help nonsmokers and smokers to coexist at work, the mechanics and costs of machine-mediated airspace could just as easily create other problems.

To keep the air moving and prevent the accumulation of smoke in offices, workers and employers typically depended on building ventilation systems and exhaust fans to do much of the work. But for these machines to substantively reduce the presence of cigarette smoke, managers usually needed to concentrate smokers near available air intake vents. At Weyerhaeuser's corporate headquarters "the ventilation system is more effective than many," a visiting journalist observed in 1980. Every ceiling lighting installation featured an intake air vent, with each situated only a few feet apart. The intensity of Weyerhaeuser's ventilation could actually be adjusted on a panel-by-panel basis, allowing management to concentrate smokers in particular locations in the office with the use of increased air intake "above a cluster of smokers." The system, managers pointed out, helped to minimize conflicts between nonsmokers and smokers without implementing a ban at work that would surely anger the smokers.[48]

In older office buildings and industrial workshops that lacked good ventilation, employers had to rely on more primitive exhaust fans to change the smoky air. An exhaust fan pulls air out of the room and expels it through a piping system that leads to the outside, with the exhaust port(s) often located on the roof. Joe Cenci of the National Interagency Council on Smoking and Health observed that smoke-weary employers he knew of who operated in older buildings usually tried to locate nonsmokers upwind from the smokers who would be placed close to the exhaust fan. Conflicts between smokers and nonsmokers could be minimized by carefully situating smokers and nonsmokers in relation to exhaust fans, but employers would need to vigilantly manage these delicate arrangements, and workers would need to exhibit considerable patience if trouble arose over the continued presence of smoke.[49]

While ventilation technologies could help employers mitigate the tensions between nonsmokers and smokers, the use of technology sometimes proved to be more problematic. Exhaust fans and air ventilation systems, for instance, were sometimes noisy and bothersome and might sometimes work so powerfully that they could suck the papers off nearby workers' desks. Other technologies that were intended to alleviate the presence of smoke indoors could be equally frustrating or simply inaccessible. Often found in bars and bowling alleys, "Smokeeter" tobacco-smoke-removal systems, for example, were expensive. For a small ten- by fifteen-foot room that contained fifteen workers, a Smokeeter machine cost $335 in 1980; for the largest version, which could guarantee smoke-free air for a significantly larger room containing sixty or more people, the price was $1,200. Companies surely balked at the prospect of investing so much capital in machines whose only purpose was to filter tobacco smoke. In a study of secondhand smoke and indoor filtration systems, James L. Repace of the EPA estimated that heavy-duty room air cleaners cost $1,800 each, an "uneconomical proposition" that made the widespread application of these machines to office environments a "completely impractical" goal.[50]

With limited capital at their disposal, some worker-smokers bought the cost-effective "smokeless ashtray" to limit their production of sidestream smoke. This popular device of the 1970s and 1980s was intended to absorb the release of most sidestream smoke into the air, but the device had several problems. The smokeless ashtray was not actually smokeless since it could do nothing about the environmental tobacco smoke that was actually exhaled by the smoker or emitted from a lit cigarette as the smoker lifted it from the ashtray to her or his mouth and put it down again. The small fans they contained pulled smoke in through a filter, but the mechanisms were a source of a low droning noise that some found annoying. Some smokeless ashtrays actually emitted cover-up scents such as lemon or cinnamon that "people find noxious when it mixes with the odor of smoke." The smokeless ashtray's tiny filtration system would also become dirty (and thus ineffective) over time without diligent maintenance, or it would simply break down after prolonged use, rendering the device useless. Another portable machine—the conventional electric fan—moved air along, but moved smoke along as well. Fans also created air currents that gave some neighboring workers chills or disturbed loose paperwork.[51] In certain contexts, technology could help to alleviate the presence of smoke and the tensions among smokers and nonsmokers, but the flaws found in many devices ensured that technology could not close the divisions that existed between those who wanted to smoke their cigarettes at work and those who resented the practice.

Getting Personal: Managers' Views of Smokers

Cigarette smoking not only burned wedges between smoking and nonsmoking coworkers; it also created considerable tensions and problems between workers and members of management. Managers' personal feelings about smoking and smokers greatly determined how workers related to the issue of cigarettes in the workplace. In addition, managers' attitudes toward tobacco determined how working people experienced social class at work, as smoking (or even *not smoking*) brought workers into conflict with supervisors, managers, and company owners.

During the 1970s and 1980s, as the public increasingly recognized the health dangers caused by smoking and sidestream smoke, tobacco users sometimes struggled to get along with those supervisors who disapproved of the habit. The tobacco industry lobbying group, the Tobacco Institute in Washington, D.C., received many letters from frustrated smokers during the 1980s and collected newspaper articles from throughout the United States that documented numerous instances of conflicts between smokers and nonsmokers in the context of labor-management power relations.

Antismoking supervisors and managers could make smokers' workdays difficult. Worker-smokers wrote to the tobacco lobby about managers who spoke in professional terms and concerned tones about curtailing smoking privileges due to the need to guarantee the health of nonsmokers, and the feelings of injustice that resulted. "We don't understand why our rights as smokers are being taken away," office worker Becky Smith complained to the Tobacco Institute in 1989. "Our Supervisor keeps telling us about the non-smokers' rights to be in a clean environment."[52] In another case of management's concern for staffers' health, Mrs. R. Faviano wrote about the actions of her boss, a man who ran a small business with twelve workers, and his threat to ban smoking when his daughter (who also worked there) became pregnant. He told the staff that the smoking rules would have to change because "the smoking is irritating to his allergies," but Faviano and her coworkers knew otherwise: they knew about the pregnancy. In addition to the prospect of losing smoking privileges at work, what frustrated Faviano was the feeling that her nonsmoking boss made a show of his power to make the final decision whenever he was ready. "Our employer is contemplating a ban on all smoking in the office," she wrote, "or the following alternatives: 1. Go for a walk and smoke outside. 2. Smoke in a room with the door and windows closed. 3. Smoking period of every two hours." Faviano and other smokers waited anxiously for his decision.[53]

Managers who had a more personal disdain for cigarette smoke acted more provocatively. Joseph Guillemette wrote to the Tobacco Institute about the increasing anger and impatience among supervisors and nonsmokers in the government office where he worked. At the moment, Guillemette noted that managers allowed smokers to congregate in the large hallway outside the main office. "Thus, at regular intervals we go out in the hall for a smoke," but nonsmoking coworkers despised them for doing so, seeing their smoke breaks as a "flagrant abuse" of the federal government's time and money. While most of the supervisors in the office were tolerant of the smokers' habits, "the more vocal ones" began to circulate a policy memo to the staff. This group wanted to limit smoking breaks to only ten minutes in the morning and ten minutes in the afternoon. Guillemette was certainly worried. First chased out of the office and into the hallway, worker-smokers now faced the possibility of compressing their real needs for nicotine into very limited time slots. If the antismoking supervisors had their way, the rules would surely change and smokers would have to somehow adapt to cigarette-starved workdays.[54]

The Tobacco Institute also learned of outright managerial disdain, such as the incident referred to them by Margaret E. Cook of Michigan in the late 1980s.

From a small police department office in upper Michigan, smoker Margaret E. Cook wrote to the Tobacco Institute about a supervisor who verbally abused smokers, constantly telling them "you stink" and "you're disgusting." Even though cigarette smokers were permitted to smoke in the station break room, the anti-smoking supervisor began to up the ante. The man "now fogs the room and/or the smokers with an industrial disinfectant deodorizer spary [sic]." He made a habit of walking into the break room while spraying heavy disinfectant into the air as the smokers congregated near the coffee pot. "The spray is strong enough for the people in the room to actually 'taste' the chemicals in the air," Cook wrote, and, as she noted, in the coffee.[55]

When managers themselves smoked, power could function in equally arbitrary ways. In 1987, a nonsmoking Barclays American/Financial, Inc. receptionist named Marie Bueche filed a lawsuit against her supervisor, Eugene Allred (a smoker), and the company. During the time she worked for Barclays, Allred taunted Bueche by smoking in her presence and even "exhal[ing] smoke into her face," according to the lawsuit.[56] Office manager Claudia Marshall sued her employer, Landsberg & Associates of San Francisco, when the owner of the company fired her for complaining about smoking in her presence. The company owner was Sharon Robertson, a smoker and source of frequent frustration for Claudia Marshall. Robertson often smoked in the closed room where Marshall worked, causing her painful headaches. Marshall tried "subtle hints" at first: opening the windows when the boss entered with a cigarette and saying, "Gee, it's stuffy in here." But after nothing appeared to help, Claudia Marshall typed a short note and silently delivered it to Robertson. "I request that you don't smoke in the work place, as this is unhealthy," she wrote. "Thank you for your cooperation." Sharon Robertson fired Marshall "on the spot," according to a subsequent lawsuit.[57]

In the decades after the 1964 surgeon general's report, conflicts between nonsmokers and smokers roiled offices throughout the United States. The site of the postwar office itself, and its particular spatial characteristics, often belied any hope for an easy solution that would please both sides of this burgeoning divide. Nonsmokers' experiences with secondhand smoke in office settings greatly heightened their resentments toward smokers' behavior. Possible solutions (such as segregation or the use of technology) presented too many flaws to fully preclude conflicts over smoking. In addition, conflicts occurred not only among workers, but also within the context of managerial power, as supervisors' feelings about smoking greatly determined the extent to which nonsmokers (and smokers) received civil treatment. As a result of continued suffering and discomfort at work, nonsmokers would turn to the courts and activism to effect change in their workaday situations.

Nonsmokers v. Workplace Smoking

Heated struggles over tobacco use that began among nonsmoking and smoking workers and managers on white-collar shop floors sometimes reached the dockets of US courts, a development that played an important role in undermining the postwar "triumph of the cigarette." Armed with medical knowledge of smoking's health hazards, some nonsmokers challenged the legal system to choose sides between healthier airspaces at work or worker-smokers' tendency to saturate offices with sidestream smoke. Court decisions provided further sanction against smoking at work, reinforcing the medical profession's warnings about tobacco. Key legal decisions from this period provided additional moral and legal authority to the nonsmokers who intended to press their employers for cleaner airspace. When historians of smoking talk about the history of tobacco litigation, they focus on tobacco companies' misrepresentations of their products, their distortions of medical evidence, and corporate advertising practices; these scholars largely overlook the prominence of working people and the site of the workplace in the legal fight against tobacco. The years between 1975 and 1984 were crucial in the history of postwar smoking: In the courts, nonsmokers and the judges who ruled on their cases began to slowly roll back the "right" of smokers to determine the substance of the airspace at work.

Customer service representative Donna M. Shimp's 1976 lawsuit against New Jersey Bell was the most important case that reached the courts during this period. She sued her employer for not protecting her from a "toxic substance" (tobacco smoke) in the workplace that, as she claimed, negatively impacted her ability to do her job. Shimp argued that the company acted wrongly since it was entirely within their power to remove the source of this toxicity (cigarettes) from the office environment. The case not only highlighted how nonsmokers such as Donna M. Shimp rightly wanted to improve air quality at work, but also how nonsmoking workers wanted the courts to create a level playing field with employers. As Shimp's suffering at work worsened during the first half of the 1970s, New Jersey Bell apparently tried to get rid of the problem by running her out of the office. In June 1975, after Shimp's allergy doctors reported to the company management on the horrific air quality of the Bridgeton office where she worked, the office manager, R. C. Belleville, told her to "remain at home until further notice." Shimp angrily responded with a proposal to the company leadership for a ban on smoking in the office. In July, managers responded by giving Shimp an ultimatum: take a demotion to a lower-paying job where there was no smoking or accept dismissal. The possible firing was necessary, Shimp's supervisors said, "in order to protect my health, as the doctors all agreed on a smoke free work environment."[58] After haggling for months with supervisors and coworkers over unused ventilation systems and fans that were not turned on to circulate the smoky air, and battling against local union stewards that showed no interest in the problems of a single nonsmoker, Shimp filed her lawsuit against New Jersey Bell in 1976. "Now people who for years thought it was hopeless—why bother to speak up—know it's not true," she said. "People have put up with it. My argument has been that they shouldn't have to, and . . . now they don't have to."[59]

Donna Shimp found justice in the courts, as the superior court in New Jersey ruled in her favor. New Jersey Bell would have to provide a "safe working environment" for her by banning smoking in the office so that she could continue at her job. The court decision readily acknowledged the prevailing medical opinions about the dangers of smoking and "its well-known association" with deadly illnesses such as emphysema, cancer, and heart disease. Going further, the court nodded to the opinions of allergists, immunologists, and specialists in industrial medicine that smoke was a "hazard" and a "pollutant" that poisoned the work environment.[60] Judge Phillip A. Gruccio of the superior court chastised the company for privileging electronics over workers, noting that New Jersey Bell managers banned all smoking around any of its sensitive electrical and computer equipment. "Human beings are also very sensitive and can be damaged by cigarette smoke," Gruccio wrote in his opinion. Utilizing the techno-speak of New Jersey Bell managers against them, he continued, "If a circuit of wiring goes bad, the company can install a replacement part. It is not so simple in the case of a human lung, eye, or heart. The parts are hard to come by if indeed they can be found at all. A company which has demonstrated such concern for its mechanical components should have at least as much concern for its human beings."[61] At New Jersey Bell, the needs of a single nonsmoker mattered, according to the Superior Court of New Jersey. All workers in the state had a common law right to a job setting that was free of environmental health hazards.

The Tobacco Institute did its best to downplay the importance of the Shimp decision. In an editorial titled "Tobacco and the Law," Paul Knopick pointed out that the case was "the single one in which a court has found an employee has a 'right' to a smoke-free environment." He complained that the New Jersey Bell Telephone Company chose not to dispute the case or appeal, which explained why Donna Shimp won this unusual decision. "She won," he wrote, "virtually by default." Knopick took on the job of damage control. He went on to isolate the importance of the case by drawing attention to its legal limitations. In 1977, he pointed out, another New Jersey Bell worker named John B. Mitchell sued the company for a smoking ban and failed, the result, he pointed out, of spirited corporate resistance in the courts. Knopick also pointed out that the "one-sided nature of the litigation" in the Shimp decision would undermine its potential as a case to be used as a precedent in other future cases against smoking privileges at work. For the tobacco lobby, the final line of argument against the significance of the case was to raise questions about Donna Shimp's motives and background. The editorial suggests that she was a hypocrite (or Judas?) since she was a "former smoker" and an attention seeker since she became an "instant celebrity." Knopick suggested that Shimp was a shoddy worker, a whiner who "complained" not only about cigarettes but also about the company's efforts to give assistance, such as supposedly offering her an electric fan.[62] While the favorable ruling in the Shimp case was credited to the work of a maverick court and the company's lack of interest in its own affairs, Knopick admitted that the case seemed to electrify nonsmokers and "stirred interest around the country."[63] Coverage of the Donna Shimp case appeared in newspapers and periodicals throughout the United States. The Tobacco Institute collected at least 685 newspaper articles and other documents that contained the details of the case, including affidavits, interview transcripts, and nonsmoker organization newsletters.[64]

Many other frustrated nonsmoking workers appeared to follow Donna M. Shimp's lead in the years that followed. Engineering associate Paul E. Smith of the Western Electric Company in Missouri wrangled unsuccessfully with his employer about the need to curtail smoking in his office for several years during the 1970s and early 1980s, only choosing to file a lawsuit against Western Electric after all other attempts to gain clean airspace failed. As indicated in the wording of his 1981 lawsuit, Smith and his attorney, Morley Swingle, used the 1976 Shimp case as a precedent. His attorney characterized the Shimp ruling as "a helpful and instructive precedent."[65] Western Electric countered their claims with the assertion that the Shimp case failed to work as an acceptable precedent since the case presented to the court in New Jersey was entirely "one-sided" and that it was not followed in the later John B. Mitchell case that was thrown out by the same judge who ruled in the Shimp lawsuit.[66]

The core of the Western Electric Company defense against Paul Smith's lawsuit was the company's assertion of its need to maintain authority over the rank and file of workers at its western Missouri facilities. If the company restricted smoking to designated areas, it would force workers to demand more "time for breaks" during the workday, a transformation, they claimed, that equaled "labor trouble" and would result in what they called a "drop in productivity" for the company. Western Electric tried to protect its sovereignty over the white-collar shop floor by blurring the issue of jurisdiction. The company insisted that the courts did not have authority over the issue of workplace smoking, as it was the state legislature that would have precedence over the matter since it (not the courts) passed laws. (Coincidentally, a pair of recent antismoking bills failed at the state level in Missouri, which surely led Western Electric to conclude that the state lawmakers would not prohibit smoking at its offices.)[67]

While the trial court dismissed the initial lawsuit in 1981, the Missouri Court of Appeals overturned the judge's ruling in 1982, ruling that workers in Missouri had a right to sue employers for not providing "a safe and healthy workplace." Citing the common law principle of company obligations to provide for the health and safety of workers in their employ, the appellate court's presiding judge, Robert Dowd, ruled that the Western Electric Company "breach[ed] its duty to provide a reasonably safe workplace," an affirmation of the Shimp ruling. The company, he argued, failed to exert proper control over activities in the workplace and take up responsibility for the prompt removal of hazardous substances. "Hailed as Victory for Non-Smokers Rights," the Paul E. Smith case required Missouri companies such as Western Electric to modify company practices to address nonsmokers' demands for cleaner air.[68]

The case thus challenged Western Electric's (and other Missouri firms') power over the shop floor. The appellate court judges imagined their ruling as social justice not only for nonsmokers but also for working people more generally. "It [the lawsuit] arises from a continuing wrong to the plaintiff," the court wrote of Paul Smith's troubles with Western Electric management. "The plaintiff should not have to wait to be disabled, or to bear the risk of it, before getting redress." In the Smith ruling, the appellate court decided *for* Western Electric managers that they were ultimately responsible for overturning the stubborn work culture of smoking in the office and protecting the health of workers.[69]

In these cases against smoking at work, public health and clean air were not the only issues at stake; the extent of worker power in shop floor matters was at stake as well. This can be seen even in the 1984 Claudia Marshall lawsuit in San Francisco, a case that stemmed more from the personal animosity among the parties involved and a likely desire for revenge than the issue of securing smoke-free air at work. After company owner Sharon Robertson fired Marshall over a tersely worded note about smoking, the jilted office manager filed a $100,000 lawsuit for lost wages and damages. Claudia Marshall surely hoped to use the courts to push back against Sharon Robinson's use of her power.[70] Despite a spate of newspaper articles on the case, Marshall's lawsuit very quickly dropped from view, as it was probably tossed out of court and not followed up by the press. But for Marshall and surely other nonsmoking workers of these years, a court ruling in their favor would have yielded a kind of rough justice. The Claudia Marshall case, for example, highlights a worker who experienced arbitrary treatment and was now trying to wrench justice from her employer. For nonsmoking litigants such as Donna M. Shimp, Paul E. Smith, and Claudia Marshall, legal proceedings followed long periods of frustrating and tense labor-management interactions, as well as personal experience and anger regarding imbalanced power relations in the workplace. In Marshall's case, she surely wanted retribution, but in all likelihood the initial coverage of the case was probably the only vindication she received.

Despite the limited impact of legal rulings, the emergence of high-profile lawsuits shows how some nonsmoking white-collar workers pursued legal action as a way to challenge the power relations that sustained smoking at work. Some, such as Donna M. Shimp and Paul E. Smith, found vindication and change before the bar. But court decisions related to smoking in the workplace never rewrote the rules on a broad scale; at most they only reshaped the local circumstances that gave rise to individual white-collar workers' grievances. For the majority of nonsmokers, their struggles against smoking continued to be debated and decided outside the legal system, often among the desks, cubicles, and partitions of the white-collar workplace itself. Even as they tried to launch, join, or shape antismoking organizations to raise public awareness about the dangers of tobacco use and to press for changes in the laws and rules that allowed smoking to continue unabated, nonsmokers returned again and again to the workplace as the central site of their battle against cigarettes.

White-Collar Workplaces and the Rise of Nonsmoker Activism

White-collar workers were a major force within antismoking activist groups during the 1970s and 1980s. In addition, antismoking organizations such as GASP (Group Against Smoking Pollution), Americans for Nonsmokers' Rights (ANR), the American Lung Association, the California Nonsmokers' Rights Foundation, Environmental Improvement Associates (EIA), and ASH (Action on Smoking and Health), among other organizations across the United States, often zeroed in on the white-collar workplace as a crucial battleground in the social, political, and legal war against tobacco. In poorly ventilated business and government offices, with their rows upon rows of workers' desks that were often situated close to each other, nonsmoking workers experienced sidestream smoke in powerful, painful, and damaging ways. As indicated by doctors and the federal government in these years, tobacco smoke sickened and killed men and women, both smokers and nonsmokers. In the overlapping contexts of the ordinary workplace geography found in offices and the growing public knowledge of tobacco's dangers to humans, it is no surprise that concerned office workers threw themselves into organizations that aimed to roll back the "triumph of the cigarette" and create better air quality at work.

Antismoking activism of the 1970s–1990s highlights a kind of labor and workplace activism that extends our view of working-class politics in these years beyond the usual and familiar labor movement, with its bureaucratic institutions, dissident factions, and problems with established political parties. With a stubborn (but fruitful) focus on unions in the workplace as the centerpiece of working-class activism, US labor historians have neglected other forms of bottom-up organizing directly related to the shop floor that helped working people to confront unequal and difficult circumstances in their daily lives.[71] At the same time, historians of postwar cigarette smoking and tobacco have neglected the importance of the workplace in antismoking activism.[72] In order to achieve the goal of smoke-free, clean air in the workplace and in public, nonsmokers needed to confront the power relations and work cultures that governed and shaped their day-to-day work situations.

Nonsmokers' organizations devoted a significant amount of time to giving advice and information to nonsmoking workers who were looking for ways to combat smoking in their workspaces. The California Nonsmokers' Rights Foundation (CNRF) published pamphlets during the 1970s and 1980s that spelled out several suggestions for confronting smoking. First and foremost, the CNRF urged workers to document the extent of the problem. Workers were urged to maintain a detailed diary that catalogued the "physical problems" caused by sidestream smoke, the numbers of hours of exposure to cigarette smoke at work each week, the number of smokers and nonsmokers in the vicinity of their work area, the type of ventilation (if any) in the office, managers' "response or lack of response" to workers' queries and complaints about smoking, and the advice given to them about air quality and health by physicians during doctor's office visits. In addition, the CNRF urged nonsmokers to draw schematics of their office layout, highlighting the arrangement of desks, windows, vents, air conditioners, doors, etc. that influenced worker troubles with cigarette smoke. When building a case against company policy, nonsmokers' groups urged would-be militants to initiate political action only when evidence was collected and ready.[73]

Nonsmoker organizations urged caution with managers and discretion as the better part of valor in the likely struggles that would result from challenges to smoking privileges in the white-collar workplace. The CNRF told nonsmokers to be "prudent, compromising, and polite" with management in all dealings. Workers who challenged the presence of smoking at work took on the potentially difficult balancing act of challenging smokers' behavior, pressing employers to change their policies, and avoiding the ostracizing or even job-threatening labels of "troublemaker," "rabble rouser," and "complainer." To engage management in the least threatening way possible, the CNRF urged workers to not only use specific and carefully compiled evidence, but to also carefully emphasize the "seriousness" of smoking as "a health hazard." Workers who complained to management about smoking needed to stress their hope to merely contribute to "a healthier workplace," not to the disruption of company business, internecine shop floor struggles, or the usurpation of managerial authority. When questioned or challenged, the nonsmoking activist needed to emphasize the "right of all people to breathe clean air." In this way, nonsmokers could create some semblance of common ground among the various factions. "It is important to be reasonable, calm, and diplomatic," the CNRF warned. "No one responds positively to sarcasm or hostility." To achieve the desired result of new company smoking restrictions (and to remain gainfully employed), nonsmokers needed to avoid any semblance of a confrontation with managers or coworkers. When dealing with either smoking workers or the members of management, nonsmokers' organizations urged working people to "be verbal" and to "speak up" at work, but to remember that a continued focus on "compromise" with others was likely to be essential for any change to occur and for other troubles to be avoided.[74]

The activities of workplace antismoking activists, however, did contribute to the palpable tensions between smokers and nonsmokers in the office. At the MSI Insurance Companies offices in St. Paul, Minnesota, nonsmoker Myrna Larry's organizing efforts in the late 1980s led to numerous personal conflicts with smoking coworkers. She received anonymous phone calls at night, some colleagues stopped speaking to her, and other coworkers began to openly mock her "weight problem." In one instance, there was an "unpleasant hallway confrontation" between Larry and another worker. She became well-known "as a hard-nosed militant" among the 699 workers in the MSI St. Paul office, yet she managed to keep her job while bringing about a new no-smoking policy. Eventually, the verbal attacks of coworkers quieted down and Myrna Larry could work at her desk without smoke in the air. In Marblehead, Massachusetts, veteran police officer Craig Cole launched an unpopular petition drive against smoking privileges in his precinct and even filed for a transfer away from his partner, a long-time smoker. Cole himself used to smoke, a habit he brought home with him from Vietnam many years earlier. But now that he had finally quit, he could no longer tolerate the currents of cigarette smoke that lingered or blew around inside of his police cruiser (when his partner rolled down the windows for him) and in the precinct itself. "The mounting drive to limit public smoking," a writer for the New York Times surmised in 1987, "is complicating many personal relationships and creating some serious tensions in the nation's workplace [sic]."[75]

The experience of discrimination also brought nonsmokers to activism. After grocery clerk Jack Hamm of San Francisco complained repeatedly to his supervisors in 1978 about customer disregard for the store's no-smoking rules, they fired him. Hamm left the store and joined the ranks of the Group Against Smoking Pollution (GASP). He lost one job but gained another: organizing petitions to limit public smoking in the city of San Francisco. On average, Hamm worked at collecting signatures ten hours per day on the streets (or in the airport if poor weather settled over the Bay Area). The experience of discrimination at the store galvanized his disdain for smoking in public and his determination to do something about it in the city where he worked. Hamm was determined to push back against those arrogant smokers who poisoned the airspace and contributed to the loss of his job at the grocery store, as well as against the employer who sided with smokers instead of nonsmoking labor.[76]

Donna M. Shimp's long ordeal with supervisors and coworkers at the New Jersey Bell Telephone Company, as well as her concerns about other workers' troubles, galvanized her own interest in continuing her fight against smoking in the workplace. After she won her court case in 1976, frustrated workers and uneasy employers wrote numerous letters to her and called her on the telephone at home, asking her for advice about how to fight smoking in their own places of work. With the help of her attorney, she helped to form a nonprofit corporation called Environment Improvement Associates (EIA) to provide a clearinghouse for information that nonsmokers could use to challenge smoking privileges in the workplace and to more effectively engage employers and the state on the need to pursue policies that restricted the prevalence of smoking at work. She imagined the EIA as a "catalyst" organization that would push other groups such as the government, industry, organized labor, and the American Lung Association "to do something" about "the great need for smoking restrictions in the workplace." Smoking was a pollutant, as dangerous as coal dust or asbestos. "Pollution is pollution," Donna Shimp insisted, "whether it's coming from human chimneys or impersonal, industrial smokestacks." After her difficult and frustrating experience at New Jersey Bell, she did not shy away from using incendiary language to characterize smokers and their behaviors on the job.[77]

Like other antismoking activists, Shimp believed in the importance of directly engaging company management to effect change. To maximize the chances that supervisors would respond favorably to nonsmokers' lobbying efforts, Shimp emphasized the importance of driving home the point that smoking at work threatened the efficiency, effectiveness, and most importantly the profitability of the enterprise. Nonsmoker activists would need to focus continually "on the bottom line" in their dealings with managers. She provided data and other information that nonsmoking activists could use in their conversations with supervisors. For example, Shimp explained that worker-smokers spent between 88 and 109 million days in bed every year due to smoking-related illnesses, and smokers *and* nonsmokers lost 399 million workdays every year as a result of illnesses that resulted from exposure to smoke. Smokers also became sick three and a half times as often as nonsmokers, which made them more sickly than other workers; smokers also experienced twice as many as workplace accidents, suggesting that smoking led to worker carelessness. Shimp also estimated that worker-smokers wasted somewhere between 2 and 10 percent of every work day "just in the mechanics of smoking": lighting up, taking breaks, walking outside, puffing on cigarettes, disposing of the butts, etc.[78]

In their battles with employers and smoking coworkers, nonsmoking activists frequently deployed a language of "rights" to press for clean air at work. For instance, the American Lung Association issued a "Non-Smoker's Bill of Rights" in the 1970s that insisted on the absolute right of nonsmokers to have smoke-free air at work and in public. It also claimed the "right" to speak up against smokers and to use "legislative channels" and "social pressures" to prevent smokers from "polluting the atmosphere" and to seek the restriction of smoking in areas other than smokers' own homes.[79] Just as smokers used a language of "rights" as an embattled "minority" in their protests against smoking prohibitions at work and elsewhere, nonsmokers claimed they had "rights" to a clean environment. Smokers' and nonsmokers' use of "rights" rhetoric in their respective causes highlights the cultural impact of civil rights struggles during the 1960s and 1970s.[80] The activist politics of nonsmokers suggests how the emerging environmental movement impacted the strategy of nonsmokers in the workplace. Nonsmokers insisted that a cleaner and safer environment was a goal not only for outdoor spaces but for indoor spaces as well. The Clean Air Act and the Occupational Safety and Health Act of 1970, which set air quality standards and restrictions on pollutants and promised workers "a right to a safe and healthy workplace," respectively, surely set the tone for the decade. Between the 1970s and 1990s, outdoor smoke pollution fell by 80 percent, while lead pollution fell by 98 percent. Between 1970 and 1985, participation in environmental groups expanded from 500,000 to 2.5 million. The simultaneous rise of nonsmoker activism suggests that serious concerns about clean air and a healthy environment, at work and elsewhere, contributed to the movement against smoking at work during the same period.[81] For nonsmoking activists of the 1970s, their decision to participate in shop floor struggles against smoking thus stemmed from both personal experiences in the white-collar workplace and broader conversations about the environment and "rights" in American culture.

Those who joined nonsmoker activist organizations were frequently office workers, individuals who recoiled from the prevalence of smoking at work. This type of activism should be acknowledged as a significant facet of labor activism in the 1970s, as nonsmokers' struggles against smoking forced them to engage employers directly and negotiate over conditions of work and rulemaking in the shop. Nonsmoking activists wanted to empower workers with information and strategies they could use to press employers for change.

By the 1980s, it was clear that nonsmokers were winning the argument about smoking in American culture. "It used to be you were on the outside looking in if you weren't a smoker," an ex-cigarette smoker recalled in 1984. "But today," the *Los Angeles Times* noted, "it is the smokers who sometimes find themselves on the outside looking in—banished to porches and patios by anti-smoking hosts, to company parking lots or steps by employers who prohibit smoking, to hallways outside public meetings and entertainment events."[82] Workplace smoking bans proliferated throughout the decade, the result of the bottom-up activism of nonsmoking workers, top-down legislation on behalf of the public good, and new employer policies.

As smoking bans at work increased throughout the 1980s, bewildered smokers continued to write letters to the Tobacco Institute in Washington, D.C. Louise M. Mockaitis of Philadelphia, for example, wrote to the tobacco lobbyists in June 1989 to ask for any information and advice the group could share that might help her do something about her employer's wide-reaching smoking ban. "My company is instituting a no smoking policy on 7/1/89," she wrote. "They are not providing smoking breaks or smoking areas. They are prohibiting smoking in the halls & restrooms also." Mockaitis assumed this change must be "illegal," as it appeared to her that the company management was usurping the "rights" of smokers.[83] Turns such as this one toward more comprehensive restrictions on workplace smoking signaled a major power shift in labor-management relations, as employers moved more and more against workers' shop floor smoking privileges and established important new rules that would govern everyday life in US workplaces. Worker-smokers increasingly discovered they could do little to stop the expansion of "no smoking" rules.

Ironically, the ubiquity of smoking in the postwar years (almost half of Americans smoked at the time of the 1964 release of the surgeon general's report) and the fact that more and more men and women worked in the poorly ventilated and compressed spaces of open-plan offices likely ensured that criticism of tobacco use would come to the fore in American culture.[84] Many nonsmoking workers struggled with recurring irritation to their eyes, noses, and lungs, as well as deeper concerns about the possibilities of cancer, lung disease, and heart disease as a result of daily exposure to sidestream smoke. While many employers and workers threw themselves into segregation schemes in order to accommodate smokers' and nonsmokers' competing interests and demands, these efforts to negotiate the relationships between smoke, office workspaces, and work cultures were difficult to manage because of the continuation of smoking in segregated offices or because they were implausible because of building design and technological limitations. Nonsmokers organized antismoking groups that educated working people and the broader public on the dangers of smoking and pressed for managers to overhaul workplace smoking privileges and stand behind nonsmokers' demands for clean air.

Many employers embraced the pursuit of clean air in the workplace during the 1980s and 1990s. Their reasons included insurance cost benefits, increased daily efficiency, and better overall worker performance as a result of better health. But the pursuit of smoke-free breathing space not only contributed to improved public health; it also deeply affected late-twentieth-century labor relations. For worker-smokers in particular, they experienced acutely the changing dynamics of power in the workplace, as the rise of new smoking bans reflected the ability of most employers to institute sweeping changes on the shop floor and the real powerlessness of labor (organized or not) to respond.

5

"EXILED SMOKING" AND THE MAKING OF SMOKE-FREE WORKPLACES

Employers can take many steps to reduce smoking-related costs and the human toll of tobacco use.

—American Cancer Society

The literary and cultural theorist Edward W. Said argued that exile was a significant reality in many lives throughout the twentieth century. On one hand, exile is a lived experience that is shaped by historical, political, and cultural circumstances and influences; at the same time, Said noted that the concept of exile matters greatly in terms of symbolism and as a prism for understanding and constructing culture, place, and self. Said was born a Protestant Christian in the contested city of Jerusalem in 1935, and his early life was characterized by frequent moves from Palestine, to Egypt, to Lebanon, and to the United States. He noted that disorientation and displacement infused his entire life, and he was separated from any enduring sense of home or lasting presence in a "native land."[1] Said defined exile as "the unhealable rift forced between a human being and a native place, between the self and its true home." He continued by saying that its "essential sadness can never be surmounted."[2] The "essential sadness" Said wrote about resulted from the exile's "anomalous and miserable life" on the outside looking in. In addition, exiles confront the "stigma of being an outsider" in every location they reside.[3]

Many cigarette smokers of the late twentieth century and numerous observers who commented on their experiences seized upon the symbolism of exile as they responded to employers' efforts to curtail smoking at work and to oust smokers from the workplace. Working-class smokers of the 1980s and 1990s imagined a sustained and frustrating process of disruption and banishment, as smoke-wary managers moved decisively against worker-smokers' post–World War II connections to indoor spaces of work and rest. New smoking restrictions pushed tobacco use out of workplaces and relegated smokers and their habit to sidewalks, streets, porches, parking lots, picnic tables, makeshift outdoor shelters, and other locations.[4] As several scholars of public health wrote in 1999, smokers' need for nicotine "causes them to be . . . exiled from the comforts and routines of their workplaces." Cast out and away from the workplace by new smoking bans, many smokers of the 1980s and 1990s experienced their own version of what Edward Said called the "sorrow of estrangement."[5] Ronnie Cervenka of Washington, D.C., certainly felt estranged from the indoor world of work. "I didn't like the idea at all," she said of her employer's new smoking restrictions. "Previously we could smoke at our desks. When we moved to a new office, we were limited to smoking in a lounge, and now we can only smoke outside the building."[6]

This chapter details how antismoking politics and management power overlapped in the reshaping of space, environment, and labor-management relations during the late twentieth century. In particular, it considers how and why employers established sweeping new bans on tobacco use on the job, a development that signaled the increasing overall powerlessness of working men and women in the 1980s and 1990s. Working-class smokers viewed smoking restrictions not as a sign of social progress or improving public health, but rather as new forms of discrimination and harassment from above, and, as workers' testimonies indicated, their complaints were not without merit. Employers' extensive power to reshape rules and workers' actions could also be seen in the ability of some companies and organizations to compel workers to quit smoking entirely, as was the case at the Chicago-based USG Acoustical Products Corporation in 1987. Smoking bans of the 1980s and 1990s initiated the process of banishment and began smokers' experiences as exiles, creating an "unhealable rift" between cigarette smokers and the indoor spaces they once occupied. Now forced outside to smoke, many smokers lamented their exclusion from the workplace and struggled to manage their need for nicotine in the face of expanding employer authority and public disapproval of smoking.

New Smoking Restrictions: Reasons, Agendas, and Reactions

Widely accepted public health concerns about smoking greatly enabled managers' assertions of power over the workplace, as employers exercised and strengthened managerial clout over labor through new smoking controls. Public health condemnations of smoking helped to clear the air at work, but at the same time it led to new scrutiny of worker behavior and strengthened employers' restrictions of worker choices and actions that were deemed injurious to individual and public health. Worker-smokers experienced new smoke-free airspaces not as the wise achievement of a healthful environment, but as a decisive employer intervention in opposition to the privileges they claimed on the job.

Throughout the 1980s and 1990s, the number of workplace smoking bans began to significantly increase. A 1986 study conducted by the Bureau of National Affairs and the American Society for Personnel Administration, for example, found that 85 percent of existing bans had been established since 1981, and 60 percent were less than two years old.[7] They surveyed 662 companies nationwide and found 239 (36 percent) with smoking restrictions in work areas. As the report pointed out, "scores of major corporations" featured new smoking bans, including the Ford Motor Company, General Motors, Campbell Soup, Boeing, Bank of America, Proctor & Gamble, and Merck.[8] The *Washington Post* pointed out that the growth of smoking bans throughout the 1980s was "unmistakable."[9]

In addition to prevalent public health concerns about tobacco use, the trend of declining union power enabled this rapid transformation of smoking policies at work. While the erosion of union ranks and influence does not explain the expansion of smoking prohibitions, there is no doubt that workers of the 1980s and 1990s had fewer mechanisms that could check the actions of employers who instituted new smoking restrictions. As the discussions of smoking restrictions among labor and management indicate, workers often had to cede broad powers on the shop floor to their employers, and in the 1980s and 1990s they increasingly lost the ability to claim them, trends ensured by the general decline of union clout.

Institutionally and politically, organized labor had been considerably weakened by a lack of grassroots organizing, sustained employer opposition, deindustrialization and capital migration, racial divisions, and even workers' own ambivalence in the post–World War II period.[10] By the 1980s and 1990s, much of organized labor was in retreat as membership eroded. In 1980, 23 percent of all US workers belonged to a union; four years later, the number was 18.8 percent. An estimated 15.7 percent of women were union members in 1977, but the number had dropped to 13.8 percent by 1984. For men, 29.6 percent were organized in 1977, declining to 23 percent by 1984. As a whole, the labor movement enjoyed its peak during the 1950s as memberships increased to 35 percent of workers in 1955. But the numbers slid downward during the next four decades, sinking to less than 22 percent in 1981 and 16 percent in 1990. Only an estimated 12.3 percent of US workers were thought to be organized in 2009. In the manufacturing sector, the numbers illustrate an even larger collapse: 50 percent of industrial workers belonged to a union in the 1950s, but only 19 percent did in 1993.[11] Available statistics for individual unions dramatically highlight the substantial scale of evaporating membership. The United Steelworkers of America (USWA) lost a staggering 42 percent of its members during the late 1970s and early 1980s, while the United Rubber Workers of America and the United Automobile Workers (UAW) lost 31 percent and 27 percent respectively.[12] As union power faded, workers tactically backed away from political struggles and controversies with managers in the shop, as statistics show. For example, the number of strikes in the United States that involved one thousand workers or more plummeted from 235 in 1978 to 35 in 1992.[13] In addition, workers increasingly voted down unions in representation elections. While unions won between 65 and 75 percent of elections in the 1950s, they only won an average of 50 percent of elections "that they themselves had called" in the 1980s.[14] Throughout the 1980s and 1990s, workers' longtime twentieth-century ally on the shop floor—organized labor—became weaker and weaker. As historian Melvyn Dubofsky notes, the United States at the end of the 1980s had a "smaller proportion of its labor force unionized than any other advanced industrial nation."[15] There were fewer institutional barriers, both real and potential, to those employers who intended to roll back smoking at work, which managers and employers of the late twentieth century were very eager to do so.

Convincing statistical analyses made by antismoking organizations, business schools, and managers themselves of the business costs of allowing smoking provided a powerful reason for eliminating tobacco use from the workplace. When comparing smoking and nonsmoking populations in the workplace, observers noted significantly higher costs per smoker for health insurance, fire insurance, cleaning, damage to property, and worker absenteeism, and they noticed diminished day-to-day productivity due to cigarette breaks. In numerous studies, scholars and employers stated that the banning of smoking would be a straightforward way to save money. For example, William Weis of Seattle University's business school wrote in 1983 that any "smoke-free business" enjoyed "substantial cost savings," and he compared the financial wisdom of managers in smoke-free businesses to the "thousands of dollars per smoker per year" that other companies needlessly lost. By permitting worker smoking, companies carried what were increasingly regarded as unnecessary costs.[16]

Citing a study conducted by the business faculty at State University of New York at Stony Brook, the American Lung Association broke down on a dollar-by-dollar basis the costs to business of smoking. In a pamphlet from the early 1980s, for example, the organization claimed that a smoking worker cost her or his employer an estimated $624 every year. Insurance costs for these unhealthy workers hurt employers the most, as smokers needed $204 in health care, $40 in worker's compensation, and $20 to $35 in life insurance and disability. Lost productivity was the second most expensive problem brought about by smoking, according to the American Lung Association. Smokers cost managers $166 every year in lost time and effort every day to eye irritation, diminished concentration, and "lowered cognitive and exercise capacity" caused by the carbon-monoxide-rich environment that smokers produced with every puff.[17] Other estimates adjusted the dollar amounts significantly higher, though they pointed to the same kinds of losses. William Weis calculated that workplace smoking led to the annual loss of a staggering $4,789 per smoker. He pointed to lessened worker production, diminished profits, high medical costs, property damage, and cleaning costs as the greatest financial injuries perpetrated by smokers. Overall, according to Weis, worker-smokers cost their employers an estimated $6.5 billion in health care costs every year and an additional $21 to 25 billion in lost productivity and wages.[18]

While no-smoking policies promised to allay labor costs and protect profits, company policy statements often framed the official rationale in paternalistic terms. In particular, policies usually stressed managers' concern for workers' health. The 1989 smoking restriction policy at the Chrysler Corporation announced to employees that smoking would be limited within the company to only those spaces with ample ventilation and total enclosures (e.g., private offices). "The purpose of the policy is to allow employees to work in a clean, healthy environment," stated Anthony P. St. John, vice president of the Human Resources department, "recognizing that smoke from tobacco affects the health of smokers and nonsmokers alike."[19] The 1992 policy of the Old Dominion Power Company in Kentucky explained that employees were "the most valuable resource," and thus the company's new smoking ban was intended to "ensure the highest standards of health and safety for all employees."[20] In business periodicals, sample policy statements echoed the paternalistic language of employers. The company "is concerned about the apparent danger smoking presents, not only to the smoker, but also to the health of non-smokers," one policy read. "We also take seriously our obligations as a Company to provide a safe and healthy workplace."[21]

But official proclamations from above, which were drafted and put forward by company managers, scholars, and newswriters, obscured the ways smoking restrictions were significant expansions of management powers over labor in the workplace during the late twentieth century. New smoking policies signaled decisive managerial interventions in the everyday privileges of workers and fundamental disruptions of work cultures and worker activities. Many worker-smokers disavowed managers' cost-cutting goals and paternalistic concerns for their bodies and well-being. Worker-smokers experienced the changing smoking rules of the 1980s and 1990s as intrusive impositions of management power, often referencing their changing workplace smoking situations in the languages of discrimination, humiliation, and subjection. "No smoking in the workplace is the latest form of discrimination," smoker journalist Alice Schultze lamented in 1988, while Carole F. Erickson, who worked at a large office in Illinois, angrily complained in a 1989 letter to the company's chairman of the board: "To arbitrarily put into effect a smoking ban is unfair harassment and *discrimination*."[22]

The new workplace smoking restrictions of the 1980s and 1990s abruptly transformed worker-smokers' relationships with supervisors and employers and upended daily routines and personal habits. In addition, these policies typically displaced worker-smokers from their usual spaces of rest. As new smoking restrictions became the norm during the late twentieth century, working-class smokers reported upsetting experiences with prejudice in hiring policies, employer intimidation, and occasional harassment by coworkers. Worker-smokers argued that employer efforts to clear the air greatly (and suddenly) undermined workers' claims to various rights on the job, such as the expectation that managers would permit workers to exercise some personal choice, have access to certain spaces, and enjoy some individual comforts on the job. Workers' discussions of their experiences with smoking restrictions during the 1980s and 1990s suggests how public health concerns were not the only reasons for management to limit smoking at work; instead, new smoking prohibitions helped employers exercise greater authority over workers' behaviors, bodies, and spaces.

The most common restrictions to smoking at work involved sending smokers to break rooms or outdoors and limiting cigarette smoking to official times of rest. Smokers themselves voiced dislike for the new hassles created by managerial policy making. From a textile factory in Virginia, Wanda Quesenberry wrote to the Workplace Smoking Group of the Tobacco Institute in 1991 to explain that management abruptly "posted a memo" about its new smoking policy. "There will be a new smoking area," she explained, "but it is in the basement and the only time you can do it is on your break, and it takes about 10 minutes to get down there." In addition to abstaining from smoking for extended periods, Quesenberry and her coworkers had to use most of their break time making the long walk to this subterranean smoking space. Work became a daily trial as workers labored all day in a near-constant state of withdrawal and unfulfilled cravings. In Kentucky, Douglas Hammerick described how the "new rule" at the factory where he worked created great inconvenience and offended his coworkers, as smokers were now obligated to walk several minutes to the very end of the factory, where smoking was permitted (beyond the "red line in the corner") in brief three-minute intervals. In addition, workers were not allowed to "lean on the wall" as they smoked. Hammerick, however, noted that workers were allowed to smoke in the company break room when their official rest periods began. Still, these changes in the rules and the new limitations of smoking angered Hammerick's coworkers, "and several people quit" their jobs as a result.[23]

Numerous letters to the Tobacco Institute suggest that employers' smoking restrictions usually displaced worker-smokers from indoor spaces and sometimes company properties entirely. Regardless of weather conditions—"rain, shine, hail, or snow"—David Stacy of Tennessee noted that smokers were now obligated to "go outside" and endure every possible form of meteorological distress as though they were mail carriers, and this was just the beginning of the changes at the company where he worked. Managers dislodged smoking from the company grounds altogether. "Rumor has it," Stacy told the Workplace Smoking Group of the Tobacco Institute in 1991, that "smoking will banned [sic] from the gate-on; no smoking on the property," a prospect that meant smokers would need to venture even further afield in the out-of-doors to satisfy their cravings. "Please call me regarding this," he begged the lobbyists.[24] In the early 1990s, letters from exiled worker-smokers throughout the United States poured in to the Workplace Smoking Group about bans on smoking on company properties. For instance, the Cleveland Illuminating Company in Madison, Ohio, adjusted its smoking restrictions from forbidding tobacco use both inside the plant and within fifty feet of the building to a total ban of smoking "anywhere on the grounds." Barry Storey at Cleveland Illuminating noted that when smokers queried managers about the decision to ban tobacco use, they "said it was for our health and safety." Storey rejected that claim, however, noting "they send people into nuclear reactors to make adjustments so they can't be too concerned about us."[25]

Worker-smokers especially lamented how some managers unexpectedly issued orders that smoking would no longer be allowed at all during breaks, whether it was inside the workplace, outdoors, or beyond the property boundaries of the business. Throughout their days (and night shifts) at work, workers were sometimes denied entirely the opportunity to smoke. Judy Meadows of Willoughby, Ohio, noted in January 1991 that the company where she worked "is going totally smoke free" and had taken the customary rest times when workers usually left the building to smoke. "They don't even give us breaks so we can go outside to smoke," she noted. Sharon Mitchell concurred, noting that the Texas firm where she worked banned smoking indoors and denied it to workers, even when on their own time, by not allowing anyone to leave the building during breaks. "We can't even go outside during breaks," she wrote. "What can be done. [sic]" Another worker in Philadelphia wrote to the Tobacco Institute to inquire about the legality of smoking bans after her employer unexpectedly announced the elimination of "smoking breaks" and "smoking areas," changes that were set to begin three weeks later.[26]

Smoke-wary employers asserted more of their authority over workers' rest times by declaring that smokers were not allowed to smoke inside their cars. This new rule frustrated many worker-smokers who imagined their automobiles as uniquely private domains amid those spaces governed by management. In letters to the Tobacco Institute, smokers emphasized their disbelief at this extension of employer power. "Not even in our cars," Johnny Creech of Coffee Springs, Alabama, complained in 1991. Charles Elmore and Cathy Hooper, also from Alabama, pointed out the same problem in their own letters. "My company, Hughes Aircraft, just went from allowing us to smoke anywhere in the building to a total smoking ban," Cathy Hooper noted of the swift changes where she worked. "We now cannot even go out to our cars on break and smoke there." For her and others, this was an inappropriate and outrageous extension of managerial authority into workers' personal rest times and private spaces.[27]

Working men and women lamented the struggles with employers over whether or not smoking in their own automobiles was within the purview of managerial authority. In these discussions, worker-smokers feared the considerable power that employers now readily wielded over workers' actions on their own time and in their own space. The concerned spouse of worker David Howard in Schenectady, New York, feared that her husband's days in the employ of Blue Cross/Blue Shield were rapidly coming to an undesired end. As she looked to the immediate future, potential trouble loomed ahead for both her and her partner. "My husband is close to being fired for smoking in his car and leaving the premises during his break to smoke a cigarette," she wrote. Grocery store worker Patricia Howlett in Oklahoma relayed her trying experience with a manager who penalized her for smoking in a car while it was parked some distance from the location where she worked. "I work for Pratt's Food store," she wrote. "Suddenly they [management] decided smoking would not be allowed anywhere around the store. Recently I was in my car, parked 2 blocks away from the store, smoking. I got written up!! . . . This is getting out of hand," Howlett said. In response, the Tobacco Institute inundated her mailbox with information about ways to respond, such as "info" about state laws that prohibited discrimination and recommendations that she contact state officials.[28]

Worker-smokers who questioned or criticized employer policies or failed to comply with new smoking regulations frequently spoke of experiences with management intimidation, threatened reprisals, or actual reprisals from above. In the enforcement of no-smoking rules, managers expressed and deployed (in ways both subtle and not) their expanded power. When an Ohio social worker urged her supervisor to notify the entire office staff after the hushed introduction of new smoking restrictions, she was "suspended for insubordination" for a week. "I did not raise my voice even though he was badgering me about smoking," the worker noted of the incident. "The policy was never negotiated they just said there will be no smoking." The supervisor's use of his power to clamp down on worker-smokers' actions and voices stunned her. "It's a very stressful job," the social worker insisted.[29] In Texas, George Keenom approached a supervisor to ask why smokers had to go outside when only two nonsmokers had voiced any disapproval of smoking in the workplace. As they talked, Keenom heard that he would likely be "fired for 'something'" if he pressed forward with his complaint. The worker was both surprised and scared and ended his brief note with an alarmed exclamation point.[30] Other workers reported potential employers who, during their interviews, pushed them to sign the no-smoking equivalent of a yellow-dog contract, pledging they would not smoke on the job nor smoke outside of work. Some worried smokers who called the Tobacco Institute for information and advice about responding to smoking policies begged the group not to use their names, fearing reprisals from managers if their complaints became known. "I am very sorry that I cannot even allow you to use my name," wrote Margaret Louise Clark in 1988. "I need my job."[31]

Some workers noted that the new smoking rules in workplaces seemed to bring out unexpected examples of arbitrary behavior from above, as managers now seemed to have real leverage against those workers who smoked and were not well-liked. In Tonawanda, New York, for instance, smoker Jim Hope wrote to ask for help with a manager who now seemed to have it in for him. Not allowed to smoke on the job, the worker was angered because his boss continually claimed to smell smoke on him, vowing to write him up and send him home. One day, despite Jim Hope's protests, the supervisor followed through on his ongoing threat and penalized him by ordering him out of the workplace. Hope worried because workers at the company could be fired if they were written up for rules violations three times. "He has never once seen me smoke," he complained. "He just keeps saying he smells it."[32] Smoking restrictions gave management new powers over the men and women in their employ. Kay Culiton of Kentucky remarked in 1991 that talking to her immediate supervisor about unkind comments from nonsmokers would do no good since "he is the one who gives me the most trouble."[33]

Not only did the new smoking restrictions of the 1980s and 1990s redraw the boundaries of acceptable worker behavior and redefine workers' conduct within spaces of work and company properties; it also led to the establishment of new boundaries between acceptable and unacceptable job candidates in the hiring office. At the Blue Cross and Blue Shield offices in New Haven, Connecticut, for example, managers bluntly explained that they avoided hiring tobacco users since they posed numerous problems for management, such as increased health insurance costs, but, more interestingly, ready-made opposition to pre-existing smoking restrictions in the workplace. "We don't want people who smoke at all," human resources manager Richard Recht noted of the mood at Blue Cross. "[B]ecause through tension or pressure," he said, "they could end up smoking here," trying to smoke on the sly, defiling both the indoor air space and the company policies that commanded workers not to use tobacco.[34] During the 1980s, an estimated

6 percent of US companies admitted that they refused to hire smokers. While new laws in twenty-eight states during the early to mid-1990s forbade employer discrimination against smokers in hiring, managers admitted they accomplished the same result (a workforce of mostly nonsmokers) as a result of stringent smoking restrictions and health insurance penalties (higher premiums) for smokers. John Banzhaf, a law professor at George Washington University and head of ASH (Action on Smoking and Health), observed that when companies vigorously pushed smoking out of the workplace, they accomplished what state laws of the 1990s could only try to interdict, which was the nicotine detox of the workforce.[35]

As managers asserted themselves between working men and women and their cigarettes, the expanding archives of the Tobacco Institute catalogued the disaffection of many worker-smokers. In May 1989, for example, an "Important Message" taken by phone "While You Were Out" to Sharon M. Stuntz asked the lobbyist to "Please Call" about "fight[ing] a ban on smoking."[36] By phone and by mail, angry, stunned, and worried cigarette smokers queried the Tobacco Institute for advice on how to best fight new workplace smoking restrictions, referencing in their requests for advice their own efforts to organize petition drives or pursue forms of collective action against management policies. Truman Strasser of Missouri wrote to the tobacco lobbyists a short message that was subsequently labeled "Urgent": "Workplace is getting ready to ban smoking entirely on the premises and will not hire smokers from now on. We have approached our employer with petitions and suggestions to no avail." Struggles against no-smoking rules began locally, only later expanding outward after employers disregarded their demands. In Maryland, Garolyn Buchanan wrote about a failed collective protest that was organized by herself and coworkers in the business where she worked in Denton. "The smokers in our company joined together," she wrote of recent efforts to gain "new smoking areas at work," only to be bluntly rebuffed by management.[37] Letter after letter arrived on the desks of tobacco lobbyists in the late 1980s and early 1990s, steadily expanding an archive that documented increasing management power over workplaces and shop floors and widespread worker frustration and opposition to the expansion of employer power.

For smokers, these new smoking restrictions guaranteed the pains and stress of withdrawal. As more and more employers banned smoking indoors and on company properties altogether, smokers became acutely aware of the long droughts without nicotine, which sparked havoc on the dopamine-deprived, pleasure-seeking receptors of the brain. For addicted tobacco users, nicotine deprivation produces forceful cravings, restlessness, irritability, difficulty concentrating, depression, increased hunger, and the inability to sleep or rest.[38] In a Bangor, Maine, newspaper office, writer Clarence Page was struggling to quit smoking and frequently contemplating the chance to "bum a cigarette" from a "holdout" smoker in his office, referencing the "persistent taunting, tingling agony of nicotine withdrawal." "We are hooked," he pondered. "We are junkies."[39] Ex-smoker "Kay" would have identified with Clarence Page's frustrations. "Physically I didn't feel any better for not smoking and emotionally I was a wreck," she said. "I almost lost my job because my emotions were so crazy that I created a scene at work and got into big trouble."[40] Even union men on a long bus trip insisted that the bus pull over every ninety minutes so the men could smoke.[41] Smokers noted that yawning gaps of time between cigarettes now overshadowed their workdays. Upon arriving at work in the morning, smoker Elaine Saunders of Wisconsin reported, "We cannot leave the work area for a full 8 hours," which guaranteed a long day of unfulfilled cravings. In 1991, Deanna Thompson wrote about the twelve-hour shifts at the company in northern Kentucky where she worked and the long wait until the thirty-minute lunch period where she could find relief in smoking a cigarette.[42] The pains of withdrawal were common in the late-twentieth-century workplace as times and spaces for smoking dwindled. As the plant manager of Scott Paper Company in western Kentucky pointed out, his employer banned smoking on the entire two-mile campus, forcing any smoker who wanted a cigarette during his or her twelve-hour shift to leave the grounds. Nonetheless, this was a distance that had to be traveled to secure any relief from nicotine withdrawal. Of smokers, he noted "they leave the plant for their lunch break and drive at least a mile and half off the property." If not, they confronted the gnawing, unrelenting torment of "abstain[ing] for 12 hours."[43]

In addition to banning smoking, employers sometimes moved against sources of supply. By the early 1990s, various employers such as Coca-Cola had removed cigarette vending machines as part of their ouster of tobacco use from the workplace. Betty Frankenfield was deeply frustrated by Coca-Cola's removal of smoking and cigarette supplies from the distributor where she worked in Kansas City, Kansas. Managers implemented their purge of workers' tobacco sources "because some vice president had a heart attack and it was possibly brought on by him smoking." She wished the cigarette companies would turn the tables on Coke. "I think that if Coca-Cola is not allowing us to smoke and they have taken out the cigarette vending machines," she complained, "maybe the cigarette companies shouldn't have Coke machines on their premises." Not only did this amount to rough justice, but the high volume of caffeine in soda was "dangerous to ones [sic] health."[44]

Many employers and managers of the 1980s and 1990s moved decisively against workers' habits and behaviors as they pursued new smoking restrictions. The implementation of smoking bans signaled the extension of management power into new areas, and no-smoking rules gave management ways to forcefully redefine acceptable working-class behaviors in areas that were thought to be private, personal, and off-limits in the mid- to late twentieth century. The reactions of worker-smokers to new smoking prohibitions suggests that employers of the 1980s and 1990s were not motivated to roll back smoking solely by public health considerations; rather, we see numerous examples of managers developing and exercising new controls over space, time, and behavior. While working-class men and women gained healthier air space, no-smoking policies signaled the erosion of their power at work.

Forcing Workers to Quit Smoking: USG Acoustical Products and Others

Managers' views that smoking was a wholly unnecessary source of high health care costs, absenteeism, and diminished productivity surely justified these assertive new moves to reshape workers' actions. The extensive physical harm to worker bodies caused by cigarettes, after all, threatened employers' bottom lines of revenues, expenditures, and profits. Management's battles against smoking during the 1980s and 1990s, however, transcended the immediate realm of the workplace; by the late 1980s, companies had begun to implement no-smoking policies that extended into employees' personal lives beyond the spaces and times of work. Total smoking bans—requirements that working men and women quit smoking entirely—became increasingly common workday realities during the late 1980s and early 1990s. Despite the widespread unpopularity of these new policies, managers often discovered they could do much to mold workers' behaviors *in absentia*. The most significant early example of a total smoking ban is found at the USG Acoustical Products Corporation, a major manufacturer of ceiling and soundproof tile. In this case, management's worries about financial losses due to mounting worker lawsuits led to a sweeping new plan to divest smokers of their unhealthy (and costly) use of tobacco.

The Chicago-based USG Acoustical Products Corporation instituted its January 1987 ban in all of its manufacturing facilities nationwide, affecting working men and women in cities and towns such as Gypsum, Ohio; Wabash, Indiana; Walworth, Wisconsin; Red Wing, Minnesota; Cloquet, Minnesota; Tacoma, Washington; Greenville, Mississippi; Birmingham, Alabama; and Corsicana, Texas. While workplace smoking restrictions had become more and more common during the 1980s, the scope of USG's ban was nearly unprecedented: it not only forbade all smoking on the job but also in workers' personal lives beyond the factory grounds. Worried about lawsuits against the company for lung disease as a result of materials handled in the workplace, managers required all employees who smoked to quit entirely, theoretically helping managers to engineer a healthier workforce that would help keep the firm out of court. Not smoking became a prerequisite for employment. USG managers' authority and influence now reached further into workers' lives than ever before and hastily forced worker-smokers to confront their addictions to nicotine and to jettison one of the most routine and necessary features of their lives: their cigarettes. "It's the principle of the matter that upsets me," Mark Grace, a smoker and electrician at the USG Acoustical Products Walworth, Wisconsin, facility, told a reporter. "They can tell me what they want on company time, but not on my time. They're only paying me during the hours I'm there."[45]

But Mark Grace was mistaken; the announcement of the smoking policy showed how USG management *could* determine much of workers' behavior, even when they went home. The total smoking ban at USG Acoustical Products powerfully highlights the trend of worker powerlessness during the 1980s and the quiet role of smoking bans in many employers' control over the shop floor and workers' behavior. The USG case illustrates the significantly expanding of freedom of action enjoyed by managers in many 1980s workplaces.

Worried about precluding worker lawsuits against the company for exposure to lung contaminants in the manufacturing of tile, managers chose not to revisit the materials they used (especially rock wool) but rather the issue of smoking among its workers. (An estimated 30 percent of USG's three thousand workers smoked cigarettes.) In the new company policy presented to workers, managers cited the findings of a 1986 World Health Organization conference that concluded that persistent cigarette smoke exposure destroyed the cilia that helped the lungs filter out airborne irritants that cause illness. Management insisted the World Health Organization's findings did not concretely prove that inhaled "man-made mineral fibers" harmed working men and women, but it admitted that exposure could create a "small increase in the risk of lung disease." Management claimed the "cause is unclear." Managers at USG insisted that lung tissues could safely filter airborne contaminants (such as the fiber particles used in the making of tiles) if healthy cilia could function properly. Thus, to protect its workers from environmental irritants and lung disease hazards in the workplace, managers banned smoking not only at work but also at home; working men and women would have to quit smoking entirely to maintain their employment at USG.[46]

Founded in 1920, the United States Gypsum Company (called US Gypsum, the later parent company of USG Acoustical Products) had been built on the fire-resistant products made possible by rock wool as well as by asbestos. US Gypsum's long history of asbestos use set the stage for its legal dilemmas of the 1980s. The term "asbestos" describes certain minerals, composed of fibrous material, that are naturally resistant to fire and able to be woven. Chrysotile is the most common form of asbestos, used most often commercially as a fire safety agent.[47] Ancient civilizations first recognized the fire-resistant qualities of this substance, as historian Rachel Maines pointed out. By the early twentieth century, to enhance fire safety in crowded turn-of-the-twentieth-century cities, builders wove asbestos fibers into matted fabric or mixed it with cement, hoping to lessen the likelihood of catastrophic fire in new urban structures. The era of wooden construction was fading away, replaced more and more with concrete, steel, and asbestos. For much of the twentieth century, asbestos became an every-day fire safety precaution in all forms of building construction.[48] Until the late 1970s, US Gypsum manufactured thirty-six everyday construction materials that contained asbestos, including tape, mortar, spackling putty, paint, plaster, joint compounds, shingles, ceiling tiles, roofing tiles, and pipe coverings.[49] While USG stopped working with asbestos in 1978 (the substance was widely recognized as a carcinogen by the 1970s), the company continued to market products that featured rock wool (such as acoustic tiles) well into the 1980s. Some forms of rock wool elevated the risk of lung disease among workers who handled them regularly, though likely to a lesser extent than asbestos, as recent studies show.[50] A 1982 article in *The New Scientist* magazine that examined home insulation described rock wool "literally" as "a wool made by heating volcanic rock until it melts and spinning it into fibres; it's rather like candyfloss [*sic*] [cotton candy] made from rock."[51] Rock wool nicely insulates against high heat and absorbs sound, which explains its importance to USG's tile business. While not as danger-ous to human tissue as asbestos, rock wool does present certain risks, specifically painful irritation of the lungs, eyes, and skin, as well as the elevated risk of lung diseases and even the possibility of cancer as a result of chronic exposure.

By the 1970s and 1980s, the public outcry over the occupational hazards posed by asbestos brought sustained scrutiny on companies that relied heavily on asbestos and related substances in their businesses, companies such as US Gypsum. During the 1980s, US Gypsum managers were desperate to protect the company and themselves from the many lawsuits that resulted from their long use of asbestos products in their enterprises. Efforts such as the 1987 ban at USG Acoustical Products were very much in response to the tidal wave of legal actions pending against US Gypsum. Managers' actions to stay out of court were too little too late, however, as the company faced hundreds of asbestos lawsuits by 1987. There were 112 lawsuits working their way through the courts from US Gypsum factory workers in twenty-five different states that alleged that the company "cre-ated a health hazard in its manufacturing plant[s]"; and US Gypsum was the defendant in "many" of the forty thousand pending lawsuits from asbestos prod-uct installers "who have contracted lung disease or cancer from the fiber" as a result of their work with USG products. South Carolina attorney Charles Patrick, who pursued ten thousand asbestos cases on behalf of working men and women during the 1980s, asserted that USG Acoustical Products imagined its smoking ban as a way to minimize its own future legal liabilities. "It sounds like a defensive posture," Patrick told the *Chicago Tribune.* "It seems to me that they are trying to protect themselves from some type of future lawsuit, possibly trying to lay the groundwork to blame future lung disease of its workers on cigarette smoking rather than on potentially hazardous fibers in the plants."[52] In other words, by pointing to the protracted history of smoking among many of its employees, the company could create reasonable doubt that its materials, past or present, were to blame for lung disease among workers.

USG managers intended to re-engineer worker bodies to minimize the chance of inconvenient and costly lung disease. Effective on 1 January, workers could no longer smoke in USG Acoustical Products facilities. Much to workers' and observers' chagrin, the ban did not apply to the company headquarters in Chicago. Still, management required all workers to be entirely smoke-free within three months, monitored by annual health and lung screenings (especially a "pulmonary function examination") designed to ensure employees' ongoing compliance with the policy. USG established an in-house program to help smokers quit and offered them the opportunity to choose another smoking cessation class. USG management promised to reimburse smokers up to the full cost of the company's own program. At the end of the three-month grace period, however, any workers would be immediately fired if found to be smoking. In addition, managers announced they would no longer hire smokers. Company spokesman Paul D. Colitti even said that if any employees were observed smoking in a bar their job at USG Acoustical Products would be in real jeopardy.[53]

USG managers' bodily paternalism went even further. They introduced new coveralls and respirators that would be required for all employees as another condition of their employment. To protect workers from airborne hazards, and the company from costly legal liabilities, management encased workers' bodies with several layers of protection. And to ease this transition to closer regulation of the shop floor, managers promised the new equipment and clothing would be free of cost and laundry services would be provided on-site for their convenience.[54]

Numerous companies throughout the United States, as well as employers in state and local government, followed USG's example and required working men and women to avoid smoking entirely as a precondition for hiring and employment. In the years that followed the USG ban, the most controversial policy totally prohibiting smoking appeared in Wabash, Indiana, at the Ford Meter Box Company in 1989. Managers fired office worker Janice Bone after a routine drug test revealed trace amounts of nicotine in her urine, a violation of the company's

recent policy that banned smoking "at any time," including in "their [workers']
own homes."[55] Bone admitted that she smoked despite the ban, but not on the
Ford Meter Box Company's property nor during her time spent on the clock.
In addition, management fired her son Sean, who also smoked. Indiana state
legislators and newspaper editorial pages railed against this "life-style discrimination," where institutions used their power to shape employees' private lives
beyond the workplace.[56] In response to the widely criticized firing of Janice Bone,
Indiana legislators passed a law in 1991 that forbade the firing of working people
who smoked cigarettes when they were not at work. Governor Evan Bayh noted
that the purpose of the law, dubbed the "smokers' bill of rights," was to protect
working men's and women's privacy when they were away from the establishments where they worked.[57] Many other states followed suit. By December 1992,
thirty-three states had passed various laws to protect workers from "job discrimination" as a result of smoking or other "personal lifestyle decisions," such as
drinking alcohol or eating unhealthy food.[58]

Despite this nationwide legal challenge, numerous employers continued to
demand total abstinence. Media magnate Ted Turner's Turner Broadcasting
System, based in Atlanta, unapologetically defended its policy of hiring only
nonsmokers. Since the state of Georgia did not pass any laws that forbade the
practice, the management at TBS could turn away tobacco users simply because
of their personal decision to smoke cigarettes and their backgrounds as smokers. "We think we have the right to employ the kind of person we want to have,"
Turner vice president William M. Shaw claimed, "and that's a nonsmoker." Also,
all new Turner Broadcasting System employees signed increasingly common
"no-smoking agreements" as a precondition of their employment.[59] The American Civil Liberties Union (ACLU) argued throughout the early 1990s that this
de jure expansion of corporate power into workers' lives at home constituted
a breach of the principle of privacy since smoking was a legal activity that was
conducted in the context of employees' time away from work. "Smokers should
be judged individually on the basis of their ability to perform their jobs safely
and satisfactorily," the ACLU noted. "Discrimination by employers for off-the-
job activities, including smoking, is a profound violation of their right to privacy,
and such discrimination should be prohibited by law."[60]

Despite significant opposition to employer efforts to prevent workers from
smoking at home, state and local governments increasingly required police officers and firefighters to quit smoking entirely, promising to never smoke tobacco
whether they were at home, at work, or anywhere else. The Oklahoma City Fire
Department fired a worker who "took three puffs of a cigarette during a lunch
period," later admitting to superiors that he still smoked despite the OCFD's
total ban. The Tenth Circuit Court in Oklahoma defended the firing of the

lunchtime smoker, claiming that "state and federal governments, as employers, have interests sufficient to justify comprehensive and substantial restraints upon the freedoms of their employees that go beyond the restraints they might impose on the rest of the citizenry."[61] What were these "interests"? In other words, the state could command a firefighter or police officer not to smoke since their jobs demanded optimum physical health; other people depended on their ability to perform their perilous jobs at the highest level possible.

According to polling data, the American public recoiled from employer assertions of managerial will in working men's and women's lives away from the job. In 1990, 76 percent of Americans strongly agreed that employers did not have the right to refuse employment to someone just because they smoked; 74 percent believed that employers did not have the right to ask about workers' smoking away from the workplace; and 74 percent claimed that managers did not have the right to require job applicants to quit smoking.[62] But at USG and elsewhere, workers continued to face sweeping changes in key aspects of their work and, for smokers, of their personal lives both in and beyond the workplace. Smokers faced stressful withdrawals from nicotine or, if they chose to disobey these total smoking bans, a struggle to somehow keep their habit a secret. These were difficult new realities not of their own choosing, as managers created wide-reaching policies and swiftly implemented them.

"Exiled Smoking"

In the late twentieth century, worker-smokers experienced improving public health as an unwelcome extension of managerial authority in the workplace. Many smokers resented the changing circumstances and spaces of smoking at work, citing feelings and experiences of exile and marginalization. Many worker-smokers resented what medical researchers of the 1990s now called "exiled smoking," the requirement that smokers leave indoor workplaces to smoke outside.[63] For smokers, "exiled smoking" made clear their powerlessness as workers. These "exiled" smokers of the 1990s tried to call attention to their feelings of injustice in the hope of challenging the new rules that ousted smoking from indoor workspaces. They wrote letter after letter to the Tobacco Institute and voiced their anger to reporters who were curious about the new communities of lonely smoker-exiles that congregated on the sidewalks and in the doorways of office buildings. "Step outside just about any office building and you'll smack into a pack of them," a curious Laura Blumenfeld of the *Washington Post* wrote in the early summer of 1991. "The pavement people. The banished ones. Leaning, pacing, chatting or maybe just staring vacantly. But most important, smoking."[64] Surveying downtown Washington, D.C., she observed how "clumps of smokers now line the streets," the result of the widespread smoking bans in offices. They now acquired their "nicotine fix" amid the foot traffic on the sidewalks. As Keith Maxwell, a staffer at the American Psychiatric Association, noted, "They've [employers] driven us outside." Unwanted indoors, worker-smokers had been cast out. The workplace was now a conspicuous nonsmoking space.[65]

Even if frequently venturing outside at the behest of management was the only option available to addicted smokers, it was still absolutely necessary in order to maintain blood nicotine levels that precluded (or at least minimized) the pain of withdrawal. In a 1995 survey of 669 smokers, 9 percent claimed they experienced "a strong need" to smoke on the job, while 71 percent reported either an "occasional" or "mild" need to smoke at work.[66] "Exiled smoking" proved to be the only way for smokers to "minimize the effects of workplace smoking bans on their daily consumption."[67] In the study of 669 smokers, 39 percent reported retreating outside at least once per day to smoke on nonbreak time. In addition to journalist Laura Blumenfeld, numerous observers remarked on the subsequent changes to the peopling of outdoor streetscapes: "We now witness smokers huddled outside no-smoking buildings attempting to smoke during brief work breaks," noted one, and another, with a witty sense of irony, said, "Smokers shiver outside their workplaces, pariahs in a country where the father of which was a tobacco farmer."[68]

Exiled smokers resented their changing relationships to company space, as managers directed them to new (but rudimentary) shelters outside. The exile shaped smokers' feelings of ostracism and marginality, and so did the lackluster physical condition of smoking shelters that some companies provided for working men and women. Surrounded by hastily arranged structures of Plexiglas canopies or "little covered sheds," smokers could see the physical evidence of their lowly state, banished from the indoors, in the threadbare surroundings of employers' shelters. George Keenom complained to his supervisor at a Texas factory about "making us smoke outside under a 2-sided flexiglass shelter," only to be cautioned that he could be fired if he complained to others. An Arkansas smoker was angry about the "shelter" her boss improvised for smokers' use: a "roof to smoke under." She wondered, "Can they do that?" In response, management issued a subtle warning. They reminded smokers they "were lucky to get that." If managers wanted, they could reverse their generosity.[69] But even as some smokers criticized managers for their arrangements of outdoor space, others saw shelters as an improvement over their lonely wanderings in the wide-open spaces outdoors. After American Yard Products of Swainsboro, Georgia, implemented a ban on smoking inside the plant, Glenda Hooks approached her supervisor about building a "sheltered smoking area," but she received no reply.[70]

The majority of employers who continued to allow smoking on company grounds did not build shelters for exiled worker-smokers, but they sometimes designated specific entrances, porches, or other areas as smoking spaces. Here, too, smokers read spaces as markers of their status as outsiders (figuratively and literally). Some embittered smokers talked about the "small side porches" and "back porches" where managers allowed them to smoke, while others described how smoking amid outdoor surroundings at work produced uneasy feelings of declining status within the working class. For instance, "It makes you feel like street people," noted one working woman outside of City Hall in Chicago.[71]

The most common complaint that exiled smokers voiced was their struggles with poor weather as they ventured outdoors to calm their cravings for nicotine, an issue that highlights the interplay of bodies, spaces, environments, and power in shaping the experience of class at work and within the working class more generally. When temperatures edged downward, sometimes precipitously, and as rain, sleet, or snow descended from above, workers who smoked were uncomfortably reminded of their lonely identities as banished smokers. At a Long Island office in 1987, the "butt bucket" filled up quickly near the back door area where numerous workers smoked during their lunch hour and on their breaks. "Rain, wind, snow, sleet, I'm out there smoking," said a computer operator. Looking at her cold and ashy surroundings that February in 1987, she noted, "I plan to quit when I have a little more peace and contentment in my life, but now I still go out."[72] Smokers complained in the early 1990s to the Tobacco Institute about how their employers demonstrated no regard for their ouster to the inhospitable weather outside. At a South Carolina hospital, a staff member lamented that "we have to go outside to smoke no matter what, there is no kind of protection from the elements," while a Mississippi worker at a medical answering service criticized the exposed back porch area where her boss permitted smoking, saying that the spot "gets rained on and is cold in the winter."[73] A Minnesota smoker noted that the subzero winter weather of his state made the experience of smoking outside an oppressive burden. As exiled worker-smokers caught colds as a result of repeated exposure to cold and wet weather, at least one annoyed employer threatened to fire those smokers who missed any days of work as a result.[74]

Some exiled smokers insisted that the need to leave work to smoke exposed them to certain dangers on the mean and busy streets of urban America. Some smokers tried to force employers to rethink policies that exiled tobacco users to the streets by insisting that smoking outside was dangerous, citing the safety threats posed by automobile traffic and urban crime. When employers banned all smoking on company property, some worker-smokers found it necessary to smoke alongside busy streets, as was the case at the National Wildlife Federation office in Virginia. Other smokers in urban or downtown settings insisted that smoking outside the office exposed them to "high crime areas." Jim Brent of Wheaton, Maryland, asked the Tobacco Institute what his employer's liability was "if we go outside to smoke and get raped, mugged, or killed because we couldn't smoke inside the building."[75] For some smokers, the experience of exile engendered not only feelings of separation, isolation, and discomfort, but also of danger because of their ouster from indoor work space.

Forced outdoors, smokers found it nearly impossible to overturn smoking bans. While they certainly engaged supervisors directly over the creation of acceptable smoking spaces in the workplace or at least near it, they were typically rebuffed or told that changes were not possible. Deliberate protest efforts by smoking workers (such as petition drives) against their relegation to the outdoors at work gained no ground during the late 1980s and early 1990s. For example, Edward T. Huck, who did not want to smoke outside, organized a petition drive in the late 1980s to challenge the indoor smoking ban at the Department of Environmental Regulation (DER) in Tallahassee, arguing that the DER rule violated the tenor of Florida's Clean Indoor Air Act of 1985 as it banned smoking throughout both the office workplace as well as in official staff vehicles. In other words, the DER went beyond the wording of the law that said smoking was to be prohibited specifically in the workplace, "an enclosed indoor workplace," as the act explained. Huck (and others) wanted to end their days of exile and return to the indoors of the office where he worked. Tampa employees of the DER tried to join the petition drive, but the effort was quickly stymied by the state. The state of Florida's hearing officer, Arnold H. Pollock, pointed out to the complainants the established medical knowledge that linked tobacco use to cancer and heart disease. As a result, the DER's total ban on smoking would remain.[76] Exiled smoking continued.

Lighting up inside the walls of the smoke-free workplace proved to be the ultimate act of conscientious objection to indoor smoking bans, often leading to serious consequences for workers if discovered. A woman who worked at a small video cassette rental store in Benton Harbor, Michigan, wrote to the Tobacco Institute to report that she and a coworker lost their jobs soon after the owners banned smoking at the store. While the owners of the video shop told the women to smoke outside during their break times, these workers continued to smoke indoors. Upon discovery, the operators swiftly fired both of them. The woman who wrote the letter assumed this outcome was not supposed to be happen and questioned the legality of the store owners' policy and actions. The Tobacco Institute staff explained to her that companies had the right to "form their own smoking policy," but the now unemployed video store clerk continued

FIGURE 5.1 American Cancer Society advertisement for the "Great American Smokeout," 1990. Courtesy Stanford Research Into the Impact of Tobacco Advertising.

to be overwhelmed and stunned by the response of management to her tiny rebellion. "I don't think this is fair," she said. "One day everything was fine and the next day, no smoking."[77]

Smokers claimed that bans on smoking on the job led them, ironically, to smoke more during those times of the day and in those spaces where they *could* smoke. Deprived of opportunities to smoke throughout the working day at Merle Norman Cosmetics in Los Angeles, Robert Altman "made up for deprivation in the office" by "chain-smoking" cigarette after cigarette during his lunch hour. "I knew it was the only time I could smoke," he wrote, "so I would store up for the two to three hours that I couldn't smoke at my desk." As time went on in this manner, Robert Altman quit smoking altogether rather than continue navigating this maddening pendulum that swung between the poles of total saturation and stressful withdrawals.[78] In 1990, Veterans Affairs staffer Dottie Bolyard remarked that now she usually smoked two cigarettes during every break instead of one because of how long it now took to make her way down to the street, a lengthy trip necessitated by her employer's ouster of smoking from indoor space. "Aggravations are greater by the time you take the elevator and come out here," she said, alluding to the lengthy nicotine droughts that accompanied life inside, which were unduly extended by these long pilgrimages to the outdoors. Other smokers, such as Lorraine Mitchell, who worked at a pharmaceutical company on Long Island, discussed how they addressed their daylong nicotine deficits by chain-smoking more cigarettes during the drive home.[79] Addiction specialists in the late 1990s corroborated smokers' claims, as one study of 143 office smokers and 113 "social" smokers noted that "smokers outside buildings with workplace smoking bans" puffed 18.7 more times on their cigarettes than "the social settings group" who smoked elsewhere with acquaintances.[80]

As worker-smokers journeyed outside to satisfy their cravings, management warned some not to let absences from the workplace affect their daily job performance. The management of the establishment where Sue Farmer of Dothan, Alabama, worked in 1991 issued the vague threat that "our production had better not drop" just because she and others frequently needed to go outside to smoke. From management's point of view, productivity superseded workers' needs to maintain steady and sufficient levels of nicotine in their bloodstreams. Farmer was worried about how her smoking habit might actually end up jeopardizing her position in the company. A week earlier, workers could apparently smoke indoors; one week later, "as of today," the workplace was now "smoke free." At the same time, smokers' personal needs to satisfy cravings might now put their jobs at risk. In only a few days, smokers saw the banishment of smoking from the workplace and the vague imposition of as-yet-unknown consequences for smoking outdoors.[81] As some smokers faced the prospect of exile to the outdoors, they tried to invoke the importance of worker productivity to managers in their arguments against smoking bans in the workplace. Reporter Vinny Kuntz of the *Tallahassee Democrat* argued that his employer's new ban of smoking "will force me to do a poorer job," since, as he noted, "On deadline, I'll have to get up and go outside if I want to smoke."[82] Did employers really want to risk losing the productivity of their smoking workers by sending them outside?

While exile produced feelings of separateness and ostracism among worker-smokers, the experience of exile created the basis for new social group-ings among some workers. When queried about their exile by journalists, some smokers insisted they were not alone in their frustration with bans on smoking; there were other members of this "endangered species." At the Veterans Affairs office in Washington, D.C., staff member and smoker Karen Dewey remarked that she got to know many other smokers outdoors where she smoked on her breaks. She talked about how the smokers she knew "meet outside" on their breaks and during lunch hours. At a Washington hospital William Martin agreed, saying that he "met a lot of people outside those exit doors." In particular, lunch time was a great time to gather outside with other smokers because after a meal "most smokers have to have a cigarette."[83] In the waning moments of their lunch breaks, exiled smokers created community.

As smoking in the new era of restrictions transformed tobacco users into exiles, some worker-smokers resigned themselves to the necessity of cutting back or quitting entirely. Enise Latino of Worcester, Massachusetts, remarked that she now no longer smoked during her workday. "I feel it's right," she said of smoking bans. When Latino worked, she aided her health by not smoking at all. Appar-ently not bothered by nicotine withdrawals, she concluded that her dissipating relationship with smoking was "a good idea" for her. Other smokers grudgingly adopted the same approach, though with significantly greater discomfort. Lisa Guinette, also of Worcester, remarked that she was "less than enthusiastic" about not smoking on the job, "but you get used to it." She said that while she certainly wanted to smoke, it was necessary (for reasons not given) to avoid cigarettes while at work. Guinette consoled herself by saying that her pack-and-a-half-a-day habit was dwindling to less than a full pack.[84] For some smokers, efforts at accommodation blunted feelings of alienation when managers instituted bans on smoking.

The emergence of "exiled smoking" in the 1980s and especially the 1990s sig-naled not only improving air quality indoors and growing concern for public health, but also the changing power relationships of the late-twentieth-century workplace. The powerful movement against smoking at work showed the great extent to which managers could institute sweeping new rules that reshaped workers' behavior at work and beyond, as the USG Acoustical Products total smoking ban illustrated. As they ventured outside to smoke in accordance with new antismoking rules, they experienced improving public health not as a benefit but more typically as discrimination and estrangement. Smokers were exiles within the worlds of work and public health during the 1980s and 1990s.

If worker-smokers had ever encountered Edward Said's *Reflections on Exile*, his thoughts on banishment and estrangement would have been very familiar. The displacement of smokers from US workplaces and their consignment to the outdoors beyond the boundaries of the workplace rendered them exiles among the working class of the late twentieth century. The "nomadic, decentered, contrapuntal" experiences of these exiled smokers highlighted their increasing powerlessness as workers.[85] Employers gained extensive authority over working-class bodies and spaces during the 1980s and 1990s, as smokers' struggles to manage their need for nicotine illustrated.

As the history of exiled smoking in the 1980s and 1990s shows, worker-smokers struggled to challenge in various ways the power relations of the changing rules in the workplace. They questioned management, lobbied for spaces where they could smoke, organized petition drives, quit jobs, and wrote angry letters to tobacco lobbyists in Washington, D.C. Their various efforts failed. Working-class smokers never found the organizational means to limit managers' abilities to establish inconvenient, unwelcome, and life-changing regulations. Only the Tobacco Institute remained a constant ally through the significant changes that were taking place in the late-twentieth-century workplace.

While the Tobacco Institute's concern for smokers' rights led them to voice their own critiques of employer policy making and give advice to worker-smokers, their institutional focus on tobacco use ensured they would be unlikely to significantly recognize (let alone respond) to the broader problems that led to the curtailing of smoking privileges at work: managers' hopes to secure decisive power over worker behaviors, spaces, and bodies at work and beyond; unions' decline; and the real antipathy between many nonsmokers and smokers. Since frustrated worker-smokers recognized the power politics of class that undergirded managers' smoking restrictions, why did these workers (many unorganized) spend so much time and effort seeking out the tobacco lobby for assistance rather than take their workplace-based problems and complaints to the representatives of organized labor? The next chapter will examine the tensions between the labor movement's actions in defense of smoking on the job (and thus privileges in the workplace more generally) and many worker-smokers' political choices, typically informed by a powerful language of "rights" that precluded collective action.

6

ORGANIZED LABOR AND THE PROBLEM OF "SMOKERS' RIGHTS"

Unions are mandated to represent all members, including smokers and nonsmokers.

—hazards.org

ALCOA metal worker Joe F. McNeely had had enough. As he considered recent management actions in 1989 to restrict smokers' habits in the southern Indiana factory where he worked, his intense frustration led him to write a scathing letter of rebuke. Reminding managers of his status as an adult, as well as his "rights," McNeely insisted that smoking was his "free choice." For two typed single-spaced pages, he complained that the new limitations on smoking at ALCOA equaled petty "harassment," was a sign of the "self-righteous exhibition of moral superiority" among "vocal" nonsmokers, a blasphemy of his "right to smoke," and a violation of collective bargaining procedures, which he referred to as the "long-established freedoms to settle issues in the normal course of contract negotiations." McNeely's "smokers' rights" diatribe urged the top brass at ALCOA to reverse course, arguing they had become too involved in his and others' personal choices. "I mean what's next?" he complained. "Candy bars? Next must we fight for the right to choose what we eat?"[1] He mailed a copy of his letter not only to the management at the plant where he worked, but also to the leadership of Local 104 of the United Steelworkers of America, the union that represented McNeely and the many other metal workers at the Aluminum Company of America.

Joe F. McNeely's fiery "rights talk" on the matter of tobacco use was emblematic of many working-class smokers' attitudes about politics and rights in the late twentieth century. McNeely and other incensed smokers of the 1980s and 1990s drew upon and shaped a narrowing language of "rights" that demanded the maintenance (or restoration) of smoking privileges at work. Despite the power politics of social class that enabled swift managerial actions against tobacco use, angry working-class smokers returned again and again to their own political and personal goals, voiced increasing antipathy toward nonsmokers, and viewed labor unions as only the occasional custodians of shop floor privileges, expected to act in the episodic periods when they collectively bargained. "Smokers' rights" in late-twentieth-century workplaces thus led workers to overlook class politics and neglect the labor movement.

Despite what appeared to be working-class smokers' preoccupations with personal politics rather than class, unions continuously grappled with smoking disputes. Focusing on the intersections of smoking politics and organized labor in the late twentieth century, this chapter explores three questions: Did smoking disputes in the 1980s and 1990s bring new energy to the labor movement from below? Did union engagement with smoking controversies empower working people? Did smoking disputes spur unorganized workers to join or build unions?

The politics of smoking in the late twentieth century undercut class politics and union politics on several levels. As unions grappled with employer assaults on shop floor traditions and privileges, including smoking privileges, the local and narrow terrain on which these battles were often fought seemed to negate more expansive forms of solidarity and action. Despite ongoing smoking controversies at work, these disputes never produced the purposeful class consciousness that emerged among the militant workers at the Staley corn processing plant in 1990s eastern Illinois or the inclusive rank-and-file movements for social justice at Boeing, two cases of inclusive working-class activism that highlighted the new thinking and energy of labor's rank and file.[2] Among organized and unorganized worker-smokers, worries about "Big Brother," of intrusions into workers' lives from above, led not to creative and inclusive engagement with employer power, but frequently to self-interested talk about "smokers' rights." For working people and the labor movement, the politics of smoking proved to be cancerous.

All Politics Is Local

When Thomas "Tip" O'Neill first ran for office (the Cambridge City Council) as an upperclassman at Boston College, he lost the election. In the aftermath of the defeat, his father took him aside and told him, "All politics is local. Don't forget it."[3] The senior O'Neill's uncomplicated life lesson for his son applies to the realm of union politics as well, as organized labor's engagement with members is the only way to maintain support, whether one is talking about the "sped-up" auto plants of Flint, Michigan, southern California canneries during the Great Depression, or the "medieval" mining towns of turn-of-the-twentieth-century West Virginia. In the years after World War II, those unions facing a decline in numbers and relevance were not only brought low by deindustrialization, capital mobility, and employer opposition, but sometimes by the political and social divisions that accompanied unions' transitions from social movements to bureaucratic institutions. This was a noticeable problem for workers and unions in the late twentieth century, one that gave rise to dissenting rank-and-file movements and labor historians' pursuits of a usable past that would offer new ways of thinking about union revitalization. Michael Moore's film *Roger & Me* (1989), for example, bluntly displayed working people's frustrations with an established union of autoworkers that had ceased to work for them. Flint workers at General Motors complained to Moore's camera about a United Automobile Workers union that operated too much as an extension of management, far removed from workers' everyday problems in an industrial community that was abruptly (and precipitously) descending into hard times. Here was a union that was no longer the vital backbone of the Congress of Industrial Organizations (CIO), as it had been during the "sit-down fever" years of the Great Depression.[4]

The intersections of smoking politics and union politics, however, illustrate a more complex narrative of union engagement with rank-and-file members. Even as labor unions confronted declining overall numbers and diminishing strength in the 1970s, 1980s, and 1990s, unions were often engaged at the local level with those employers who were expanding their abilities to institute updated (and sometimes unwanted) work rules, such as new restrictions on tobacco use. Also, local unions repeatedly battled with employers who seemed to be selectively using public health concerns (such as smoking indoors) to cast aside the procedural mechanisms of collective bargaining and formal grievances, the democratic checks and balances that the labor movement brought to unionized workplaces. Union leaders and shop stewards employed an "all politics is local" practice of their own as they tried to maintain as much control as possible over shop floor privileges (including workers' ability to smoke), sometimes struggling to juggle the contradictory demands of smoking and nonsmoking memberships. The labor movement can be seen fighting for smokers and sometimes for nonsmokers at the end of the twentieth century, a pattern that reflected local unions' efforts to respond to the pressures put on them from below.

Unions regularly supported smokers, as they increasingly had to worry about how to preserve workers' on-the-job privileges, and smokers' problems in the workplace seemed to warn of unions' diminishing power. For instance, representatives of organized labor boycotted a 1979 conference at Rutgers University on the subject of smoking at work that was convened by the American Lung Association and the Cooperative Extension Service of Rutgers; in response to the event's no-smoking politics, an estimated one hundred union members in attendance flicked on cigarette lighters during one session to show their continued support for smoking privileges in the workplace. The nonsmoking advocate and veteran of workplace smoking battles, Donna M. Shimp, who successfully sued New Jersey Bell in 1976, attended the Rutgers conference and was annoyed by what she thought was irresponsible union opposition to nonsmokers' demand for cleaner air. "No one has the right to make me sick," Shimp, herself a member of the Communication Workers of America, told the *Newark Star-Ledger*.[5] This was a new era of debate in the unionized workplace. Both smokers and nonsmokers hoped to influence smoking politics within the labor movement; some wanted labor to stalwartly defend working-class claims to shop floor traditions (as smokers did), or decisively break away from harmful habits to establish safer environments.

In the mid-1980s, several national leaders in the labor movement responded collectively to what they perceived to be gratuitous government attention to smoking at work, as the federal government seemed to condemn workers' smoking habits but let the larger issue of managers' neglect of workplace air quality alone. The catalyst was C. Everett Koop's *The Health Consequences of Involuntary Smoking: A Report of the Surgeon General* (1986), where the surgeon general suggested that tobacco smoke constituted the most urgent and dangerous contaminant of workers' surroundings, as it was clearly linked to the development of lung cancer and other illnesses among those exposed to mainstream and sidestream smoke.[6] Several union presidents—Patrick J. Campbell (United Brotherhood of Carpenters and Joiners of America), James L. Walker (International Brotherhood of Firemen and Oilers), Edward J. Carlough (Sheet Metal Workers International Association), John DeConcini (Bakery, Confectionery and Tobacco Workers International Union), and William W. Winpisinger (International Association of Machinists and Aerospace Workers)—crafted a long letter that criticized Koop for shifting the responsibility for clean air on the job to workers themselves (especially smokers whose habit sullied indoor environments). Because of the supposedly "political" focus of the Koop report, the authors argued that the surgeon general let employers off the hook for environmental conditions in workplaces. These leaders of labor insisted that scrutiny needed to be shifted from the single issue of smoking to the broader problem of historically poor ventilation in many workplaces, a responsibility, they insisted, employers had long neglected. The war on tobacco smoke, they argued, distracted everyone concerned from the real battle to be fought over the need for re-engineered indoor workspaces that featured better ventilation, which would not only remove smoke but other airborne toxins as well. This cohort of labor leaders did not want to see tobacco smoke privileged as a workplace contaminant, thereby taking away from concerns about other serious on-the-job contaminants such as asbestos.[7]

The leadership of the AFL-CIO worried that any move by the state against workplace smoking privileges was a threat to organized labor as a whole. Looking at the pressures put on smokers from above, the labor movement worried that state intervention in smoking controversies would overturn the role of union-management collective bargaining in determining the rules that governed unionized workplaces. As a result, organized labor repeatedly insisted that unions and management would have to decide these issues, not state, local, or federal governments, however well-intentioned they may be. "Unions are faced with legislation or unilaterally imposed employer policies that forbid smoking on the job and infringe on the rights of workers who smoke," AFL-CIO officials explained in 1986. "The AFL-CIO believes that issues related to smoking on the job can best be worked out voluntarily in individual workplaces between labor and management in a manner that protects the interests and rights of all workers and not by legislative mandate."[8] Labor leaders were determined not to throw smokers under the oncoming bus of employers' smoking bans, as their fate seemed to foreshadow the demise of organized labor's clout.

Preserving unions' relevance through the maintenance of collective bargaining and disapproval of state interference in the determination of work rules remained signposts of the labor movement's overall stand toward smoking. By the early 1990s, representatives of the AFL-CIO continued to invoke the wording of the 1986 joint union statements on tobacco use, dusting off the decades-old rhetoric of American Federation of Labor president Samuel Gompers and emphasizing that the state's "legislative mandate" solution to smoking issues negated workers' and unions' historic abilities to "voluntarily" shape work rules through negotiations with employers.[9] Sometimes, major unions such as the United Automobile Workers supported workers' demands for rule-protected smoking privileges with more than words, even as permission to smoke at work ebbed to all-time lows at the turn of the twenty-first century. In 2008, the UAW and production workers at Caterpillar in Illinois challenged in court management's decision to ban smoking at its manufacturing facilities, citing management's violation of the collectively bargained labor contract. At the same time, however, the union did not fight only for smokers. In New Jersey casinos, the UAW called for a ban of smoking (and won) in order to safeguard the health of card dealers and other workers who labored for long hours near gamblers as they idly puffed away on cigarettes, generating extraordinary amounts of secondhand smoke in the process.[10]

Organized labor presided over unionized workers who were sometimes deeply divided over smoking. While polling data in the 1980s and 1990s showed that both nonsmokers and smokers favored smoking limitations in the workplace, there were reports throughout these years of conflicts that brought tobacco use to the fore of shop floor politics.[11] In the 1990s, for example, at the Transcon Lines facility in El Segundo, California, the construction of a new building to replace the old (now classified as nonsmoking) led several smokers to file a grievance against the "new rule." At the same time, nonsmoking members of the local Teamsters union protested the smokers' efforts to keep their smoking privileges, leading the Tobacco Institute to note that "there seems to be some unrest which might eventually foil their [smokers'] efforts." The lobbyists concluded that the smokers' grievance would fail if the Teamsters caved in to the nonsmokers' opposition. The Teamsters represented a local workforce of El Segundo truckers that consisted of competing caucuses of smokers and nonsmokers, divisions now angrily sharpened by management's efforts to reshape Transcon smoking rules. At an unnamed factory in Port Wentworth, Georgia, worker Joe McCullough complained to the tobacco lobby about a single nonsmoker's claims of indoor allergy problems after the local union in the plant negotiated for, and won, the establishment of indoor "designated smoking areas." Now it seemed the hard-won concession that led to protected indoor smoking spaces was in jeopardy, as the company doctor reported to the workers and the union stewards that environmental tobacco smoke was the cause of the nonsmoker's breathing problems. Smokers were up in arms. McCullough wrote to the Tobacco Institute to vent the smokers' frustrations and inquire about information they might somehow use to defend their smoking lounges in the factory. After smokers had secured management's permission to smoke inside, a single nonsmoker's grievance now threatened to ruin the smokers' victory.[12]

Local and national unions, however, often remained very much aligned with smokers throughout much of the postwar period, a result no doubt of the long history of intersections among workers, labor, and tobacco use. As early as the 1960s, re-emerging controversies over smoking in the workplace affirmed local union ties to the workers in the shop. In 1965, roughly one year after the 1964 surgeon general's report, United Rubber Workers Local 721 at the Samsonite Corporation facility in Denver, Colorado, backed a rank-and-file "rebellion" against a ban on smoking that had been extended from areas that handled flammable materials to every area of the factory: shop floors, offices, visitors' areas, waiting rooms, cafeterias, bathrooms, everywhere on the grounds. The president of Local 721, Charles Griffin, called the expansion of the no-smoking rule "unfair, unjust, and discriminatory." Faced with a now-allied and animated union and rank and file, management hastily revoked the expanded smoking ban.[13]

Samsonite was a dramatic case, but the politics of smoking in workplaces gave rise to similar examples of union and smoker solidarity. Workers' letters sent to the Tobacco Institute in the early 1990s, for instance, indicated that worker-smokers and union representatives sometimes intended to work together inside union shops to challenge employers who instituted new smoking prohibitions. When management tried to impose these rules, smokers often responded by insisting that any changes would have to be handled within the mechanism of collective bargaining. Here, the framework of bureaucratic unionism could add strength to worker self-activity by forcing management to negotiate new rules.[14]

Smokers in union shops often filed grievances as a way to wed their concerns about rule changes to union politics. At the United Airlines operation center in San Francisco, for instance, several smokers pursued a grievance when their supervisor instituted his own ban on smoking. Other workers at the airline facility, however, could continue to smoke, as the new rule did not apply to them. Workers claimed that personal animus fueled the supervisor's private war on smoking, as he was "an anti-smoker now," a supposedly hardcore, intolerant militant who allegedly targeted for banishment the smokers in his charge. In this unionized workplace, the group of smokers at United Airlines went to their union, hoping to undo the supervisor's use of his position to institute a significant change in the rules. Workers claimed that smoking privileges were to be contractually determined on a company-wide basis.[15]

Monthly union meetings provided regular occasions where workers and shop stewards could discuss and plan responses to new smoking policies that were planned or had been implemented from above without consulting workers' bargaining representatives. Paul Hays, who worked for an unnamed employer in Mt. Vernon, Ohio, wrote to the Tobacco Institute to request information about how to best formulate a response to the "just implemented" indoor smoking ban. Now smokers had to venture outside, a new rule that apparently angered much of the rank and file. "We are having a union meeting," Hays noted, "and we would like to have some information." At the upcoming meeting, the membership intended to hold a strategy session on how to challenge the ban. Hays' consistent use of the pronoun "we" in his note to the Tobacco Institute suggests that he was part of a cohort of smokers in the shop and that smokers' privileges (or the lack thereof) was legitimate union business.[16]

Workers' identities as smokers or nonsmokers—and their own experiences with the issue in relation to union actions—influenced their feelings about the union organizations that represented them. Depending on the contexts of local disputes, smoking could either enhance the engagement among local unions and the rank and file or create considerable division.

The background of the Donna M. Shimp lawsuit of the mid-1970s highlights the schisms and tensions created by the issue of smoking in the workplace and the union hall during the late twentieth century. A nonsmoker with painful respiratory and eye reactions to environmental tobacco smoke, Shimp tried to lobby her long-time employer, New Jersey Bell, her coworkers, and the local union, the Communication Workers of America (CWA), for help in clearing the air of the permanent haze of smoke. As Shimp testified in court, the majority of Bell workers at the New Jersey office smoked on the job, making the air thick with smoke.

Coworkers decried her demand that fans be turned on because they lowered the temperature inside the offices. At the same time, managers and the union had no desire to cause a conflict with the smoking working-class majority at New Jersey Bell. By 1976, Donna Shimp had been suspended from work, as it was the only way, management claimed, to safeguard her health.[17] During the mid-1970s, Shimp's enduring struggles with CWA Local 1021 leaders were overlooked in press coverage of her 1976 lawsuit that forced New Jersey Bell to prohibit cigarette smoking indoors.

As Donna Shimp struggled to reconcile her disdain for smoking at work with her hope of resuming her career at New Jersey Bell, she filed numerous grievances with her CWA local union. Herself a steward during the 1960s, she understood that the mechanisms of grievance were supposed to provide a legitimate pathway to redress in the face of managerial inaction. The union, however, viewed Shimp as a bothersome troublemaker who rocked a boat whose occupants were entirely content to drift on the issue of smoking. Throughout the early 1970s, Shimp filed grievances related to a demotion, a transfer, and a suspension, the ban of smoking in the Bell offices, and the need for functioning ventilation in company workspaces. All her grievances were denied by the local union leadership, whose members agreed with the company that "major employee unrest in these difficult economic times" would result if any union action were taken in opposition to workers' smoking privileges. Shimp was subjected to protracted bureaucratic delays and harassment as she filed repeated grievances with the union.[18] For instance, Local 1021 president Warren Pangburn purportedly smoked a cigarette in front of Shimp during a meeting about a grievance despite Shimp's request that he refrain from lighting up. Feeling slighted by both the Local 1021 leadership and the management of New Jersey Bell, she even lodged a complaint with the National Labor Relations Board, only to be told that nothing could be done unless deliberate "malice" could be proved.[19]

Donna Shimp nonetheless remained active and continued to press the union to do something. As she tried to push for change through grievance channels, the CWA stymied Shimp's hope that a ban on smoking could be added to the list of issues to be collectively bargained between the union and the company. Her energy from below, from the smoke-stained rank and file, ran headlong into a union bureaucracy that functioned as a "professional organization," in the words of CWA member Joseph Beirne. As the Shimp case showed, the CWA (among other major unions of the 1970s) occupied itself with "rational interests" to be "hashed out" at the bargaining table.[20] Smoking, however, would not become part of the bread-and-butter wages and benefits conversations that underpinned the episodic contract talks between management and the union leadership at Bell. Shimp creatively tried to enlist the established mechanisms of bureaucracy on her own behalf, but the local union and national leadership blocked her efforts. After approaching her local, only to be bluntly rebuffed, she contacted the national union directly. But John Carroll, the executive assistant to CWA president Glenn Watts, told her that the "union's position" was to "favor the right of the employee to smoke wherever and whenever they wanted."[21] The Communication Workers of America would not align themselves with one nonsmoker, especially since it seemed that the majority at New Jersey Bell wanted very much to carry on with their tradition of smoking in the office. In this era of deepening recession and growing union reticence, it makes sense that the CWA tried to avoid confrontations that would interdict the entrenched shop floor culture of smoking at New Jersey Bell and arouse the ire of worker-smokers.[22]

It would be wrong, however, to conclude that labor unions of the late twentieth century only sided with those members who smoked. Throughout the 1970s through the 1990s, organized flight attendants, for example, worked extensively to limit in-flight workers' exposure to the smoke-saturated airspaces that predominated on commercial flights. Speaking for all flight attendants in the industry, Margaret Brennan of the Joint Council of Flight Attendant Unions and vice president of the Independent Union of Flight Attendants (IUFA) noted in a 1985 hearing how the toxic airspaces on commercial flights (fueled by cigarette smoke, cleaning chemical residues, and poor ventilation) caused a laundry list of occupational illnesses, from colds to coughing up blood ("blood in the throat"). The lobbying of flight attendants' unions helped to bring about the end of smoking on all US flights in 1990, after workers' testimonies, union leaders' statements, passengers' complaints, and medical researchers' investigations made clear the damage done by environmental tobacco smoke to the health of in-flight workers and passengers. In the busy flight paths over the United States, organized labor actively tried to safeguard the health of nonsmoking workers (and worker-smokers themselves) by prohibiting smoking in the close spaces and still air of the airplanes where they labored day after day for many years.[23] Unions helped to make the friendly skies friendlier (and safer) by improving the air quality on board. The same can be said of union actions in New York City, where consumers' and workers' support for city-wide smoking restrictions in restaurants and other public places where service workers toiled, and organized labor's endorsement of cigarette taxes, hastened the legal ouster of secondhand smoke as a significant occupational hazard for restaurant workers in 2001. Tobacco Institute campaigns that lambasted the New York City cigarette tax as a form of economic discrimination against working people failed when influential union leader and Democrat Dennis Rivera of 1199SEIU (a union of health care workers in New York) announced his support for the new tax on cigarettes, a product still very much coveted by New York smokers.[24]

On rare occasions, smokers complained about alienation from unions that seemed to be dominated by nonsmoking members. Unionized college faculty members of the early 1990s voiced these apprehensions. Smoker-professor Robert Storch of Lock Haven University lamented the impending arrival of a smoking ban on the campus and how the faculty union did not represent his and other smokers' concerns since "most of them are nonsmokers." As he contemplated how best to begin on-campus opposition to the ban, he dismissed the faculty union as a vehicle for organizing concerned academic workers. More than sixteen years later, he was still battling his campus's ban on smoking on the grounds. "I find it ridiculous," he said in 2008, when all fourteen state campuses in Pennsylvania banned smoking indoors *and* outdoors to comply with the Clean Indoor Air Act. "You feel like a leper. It's very demeaning." But this time the union of faculty members, APSCUF (Association of Pennsylvania State College and University Faculties), was unmistakably vocal in its opposition to the smoking ban. Kevin Kodish, the union spokesman, told the *Pittsburgh Post-Gazette* that the state of Pennsylvania needed to negotiate the implementation of any smoking restrictions since they were major revisions to work conditions.[25]

Nonunionized workers sometimes voiced frustrations that they were without any union to represent them and their concerns about smoking rules, especially since open-shop employers could so swiftly introduce new and powerful rules that prohibited smoking. Unionized workers, on the other hand, had some formal mechanisms for responding to grievances. Smoker Peter Lewandowski, an office staffer at a General Motors plant in Michigan, complained to the Tobacco Institute that the top brass in the company were systematically winnowing tobacco smoke out of the entire campus, instituting "several stages of non-smoking actions" that left only one smoking lounge intact. As Lewandowski anxiously watched the lit cigarettes fade from view in his work area, he knew that further changes were soon to come. While unionized workers might be able to somehow limit the GM offensive against smoking in the next contract negotiation, Lewandowski saw no bureaucratic means for unorganized white-collar executives to press for a halt to the advance of no-smoking rules. "I'm not a union member," he complained in his letter. "What can I do?" Lewandowski remarked, "I've worked here for 28 years and now they won't let me smoke." A UAW member might have a reason to hope; others saw no cause for optimism.[26] At the same time, the executive tier at the GM Tech Center campus in Warren, Michigan, instituted a smoking ban in their office buildings. There, too, executives complained that a lack of unionization guaranteed their powerlessness in the face of management's decisions. While the members of the United Automobile Workers could hope to shape work conditions and rules through collective bargaining arrangements, even in this era of UAW concession bargaining, nonunionized white-collar staffers could only let themselves be pushed in the new directions imposed by management.[27]

Whether they themselves smoked or not, shop officials often felt obligated to fight for smokers. "I think they are thinking of changing their policy," said a United Electrical Workers committeeman at a General Electric facility in New Jersey, "and I want to be ready." Union representatives disliked the speediness they observed in these newest examples of managerial policy making. Non-smoker Dale Haught, who represented workers in the local union at the Champion Sparkplug factory in Toledo, Ohio, learned in 1991 that the new ownership of the company was soon to make the workplace completely smoke-free after thirty-eight years of allowing smoking indoors. He could not quietly accept this since managers had announced the new policy without any consultation with the union. "I am looking at the different avenues that I can take to fight this on the local level," Haught pointed out, "but this is a corp. policy." This would be a difficult fight since the Champion Sparkplug firm was now owned by Cooper Industries, Inc. in Houston, Texas. If the new owners in Houston would abruptly change long-standing rules, then what else would they alter? Dale Haught intended to formulate the strongest possible response to management's actions that seemed to test the union's strength. Elsewhere, union representatives spoke of their intent to "fight" smoking bans since the issue seemed to both ignite and encapsulate new struggles over who ruled in the workplace.[28]

Some letters to the Tobacco Institute explained smokers' frustrations that local union leadership claimed helplessness in the face of new smoking restrictions. When managers upended indoor smoking rules, working men and women expected the union to respond with a seriousness that matched their own. "We've gone to the union," Josephine Fidda wrote after her employer, Bell Telephone, insisted that smokers would have to leave the building to smoke, but the local union leadership "say they can't help us." She and others approached the company on their own, only to be told that smoking bans kept insurance costs down. "Is there anything we can do?" The representatives of organized labor stayed out of the fray.[29] As the union bowed out, smokers took up grievances on their own. Maurice Edwards and other smokers in a Norwalk, Ohio, workplace would not give up the hope of having one of the break rooms made into a smoking area after the union effort was rebuffed by management. Continuing the struggle, Edwards contacted the Tobacco Institute for advice about how to win a fight the union had quietly lost.[30]

The powerful rationale of ensuring public health and workplace safety through the creation of smoke-free airspace, however, continued to propel anti-smoking measures. Smokers brought grievances to unions, but smoking bans enjoyed considerable support among many workers, employers, and the public.

Employers found they could clear the air, as cigarette smoke was wisely condemned as an unpleasant and deadly pollutant. Workplace smokers of the 1980s and 1990s could only shout at the winds of change. In 1986, 45 percent of working adults worked for employers with some form of smoking restrictions, but only 3 percent worked in a smoke-free workplace. A decade later, 86 percent of these adults worked for employers with some form of limitation on smoking, while 63 percent worked in smoke-free environments. In 1999, 70 percent of all indoor workers in the United States worked in a smoke-free workplace, a sizeable increase from 46 percent in 1993.[31] Even as some local unions gave help to smokers on the front lines of antismoking politics, employers' no-smoking measures steadily advanced.

"Big Brother": Reactions to the 1987 USG Acoustical Products Smoking Ban

The total ban of worker smoking at the Chicago-based USG Acoustical Products company, which mandated that factory employees quit smoking entirely, provoked an unusually broad conversation in the press about the extent to which employers could prohibit working-class smoking on the job and how far corporate power should reach into working men's and women's daily lives in the workplace and beyond. Workers' and commentators' discussions of the 1987 USG smoking ban tellingly highlighted how many workers' views militated against collective action, organization, and unionization. Despite the worrisome sign that companies of the late twentieth century could do much to reshape the supposedly individual choices and private lives of workers, the extensive body of rants from the bottom-up about a mythic "Big Brother" and dwindling personal "rights" pointed to the symbolic importance of *the individual*—in the personal, private, and solitary spaces of the home, bedroom, car, etc.—as the basic lens through which many working men and women responded to smoking bans. For the workers in the open-shop operation at USG and even beyond, there were few signs that action would materialize.

The unpopularity of the smoking ban at USG exposed many workers' basic assumptions about their relationships with employers and their work. In particular, the total smoking ban led many workers at USG's factories to insist that a boundary separating private and working lives had been grossly violated. At USG's Cloquet, Minnesota, facility, worker Walt Marotz complained, "They're [USG managers] starting to pry into our personal business now. I'll stop smoking at work, but what I do at home, there's no way they can stop me."[32] Marotz's words shed some light on worker expectations of their employers during this era of declining rates of unionization and the subsequent erosion of worker clout on industrial shop floors. He suggested that workers like him readily accepted employer control of the workplace in exchange for management's respect for the sanctity of worker "personal business" beyond the factory gates. At work, Marotz submitted; at home, he would not. His comment suggests how workers tried to accommodate themselves to the changing landscape of labor's power during the 1970s and 1980s: workers had largely retreated from rulemaking in the shop, conceding the renting of their bodies and hours to employers during their shifts. But the boss's authority was to end when the factory whistle blew at the end of the day. After USG announced the ban, a worker "promptly" pasted a "Sex Is Next" bumper sticker to his car, apparently determined to voice opposition to any employer who would scrutinize other (and even more personal) activities.[33] In addition to USG workers themselves, their friends and acquaintances beyond the factory walls shared their expectation that the reach of the employer must end at the punch clock. Denver Freeman, the owner of a bar near the Gypsum, Ohio, plant, remarked that workers from USG "are really upset." He continued, "I could see, maybe, not smoking in the plant, but you can't make a guy quit smoking at home."[34]

USG worker-smokers' frustration over the ban stemmed not only from their resentment of the company's intrusion into what they imagined was a personal choice on private time, but also from a dislike of USG's pattern of heavy-handed interactions with workers. On the open-shop factory floors at USG, managers assumed that their historically nonunion labor force would quietly submit to policy changes, as suggested by their handling of worker frustrations over the 1987 ban. When workers openly questioned the new policy during conversations with managers, bosses curtly reminded workers that they, not labor, controlled rule making within the company. A worker sarcastically told a USG manager, "Hey, this seems like another place I've heard of called Moscow," after the company imposed the ban on smoking. The boss's reply drew a sharp distinction between managers' power and the powerlessness of the unorganized laborers at USG. "If you think you can find a job there," he said, "go ahead."[35] As reporters trailed "tight-lipped" workers at various USG plants to ask about their opinions, some workers noted that the company had commanded them not to discuss the matter with the press.[36] But as an unnamed USG worker admitted of the smoking ban, "I think it stinks."[37]

The critiques of corporate power raised among workers at USG gave rise to scattered voices of opposition and concern from workers at other plants and offices who viewed their own precarious situations through the prism of events at USG. For instance, a gay man from Macomb, Illinois, worried that if a company could regulate workers' behavior at home through something like a total smoking ban, then what was to prevent an employer from punishing him on the basis of sexual identity? At a private open-shop company such as USG Acoustical Products, where men and women worked at the pleasure of their superiors rather than by union contract or formal agreement, management could terminate a worker's employment without necessarily violating her or his legal rights. "The action by USG Acoustical Products Co," the man wrote to the *Chicago Tribune*, "in attempting to stop its employees from engaging in a legal activity is not unprecedented. Far from it. The specter more frightening than Big Brother hangs every day over the heads of most gay workers. No authority prevents private companies or government agencies from attempting to regulate the personal lives of their gay employees."[38]

The image of George Orwell's "Big Brother," from his novel *1984* (and the major motion picture version of the story, actually released in 1984), provided a key symbolic framework for many workers and other observers to interpret, and ultimately condemn, USG's policy. Orwell's figure of Big Brother embodied the vast power of the twentieth-century totalitarian state to repress and overwhelm human beings. The main character, Winston Smith, who resides in the fictional superstate of "Oceania," despises the constant, stifling, and demanding presence of Big Brother, whose fearsome image stares down at him from posters and "telescreens" throughout Airstrip One (once known as London, England). Winston lives without privacy or pleasure. Big Brother's presence is felt even in his own home as authorities watch him and command him from behind the telescreen in his apartment. He ultimately rebels against this repression, pursuing sexual excitement, closeness, and privacy with a young woman named Julia. In time, he and Julia are discovered, jailed, tortured, and broken by the vengeful power of Big Brother and his agents. Winston survives, but his emotions and innermost thoughts (once his own) now belong to the regime. He "loved Big Brother."[39]

As a result of the total smoking ban, USG Acoustical Products surely appeared to workers and other observers as the archetypal Big Brother: an overreaching, insidious, and powerful institution that demanded total obedience. The editors of the *Chicago Sun-Times* suggested that the ban encapsulated a worrisome trend among twentieth-century institutions, both public and private: their tendency to reach for expansive forms of undemocratic control, even when they claimed to do so for the sake of others' best interests. "This is the kind of benevolent authoritarianism," editors noted, "that people won't tolerate when it is dished out by their government. They should not have to accept it from their employers either." *Sun-Times* editors insisted that USG "paternalism" had no place in the late twentieth century because it threatened to impose on working people a childlike form of dependence. "This kind of company paternalism doesn't work because the grand designers fail to recognize that employees, having all the rights and responsibilities of adults, should and can insist on making decisions about how they live their lives in their own homes."[40] The deployment of Big Brother imagery resonated strongly with the underlying popular assumption that employer power must end at the factory exits. "Cigarette smoke is offensive," the editors of *The Tennessean* conceded, "but so are Big Brother policies concerning private behavior."[41] The editors of a newspaper in Roanoke, Virginia, so close to the heart of piedmont tobacco country, commented, "As a private company, USG Acoustical Products has a right to limit or ban smoking on its property. But its control over its employees ends at the factory gate. It has no right to follow them home and tell them to snuff out their cigarettes." They concluded, "So butt out, Big Brother."[42] An ABC-TV viewer poll registered 89,248 callers who opposed the USG ban; only 17,974 approved.[43]

Even as Orwell's symbolism offered a stern, yet simple way to castigate USG, the prevalence of Big Brother imagery in press critiques of the USG ban actually (and subtly) militated against collective possibilities and identities for workers who resented this bothersome expansion of corporate power into private life. The criticisms of USG's action reinforced the idea that employees' struggles with their bosses were individualized and personal. For instance, a March 1987 cartoon printed in the *Tobacco Observer* publication showed a lone husband and wife smoking in bed while the gigantic, bloodshot eye of Big Brother glares at them through the open window. "First, there was no smoking in the caf. [*sic*]," the man remarks. "Then, smoking was banned at work." He feared, "WHAT NEXT?" Not unlike Winston, the man would have to confront this struggle against corporate Big Brother on his own, in the context of his home. His only ally would be his spouse. By defining the intimate spaces of the home as the key battlegrounds against company authority, Orwell-inspired critiques of USG symbolically walled off frustrated workers from one another and suggested that the public was a space where Big Brother ruled.[44] The deployment of Big Brother as a cultural touchstone in this debate also reinforced the prevailing view among workers that employers rightly held sway over the shop floor in exchange for presumed autonomy of workers elsewhere.

Reagan-era criticisms of the Soviet system throughout the 1980s surely fueled, to a significant degree, the Orwellian rhetoric surrounding opposition to the smoking ban at USG. As president, Ronald Reagan used the White House as a bully pulpit to press for a vigorous defense and assertion of American power and cultural ideals on the contested world stage. After the embarrassing US withdrawal from South Vietnam and the inability to end the 444-day hostage crisis in Iran, worried Americans responded favorably to Reagan's unequivocal condemnations of the political repression found in the "Evil Empire" and his celebrations of American freedom and assertions of US might.[45] Historian Gil Troy argues that Reagan was more than a chief executive; he was a cultural phenomenon. "Reagan's aggressive foreign policy and assertive patriotism," Troy writes, "captured the popular imagination."[46] The cultural and political conversation about the Soviet system during the Reagan years, which drew stark parallels between the professed openness of American life (with its individual liberties and "free" markets) and Soviet totalitarianism (a repressive and closed system looming behind an Iron Curtain) readily lent itself to Americans' views of any suppressive policy as Soviet-styled. During these years, when political leaders and producers of culture taught Americans to fear totalitarian repression as though it were the peak years of the Cold War during the 1950s, it is not surprising that Americans recoiled from institutional intrusion into private life and derisively labeled it "Big Brother."

Reagan-era rhetoric about the sharp contrasts between American freedom and Soviet repression sharpened fears about intrusion from above into supposedly private matters, and it also provided workers and observers with a language of resistance. "USG's action," the *Newport News Press* editorialized, "represents a type of economic tyranny," and the AFL-CIO in Washington State noted of the ban that "the red flag is up."[47] Like the worker previously mentioned, on the shop floors at USG plants, workers labeled the company "Moscow," while another USG worker noted, "Did I wake up this morning in the Soviet Union?"[48] In a letter to the local newspaper, John Snyder of Fort Wayne, Indiana, condemned the USG ban as a frightening form of communist-style repression that coldly betrayed the hard-fought freedoms that defined his understanding of American national identity. "Communism. What is it?" he wrote. "Well, a good place to look for it close to you would be at USG Acoustical Products. Company officials, you have the right to end smoking in your plants and on your property, but you have no right whatsoever to make employees quit smoking at home or anywhere away from work." Snyder suggested that "communism" equaled repression everywhere in the world, whether it was the USSR or USG in the USA. "Yes, I have a knowledge of communism since I am a Vietnam vet," he wrote, "and to me, you are no better than what all the good men and women who have died and shed their blood to prevent that from happening." He continued, "You are trying to slowly bleed freedom from Americans. May I say to all the employees of USG Acoustical Products, if you do not wish to stop smoking when you are away from work, then stand up for your rights. Fight this and any other rule by the company that infringes on your constitutional rights our brothers and sisters have died to give us."[49] During a sidewalk interview for a local paper, a woman from Indiana complained that the USG policy meant "we are in a dictatorship society."[50]

But the boundaries of Reagan's rhetoric, as well as his policies, made no room for workers to view unions as emblems of American freedoms or pathways to improved opportunities on the job or at home. For Reagan, organized labor stood in the way of conservatives' faith in free markets and individual opportunity in the labor market and the economy as a whole. In August 1981, the new president locked out 11,350 PATCO (Professional Air Traffic Controllers Organization) workers for their decision to strike, a decision that netted him a hefty 64 percent approval rating in an NBC News poll. (Even a reported 52 percent of union members nationwide approved.)[51] Reagan sternly punished these workers, who struck against working conditions they claimed were unsafe for fliers, and the president promised there would be no chance for the controllers to rejoin the Federal Aviation Administration (FAA).[52] The Reagan administration viewed unions as anachronistic, a relic of past conflicts that conservatives claimed were now over. When secretary of labor Raymond J. Donovan traveled to Florida in 1983 to confer with leaders of the AFL-CIO at their policy making convention in Bal Harbour, he insisted that organized labor had "a shared interest" with the Reagan White House. "There is no longer the old confrontations of the past," he said, dismissively ignoring the recent PATCO controversy.[53] Donovan's remarks suggest how some Americans of the 1980s saw organized labor not as a way to press for democratic rights in the workplace, but as an unremarkable part of the political establishment; it would be easy to ignore or overlook the labor movement if it was implicitly viewed as indistinct in the American political landscape. At USG Acoustical Products, the widespread Reagan-era rhetoric about freedom did not lead frustrated workers to consider organizing as a way to confront the managerial Big Brother in the shop.

Some union leaders themselves addressed the USG controversy. The lengthiest union indictment of the smoking ban at USG appeared in North Carolina, where Christopher Scott of the North Carolina state AFL-CIO issued a press release that reminded workers that USG's policy embodied the dangers of "employment at will" laws. Under such laws, without contracts behind them, any worker could be fired by their employer without justification.[54] Scott reminded union members, "It is true that a worker could work for 25 years to the total satisfaction of the employer and be fired for some personal habit, as in the case of USG, that has no effect on the work. USG could have just as easily decided to fire any worker who eats meat, owns cats or plays the piano—and could legally get away with it." But union leaders' remarks remained only remarks. "We are outraged by the announcement of the USG Acoustical Products Company that it will fire any of its employees who do not quit smoking—not only on the job, but also at home," Scott continued. "We are outraged because this action represents a corporate imposition of a private morality on working people." He went on to demand that "North Carolina must say no to USG, and all the petty tyrants who would impose their own morality on our working people." However intense the rhetoric, though, any call for organizing (in the shop or elsewhere) or political action remained largely absent from the debate.[55]

The unpopular policies at USG could not significantly bridge the gaps among its workers. For example, nonsmokers at USG plants vocally sympathized with worker-smokers' newfound problems with management's policy making, but these expressions of sympathy failed to significantly bridge the increasingly politicized social and health differences between smokers and nonsmokers that had emerged in the United States during the 1970s and 1980s.[56] The strained relationship between workers and USG managers, now intensified and exposed publicly by the smoking ban controversy, failed to produce any sustained criticism or condemnation of management. Nonsmoker and USG worker Carl Matthews simply called the situation "bad" for smokers. "I can see it in the plant," he noted of the ban, "but not at home," an echo of the growing chorus of fears of a corporate Big Brother that would further intrude into workers' personal lives.[57] Nonsmokers at USG could sympathize with smokers, but they were not pressed by the situation to join forces with their smoking colleagues against managers' grab for power. "I feel sorry for some of these guys who have smoked for 30 years," USG worker and nonsmoker Jude Fitzthum said of some of his coworkers. But he quickly redirected his concerns back to himself: "I'm just thankful I didn't start smoking." In the end, the USG ban did not impact nonsmokers' daily lives in any bothersome way. Their objections, so casually expressed, resonated with a noticeable sense of detachment from the subject of smoking prohibitions. Some USG nonsmokers, however, did offer more pointed indictments of bosses' actions. A woman at USG's Corsicana, Texas, plant near Dallas told reporters that "it ain't nobody's business" if a worker, at USG or elsewhere, chose to smoke on his or her own time away from work.[58] Still, at USG Acoustical Products, nonsmoker disapproval of the total smoking ban never extended beyond the level of a few informal remarks to visiting journalists.

Without recourse, many of the worker-smokers at USG resigned themselves to giving up smoking. Leon Howerd, a long-time smoker and fifty-two-year-old veteran employee, simply told a reporter, "I'll quit." Fortunately, he had "quit before" and thought he could "quit again."[59] But if Howerd's attachment to nicotine waxed and waned throughout his life, he would now have to permanently set aside his cigarettes in order to keep his job. Another USG worker, twenty-one-year-old Jim Dages, coped by adopting the view that the policy offered him a "chance" to quit. He had smoked since he was eleven years old. Only recently hired at USG after a six-month stint without a job, Dages said the steady paycheck was reason "enough to do it." He told a reporter, "I've wanted to quit many times," but, "I'm not going to try to quit cold turkey."[60]

The scope of joblessness during the 1980s surely shaped workers' willing-ness to abandon their smoking habit in order to protect their jobs. When asked, "Would you quit smoking to keep your job?" in a *Chicago Tribune* "photopinion" poll, three of four interviewees reported they would. Kenneth Holmes noted, "Yeah, most definitely. If I were told I had to quit or lose my job, I would quit. There are some things you have to stand up and fight for, but I can't see where cigarettes are one of those things. It's just not worth it." Financial analyst Inge Serpe said, "If I were a smoker and given the alternative to quit or lose my job, I would see that as a really good reason to quit." Retiree Frank Stuart's response to the question suggests how working people were willing to significantly mod-ify personal habits to stay in their jobs after the "Reagan recession" of the early 1980s, when unemployment exceeded 10 percent.[61] "Yes, I would prefer to give up smoking as opposed to giving up my job," he said. "Cigarettes are a hindrance to your health; why wouldn't a person give them up to keep his job? A job is a lot more important than cigarettes."[62]

In the weeks and months that followed the 1987 smoking ban at USG, the number of employers that established their own smoking restrictions continued to increase, leading the press to exclaim, "Smoking Rules Spread Like Wildfire."[63] As journalist Michael Abramowitz of the *Washington Post* reported in Decem-ber, the estimated number of US companies that adopted no-smoking policies increased by 50 percent from 1986 to the end of 1987. These companies' policies, he noted, included prohibitions of smoking in work areas to "outright bans on smoking." He surveyed 623 businesses and found that the number of employers that prohibited smoking in "all open working areas" increased from 41 percent in 1986 to 51 percent by December 1987. Abramowitz noted that 12 percent banned smoking entirely from the grounds.[64] By 1989, 70 to 80 percent of corporations in the United States established (or planned to establish) smoking prohibitions in their workplaces; and thirty-two states and "scores" of cities restricted or banned smoking in 6,800 government buildings.[65]

The USG comprehensive smoking ban was the most dramatic example of employers' burgeoning opposition to smoking in the late twentieth century. Managers at USG went significantly further than their contemporaries, forbid-ding smoking not only on the job but also requiring employees to quit smok-ing altogether, extending the scope of company power far into the daily lives of working men and women. While the company proclaimed that its decision was motivated by workers' health, management wanted to gain greater control over the present and future of the company; it wanted to insulate the firm from any legal liability or financial damages incurred as a result of worker lawsuits. Those who defended USG reiterated then-common knowledge about the health risks of cigarette smoke. In Everett, Washington, where USG operated one of its several factories in the United States, local resident Maria Lopez acknowledged that "the company shows great concern for their [workers'] health." They were acting decisively to prevent cancer, emphysema, and heart disease.[66]

But the expansion of smoking restrictions in 1980s America did not stem only from widespread concerns about healthier air. Workers and even casual observers noted the managerial power politics that facilitated smoking bans in the workplace. As Maria Lopez herself noted of USG's policy that affected so many workers in her hometown, "I call it blackmail." In her view "it . . . shows a lack of concern for the employees' rights. People smoke by choice. People should quit also by their own choice. USG has the right to make a policy that employees may not smoke while on the job, but as soon as that employee punches out, that policy should not apply."[67] The USG controversy illustrates how worker-smokers and even nonsmokers reacted to the changing situations they faced. Amid the erosion of union density, workers expected employers to respect the imagined boundary between the workplace and their personal lives in exchange for cooperation with employer authority. At USG, working people responded with disbelief and dismay. They failed to realize that USG's swift imposition of the smoking ban was facilitated by its open-shop operation and the disorganized powerlessness of working men and women. While smokers and nonsmokers related very differently to tobacco, they both had to confront the reality of declining influence in the workplace that could be seen in new no-smoking policies.

Smoking at Work and the NLRB in the Late Twentieth Century

While tobacco smoke dirtied and poisoned airspaces at work up to the final years of the twentieth century, management's use of no-smoking rules against organized labor and unionized workers added yet another form of toxicity. Employers infused workplaces with stress, frustration, and anger by moving against the privileges of workers in union shops, fostering work environments that endangered freedoms of assembly and speech. Employers' disdain for both smoking and organized labor sometimes overlapped. In 1991 at the Highland Yarn Mills in High Point, North Carolina, for example, members of the management staff regularly eavesdropped on workers' off-the-clock conversations in nonworking areas (especially the smoking lounges) about the need for unionization at the factory, and they inserted themselves into informal gatherings of smokers on break, illegally "trying to make sure that they were not talking union on the job."[68]

By the turn of the twenty-first century, bullied workers and embattled unions reported employers to the federal government with increasing frequency. As noted by management scholar Bruce Barry in *Speechless: The Erosion of Free Speech in the American Workplace* (2007), the volume of federal cases related to workplace discrimination increased by 2,100 percent after 1970, while the overall federal caseload only expanded by 125 percent.[69] In these years and those that followed, there were numerous cases on the National Labor Relations Board's agenda that dealt directly with smoking rules. Working men and women, union representatives, managers, and the NLRB struggled over the extent of employers' ability to determine the power relations of workplace environments.

Labor unions and working men and women, however, only found intermittent redress as a result of the NLRB's investigations in the 1970s through the 1990s. In labor disputes where managerial abuses could be confirmed by convincing testimony, the board and its appointed representatives could most fully enforce the National Labor Relations Act. Even as the board could be counted on to plainly follow (sometimes to a fault) the written rules enshrined in the Wagner Act, it was not always so "conservative" or "anti-union."[70] Under both Republican and Democratic administrations, the NLRB's decisions were still greatly shaped by the evidence that could be gathered rather than by politics or partisanship. As a result of the board's disciplined work, its rulings laid bare numerous employer offensives against the labor movement in the final decades of the twentieth century.

The legitimate and increasingly well-understood public health dimensions of the need to roll back smoking at work surely encouraged some managers to sidestep negotiations with unions over smoking-related rules, as the reality of tobacco's dangers were now common knowledge, even as many smokers remained in denial about the health risks, and the tobacco industry struggled to muddle the warnings of the medical profession and the government.[71] At the Allied-Signal Company in Kansas City, Missouri, for example, management had been working since the late 1980s to institute smoke-free workplaces at its plants and offices, a policy that was to fully take effect in February 1990. They hoped to accomplish this without interference from members of the International Association of Machinists (IAM) that represented nearly 3,200 workers there. Allied managers deployed a new top-down approach to rule making when they instituted the smoking ban, stepping around the established practice of collective bargaining. Now working in secret with a committee of hand-picked workers, management devised its new policy, which included a series of punishments for smokers (called the "smoking ban enforcement policy") who were caught in violation of the new rules; first offenses received written reprimands while the fifth (and final) offenses led to the termination of employment.

The International Association of Machinists and the NLRB complained that managers' handling of the smoking ban created a new aura of secrecy and uncertainty at Allied-Signal and that management had dropped its obligation to negotiate with union representatives over work rules and failed to inform the IAM of the existence of the smoking policy task force. The unionized workers were fuming over the abrupt changes that were afoot in managers' dealings with labor. "We've been able to do it [smoke] for 35 years, and we should continue to do so," machinist Danny Daniels said of the brave new world at Allied-Signal. The National Labor Relations Board ruled against Allied's new unilateralism in 1992, obliging management to submit its policy changes to the IAM for negotiation. Furthermore, as suggested by the board's examinations of managers' actions in its written decision, the NLRB rebuked Allied-Signal for its effort to transform labor relations in ways that curtailed the voice of the union in shop floor governance and kept hidden the workings of policy deliberation.[72] The board ordered Allied-Signal management to post a "Notice to Employees" in its factories and offices that recanted recent anti-union measures:

> The National Labor Relations Board has found that we violated the National Labor Relations Act and has ordered us to post and abide by this notice. WE WILL NOT refuse to bargain collectively with District 71, International Association of Machinists and Aerospace Workers, AFL-CIO as the exclusive representative of our employees, by bypassing it and dealing directly with bargaining unit employees. WE WILL NOT in any like or related manner interfere with, restrain, or coerce you in the exercise of the rights guaranteed you.[73]

The NLRB ruled the same way in other cases related to smoking and collective bargaining after several other employers followed similar courses of action. For instance, Youngstown hospital workers (members of SEIU627) challenged the leadership of Youngstown Hospital Association, Inc. when it bypassed SEIU representatives and implemented a total smoking ban in all of its area facilities. The hospital workers and SEIU627 cried foul as an estimated 25 percent of the YHA workforce were regular smokers. Managers responded to workers' complaints that its policy was "fair and reasonable" and "did not violate the rights of the employees," but the National Labor Relations Board ordered a complete reversal since the company had not bargained with SEIU627 over new work rules and had "unilaterally discontinued an employee privilege." The NLRB ordered YHA to "cease and desist." In posted notices, management had to publicly admit their guilt. "WE WILL notify and bargain collectively with the Union, on request," the notices read, "concerning changes in policy with regard to smoking inside the facilities by unit employees.... WE WILL rescind the April 1, 1990 policy regarding smoking inside the facilities by unit employees, and restore the policy as it existed prior to that date."[74]

As these disputes showed, the NLRB could be a bulwark against unionized employers' attempts to maneuver outside of collective bargaining arrangements by instituting new smoking restrictions. And as a result of the board's strict focus on the law, organized labor could make its most effective responses to anti-union uses of smoking rules. Still, some employers continued to bully unionized workers with new or pre-existing smoking regulations. At Frank Leta Honda, a Bridgetown, Missouri, car dealership with forty-seven employees, an August 1994 wage increase failed to materialize and all but five of the workers struck their employer, leading to retribution from management. As the strike dragged on for several weeks into the autumn, Frank Leta used scab laborers in numerous areas of the operation, including repairs, office work, and sales. When the strike finally ended, Leta instituted what the board called a "stricter no-smoking policy" that was intended to punish the strikers, who were themselves oblivious to the rule change. According to the NLRB, service manager Rick Witges told scab workers at the dealership to be on their best behavior in the coming days because the Frank Leta management intended to "strictly enforce the rules" so much that many of the returning strikers would be fired, punishing those who had walked off the job and rewarding the replacement workers who had assumed their places. The 1996 NLRB ruling on the case, however, ordered Frank Leta and his management team to renounce their "egregious and widespread" actions, which included the use of new smoking rules to punish workers. The NLRB also forbade the use of informants, harassment of auto service department workers for their membership in the International Association of Machinists and Aerospace Workers (IAM), and the institution of several rule changes and new wage rates without the transparency and procedures mandated by the pre-existing collective bargaining process.[75]

Several employers with nonunion operations deployed no-smoking rules to intimidate and oust union organizers and union supporters. In West Virginia at the Mullican Lumber Company, a manufacturer of wood flooring materials, managers fired worker and Teamsters supporter Patrick Garrett in June 1991 for smoking several cigarettes inside the plant near the loading dock, an offense that mandated immediate termination of employment. Garrett, however, was more likely fired for his support for unionization at Mullican Lumber; he was the actual worker who made the initial contacts with the Teamsters Union and helped lead the subsequent unionization effort inside the factory. In May 1991, management learned of the union discussions and announced several new rules soon after, including a harsher indoor tobacco use policy whereby offenses for smoking inside the plant would no longer receive written warnings. Instead, workers caught smoking would be summarily fired. As Garrett smoked on the loading dock inside the plant, he was spotted by a supervisor, who promptly reported the event to plant operations manager Steven Lafon. Garrett was immediately dismissed. Queried by the NLRB, Lafon testified that the dismissal of Patrick Garrett was simply a matter of diligent enforcement of an important rule. "We [management] talked about it and felt that there really was nothing we could do other than to terminate him," Lafon claimed. "We had already had a couple of meetings involving the smoking policy. We felt like if we didn't do something in this case then there was no way we were ever going to have a smoking policy."[76]

Patrick Garrett walked into the damning web of new rules at Mullican Lumber, policies that allowed managers to avoid acknowledging what was probably an effort to get rid of Garrett and hamper the union organizing inside the plant. In its ruling, the NLRB sided with the leadership of the Mullican Lumber Company, who claimed they had not wrongly fired Garrett. He was supposed to have known the harsh penalty for smoking as a result of managers' informational meetings with employees, written policy statements, and posted signs throughout the factory.[77]

As the Patrick Garrett case suggests, working men and women who claimed they were punished by employers for their support of unionization sometimes found it difficult to meet their burden of proof. In the absence of documentable proof or convincing testimony from witnesses, the NLRB tended to uphold employers' claims that they were only enforcing the rules when they punished workers for smoking. Several workers on the front line of a unionization fight at the Howe K. Sipes Company in Memphis, Tennessee, a manufacturer of baseball uniforms and varsity letter jackets, failed to prove managers' possible prejudice against their pro-union sympathies in 1994. Their claims were contradicted by others' testimonies, and they lacked any proof that management acted prejudicially or deliberately against them. Instead, management at the company could claim they acted entirely according to pre-existing employment policies. The NLRB's investigation of incidents at the Sipes firm highlighted a potentially lengthy history of shop floor tensions and conflicts that prevailed among the employees and within the context of labor-management relations. Smoking and unionism were at the heart of the instances uncovered and examined by the NLRB. The International Union of Electronic, Electrical, Salaried, Machine and Furniture Workers (IUE) of the AFL-CIO tried and failed in 1993–1994 to win a contract for the workers at the company. They subsequently lost their support and were decertified by a majority of the workers, but tension-filled memories of the period lingered. Some supporters of the IUE claimed in the months after the September 1994 decertification process that they were the targets of managerial harassment; they found themselves on the receiving end of written warnings and suspensions for actions such as smoking in the plant (a long-standing company policy) and verbal insubordination.

Employee Shirley Jones argued that she wrongly received a written warning from management for smoking in the women's restroom, a punishment, she claimed, that was really for her known support of the union. In March 1994, Jones lit a cigarette in the women's bathroom that was adjacent to the manufacturing room floor. The mostly female workforce had often done this—in violation of company no-smoking rules—as they reportedly wanted the space and time away from the men who supervised them and to quickly smoke during nonbreak times.[78] (Officially, they were only permitted to use the break room for smoking.) On this occasion, busy custodian Karen Ellis raged against Jones' untimely intrusion in the restroom. As the pair argued, the melee brought company owner Howe K. Sipes himself to the scene, where he supposedly told Ellis to "whip her ass" if Shirley Jones ever interrupted her work. In other instances, Sipes reportedly called the smokers "trash."[79]

While Shirley Jones insisted that Sipes' written reprimand for smoking was the result of his anti-union politics, the NLRB disagreed. They dismissed Jones' claim that she had been targeted for pro-union views. Instead, the board concluded that Howe K. Sipes and the management of his company had long been rightly aggrieved by the wide extent of illicit smoking inside the tiled confines of the women's restroom, a claim that was affirmed in numerous sworn testimonies. In fact, the board excused Howe K. Sipes for his harsh language, remarking that his words must be understood within the context of his admitted and genuine anger ("utterly frustrated") toward smokers.[80]

The boss's pursuit of revenge was not always so subtle or ambiguous. In 1987, as the Teamsters stood to win (in a blowout) an upcoming representation election at the Missoula, Montana–based USA McDonald Corporation's manufacturing plant for school and office furniture, the company president, James McDonald, seethed in disbelief that his coveted factory operation was soon to become a union shop. He grumbled and complained openly and often about his angry determination that the "union would not work at [his] facility." If the Teamsters won the representation election in February 1987, he vowed to "make the employees' lives miserable by turning off the heat in the wintertime, turning off the fans in the summertime, and locking the bathrooms." More urgently, he threatened to reduce sales so he could justify firing the employees who voted union; he even said he would "shut the place down."[81] McDonald's gruff talk signaled his determination to hold no quarter with the unionized workers, and his public statements to workers contained within them a plan of action that would violate the Wagner Act, since it was illegal for an employer to dismiss workers for unionism or to shut down an enterprise in order to punish workers for organizing themselves into a union for the purpose of collective bargaining.

When the Teamsters won the election, James McDonald quieted his rhetoric but pursued with deliberateness his plans for settling the score. He summarily laid off fourteen workers and issued a modified employee handbook with new rules that included an indoor smoking ban. At the same time, McDonald refused to bargain with the new union about seasonal layoffs. After its investigation, the NLRB threw the book at McDonald, finding him responsible for making threats (including shutting down the plant) and for illegally firing workers who voted to unionize.[82]

The indoor smoking ban was likely a component of James McDonald's reprisal against workers for their support of the Teamsters. While Jay R. Pollack, the administrative law judge appointed by the NLRB, noted in his written decision that McDonald issued the new handbook with its no-smoking rule only after learning of the election results (he ordered the book retyped) and did not communicate its contents to the new union, it did not rule against the company for these actions. Pollack justified this unusual NLRB reading of events and the provisions of the National Labor Relations Act by saying that in his opinion the no-smoking rule and the handbook changes were not in and of themselves evidence of "changes in established working conditions." "Although there were changes in the new handbook from the old version regarding no smoking, vacation time, and seasonal layoffs," he wrote, the shop floor was not actually altered to any degree significant enough ("change has not been proven") to justify the need to collectively bargain over the new conditions of work. Pollack ordered that the laid-off workers be reinstated with back pay, but the new assortment of rules (smoking ban included) remained in place.[83]

In the late 1970s, however, the board ruled against Nyari Odette, Inc. (a company that ran the Chez Odette restaurant in the tourist destination of New Hope, Pennsylvania) for its own creation of new smoking rules to punish workers who voted for unionization in an NLRB election. After the election, management struck hard at its workforce of dishwashers, waiters, waitresses, bartenders, kitchen staff, and coat check employees. Owner John Nyari posted new rules for all staff. He abolished indoor smoking privileges, required all workers to remain at their designated workstations throughout their shifts, and required the use of hairnets by waitresses. In testimony, the board also heard workers' claims that Nyari snatched beverages out of the hands of thirsty waitresses and forbade workers to loiter in the restaurant at closing or after their shift. Lastly, the staff complained to the NLRB that Nyari's used rude language and dubbed them "lousy" and "sloppy."[84]

Because working conditions became so restrictive so quickly, the workers at Chez Odette walked out on strike in February 1976.[85] The last straw was John Nyari's firing of hostess Charlotte Besson. As Saturday night approached—Valentine's Day, February 14—Nyari told the usual hostess (who had signed a union card earlier) that she need not come to work that night because he expected a small number of customers. (During the off-season months, fewer customers visited the restaurant.) Instead, he moved another worker into her position, William Soriero, whom he personally favored. When Besson stopped by the restaurant with her daughter to see how things were going, she was stunned to see Soriero working. When Besson called John Nyari on the phone to ask what was going on, he told her that he could hire and fire whomever he wanted because it was "my business what I do with my restaurant." Besson protested, but "[w]ell, that's the way it goes."[86] In this case, the Board ruled against the boss, giving credence to consistent testimony from workers, dismissing inconsistent testimony from John Nyari, and seeing a pattern of wrongdoing in the series of events, in particular, Besson's signature on a union card immediately preceding her dismissal.

As the restaurant staff began picketing, John Nyari went into action. He fired thirteen more workers for their participation in the walkout, leaving only a skeleton crew of three. The Chez Odette strikers struggled for weeks to maintain a picket line of at least three persons on the edges of Nyari's parking lot. Nyari continued to keep the restaurant open with apparently whatever workers he could find, and he tried to secure a court injunction against the pickets since, as he claimed, they physically interfered with auto traffic in and out of the lot. The strike quietly paused in May 1976, but its real conclusion did not come until the NLRB's ruling on the case in April 1977. The strikers won their full reinstatement, and the board ruled that John Nyari would have to bargain in good faith with Local 274 and refrain from interfering with union business and punishing the workers who participated in a legal strike.[87] As suggested by the NLRB's written decision, the smoking issue and other new work rules would have to be revisited within the framework of collective bargaining between the unionized employees and management.

These smoking-related NLRB cases of the late twentieth century offer revealing discussions of otherwise unknown anti-union measures by numerous employers, and they also show how the issue of smoking rules in the workplace related to many of those actions. As the end of the century approached and union power continued to dissipate, many working men and women confronted what must have been for them a disquieting mixture of punitive employer actions and arbitrary rule. While the NLRB's consistently legalistic approach to workplace struggles could provide leverage to embattled workers, it could also undercut the ability of the federal government to apply fully the provisions of the Wagner Act. Written policies (such as no-smoking rules) provided a way for some employers to challenge the presence of unions and harass organized labor's supporters, and the application of no-smoking policies also provided managers with a way to hinder outsiders' ability to censure anti-union bullying.

These instances of anti-union bullying help to illuminate some of the lesser-known forms of opposition that organized labor and union supporters faced in late-twentieth-century workplaces. NLRB cases that related to smoking rules, for example, highlighted several unions and many workers who existed daily on the defensive, hoping the board could help them secure parity in labor-management relations. Union supporters often complained of harassment on the job for their politics (and sometimes for smoking). Employers were ready to wield the upper hand in their dealings with labor, apparently feeling empowered in the above instances to test workers, unions, and federal law. While employer opposition to the labor movement was by no means new or somehow more problematic in the 1990s, the cases explored here suggest how the convergence of anti-union politics and antismoking politics enabled the shoving of workers and unions into a defensive position, and sometimes out the door.

"Rights Talk"

Talk about workers' "rights" pervaded the late 1980s debate over the USG ban, fueled by Ronald Reagan's energized Cold War rhetoric about liberty and the history of civil rights struggles in the United States. Frequent references to "rights" during the 1987 USG controversy show the extent to which the civil rights upheavals of the 1950s to the 1970s transformed the language of politics and Americans' political sensibilities.[88] For example, in Chicago, Louverne Crosby reasoned, "What right does an employer have over whether an employee smokes away from the job? Aren't we a free nation? Big businesses, privately owned—it's an infringement upon our civil rights!" Another Chicago resident asked of USG managers, "What happens to their human rights? I believe USG is way out of line on this issue." She concluded, "USG should not be permitted to get away with this unfair practice, not in these United States, now or ever!"[89] When asked about the USG ban, a former three-pack-a-day smoker recalled that "as early as '79" he had "begun to [himself] to be part of a tiny, embattled minority. Indeed, what with gay rights and women's lib in the mainstream, smokers had become the last social group which it was acceptable to despise."[90] This hate of smokers, he believed, now bore its bitter fruit. "Among the personal freedoms enjoyed in this country is the right to be stupid about your health," editors of the *Seattle Times* lamented. "The USG plan is discrimination, no less an affront to the Constitution than denying a person employment because of sex or race or creed."[91]

The conversation among workers, employers, and lobbyists about smokers' claim of a "right" to their vices reached across US society, much further than just the dusty factory floors at USG Acoustical Products. Rather, worker-smokers in multiple settings pressed for the maintenance of smoking privileges as a basic individual "right," insisting again and again that smoking was a matter of personal choice and conscience. At the same time, smokers of the late twentieth century contributed greatly to a culture of "rights talk" that seemed to look past any hope of collective class action in US workplaces, even as workers' "rights talk" over tobacco use was part of an overall pattern of working-class efforts in these years to hold on to vanishing privileges at work. These privileges included not only smoking privileges, but also job security, retirement benefits, health care, overtime pay, and seniority.[92]

While it is important to recognize the presence of class politics in worker-smokers' rights talk, we have to be careful not to overstate its impact or significance. Indeed, discussions of smokers' claims to "rights" should be added to historians' discussions of late-twentieth-century workers and their politics, but worker-smokers' concerns and demands typically flowed from an underlying *personal politics* rather than class politics, from individuals' anger about the disregard of their needs as smokers, not as workers.[93] They voiced a general feeling of persecution that made noise about smoking bans, but these complaints could not really engage the framework of social class that so enabled antismoking measures. "Hell, this is America," growled one angry smoker in 1985 who "snapped" at a questioning *Los Angeles Times* reporter. "Smokers have a right to live the way they want, don't they?"[94]

Political scientists and historians have often voiced their frustrations with "rights talk" in US political discourse, even as some scholars want to highlight its potential as a medium for talking about and for pressing for progressive social change. This ambivalence stems from some scholars' discomfort with the divisiveness of interest group politics and the history of conservatives' use of rights talk (e.g., property owners' rights, complaints of declining white male privilege) in their reactionary "backlash" against the race and gender changes in the 1950s to the 1970s. Probably the most critical discussion of "rights talk" appears in Mary Ann Glendon's *Rights Talk: The Impoverishment of Political Discourse* (1991), which argues that the frequent invocation of "rights" has debased and lowered US political discourse to a level where selfishness, discord, and inaction are the norm. Glendon claims that "rights talk" is "simplistic" and often an "intemperate rhetoric of liberty" that "corrodes" the need for a politics of action and change; at the same time, it "[trivializes] core democratic values."[95] The endless fragmentation into competing claims, she continues, subsequently undermines consensus building as the basis for political action. Infrequently, some scholars offer cautiously optimistic readings of "rights talk" in twentieth-century America. In his book *This Is Not Civil Rights: Discovering Rights Talk in 1939 America* (2012), political scientist George I. Lovell discovers that Americans' letters to elected officials in the late 1930s and early 1940s yielded evidence of a deeply engaged "rights talk" among everyday men and women. He found a voluminous archive of political talk that oftentimes laid out progressive goals and moral visions of a more just society. As Lovell puts it, "People deploy legal discourses not to succumb to the legal order expressed as formal law, but to express aspirations for a better legal order."[96] Rights talk, then, is an expression of hope.

To be sure, "rights talk" provided a language of resistance to embattled and embittered smokers in US offices and factories, but it was very limited *and limiting* at the same time. "Rights talk" segmented worker-smokers' politics within a niche of American political discourse that overlooked the labor movement as a vehicle for change and the possibilities for significant collective action rooted in the workplace. While "rights talk" mattered as a medium for smokers' opposition to changing work rules, it was a discourse that would never encompass more than the voicing of angst. As political scientist Jeffrey R. Dudas writes, "Rights talk is an open-textured language form that offers strategic and psychic resources," and that "all of sorts of interests . . . can be convincingly depicted as a function of one's rights."[97] This language of resistance, this "open-textured language," however, proved to be exclusive of others within the working class. "Rights talk" could not inclusively frame smokers' problems as *working-class problems*, as evidence, for instance, of employers' abilities to overturn and throw away shop floor privileges. As worker Leah R. Ware tellingly (and selfishly) wrote in 1989, "Would you please send me whatever information you have regarding MY RIGHTS as a smoker."[98]

In their own versions of "rights talk," smokers voiced self-interested resentments toward the tightening grip of employer power and its intersections with public health concerns. Their statements, however, were not so much a "backlash" against nonsmokers' demands, but rather deliberately and carefully worded efforts to somehow situate notions of individual rights as barriers to employer policies and affirmations of embattled identities as smokers in the workplace. Working-class smokers first demanded rights over their bodies and then permissible spaces and times for smoking. Despite their often heated language, they presumed that their demands were humble and reasonable. "Don't we have rights, too?" demanded the typical smoker; other tobacco users pondered how smokers could "understand, respect and accept the rights of others" but complained about "what has happened" to smokers' "rights." One worker spoke with style and urgency when he said, "We need help in combating this menace to our freedom." The Tobacco Institute's telephone lines and answering services proved to be key venues where worker-smokers voiced their "rights talk." Busy phone operators left tersely worded notes for lobbyists that catalogued smokers' struggles to connect with those who they believed could provide the means with which to fight workplace smoking bans: "Message: questions. Re: company smoking policies and his rights. Please call."[99] Working-class smokers insisted that the legal, historical, and moral domain of "rights" would protect and restore their privileges when finally recognized by management in the workplace.

Even as much of the talk about smokers' "rights" flowed directly from the pens and phones of the late-twentieth-century working class, it certainly flourished as a result of the tobacco lobby's efforts to maintain the addictive bonds between cigarette manufacturers and customers. Like workers themselves, the Tobacco Institute situated workplace debates about smoking on the high moral and historical plane of individual rights, but it included in its philosophy the conservative laissez-faire principle that individuals (rather than the state) should solve their own problems as they arose in workplaces. The Tobacco Institute's literature, for example, encouraged worker-smokers themselves to insist upon smoking as a "right" (even though there were no legal underpinnings for such claims). They actually urged worker-smokers to *create* the "right" to smoke by seeking out informal negotiations with supervisors and coworkers to create gentlemen's agreements that would satisfy all parties. In these conversations, smokers would ideally fashion compromises and solutions that would safeguard the ability to smoke. The Tobacco Institute urgently wanted smoking disputes to remain local problems that were worked out in private. This approach to "smokers' rights" would, lobbyists hoped, undercut public support for any sweeping antismoking, antitobacco measures from local, state, or federal governments. "They [antismoking ordinances and laws] take the issue of workplace smoking out of the hands of employers and employees and force action which, most often, is unnecessary and divisive," complained the authors of the Tobacco Institute's pamphlet *Smoking in the Workplace: Some Considerations* (1991). "These intrusive laws assume that workers and management are incapable of identifying problems and working out their own solutions."[100] Big Brother, stay out.

As worker-smokers and lobbyists grumbled about the demise of smoking privileges, employers were not averse to insisting upon claims of their own "rights" to determine whether or not smoking would be permitted in the workplaces they owned and operated. A 1991 survey of Southern California employers by the Orange County Chamber of Commerce yielded several pages of comments from employers who believed that local lawmakers' pressures on them to ban smoking violated their rights as business owners. They claimed that they should determine all workplace rules and regulations in all circumstances without any outside interference from state or local government. One manager (among several) insisted that the issue "should remain the province of the private sector," while another noted that "we don't feel it is the business of any government agency to tell us, especially in private industry, what we can or can't do as far as smoking goes or anything else in one's private life!!!"[101] On the first page of the Orange County report, a local employer remarked, "I feel this is in violation of my rights as a citizen and a small business owner." State interference on the issue of smoking, he suggested, impinged not only on his individual citizenship rights (as he imagined), but also on his status as an employer and stakeholder in the business community, a claim, he suggested, that counted as a kind of super-citizenship. He surely could count on the "right" to wield power and authority within his own enterprise because of his high social standing that rested upon his claims to Americanness and his class position as a business owner and employer.[102]

Late-twentieth-century employers' references to "rights talk" were the most likely to frame smokers' rights issues within the context of post–World War II conservative beliefs that freedom flowed from the convergence of the supposed mobility and opportunity that the capitalist system provided and the supposedly hands-off inaction of government that safeguarded employers' exercise of their liberty, a set of principles widely embraced by Southern Californians during these years.[103] The Orange County survey results highlight this very clearly. As one employer put it,

> We believe in FREEDOM! We make the rules in our workplaces, independent of any *artificial* rules by some misdirected government body. We are in business at the pleasure of the people in our area of interest and those people that voluntarily approve our standards join us. We will work diligently to place people in office that believe the BEST GOVERNMENT governs LEAST! Or the BEST GOVERNMENT provides for *maximum* individual *freedom*!

These employers imagined a rigid dividing line between their domains in the private sector and the power of the state. As one business owner put it, "I don't have the time or the inclination to involve myself or my company in the personal affairs of my employees. No governmental agency will ever enforce such laws in my business." Another wove in a rebuke of the Chamber of Commerce in a denunciation of state action within the workplaces of the private sector. "It is none of the government's concern how I run this aspect of my business," a respondent complained. "The Chamber of Commerce should oppose all measures to impose a smoking policy in private offices, rather than becoming a party to this gross intrusion of governmental power." Still another said, "I will not be regulated any more!"[104]

The Orange County survey results, however, highlighted dissenters within the ranks of local employers. Some business owners preferred action on the part of the state that would effectively take over the responsibility of addressing and solving the debates about smoking. This would allow employers to avoid stepping into the middle of the debate by instituting new workplace smoking rules that some workers might vocally criticize. "'No smoking' is one area government *may* be necessary," a respondent cautiously answered. Some employers believed that "voluntary" actions to clear workplace airspaces of smoking would never accomplish their goal, since they would only be inconsistently applied and not rigorously enforced. "The County *MUST* adopt smoking regulations for all business as well," a respondent wrote. "Voluntary regulation will not work." Others told the Chamber of Commerce that they intended to cooperate with local laws about smoking indoors, as they anticipated cooperative attitudes among the nonsmoking majorities and the cohorts of hold-out smokers in their employ. "The few smokers that are employed by this Corporation are cognizant of the many non-smokers in the workplace and respect their non-smoking attitude," wrote one of the calmer respondents. "Should a smoking ordinance be adopted in Orange County, we would comply with such an ordinance."[105] The nonsmoking dictates of Big Brother did not terrify every employer in the business-friendly environs of Orange County capitalism.

Smokers' "rights talk" stemmed from sources above and below, from workers, lobbyists, and employers. Despite its importance to many tobacco users, "smokers' rights" discourse was perceptibly limiting. Cigarettes divided workers, and smokers' "rights talk" offered nothing more than a perpetuation of these smoky fissures in working-class life. This discourse could not usually engage the underlying class power that made possible employers' antismoking measures.

Fights over smoking at work were a losing issue for organized labor in the 1970s, 1980s, and 1990s. Unions never overturned the divisiveness of tobacco use among workers, nor were they able to parlay the politics of energized smokers or nonsmokers into more inclusive efforts for change. At the same time, struggles over smoking in union shops remained for all intents and purposes localized struggles that played out in discrete contexts: shop floor confrontations, NLRB hearings, grievance procedures, and collective bargaining deliberations. Despite many workers' passionate feelings about smoking, despite the shrill talk of "rights," the politics of smoking in the late twentieth century failed to check employers' moves against smoking and against workers' privileges on the shop floor.

QUITTING SMOKING AND THE ENDURANCE OF NICOTINE

If you have tried to quit smoking and failed before, take comfort in the fact that most smokers fail several times before quitting successfully. Your past failures are not a lesson that you are unable to quit. Instead, view them as part of the normal journey toward becoming a nonsmoker.

—Foundation for a Smokefree America

"It has become so difficult for me to breathe that I must quit smoking," wrote John Fred Cirillo in a 1998 letter he sent to the Brown & Williamson Tobacco Corporation, Lorillard Tobacco Corporation, Phillip Morris Tobacco Company, and R. J. Reynolds Tobacco Company. He vowed to retaliate for the ruinous addiction to nicotine that overshadowed his adult life and wrecked his health. Giving up this deadly habit, he argued, meant taking on painful withdrawals, what he called "the tortures of the damned." In his earlier years, the "tortures" of withdrawal ruined several attempts to give up smoking. "I know what it is like to quit smoking," he insisted, "and it is sheer hell." Claiming "emotional distress" as a result of the drug pushing of tobacco companies to their customers, which left him hopelessly addicted and guaranteed the misery of withdrawal if he tried to quit, he threatened to sue in court unless the tobacco companies agreed to "settle." He attached a Texas statute that allowed for damages to be paid to claimants if they could prove "mental suffering" and "mental anguish" caused by the deliberate and knowing actions of a "willful" party or "wrongdoer." According to Cirillo, the tobacco industry had nurtured his addiction to nicotine and was ultimately responsible for the acute psychological suffering it caused, and he would need "the money for diversions to lessen the pain of withdrawal."[1]

Even as tobacco users such as John Fred Cirillo struggled to quit smoking for good, simply *trying* to quit would yield improvements to health. While the brain of the addicted smoker demands regular infusions of nicotine to prevent withdrawal, the smoker's blood pressure and pulse will return to normal only twenty minutes after the last cigarette. After another twenty-four hours, the smoker's likelihood of heart attack already begins to recede; after forty-eight hours, damaged nerve endings start to heal and the ability to smell and taste improves. At the seventy-two-hour mark, the ex-smoker's bronchial tubes begin to relax and lung capacity expands. Over the next two weeks to three months, the ex-smoker's circulation improves. At this point, lung function will rebound by 30 percent. By the ninth month, cilia in the lungs begin to heal. At the same time, ex-smokers will notice the decreased incidence of sinus infections, shortness of breath, and coughing. By the end of the first year, the ex-smoker's risk of dying from a heart attack or stroke declines by 50 percent. Quitting over the long-term offers the most health benefits, but quitting for even a short period is healthy and beneficial, especially if early attempts lead to long-term success later.[2] As television public service announcements in the 1980s and 1990s advised, "If you do smoke, quit. And don't quit quitting."

While 68 percent of smokers want to quit, only about half will succeed.[3] John Fred Cirillo failed before and worried that he was destined to fail again. Despite the development of behavioral and pharmaceutical assistance to help smokers give up their addictions to cigarettes, the transition from dependence to a smoke-free lifestyle can be, at least for some, "sheer hell."

Nicotine endures. Not only do many smokers struggle to permanently end their need for the drug, but nicotine now transcends tobacco itself. The new "e-cigarette," with its tobacco-free vapors, delivers potent recreational doses of nicotine to those who want them, purportedly without the lethal dangers that accompany tobacco products. Despite declining overall numbers of tobacco users since the mid-1960s, nicotine survived the "cigarette century" that was the twentieth century.[4] For John Fred Cirillo and others, nicotine addiction would remain a "trap" that defied the efforts of many to escape.

Employer Incentives for Quitters

During the 1970s, 1980s, and 1990s, employers both large and small played an important role in promoting smoking cessation. Many managers promoted smoke-free lifestyles as the worker's pathway to the rewards of individual health and profit, sometimes offering attractive monetary rewards and even counseling assistance to encourage workers to quit smoking. These new policies often accompanied workplace smoking bans, as employers understood that smoke-free workers cost them less in terms of health insurance costs, absenteeism for medical reasons, and lost productivity. Offering smokers sums of money to motivate them to pursue smoke-free lifestyles was an investment that, if successful, could yield significant long-term savings on labor costs. Estimates as to how many of these incentive programs existed in the past or present cannot be found, but a search for the phrase "cash incentives to quit smoking" yields hits on 1,380 documents in the online Tobacco Institute collection at the University of California, San Francisco's Legacy Tobacco Documents Library. A 1990 article in *Preventive Medicine* estimated that between 9 and 15 percent of US businesses offered "worksite stop-smoking programs," but the article did not provide data as to how many offered cash incentives.[5]

In the late twentieth century, employers who incentivized smoking cessation presumed that working men and women were economic beings only, a philosophical throwback to Frederick Winslow Taylor's understandings of workers' motivations and a nod to business discussions of "motivation theory" and "incentive theory" in the late twentieth century.[6] In the 1970s and 1980s, employers instituted cash incentives in the belief that the worker's constant pursuit of profit was powerful enough to destroy her or his devotion to nicotine. In the employer calculus, de jure wages for the labor of quitting smoking would "stimulate and direct workers' actions" to do away with tobacco.[7]

Employers' explanations of their cash incentive programs for quitters suggested their own paternalistic views of labor-management relations. In 1975, NBC Nightly News profiled the Leslie Manufacturing Company in Bloomington, Minnesota, a firm they believed was the first to offer workers cash to encourage them to give up cigarettes. The broadcast showed company president Leslie Renner presenting bonus checks to ex-smokers, who earned $1 per day for their abstinence. "I'm pleased to present this check to you for your quitting smoking," he said to a worker. "Very nice gesture."[8] At a Vineland, New Jersey, plumbing and heating supply business in 1985, owner Leon Lowenstern appeared in a *New York Times* photograph that showed him standing with firm arms crossed in front of a small group of workers who were participants in his $2 "bonus" program for quitters. In the article about employers getting "tough on smoking" that accompanied the photo, Lowenstern indicated that he knew what was best for workers. "Non-smokers are worth more than people who smoke," he said. "Smokers are always stopping for a pack and running out of matches." Instead, he aimed to re-engineer their bodies to better fit his fiscal priorities, as "smoking takes time from the job." He would pay them in exchange for an exacting account of their time spent.[9] In 1989, the Texas energy titan known as Enron made wellness promotion a centerpiece of its labor-management relations strategy. "The company historically has been very health-conscious," argued Brian List, the company's wellness coordinator. "Its philosophy is that it makes good business sense to have healthy employees." Enron offered quit aids (such as videos) and trivial individual incentives, such as gifts of pen-and-pencil sets. At the same time, Enron offered several smoking cessation programs. "Hard-core" smokers had the choice of working with a physician and were entitled to free supplies of nicotine gum. "We have always been conscious of the well-being of our employees," Brian List noted.[10]

As with the politics of workplace smoking bans in the late twentieth century, company policies that encouraged smokers to quit sometimes overlapped with managers' powers to discipline and punish. Worried smokers wrote to the Tobacco Institute to ask for advice about dealing with management pressures to accept offers of bonuses to quit smoking. In some contexts, urgings to quit coincided with the threat of punishment if smokers resisted. A worker in Enid, Oklahoma, noted that the $500 carrot of a bonus offered by her employer only masked the intimidating stick wielded by management. To be promoted, workers were required to accept the bonus and quit smoking right away, but Diane Faught feared that if she (and others) continued to smoke or voiced opposition to the new policy, they would be "fired on the spot." She begged the Tobacco Institute to avoid using her name in any communications with the company. The feared human resources manager at the unnamed firm, "ex smoker" Dean Henderson, justified this combination of coercive and incentivized motivation by saying, "Employers have the right to regulate the behavior of their employees if it costs the company money on insurance or lost time." For Diane Faught, Henderson's real message was simpler than that: quit or face the consequences.[11]

Employers continue to possess the ability to influence, if not determine, what workers may do with their bodies, habits, and health. When it comes to the use of prescription and recreational drugs, for example, US employers may choose to deny employment to those workers who use them, even when those drugs are prescribed by physicians or are legal to use. For instance, various state laws that permit the use of certain drugs, such as marijuana, put working men and women at odds with employer policies that regularly ban them. For workers and job applicants who are overweight or obese, employers may turn them away as unsafe investments; they may be passed over as undesirable individuals who create burdensome and unwanted health care costs. Workers in the United States today even face pressure from employers regarding their personal financial habits, as managers regularly screen job applicants for bad credit ratings as part of their hiring processes. The issue of smoking is disappearing from the workplace, but employers remain determined to shape workers' habits and bodies.[12]

Solitary Struggles to Quit

Regardless of the institutional pressure and incentives found in some workplaces, the labor of giving up smoking is a lonely and difficult undertaking. Quitting demands the untangling of bodies and emotions from the potent grip of addiction, as well as maintaining distance from sources of nicotine. This is a jarring process that creates considerable emotional and physical turmoil among many of the newest nonsmokers. Recidivism is common.[13] "A smoker's whole day is filled with cues that could trigger the desire for a cigarette," Dr. Celia Jaffe Winchell, a psychiatrist who heads the FDA's medical team that deals with addictive drugs, points out. "The first cup of coffee in the morning, sitting down to check the email, opening the paper, finishing a meal."[14]

Quitting "cold turkey"—that is, abruptly and without any type of replacement medication—is the least successful approach. Among smokers who tried to quit in the 1990s, for example, roughly 87 percent tried cold turkey, but no more than 7 percent of the smokers who did this actually remained smoke-free, according to a Gallup Poll survey of ex-smokers.[15] Instead, smokers who try to quit on their own usually find that steadily reducing their usual number of cigarettes per day over a given period is a way to partly mute the shock of cold turkey. Among the men and women who are able to stop smoking, 67 percent report that "gradually cutting down" was their method.[16] By the early 2010s, the incidence of quitting cold turkey had receded, a sign that more smokers now looked beyond the trauma of cold turkey to the help found in pharmaceutical aids such as nicotine patches, lozenges, and gum. In 2013, only 48 percent reported doing so via the "cold turkey" route.[17]

The nicotine patch, lozenge, and gum allow smokers to gradually reduce their intake of nicotine as they take on the challenges of trying to quit. Now available over the counter, these aids help to ease the suffering of those who struggle with withdrawals and cravings, as they deliver doses of nicotine for absorption into the body or the mouth. Roughly 6 percent of those who quit use nicotine replacement therapy.[18] The patch and the gum carry certain risks, however, such as the danger of overdose. If a patch wearer, for example, uses tobacco products at the same time, it is possible to ingest toxic levels of nicotine. Quitters also have the option of using nicotine inhalers. Designed to resemble a cigarette, these cylindrical devices deliver doses of nicotine orally that are absorbed into the body within twenty minutes, much like the gum. (Nicotine patches need two to four hours to be effective.) Inhalers have been found to greatly improve abstinence rates, improving by 28 percent the number of those who are able to stay smoke-free.[19] But clinicians advise smokers to use nicotine replacement therapy only on a temporary basis; they are not intended to be permanent substitutes for cigarettes. Patches should be used for no more than five months; nicotine gum should be stopped at six months.[20]

Some quitters have looked to prescription medications that help to ease cravings and withdrawals without nicotine replacement. The antidepressant Bupropion (Zyban), for example, increases levels of dopamine in the brain, which helps to suppress withdrawal symptoms. Verenicline (known as Chantix) eases

FIGURE C.1   Nicoderm CQ product advertisement, 2005. Courtesy Stanford Research Into the Impact of Tobacco Advertising.

cravings and withdrawal as well.[21] These forms of pharmaceutical assistance, however, largely depend on the prescription drug coverage that only health insurance can provide, and for 15.4 percent of men and women in the United States, health coverage remains absent.[22]

In the marketplace of medical services and therapies for quitting smoking, some health care service providers offer intensive therapy for "hard core" smokers who are desperate to quit. For a substantial fee, the Glenbeigh Hospital in Hialeah, Florida, for instance, offered a twelve-day intensive treatment program in the 1980s for those smokers who felt "helpless" in their battle to quit. The hospital used a "cold turkey approach." Smokers quit without any pharmaceutical help and developed healthier lifestyles without drugs. Not only did patients have to give up nicotine, but the Glenbeigh Hospital program was sugar-free and caffeine-free. The Mayo Clinic offered a nicotine dependence clinic in the 1990s, a $3,000 service that consisted of eight days of in-patient treatment. The patients there averaged eight previous attempts to quit, and 80 percent were struggling with health problems as a result of their tobacco use. Some individuals in the program had even been removed from organ donor lists because of their inability to quit. Patterns of desperation and frequent failure among these smokers were underlined by the Mayo Clinic's grim discovery that more than 43 percent would soon relapse after leaving the hospital.[23]

The solitary struggle to (1) quit smoking and (2) remain smoke-free is an uncertain process of trial and error. Quitters usually need 6.1 serious tries before achieving long-term success. In addition to nonprescription and prescription drug help, some smokers have tried hypnosis, counseling (even by telephone), acupuncture, acupressure, changes in diet, audio tapes, videos, self-help books, and exercise in order to preclude cravings for cigarettes and develop nicotine-free lifestyles. As clinicians suggest, a combined approach—that utilizes smoking cessation products and counseling support—offers the best chances of success.[24] Sometimes it takes a village.

"Holdouts"

By 2012, the number of cigarette smokers in the United States fell below 20 percent for the first time since the early twentieth century. While working toward quitting appears to be the new normal among most tobacco users, a significant population of men and women continue to choose smoking. In 2010, the *New York Times* labeled them "holdouts," anachronisms of a bygone era who knowingly defy the changing cultural and political landscape by maintaining their addictions. In 2013, there were more than just a few holdouts: 19 percent of adult Americans admitted to smoking at least one cigarette in the past week, and 41 percent of Americans claimed to know "a few" smokers.[25]

Holdouts' ongoing need for nicotine creates frequent inconvenience. In 2010, the price for a single pack of twenty cigarettes in New York City (the most expensive city for smokers) reached $11. Besides the immense cost, the spaces where smoking is permissible (especially in cities) continue to dwindle, "their turf con-tinually circumscribed" by rules and ordinances that prohibit smoking in bars and restaurants and even on the sidewalks where some firms (such as MetLife in Manhattan) prohibit smoking within twenty-five feet of their buildings. Smokers, however, have been "regulated into submission," quietly relocating to nearby alleys. Since the 1990s, smokers have watched their presence and privileges dissolve. As the *New York Times* noted of the changing landscape, smokers went from "big room to small room, inside to outside, public to private, acceptable to anathema."[26] Despite diminishing spaces and opportunities, as well as exorbitant prices, many smokers continue to maintain their dependence on nicotine. In 2013, more than one in ten US adult smokers (12 percent) admitted never trying seriously to quit.[27]

Many holdout smokers are working-class, rural, and poor. In eastern Ken-tucky's Clay County, for instance, four in ten residents are smokers. While the overall adult smoking rate in the United States declined by 27 percent since 1997, it did not change at all among poorer rural communities in the Midwest and South. In the heartland, tobacco companies maintain a robust presence. They donate money to local organizations and causes, concentrate many of their adver-tising efforts there, and sell products more cheaply there. (The average price for a pack is $5 in Clay County, Kentucky, less than half of the price in New York City.) According to the *New York Times*, rural residents cite smoking as "one of the few pleasures" they have in small communities that are economically depressed. "It's just what we do here," noted Ed Smith, a fifty-one-year-old smoker in Clay County. In contrast, urban areas at the turn of the twenty-first century feature more education, more access to health care, hefty prices for tobacco products, prohibitively high cigarette taxes, and local laws that limit public smoking. In cities, compared to the heartland, smoking has considerably declined. But in the heartland, smoking cessation and tobacco control are a tougher sell. "While smoking is no longer normal in big cities," noted one Kentucky physician, "it's not viewed as a problem" in places like Clay County, and "smokers aren't seen as the minority." Some residents of rural communities even view smoking as a form of harm reduction, as tobacco is thought by some to be the kinder and gentler alter-native to other dangerous drugs like heroin, cocaine, and methamphetamine.[28]

Many holdout smokers insist their smoking habit is only temporary, even in the heartland; they intend to quit altogether someday. Seeing their habit as anachro-nistic and stigmatized amid the "denormalization" of tobacco use at the turn of the twenty-first century, some smokers, such as a Vietnam War veteran interviewed by the *New York Times* in 2010, so ashamed that he wished to remain nameless, wake up "every morning determined to quit." Perhaps when everyday stressors (such as work problems) are fewer, perhaps when they have greater resolve. "Oh yeah, I'm going to quit," noted a New York travel management executive. "Eventually, when I'm ready, I'll quit."[29] Ed Smith of Clay County, Kentucky remarked, "I want to see my grandson grow up." Holdout smokers' claims of the future intention to quit suggest a desire to somehow distance their own habit from the negative social and cultural connotations that now accompany tobacco use. As one smoker noted when he lit a cigarette in the audience at a 2013 Rolling Stones concert in New York City, nearby concertgoers glared at him as if he'd "clubbed a baby seal." The durable guitar player Keith Richards smoked on stage, but the audience members' hostile gaze conveyed to at least one smoker that his rebellious tobacco habit was no longer permissible. Since holdouts often say they plan to quit smoking in the future, they are trying to present themselves as more casual users of tobacco products rather than hardcore, committed, and enduring addicts.[30]

Holdouts try to shelter their pressing need for cigarettes by promising courteousness and deference to nonsmokers, legitimizing their own use of tobacco products through the insistence that they are always considerate of nonsmokers' preferences and expectations. When talking with friends and coworkers outdoors on the sidewalk near the office where he worked, for example, one holdout reported that he always stood downwind, making sure that his secondhand smoke did not waft in the direction of his conversation partners. Another individual remarked that she never smoked indoors when nonsmoking friends visited her apartment. She purposefully embraced this sacrifice in order to safeguard the comfort of her guests (and thereby excuse her habit of smoking at other times and at other sites). These holdout smokers hoped their carefully crafted, strategic, and self-sacrificing manners would, in the end, lessen the possibility of hostile treatment from nonsmoking friends and coworkers.[31]

Though smokers' ranks declined to less than one of every five adults by 2012, nicotine addiction remains commonplace. Faced with a smoke-averse political and cultural environment, especially in cities, holdouts must often be strategic, compromising, and careful to avoid censure. The emergence of this newly constructed category is itself shaped by the declining presence of tobacco use in the United States, as journalistic observers frame the "holdout" as completely out of step with the "denormalization" of smoking at the turn of the twenty-first century. At the same time, holdouts' testimonials about their experiences and practices underline the profound difficulties many smokers face as they hope to reclaim their bodies and their health from the harmful grip of tobacco use and nicotine addiction.

E-Cigarettes

The growing popularity of electronic cigarettes among tobacco users contributes both to the demise of tobacco smoking and the endurance of nicotine. The e-cigarette is a rechargeable device with a battery-operated heating element that renders nicotine-infused fluid (contained in a small cartridge) into vapor, which is inhaled into the lungs. Cartridges for electronic cigarettes are replaceable, free of ash, and longer-lasting than the single tobacco cigarette.

Using an electronic cigarette is known as "vaping" (instead of "smoking"), and "e-cigs" are sometimes made to resemble real cigarettes, thereby recreating important elements of the experience of smoking to the fullest extent possible: holding the cigarette, bringing it to the mouth, inhaling its exhaust. Some devices are designed to look like memory sticks or pens in order to allow someone to "use the product without others noticing."[32] As cigarette taxes drive up consumer prices for tobacco products, tobacco smoke becomes widely prohibited indoors, and the lethality of cigarettes remains very real, nicotine-addicted tobacco users quickly become the main consumers of these smoke-free products: one in five smokers tried e-cigarettes in 2011, up dramatically from one in ten in 2010.[33] Their choices as consumers are legion, as some manufacturers offer sixty flavors of vapor that include Marlboro and retro Lucky Strike. "Everybody's doing it," noted a user in Clay County, Kentucky. "Young people, old people, everyone."[34]

E-cigs are big business, but not so big as to eclipse the tobacco industry behemoth. There is currently an $80 billion a year market for smoking products in the United States, but electronic cigarette sales account for only $500 million dollars a year. Worldwide, e-cigarette products account for a total of only $2 billion a year. The sum of $2 billion, however, is the result of 30 percent increases every year since 2008.[35] In the United States alone, 6 percent of adults ("not just smokers") have tried electronic cigarettes.[36]

The manufacture and sale of e-cigarette products are not regulated by the Food and Drug Administration's (FDA) Center for Tobacco Products. While the original, historic sources of nicotine are covered by federal regulation—including cigarette tobacco, smokeless tobacco, roll-your-own tobacco, and cigars—there is no bureaucratic oversight that upholds standards of safety or quality in the rapidly growing electronic cigarette industry. Users of e-cigarettes "currently have no way of knowing," according to the FDA, whether these products are safe for use, exactly how much nicotine is inhaled in each puff, or what is the complete list of chemicals that are present in e-cig vapors.[37] As Erika Sward of the American Lung Association pointedly summarized, e-cigarettes are "a complete unregulated wild west": No user is safe since neither consumers nor the state knows the full extent of the substances that are in the product or the risks that may result from short- or long-term use.[38] In 2009, FDA tests of several firms' e-cigarette cartridges found "detectable levels of known carcinogens and toxic chemicals to which users could potentially be exposed," such as diethylene glycol, which was found in one. As a result of its study, the FDA ordered a

FIGURE C.2   Actor Stephen Dorff in Blu Electronic Cigarettes advertisement, 2013. Courtesy Stanford Research Into the Impact of Tobacco Advertising.

ban of e-cig sales, claiming the cartridges had been shown to yield "toxic" and "harmful" chemicals that were potentially dangerous to users. In 2010, however, courts overturned the ban since "the FDA had cited no evidence to show that electronic cigarettes harmed anyone." In 2014, the federal government via the

Food and Drug Administration proposed modifications to the 2009 Tobacco Control Act that would put e-cigarette products under the same category as tobacco products.[39]

The technology of the e-cigarette stands squarely on the shoulders of the "smokeless" cigarette concept that tobacco companies had once struggled to perfect during the late twentieth century, as "vaping" delivers nicotine and even flavor without tobacco's risks or odors. Some major tobacco companies devoted significant resources to develop smokeless devices that would deliver the pleasures of smoking by heating (rather than burning) tobacco, thereby "reducing the risk" to smokers. British American Tobacco (BAT) led the way in the early 1960s with "Project Ariel." They patented a cylindrical device that burned "tobacco to heat a centrally arranged tube containing nicotine and an aerosol generator, consisting of material such as water, which would form an aerosol when heated and then cooled, so that the nicotine would dissolve into droplets and then be inhaled as part of the aerosol."[40] This complex nicotine delivery system was never marketed. R. J. Reynolds later invested heavily to develop its Premier brand smokeless cigarette, yet the 1988 venture proved to be a "mistake" that cost the company $300 million. Test market users complained of its inconvenient and unreliable lighting mechanism. (Premier packs featured written instructions.) Smokers also hated the "intolerable" smells and flavor. One "venturous" smoker said a lit Premier cigarette smelled "like burning tennis sneakers," while another user remarked that it created an odor like "you'd just opened a grave on a warm day."[41] Today's electronic cigarettes, on the other hand, promise the flavor, convenience, and nicotine that earlier smokeless devices failed to provide.

The links between e-cigarettes and tobacco are more than historical, technological, or cultural; they are also increasingly industrial. In 2012, Lorillard (the manufacturer of Newport, Kent, and Old Gold cigarettes) bought Blu eCigs, a firm that commanded about one-third of electronic cigarette product sales at convenience stores in the United States. In addition, Marlboro announced in 2013 its plans to roll out the "MarkTen" e-cigarette. At the meeting with shareholders to promote the new venture, company executives explained that the new product "closely resembles the draw of a cigarette," and matches the selection of flavors cigarette smokers enjoy most: "classic or menthol." Eager for a piece of the growing market in nontobacco nicotine delivery, Reynolds American (the maker of the Camel and Pall Mall brands) released its new "VUSE" electronic cigarette in 2014, part of the company's professed efforts to "[transform] tobacco" and "make the product less harmful."[42]

The e-cigarette industry's advertising practices also evoke the heyday of tobacco company ads during the long "cigarette century." For example, firms craft artful slogans to represent their products like "Cigarettes, you've met your match" and "Rise from the ashes"—modeled on classic tobacco catchphrases such as "I'd Walk a Mile For a Camel," "Tastes Good Like a Cigarette Should," and "Be Happy—Go Lucky." Also, television ads feature ringing celebrity endorsements, showing nicotine-addicted celebrities (e.g., actors Stephen Dorff and Jenny McCarthy for the Blu brand) coolly and alluringly enjoying e-cigarette products at the beach or in a night club, a new generation of Marlboro Men and Virginia Slims women for a brave new world without tobacco. "You've come a long way baby."[43]

Should e-cigarettes be subjected to the same restrictions in public spaces as tobacco cigarettes? Citing the public's lack of detailed knowledge about electronic cigarette health risks, the New York City Council voted in December 2013 to extend the city's ban on smoking in public locations such as restaurants, bars, parks, and office buildings to include the use of e-cigs.[44] Opponents of electronic cigarette bans insist that e-cigs should not be lumped with tobacco since "they pose no risk to bystanders" and "give you what you want [nicotine] in a pure, reduced harm form." These devices are not your grandmother and grandfather's coffin nails, they say. "As for the smokers," a blogger insisted, "e-cigs are a dose of something they're increasingly being deprived of: the freedom to enjoy nicotine."[45]

Electronic cigarettes currently exist in a muddled political and cultural context. While they are not tobacco products per se, they deliver recreational doses of nicotine. Opponents and some policy makers view e-cigarettes through the lens of tobacco control, seeing in e-cig vapors the potential for similar health dangers that accompany mainstream and sidestream smoke. For users and some public health experts, however, e-cigarettes are accepted as a form of harm reduction. Since all smokers cannot be made to quit through prohibition measures, e-cigarettes could curtail the many health risks that tobacco use fuels. Just as prohibition never ended heroin addiction, for example, accessible supplies of clean needles can help to lessen the dangers that drug addicts might otherwise confront, such as HIV or AIDS. Electronic cigarettes could help smokers cope with their addictions to nicotine without causing further injury to themselves or others.[46] That is, if they are actually nontoxic.

As tobacco use declines overall in the United States, nicotine paradoxically endures. Even as most smokers want to quit, many never do, and relapse is frequent. The burgeoning e-cig industry, however, might someday accomplish what policy makers, researchers, physicians, activists, and even employers could not: dissolve the bonds between smokers and tobacco. Nicotine addiction will surely remain, but there is the chance that tobacco, what King James I once dubbed the "deceivable weed," could be relegated someday to the dustbin (or the ashtray) of history.[47]

Smoking was, and is, subversive. Cigarettes brought workers into conflict with employers and created opposing needs, desires, and solidarities. Even as mainstream and sidestream smoke seriously endangered health, nicotine addiction often confounded employers' hopes to direct workers' loyalties and actions; tobacco use, in fact, became an everyday expression of workers' own needs and wants. As a result, working-class men's and women's regular smoking of cigarettes was a wellspring of challenges to employer power and management policy making. Read smokers' chronic malingering at the Hammermill Paper Company in 1915; the protest actions of the "smoke-inners" at Chrysler's Jefferson Avenue Assembly plant in 1942; the angry letters of "exiled" workplace smokers to the Tobacco Institute in 1991. Conflicting views of workers' rights and privileges were at the center of workplace battles over smoking in the twentieth century, and the wide extent of tobacco use in US workplaces underlines the profound significance of addiction in the social and cultural history of working people.

Notes

INTRODUCTION

1. Barbara Ehrenreich, *Nickel and Dimed: On (Not) Getting By in America* (New York: Metropolitan, 2001), 30.

2. On the history of tobacco, see Barbara M. Hahn, *Making Tobacco Bright: Creating an American Commodity, 1617–1937* (Baltimore: Johns Hopkins University Press, 2011).

3. *Harlan County USA*, dir. Barbara Kopple, Cabin Creek Films, 1976; *Silkwood*, dir. Mike Nichols, ABC Motion Pictures, 1983. On working people and alcohol in the nineteenth century, see Peter Way, *Common Labour: Workers and the Digging of North American Canals, 1780–1860* (New York: Cambridge University Press, 1993), esp. 163–99; Roy Rosenzweig, *Eight Hours for What We Will: Workers and Leisure in an Industrial City, 1870–1920* (Cambridge, UK: Cambridge University Press, 1983); Mark Edward Lender and James Kirby Martin, *Drinking in America: A History* (1982; repr., New York: Free Press, 1987); on narcotics, see Timothy J. Gilfoyle, *A Pickpocket's Tale: The Underworld of Nineteenth-Century New York* (New York: W. W. Norton & Company, 2006); Eric C. Schneider, *Smack: Heroin and the American City* (Philadelphia: University of Pennsylvania Press, 2008); David T. Courtwright, *Dark Paradise: A History of Opiate Addiction in America* (1982; repr., Cambridge, Mass.: Harvard University Press, 2001).

4. Kevin Boyle, "The Kiss: Racial and Gender Conflict in a 1950s Automobile Factory," *Journal of American History* 84:2 (1997): 496–523; Richard David Riddle, "The Rise of the 'Reagan Democrats' in Warren, Michigan, 1964–1984" (PhD diss., Wayne State University, 1998), esp. 259–60; Steve Meyer, "Workplace Predators: Sexuality and Harassment on the US Automotive Shop Floor, 1930–1960," *Labor: Studies in Working-Class History of the Americas* 1:1 (2004): 77–93; Steve Meyer, "Rugged Manhood: The Aggressive and Confrontational Culture of Male Auto Workers during World War II," Journal of Social History 36 (2002): 125–47; Ben Hamper, *Rivethead: Tales from the Assembly Line* (New York: Warner Books, 1992); see also Hobart Foote's revealing statements in Studs Terkel, ed., *Working* (1972; repr., New York: New Press, 1997), 170.

5. Robert N. Proctor, *Golden Holocaust: Origins of the Cigarette Catastrophe and the Case for Abolition* (Berkeley: University of California Press, 2011), 40.

6. Historians of smoking and the tobacco industry have only briefly discussed the workplace as a major site in the history of tobacco control. The best treatment of workplace issues is found in Allan M. Brandt, *The Cigarette Century: The Rise, Fall, and Deadly Persistence of the Product That Defined America* (New York: Basic Books, 2007), esp. 289–90. For other key histories of smoking, see Proctor, *Golden Holocaust*; Cassandra Tate, *Cigarette Wars: The Triumph of 'the Little White Slaver'* (New York: Oxford University Press, 1999); Richard M. Kluger, *Ashes to Ashes: America's Hundred-Year Cigarette War, the Public Health, and the Unabashed Triumph of Philip Morris* (New York: Random House, 1996).

7. Heather Hasan, *Caffeine and Nicotine: A Dependent Society* (New York: Rosen Publishing Group, Inc., 2009), 4.

8. Heather Lehr Wagner, *Nicotine* (New York: Chelsea House Publishers, 2003), 8–9; "Nicotine," http://www.psychologytoday.com/conditions/nicotine, accessed 1 February 2014.

9. Jordan Goodman, *Tobacco in History: Cultures of Dependence* (New York: Routledge, 1993), 5.

10. Stanton A. Glantz, John Slade, Lisa A. Bero, Peter Hanauer, and Deborah E. Barnes, eds., *The Cigarette Papers*, foreword by C. Everett Koop (Berkeley: University of California Press, 1996), 30, 62.

11. "Nicotine."

12. The Gallup Poll, "Tobacco and Smoking" (2013), http://www.gallup.com/poll/1717/tobacco-smoking, accessed 2 December 2013. On definitions of nicotine addiction, see Glantz et al., *Cigarette Papers*, 58; "What Is Nicotine Addiction?" (1993), pamphlet, 2023668500, Legacy Tobacco Documents Library, University of California, San Francisco, http://legacy.library.ucsf.edu (hereafter LTDL). Each document in the Legacy Tobacco Documents Library features a catalogue number that was applied with a handheld Bates stamp. The small Bates machine allows "large sets of documents to be uniquely sequenced" at a very efficient pace. The LTDL is fully searchable online; users may scan the archive (which consists entirely of pdf files) according to Bates numbers, titles, or text. On the Bates numbering of sources, see Proctor, *Golden Holocaust*, 563. For each reference to LTDL sources, I include the Bates number printed on the page.

13. "Withdrawal," http://smokefree.gov/withdrawal, accessed 4 February 2014; "What Is Nicotine Addiction?"

14. "Theories About Tobacco," *New York Times*, 14 November 1885, 2.

15. "Results of the Cigaret Habit," *Chicago Daily Tribune*, 6 February 1910, F6.

16. Henry Oyen, "Ruin and Death in Wake of Cigaret," *Chicago Daily Tribune*, 16 April 1905, E3.

17. "Circus Feels Cigaret Law," *Chicago Daily Tribune*, 18 August 1905, 1; "Cigarets, or We Perish, Governor," *Minneapolis Journal*, 18 August 1905, 1.

18. "Death and Exile in Cigaret Law," *Chicago Daily Tribune*, 20 April 1905, 4.

19. US Surgeon General, "Adult Per Capita Cigarette Consumption," in *Reducing the Health Consequences of Smoking* (1989), TIMN354119, LTDL.

20. For these statistics, see Brandt, *Cigarette Century*, 309.

21. Proctor, *Golden Holocaust*, 3.

22. Harry Braverman, *Labor and Monopoly Capital: The Degradation of Work in the Twentieth Century* (1974; repr., New York: Monthly Review Press, 1998); Robert H. Zieger and Gilbert J. Gall, *American Workers, American Unions*, 3rd ed. (Baltimore: Johns Hopkins University Press, 2002), 2–9, 11–14; Elspeth H. Brown, *The Corporate Eye: Photography and the Rationalization of American Commercial Culture, 1884–1929* (Baltimore: Johns Hopkins University Press, 2005), 23–118.

23. Susan Porter Benson, "'The Customers Ain't God': The Work Culture of Department Store Saleswomen, 1890–1940," in *Working-Class America: Essays on Labor, Community, and American Society*, ed. Michael H. Frisch and Daniel J. Walkowitz (Urbana: University of Illinois Press, 1983), 185 (quotes); see also Susan Porter Benson, *Counter Cultures: Saleswomen, Managers, and Customers in American Department Stores, 1890–1940* (Urbana: University of Illinois Press, 1986); Barbara Melosh, *"The Physician's Hand": Work Culture and Conflict in American Nursing* (Philadelphia: Temple University Press, 1982), 6–7; Patricia Ann Cooper, *Once a Cigar Maker: Men, Women, and Work Culture in American Cigar Factories, 1900–1919* (Urbana: University of Illinois Press, 1987).

24. Benson, "'The Customers Ain't God,'" 186; see also Melosh, *"The Physician's Hand,"* 6.

25. On work culture and critical readings of rules, see Cooper, *Once a Cigar Maker*, 2.

26. For a recent example, see Brian Luskey, *On the Make: Clerks and the Quest for Capital in Nineteenth-Century America* (New York: New York University Press, 2010).

27. On labor and culture in workplaces during the later years of the twentieth century, see Bethany Moreton, *To Serve God and Wal-Mart: The Making of Christian Free Enterprise* (Cambridge, Mass.: Harvard University Press, 2009); Andrew Ross, *No Collar: The Humane Workplace and Its Hidden Costs* (Philadelphia: Temple University Press, 2003).

28. "LTDL History," http://legacy.library.ucsf.edu/about/about_history.jsp, accessed 9 February 2014; see also Proctor, *Golden Holocaust*, 15–16.

29. Wagner, *Nicotine*, 8.

1. REFORMERS, EMPLOYERS, AND THE DANGERS OF WORKING-CLASS SMOKING

1. "Cigarette Fiend Won Race," *New York Times*, 16 June 1900, 11.

2. "Right to Breathe Fresh Air," *New York Times*, 15 May 1903, 8.

3. On social class and urban Progressivism, see George Chauncey, *Gay New York: Gender, Urban Culture, and the Making of the Gay Male World, 1890–1940* (New York: Free Press, 1994); Jennifer Fronc, *New York Undercover: Private Surveillance during the Progressive Era* (Chicago: University of Chicago Press, 2009); Elizabeth Alice Clement, *Love for Sale: Courting, Treating, and Prostitution in New York City, 1900–1945* (Chapel Hill: University of North Carolina Press, 2006); Cynthia M. Blair, *I've Got to Make My Livin': Black Women's Sex Work in Turn-of-the-Century Chicago* (Chicago: University of Chicago Press, 2010).

4. On the cultural power and influence of "Victorian virtues," see John F. Kasson, *Amusing the Million: Coney Island at the Turn of the Century* (New York: Hill & Wang, 1978), 4. For insightful discussions of sights, sounds, smells, and tastes in cities at the turn of the century, see Jane Addams, *Twenty Years at Hull-House* (1910; repr., New York: Signet Classic, 1981), 124, 200–204, 208–210; Jacob Riis, *How the Other Half Lives* (1890; repr., New York: Penguin Classics, 1997); Adam Mack, *Sensing Chicago: Noisemakers, Strikebreakers, and Muckrakers* (Urbana: University of Illinois Press, 2015); Timothy J. Gilfoyle, *City of Eros: New York City, Prostitution, and the Commercialization of Sex, 1790–1920* (New York: W. W. Norton & Company, 1994); Peter C. Baldwin, *In the Watches of the Night: Life in the Nocturnal City, 1820–1930* (Chicago: University of Chicago Press, 2012); Chad Heap, *Slumming: Sexual and Racial Encounters in American Nightlife, 1885–1940* (Chicago: University of Chicago Press, 2009), esp. 17–54; Andrew P. Haley, *Turning the Tables: Restaurants and the Rise of the American Middle Class, 1880–1920* (Chapel Hill: University of North Carolina Press, 2011), esp. 94, 101, 103; Laura Wexler, *Tender Violence: Domestic Visions in an Age of US Imperialism* (Chapel Hill: University of North Carolina Press, 2000), esp. 211–223; "Noises in the Streets," *New York Times*, 13 September 1899, 6; "To Open Anti-Noise Crusade," *Chicago Daily Tribune*, 21 April 1900, 9.

5. Allan M. Brandt, *The Cigarette Century: The Rise, Fall, and Deadly Persistence of the Product That Defined America* (New York: Basic Books, 2007), 49.

6. Henry Ford, *The Case against the Little White Slaver* (Detroit: Published by Henry Ford, 1916), 25.

7. On the Ford Sociological Department, see Steve Meyer, *The Five Dollar Day: Labor Management and Social Control in the Ford Motor Company, 1908–1921* (Albany: State University of New York Press, 1981).

8. "No Cigarettes for Boys," *New York Times*, 6 December 1894, 8. On urban male behavior on streetcars, see Baldwin, *In the Watches of the Night*, 147–52.

9. "Cigarette Fiends," *Los Angeles Times*, 2 February 1891, 28.

10. "Cigarette Smoking Boys," *Los Angeles Times*, 27 May 1892, 8. On smoking among newsboys, see Baldwin, *In the Watches of the Night*, 116–17; Cassandra Tate, *Cigarette Wars: The Triumph of "The Little White Slaver"* (New York: Oxford University Press, 1999), 58; "What Men Think of Boys Who Smoke Cigarettes," *Bismarck Daily Tribune*, 26 October 1915, 4; Herbert H. Smith, "No More for Me," *Continent*, 6 November 1913, 1524; "Bad Habits Among School Children," *Medical Bulletin*, June 1905, 227.

11. "Testing the Boy Who Smokes Cigarettes," *New York Times*, 27 February 1910, SM12; see also "The Cigarette Debated," *New York Times*, 22 April 1905, 10. On the connections between male bodies and manliness at the turn of the century, see John F. Kasson,

Houdini, Tarzan, and the Perfect Man: The White Male Body and the Challenge of Modernity in America (New York: Macmillan, 2002); Michael Kimmel, *Manhood in America: A Cultural History* (New York: Free Press, 1996), esp. 127, 138–39; Gail M. Bederman, *Manliness and Civilization: A Cultural History of Gender and Race in the United States, 1880–1917* (Chicago: University of Chicago Press, 1995), esp. 8, 15; E. Anthony Rotundo, *American Manhood: Transformations in Masculinity from the Revolution to the Modern Era* (New York: Basic Books, 1993), 223–24.

12. "The Anti-Cigarette Club," *Los Angeles Times*, 30 September 1894, 15.

13. Ford, *Case Against the Little White Slaver*, 15–16, 77; Brandt, *Cigarette Century*, 48. On adult male concerns about the destructive impact of professional failure on manhood, see Scott A. Sandage, *Born Losers: A History of Failure in America* (Cambridge, Mass.: Harvard University Press, 2005).

14. "Curious Result of Cigarette Smoking," *Los Angeles Times*, 18 August 1889, 9.

15. "Did Cigarettes Kill Him?" *New York Times*, 20 February 1893, 8; see also Iain Gately, *Tobacco: A Cultural History of How an Exotic Plant Seduced Civilization* (London: Simon & Schuster, 2001), 230.

16. "All Along the Line," *Los Angeles Times*, 27 July 1898, 9.

17. "Cigarettes and Crime," *New York Times*, 23 May 1899, 4. For similar conclusions, see "The War on the Cigarette," *New York Times*, 8 August 1909, SM8; "Formed by Boys," *Boston Daily Globe*, 23 April 1905, 12; Ford, *Case Against the Little White Slaver*, 27.

18. "Boy Set Fire to School," *New York Times*, 9 May 1903, 6; "Eddy Luke Held for Arson," *New York Sun*, 10 May 1903, 6; "Set School on Fire for Spite," *New York Evening World*, 8 May 1903, 2.

19. "Garrabrant Murder Trial," *New York Times*, 4 October 1900, 5; "State's Case All In," *New York Tribune*, 3 October 1900, 4; "Verdict Against Garrabrant," *New York Tribune*, 5 October 1900, 6.

20. "Crazed by Cigarette Smoking," *Los Angeles Times*, 21 December 1897, 6; "Warning to Smokers," *Salt Lake Herald*, 21 December 1897, 1; James Samuel Knox, *Personal Efficiency* (Cleveland: Knox Business Book Co., 1920), 54, 59.

21. Robert Loerzel, "The Smoking Gun," *Chicago Magazine*, June 2008, http://www.chicagomag.com, accessed 21 March 2012; Tate, *Cigarette Wars*, 41–42, 44; Perry Duis, *Challenging Chicago: Coping With Everyday Life, 1837–1920* (Urbana: University of Illinois Press, 1998), 197.

22. Tate, *Cigarette Wars*, 45.

23. Ibid., 54; "Miss Gaston Begins Anti-Cigarette War," *New York Times*, 12 September 1907, 2; "Calls Boys in Cigaret War to Be Resumed Tomorrow," *Chicago Daily Tribune*, 22 October 1911, 7; "Formed By Boys," *Boston Daily Globe*, 23 April 1905, 12.

24. Loerzel, "Smoking Gun."

25. "Lucy Page Gaston, with Boy Detective Perry Rathbun," DN-0001988, *Chicago Daily News* Negatives Collection, Chicago History Museum, http://memory.loc.gov/ammem/ndlpcoop/ichihtml/cdnhome.html, accessed 4 April 2012; "'Boy Sleuth' Is Foiled," *Chicago Daily Tribune*, 9 December 1904, 3. On the history of private surveillance and moral reform during the Progressive Era, see Fronc, *New York Undercover*.

26. "'Boy Sleuth' Is Foiled," 3.

27. "Miss Gaston a Policeman," *Chicago Daily Tribune*, 12 October 1911, 3; "Miss Gaston Deaf to Plea," *Chicago Daily Tribune*, 15 October 1911, 3; Loerzel, "Smoking Gun."

28. Loerzel, "Smoking Gun."

29. Tate, *Cigarette Wars*, 58; "Slaves to Cigarets Rush to Take 'Cure,'" *Chicago Daily Tribune*, 6 August 1913, 9; Brandt, *Cigarette Century*, 48; "Cures Women of Smoking," *New York Times*, 14 March 1914, 1.

30. Nicotine withdrawal symptoms can persist for weeks or even months. See National Institute on Drug Abuse, *Tobacco Addiction*, Research Report Series (Washington, D. C.: National Institutes of Health, 2009), 3, at http://permanent.access.gpo.gov/gpo16429/ TobaccoRRS_V.16.pdf, accessed 1 March 2012; "Withdrawal," smokefree.gov, http://www. smokefree.gov/topic-withdrawal.aspx, accessed 21 March 2012.

31. "Bad for De Troat," *Boston Daily Globe*, 18 May 1905, 6.

32. "Prisoner Lectured Court," *New York Times*, 15 September 1903, 16.

33. Len G. Shaw, "The Way of the Transgressor," in Ford, *Case Against the Little White Slaver*, 37–39.

34. Frederick James Pack, *Tobacco and Human Efficiency* (Salt Lake City, Utah: Deseret News, 1918), 142–43.

35. Pack, *Tobacco and Human Efficiency*, 138, 139.

36. Ford, *Case Against the Little White Slaver*, 29, 31, 32.

37. "Messenger Boys Without Cigarettes," *New York Times*, 30 April 1894, 9. On urban middle-class men and women's views of messenger boys, see Baldwin, *In the Watches of the Night*, 187–88.

38. "Strike Fever Hits the Messenger Boys," *New York Times*, 27 December 1905, 7; "Messenger Boys Threaten Strike," *New York Evening World*, 26 December 1905, 3; "Messenger Strike Fizzled," *New York Times*, 28 December 1905, 7.

39. On the history of the Triangle Fire, see David Von Drehle, *Triangle: The Fire That Changed America* (New York: Grove Press, 2003); Richard A. Greenwald, *The Triangle Fire, the Protocols of Peace, and Industrial Democracy in Progressive Era New York* (Philadelphia: Temple University Press, 2005); Jo Ann E. Argersinger, ed., *The Triangle Fire: A Brief History with Documents* (Boston: Bedford/St. Martin's, 2009); John F. McClymer, ed., *The Triangle Strike and Fire* (Fort Worth, Tex.: Harcourt Brace College Publishers, 1998); Elizabeth V. Burt, "Working Women and the Triangle Fire: Press Coverage of a Tragedy," *Journalism History* 30:4 (2005): 189–99; Thomas J. Kerr, "The New York Factory Investigating Commission and the Minimum Wage Movement," *Labor History* 12:3 (1971): 375; Leon Stein, *The Triangle Fire* (1962; repr., New York: Carroll & Graf Publishers, 1986); Daniel E. Bender, *Sweated Work, Weak Bodies: Anti-Sweatshop Campaigns and Languages of Labor* (New Brunswick, N.J.: Rutgers University Press, 2004), esp. 1, 189.

40. Stein, *Triangle Fire*, 207.

41. On cigarette smoking and the Triangle Factory Fire, see Drehle, *Triangle*, 118–19, 107–8; Jo Ann E. Argersinger, "Introduction: The Fire That Changed America," in Argersinger, ed., *Triangle Fire*, 16; "Croker Says Cigarette Cost 143 Innocent Lives at Asche [*sic*] Building Fire," *New York Evening World*, 10 October 1911, 20; "Fire Prevention Lessons from the Triangle Disaster," *New York Sun*, 22 March 1914, 6; "Triangle Lesson Is Lost, Says Adamson," *New York Sun*, 29 March 1914, 8. Joe Hermer and Alan Hunt describe "regulatory signs" as "government at a distance." See Hermer and Hunt's "Official Graffiti of the Everyday," *Law & Society Review* 30:3 (1996): 455.

42. Stein, *Triangle Fire*, 11–21, 73–75, 84, 95–109; Drehle, *Triangle*, 126–35, 139–59, 166–70, 181–83; Lawrence J. Epstein, *At the Edge of a Dream: The Story of Jewish Immigrants on New York's Lower East Side, 1880–1920* (San Francisco: John Wiley & Sons, 2007), 126–30.

43. Annelise Orleck, *Common Sense and a Little Fire: Women and Working-Class Politics in the United States, 1900–1965* (Chapel Hill: University of North Carolina Press, 1995), 32, 35–36; Bender, *Sweated Work, Weak Bodies*, 110.

44. All quotes from New York (State) Factory Investigating Commission, *Preliminary Report of the New York Factory Investigating Commission, 1912*, http://www.law.umkc.edu/ faculty/projects/ftrials/trianglereport.html, accessed 14 February 2009.

45. Palmer H. Langdon, "Careless Smokers," *New York Times*, 26 July 1913, 6.

46. New York Factory Investigating Commission, *Preliminary Report* (1912).

47. "Losses By Fire," *New York Times*, 5 September 1890, 5.

48. "Perfume-Laden Smoke Chokes Fire Fighters," *New York Times*, 23 December 1901, 2; "Chorus Girl's Cigarette," *Baltimore Sun*, 2 January 1902, 1; see also "Moving Picture Blaze," *New York Tribune*, 15 December 1910, 11.

49. "Nine Dead in Fire; Trapped in Factory," *New York Times*, 9 November 1909, 18; "Nine Men Burned to Death," *New York Sun*, 9 November 1909, 4.

50. On the suggestion that a cigarette or match started the Newark fire, see "Newark Fire Starts an Inquiry Here," *New York Times*, 30 November 1910, 20.

51. "23 Die, 40 Hurt in Newark Fire," *New York Times*, 27 November 1910, 1; "25 Die in Factory Fire," *New York Tribune*, 27 November 1910, 1, 2; Mary Alden Hopkins, "The Newark Factory Fire," *McClure's Magazine*, April 1911, 663–72. For an early list of those killed and wounded, see "Victims of the Newark Factory Fire," *New York Times*, 27 November 1910, 2.

52. "23 Die, 40 Hurt in Newark Fire," 1; "25 Die in Factory Fire," 2.

53. "Newark Fire Deaths Charged to Victim," *New York Times*, 7 December 1910, 2.

54. On the details of the Binghamton fire, see "50 Girls Die in a 20-Minute Factory Blaze," *New York Times*, 23 July 1913, 1; "Fifty Dead in Factory Fire at Binghamton," *New York Tribune*, 23 July 1913, 1; "Photographs of the Binghamton Fire," *New York Sun*, 24 July 1913, 2; quote appears in Langdon, "Careless Smokers," 14.

55. "Kenlon, the 'Great Fire Tactician,'" *New York Times*, 14 January 1912, 2.

56. Joseph Johnson, "New Fire Prevention Bureau Justified by First Year," *New York Times*, 23 March 1913, 8.

57. Johnson, "New Fire Prevention Bureau," 8.

58. Quotes from Johnson, "New Fire Prevention Bureau," 8.

59. For a full summary of these new laws for factories, see New York (State) Factory Investigating Commission, *Fourth Report of the Factory Investigating Commission, 1915*, http://www.ilr.cornell.edu/trianglefire/texts/reports/nyfic_1915.html, accessed 18 February 2009.

60. New York (State) Factory Investigating Commission, *Preliminary Report of the New York Factory Investigating Commission, 1912*, http://www.ilr.cornell.edu/trianglefire/texts/reports/nyfic_1912_p14.html, accessed 18 February 2009.

61. "Arrests Smokers in Auto Garages," *New York Times*, 25 February 1913, 6.

62. Ibid., 6.

63. "Woman Fire Chief for 15,000 Girls," *New York Times*, 23 June 1913, 6.

64. "The Only Woman Fire Fighter!" *Chicago Daily Tribune*, 28 September 1913, 2.

65. Ibid., 2.

66. Johnson, "New Fire Prevention Bureau," 8.

67. "Arrests Smokers in Auto Garages," 6. Originally from Chicago, Sarah Christopher became a national celebrity, largely due to her reputation as "the only woman fire fighter." See "The Only Woman Fire Fighter!" 2; "Active Women," *Los Angeles Times*, 20 October 1912, 19.

68. "Fire Law Breakers Are Fined Heavily," *New York Times*, 14 August 1913, 18.

69. Ibid.

70. Ibid.

71. "Court Rejections a Bargain," *New York Times*, 27 November 1917, 8.

72. "Subway Smokers Fill Police Nets," *New York Times*, 24 February 1912, 20.

73. Ibid.

74. Ibid.

75. On signs in tobacco store windows, see A. E. Fraser, "Smoking on Surface Cars," *New York Times*, 3 September 1914, 6; on the petition effort, see "Smokers' Petition Fails," *New York Times*, 24 December 1913, 6; "Petition of 72,000 May Restore Smoking on Cars and Trains," *New York Evening World*, 14 October 1913, 1; "Women Come Out in Smokers' Defense," *New York Sun*, 24 October 1913, 6.

76. Brandt, *Cigarette Century*, 96.

77. "Caught Gov. Foss Smoking," *New York Times*, 5 February 1911, 1.

2. SMOKING BANS AND SHOP FLOOR RESISTANCE DURING THE EARLY TWENTIETH CENTURY

1. On increasing rates of smoking among women in the late nineteenth and early twentieth centuries, see Cassandra Tate, *Cigarette Wars: The Triumph of "The Little White Slaver"* (New York: Oxford University Press, 1999), 93–94, 96–97; "New York Women Smoke Up $500,000," *Chicago Daily Tribune*, 24 January 1910, 13; "Smokes for Women," *Chicago Daily Tribune*, 13 August 1916, 4.

2. "The War on the Cigarette," *New York Times*, 8 August 1909, 8; "A Cigarette 258,169 Miles Long," *St. Louis Post-Dispatch*, 30 August 1908, B2. On the rising overall rates of tobacco use in the United States during the 1910s, especially during World War I, see Tate, *Cigarette Wars*, 65, 76–77, 91; Allan M. Brandt, *The Cigarette Century: The Rise, Fall, and Deadly Persistence of the Product That Defined America* (New York: Basic Books, 2007), 47, 48, 51–54; Elizabeth M. Whelan, *A Smoking Gun: How the Tobacco Industry Gets Away with Murder* (Philadelphia: Longman Trade, 1984), 57.

3. Brandt, *Cigarette Century*, 45–47; "War on the Cigarette," 8; Michael S. Givel and Andrew L. Spivak, *Heartland Tobacco War* (Lanham, Md.: Lexington Books, 2013), 11; Tate, *Cigarette Wars*, 55; Richard Kluger, *Ashes to Ashes: America's Hundred-Year Cigarette War, the Public Health, and the Unabashed Triumph of Philip Morris* (New York: Vintage Books, 1997), 66–67.

4. "War on the Cigarette," 8.

5. For a discussion of workers and breaks in the auto industry, see Steve Meyer, "Work, Play, and Power: Masculine Culture on the Automotive Shop Floor, 1930–1960," in *Boys and Their Toys? Masculinity, Class, and Technology in America*, ed. Roger Horowitz (New York: Routledge, 2001), 21.

6. Among many fine studies to consider, see Herbert G. Gutman's classic essay, "Work, Culture, and Society in Industrializing America, 1815–1919," *American Historical Review* 78 (1973): 531–88, reprinted in *Work, Culture and Society in Industrializing America: Essays in American Working-Class History* (New York: Vintage, 1976); Steve Meyer, *The Five Dollar Day: Labor Management and Social Control at the Ford Motor Company, 1908–1921* (Albany: State University of New York Press, 1981); Joyce Shaw Peterson, *American Automobile Workers, 1900–1933* (Albany: State University of New York Press, 1987); James R. Barrett, *Work and Community in the Jungle: Chicago's Packinghouse Workers, 1894–1922* (Urbana: University of Illinois Press, 1987); Rick Halpern, *Down on the Killing Floor: Black and White Workers in Chicago's Packinghouses, 1904–1954* (Urbana: University of Illinois Press, 1997). On the degradation of industrial work in the twentieth century, see Steve Meyer, *The Degradation of Work Revisited: Workers and Technology in the American Auto Industry, 1900–2000*, http://www.autolife.umd.umich.edu/Labor/L_Overview/L_Overview1.htm, accessed 13 March 2009.

7. In addition to the key studies cited above, great examples can be found in Tera Hunter, *To 'Joy My Freedom: Southern Black Women's Lives and Labors after the Civil War* (Cambridge, Mass.: Harvard University Press, 1997), esp. 57–64, 74–97; Robin D. G. Kelley, *Race Rebels: Culture, Politics, and the Black Working Class* (New York: Free Press, 1994),

17–34; Meyer, "Work, Play, and Power," 21, 26; Nelson Lichtenstein, *State of the Union: A Century of American Labor* (Princeton, N.J.: Princeton University Press, 2002), esp. 59–61; Thomas G. Andrews, *Killing for Coal: America's Deadliest Labor War* (Cambridge, Mass.: Harvard University Press, 2008), 162–68, 171–73.

8. For examples of the parochial tendencies of white working men and their shop floor cultures, visit scholarship that examines the automobile industry during the early- to mid-twentieth century. See Meyer, "Work, Play, and Power," 14; Steve Meyer, "Workplace Predators: Sexuality and Harassment on the US Automotive Shopfloor, 1930–1960," *Labor: Studies in Working-Class History of the Americas* 1:1 (2004): 77–93; Kevin Boyle, "The Kiss: Racial and Gender Conflict in a 1950s Automobile Factory," *Journal of American History* 84:2 (1997): 496–523; August Meier and Elliot Rudwick, *Black Detroit and the Rise of the UAW* (New York: Oxford University Press, 1979), 162, 167–68; Thomas J. Sugrue, *The Origins of the Urban Crisis: Race and Inequality in Postwar Detroit* (Princeton, N.J.: Princeton University Press, 1995), 93, 101. For a broader view of shop floor parochialism, see Lichtenstein, *State of the Union*, 73–75, 88–92.

9. Paul Michel Taillon, "'What We Want Is Good, Sober Men': Masculinity, Respectability, and Temperance in the Railroad Brotherhoods, c. 1870–1910," *Journal of Social History* 36:2 (2002): 319–38; Peter Way, "Evil Humors and Ardent Spirits: The Rough Culture of Canal Construction Laborers," *Journal of American History* 79 (1993): 1397–1428; Gutman, "Work, Culture, and Society," 544–45, 550, 557–58.

10. On "time theft," see Barbara Ehrenreich, *Nickel and Dimed: On (Not) Getting By In America* (New York: Metropolitan, 2001), 145–46.

11. See "Road Rules: 'No Cigarets,'" *Chicago Daily Tribune*, 28 August 1908, 16; "Carpenter Has No Easy Job," *Chicago Daily Tribune*, 2 June 1907, E3; Henry Ford, *The Case Against the Little White Slaver* (Detroit: Published by Henry Ford, 1916), 29; Peterson, *American Automobile Workers*, 54–55; Douglas Brinkley, *Wheels for the World: Henry Ford, His Company, and a Century of Progress, 1903–2003* (New York: Viking Press, 2003), 164, 188. For additional useful references, see Kluger, *Ashes to Ashes*, 67; "Teacher Up For Smoking," *New York Times*, 21 November 1923, 2; "On the Worker's Firing Line," *Chicago Daily Tribune*, 28 January 1912, E7; "Cigarette Habit Grows Apace in Salt Lake," *Deseret Evening News*, 21 May 1904, 27; Tate, *Cigarette Wars*, 54–55.

12. On the Homestead strike, see Paul Krause, *The Battle for Homestead, 1880–1892: Politics, Culture, and Steel* (Pittsburgh: University of Pittsburgh Press, 1992); on Pullman, see Nick Salvatore, *Eugene V. Debs: Citizen and Socialist* (Urbana: University of Illinois Press, 1982); Adam Mack, *Sensing Chicago: Noisemakers, Strikebreakers, and Muckrakers* (Urbana: University of Illinois Press, 2015), 66–70. For additional discussions of both, see H. W. Brands, *The Reckless Decade: America in the 1890s* (Chicago: University of Chicago Press, 1995), 128–60. On the history of the CIO, be sure to begin with Lichtenstein, *State of the Union*. Statistics reported in James R. Green, *The World of the Worker: Labor in Twentieth-Century America* (New York: Hill and Wang, 1980), 3, 61.

13. See Annelise Orleck, *Common Sense and a Little Fire: Women and Working-Class Politics in the United States, 1900–1965* (Chapel Hill: University of North Carolina Press, 1995), 53–63; Andrews, *Killing for Coal*; David Brody, *Labor in Crisis: The Steel Strike of 1919* (Westport, Conn.: Greenwood Press, 1965).

14. "Put a Ban on Cigarets," *Chicago Daily Tribune*, 9 April 1900, 2; "Edison Bans Cigarettes," *New York Times*, 11 May 1914, 20; Ford, *Case Against the Little White Slaver*, 29; Tate, *Cigarette Wars*, 55; see also "Prohibition of Cigarettes," *New York Times*, 14 August 1909, 6.

15. "Put a Ban on Cigarets," 2.

16. "On the Worker's Firing Line," *Chicago Daily Tribune*, 28 January 1912, E7.

17. "Off Duty, Smokes Cigarette, Ousted," *St. Louis Post-Dispatch*, 5 June 1908, 10; Tate, *Cigarette Wars*, 55; "How I Lost My Job," *Chicago Daily Tribune*, 24 December 1905, E4.

18. James Samuel Knox, *Personal Efficiency* (Cleveland: Knox Business Book Co., 1920), 56.

19. "Cigarets Put Under a Ban," *Chicago Daily Tribune*, 8 July 1900, 43.

20. Ford, *Case Against the Little White Slaver*, 29; see also "A New Angle—Written from Experience," *Ford News*, 22 September 1923, 2, where managers boasted of their success in eliminating smoking at Ford.

21. Henry Oyen, "Ruin and Death in Wake of Cigaret," *Chicago Daily Tribune*, 16 April 1905, F3.

22. Edward H. Smith, "A Talk with Two Sales Managers About the Men They Employ," *Chicago Daily Tribune*, 24 September 1911, E1; "Smokers Preferred," *New York Times*, 9 August 1903, 29.

23. "Smoking on Cars Is Over Forever," *Chicago Daily Tribune*, 1 November 1918, 17.

24. "'Let's Smoke or We'll Croak!' Is Prayer to Mayor," *Chicago Daily Tribune*, 13 November 1918, 13.

25. "Council Lifts Bar to Smoking Upon 'L' Trains," *Chicago Daily Tribune*, 24 June 1919, 7; "Smoking in Cars," *Chicago Eagle*, 10 May 1919, 4; "Smoking on the 'L' Train," *Chicago Eagle*, 14 June 1919, 2.

26. "Verdict for the Male Shirtwaist," *New York Times*, 9 August 1900, 1; "Hope of Clean Streets By To-Morrow Night," *New York Times*, 11 February 1906, 10; "Steel Car Plant Called a Prison," *New York Times*, 28 August 1909, 1.

27. Though her work examines a very different subject, I am thinking here of Wendy Anne Warren's efforts to reconstruct the racial ideologies and social structures of seventeenth-century Massachusetts, while at the same confronting prominent gaps in the available evidence. See Warren's "'The Cause of Her Grief': The Rape of a Slave in Early New England," *Journal of American History* 93:4 (2007): esp. 1031, 1049.

28. See Ernst Behrend to Carl Hofmann, 21 March 1913, Folder: "Wood Room Strike, 1913," unprocessed box, Hammermill Paper Company Collection, Lilley Library, Penn State Erie, Erie, Pennsylvania (hereafter HPCC); Ernst Behrend to Carl Hofmann, 7 April 1913, Folder: "Wood Room Strike, 1913," unprocessed box, HPCC; Ernst Behrend to Hans Schlesinger, 22 March 1913, Folder: "Labor-Management, 1913," unprocessed box, HPCC; Ernst Behrend to B. A. Behrend, 7 April 1913, Folder: "Labor-Management, 1913," unprocessed box, HPCC. In November 1913, Behrend complained about the election of "Union Labor candidates" to local city council posts. See Ernst Behrend to Carl Hofmann, 5 November 1913, Folder: "Wood Room Strike, 1913," unprocessed box, HPCC. For helpful background information on Ernst Behrend and the development of his paper business, including his concerns about labor strife, see Scott W. Daley, "An Engineer's Story: Ernst Behrend and the Hammermill Paper Company, the First Quarter Century" (PhD diss., West Virginia University, 2010), esp. 76.

29. Ernst Behrend must have been given police powers by a governor of Pennsylvania at some point during the early twentieth century, an increasingly common practice in the Commonwealth. In 1902, for example, Governor William A. Stone issued 4,512 commissions to business owners as complaints from employers about coal miner strikes increased. See Frank Morn, *"The Eye That Never Sleeps": A History of the Pinkerton National Detective Agency* (Bloomington: Indiana University Press, 1982), 168. On coal mining strikes in Pennsylvania in the late nineteenth and early twentieth centuries, see Victor Greene, *The Slavic Community on Strike: Immigrant Labor in Pennsylvania Anthracite* (Notre Dame, Ind.: University of Notre Dame Press, 1968); David Montgomery, *The Fall of the House of Labor: The Workplace, the State, and American Labor Activism, 1865–1925* (Cambridge, UK: Cambridge University Press, 1989), 335, 341; "The Strike in Pennsylvania," *New York Times*, 22 April 1894, 2; "Miners' Strike Aspect," *New York Times*, 8 July 1897, 7; "Pittsburg Short of Coal," *New York Times*, 11 April 1900, 5. William J. Burns operated the most

famous private detective firm of the early twentieth century. Burns had been a Secret Service agent, and his new company quickly eclipsed Allan Pinkerton's infamous National Detective Agency ("the Pinkertons"). In 1911, Burns and his agents captured two men with anarchist leanings, James B. McNamara and John J. McNamara, who had close ties to the International Association of Bridge and Structural Iron Workers, American Federation of Labor (AFL). They were found guilty of bombing the *Los Angeles Times* building in 1910, where twenty people were killed. See Gene Caesar, *Incredible Detective: The Biography of William J. Burns* (Englewood Cliffs, N.J.: Prentice Hall, 1968), 160–87.

30. Behrend to Hofmann, 7 April 1913; Ernst Behrend to Carl Hofmann, 12 May 1913, Folder: "Wood Room Strike, 1913," unprocessed box, HPCC.

31. On the finishing room petition, see L. M. Fratus to Ernst Behrend, 14 March 1914, Folder: "Reference to Finishing room Petition, 1914," unprocessed box, HPCC; quotes appear in Behrend to Hofmann, 7 April 1913.

32. "Paper Mills Strike Not Yet Settled," *New York Times*, 27 September 1908, 7.

33. "Glens Falls, NY," *New York Times*, 10 March 1910, 2; "Lundrigan Is Pleased," *New York Times*, 23 May 1910, 7.

34. "12,000 Workers on Lake Boats Strike," *New York Times*, 2 May 1909, 2. Also, there were earlier strikes among Great Lakes seamen in 1904 and 1906. See David Brody, *Steelworkers in America: The Nonunion Era* (1960; repr., Urbana: University of Illinois Press, 1998), 76.

35. On the history of maritime labor unrest, with a focus on the early modern Atlantic, see Peter Linebaugh and Marcus Rediker, *The Many-Headed Hydra: Sailors, Slaves, Commoners, and the Hidden History of the Revolutionary Atlantic* (Boston: Beacon Press, 2000); Marcus Rediker, *Villains of All Nations: Atlantic Pirates in the Golden Age* (Boston: Beacon Press, 2004).

36. "Shooting in Lake Strike," *New York Times*, 9 May 1909, 1.

37. "Furious Rioting Near Pittsburg," *New York Times*, 15 July 1909, 1. For overviews of labor unrest in McKees Rocks, see John N. Ingham, "A Strike in the Progressive Era: McKees Rocks, 1909," *Pennsylvania Magazine of History and Biography* 90 (1966): 353–77; Edward Levinson, *I Break Strikes! The Technique of Pearl L. Bergoff* (New York: Arno, 1935), 70–88; Robert M. Smith, "'King' Pearl L. Bergoff Invades McKees Rocks!" *Pennsylvania Heritage* 28:3 (2002): 30–37; Brody, *Steelworkers in America*, 138–139; Green, *The World of the Worker*, 68–69.

38. Levinson, *I Break Strikes!* 75.

39. "Five Killed in Strike Riot," *New York Times*, 23 August 1909, 1.

40. "McKees Rocks Strike Ends," *New York Times*, 9 September 1909, 5.

41. "Seven Shot in Riot and Three May Die," *New York Times*, 21 April 1910, 1.

42. On the Mine Wars of the early twentieth century, see David Alan Corbin, *Life, Work, and Rebellion in the Coal Fields: The Southern West Virginia Miners, 1880–1922* (Urbana: University of Illinois Press, 1981); Stephen H. Norwood, *Strikebreaking and Intimidation: Mercenaries and Masculinity in Twentieth-Century America* (Chapel Hill: University of North Carolina Press, 2002), 114–70; Elliot Gorn, *Mother Jones: The Most Dangerous Woman in America* (New York: Hill and Wang, 2001), esp. 169–225; Andrews, *Killing for Coal*.

43. Sidney Howard and Robert Dunn described the activities of Howard W. Russell's spying business in some detail. See Sidney Howard, with Robert Dunn, *The Labor Spy* (New York: Republic Publishing Company, 1924), 19, 29–31, 45, 55–56. His name would briefly appear again in a discussion of labor spying during the 1930s. See Leo Huberman, *The Labor Spy Racket* (New York: Modern Age Books, 1937), 169. For the reference to "systematic surveillance," see Howard W. Russell to Ernst Behrend, 3 August 1915, File: "Manufacturers and Merchants Inspection Bureau," unprocessed box, HPCC.

44. See Howard, with Dunn, *Labor Spy*, 29–30.

45. Russell to Behrend, 3 August 1915. In Cleveland, F. J. Heine, who managed a firm called the "Employers' Information Service" used similar wording in his company's 1911 correspondence: "Dear Sir: Are there any leaks in your plant? Of course—but you may not know it. And how are you going to find out? It is the small leaks, the loss of dollars here and there, which help to eat up the large profits. Our business is to find the leaks in your business, *and observe what is not for the eyes and ears of the boss to see or hear.*" See *American Flint*, June 1911, reprinted in Harry W. Laidler, *Boycotts and the Labor Struggle* (New York: John Lane Company, 1913), 294, available at http://historymatters.gmu.edu/d/5663, accessed 9 January 2009. Emphasis in original. For a discussion of a second spy firm in Cleveland, see Howard, with Dunn, *Labor Spy*, 14–15, 19. Since 1855, the Pinkertons had promised to root out "habits and associations of employees." See Jennifer Luff, "Surrogate Supervisors: Railway Spotters and the Origins of Workplace Surveillance," *Labor: Studies in Working-Class History of the Americas* 5:1 (2008): 52.

46. FP, Report, 21 June 1915; FP, Report, 22 June 1915; FP, Report, 23 June 1915, all in HPCC (copies in possession of the author). Ernst Behrend's copies of FP and HC's reports can be found in Box 6A. The spy reports in the Hammermill records were flawlessly typed; they were sent directly to the Manufacturers and Merchants Inspection Bureau in Milwaukee for processing, where they were probably retyped for the client. For insights into the processing of labor spy reports, see Charles K. Hyde, "Undercover and Underground: Labor Spies and Mine Management in the Early Twentieth Century," *Business History Review* 60:1 (1986): 17.

47. Hyde, "Undercover and Underground," 16–19; Gary M. Fink, *The Fulton Bag and Cotton Mills Strike of 1914–1915: Espionage, Labor Conflict, and New South Industrial Relations* (Ithaca, N.Y.: Cornell University Press, 1993), 92. Despite the deployment of two spies from the same firm, FP and HC were likely unaware of the other's work, as they never mentioned or alluded to any possible coordination of efforts or their colleague's presence in their reports.

48. HC, Report, 3 August 1915; HC, Report, 4 August 1915; HC, Report, 5 August 1915; HC, Report, 6 August 1915, all in HPCC.

49. Ibid.

50. Ibid.

51. Ibid.

52. For example, see HC, Report, 12 August 1915, HPCC; FP, Report, 15 July 1915, HPCC. Social historians have studied everyday forms of worker resistance for many years. On industrial workers' resistance to labor discipline, be sure to begin with Gutman, "Work, Culture, and Society"; David Montgomery, *Workers' Control in America: Studies in the History of Work, Technology, and Labor Struggles* (Cambridge, UK: Cambridge University Press, 1979). Also, historians of slavery in the Americas also made it possible for historians to study resistance, labor, and history from below. See the pioneering work of Herbert Aptheker in his *American Negro Slave Revolts* (New York: International Publishers, 1943); Peter H. Wood, *Black Majority: Negroes in Colonial South Carolina From 1670 Through the Stono Rebellion* (1974; repr., New York: W. W. Norton & Company, 1996); Eugene Genovese, *Roll, Jordan, Roll: The World the Slaves Made* (New York: Vintage, 1976). For additional histories from below, see Kelley, *Race Rebels*, 236–37 (notes 5–6).

53. On labor spying in US history, see Fink, *Fulton Bag and Cotton Mills Strike*; Hyde, "Undercover and Underground," 1–27; Luff, "Surrogate Supervisors," 47–74; various references in Robert P. Weiss, "Private Detective Agencies and Labour Discipline in the United States, 1855–1946," *Historical Journal* 29:1 (1986): 87–107; Stephen Robertson, "The Company's Voice in the Workplace: Labor Spies, Propaganda, and Personnel Management, 1918–1920," *Labor: Studies in Working Class History of the Americas* 10:3 (2013):

57–79; Julie Greene, *The Canal Builders: Making America's Empire at the Panama Canal* (New York: Penguin Books, 2009); Norwood, *Strikebreaking and Intimidation*, esp. 197. For an additional related study, see Jennifer Fronc, *New York Undercover: Private Surveillance in the Progressive Era* (Chicago: University of Chicago Press, 2009), esp. 145–75. Also, useful published examinations of labor spies' activities during the early twentieth century include Interchurch World Movement, *Report on the Steel Strike of 1919* (New York: Harcourt, Brace and Howe, 1920); Howard, with Dunn, *Labor Spy*; John A. Fitch, *The Causes of Industrial Unrest* (New York: Harper & Brothers, 1924), 171–84; Levinson, *I Break Strikes!*; Lois MacDonald, *Labor Problems and the American Scene* (New York: Harper, 1938), 606–9; William Z. Foster, *Pages from a Worker's Life* (1939; repr., New York: International Publishers, 1970), 201–11; Huberman, *Labor Spy Racket*. In particular, be sure to consult "Summary of Senate Sub-Committee's Report on Use of Espionage in Industry," *New York Times*, 22 December 1937, 22, a thorough overview of Senators Robert M. LaFollette and Elbert D. Thomas's special Senate subcommittee report on the workings of the labor spy industry.

54. On the early history of the Hammermill Paper Company, see Michael J. Mcquillen and William P. Garvey, *The Best Known Name In Paper: Hammermill, a History of the Company* (Erie, Pa.: Hammermill Paper Company, 1985); Daley, "An Engineer's Story"; Chris Groesch, "From Family to Frustration: Hammermill Managerial Philosophy, 1898–1920," unpublished seminar paper, Penn State Erie, in author's possession.

55. See the detailed findings of Robert W. Dunn in *Labor and Automobiles* (New York: International Publishers, 1929); and later studies by Meyer, *Five Dollar Day*; Peterson, *American Automobile Workers*, esp. 38–41, 48–56, 95–102; Roger Keeran, *The Communist Party and the Auto Workers' Unions* (1980; repr., New York: International Publishers, 1986), 52–56.

56. HC, Report, 24 August 1915, HPCC.

57. HC, Report, 26 August 1915, HPCC; HC, Report, 23 August 1915, HPCC.

58. HC, Report, 18 August 1915; FP, Report, 7 July 1915; FP, Report, 19 July 1915, all in HPCC.

59. FP, Report, 3 September 1915, HPCC.

60. FP, Report, 10 July 1915, HPCC; FP, Report, 22 July 1915, HPCC.

61. On worker uses of factory bathrooms, see Meyer, "Work, Play, and Power," 19–20.

62. FP, 22 July 1915.

63. HC, Report, 16 August 1915, HPCC.

64. FP, 22 July 1915; see also Howard, with Dunn, *Labor Spy*, 55.

65. FP, 22 July 1915.

66. FP, Report, 25 August 1915, HPCC.

67. HC, Report, 14 September 1915, HPCC; HC, Report, n.d., HPCC.

68. FP, Report, 21 July 1915, HPCC.

69. FP, 21 July 1915. On European immigrants' otherness and uncertain claims to whiteness in the late nineteenth and early twentieth centuries, see Matthew Frye Jacobson, *Whiteness of a Different Color: European Immigrants and the Alchemy of Race* (Cambridge, Mass.: Harvard University Press, 1998).

70. See Ernst Behrend to Carl Hofmann, 21 March 1913, Folder: "Wood Room Strike, 1913," unprocessed box, HPCC; Ernst Behrend to Carl Hofmann, 7 April 1913, Folder: "Wood Room Strike, 1913," unprocessed box, HPCC.

71. US Bureau of the Census, *Thirteenth Census of the United States, Vol. I, Population, 1910* (Washington, D.C.: Government Printing Office, 1913), 864–65 (Table 38).

72. US Bureau of the Census, *Fourteenth Census of the United States, Vol. II, Population, 1920* (Washington, D.C.: Government Printing Office, 1922), 764–65 (Table 17).

73. FP, 25 August 1915.

74. On "moral economy," see E. P. Thompson, "The Moral Economy of the English Crowd in the Eighteenth Century," *Past & Present* 50 (1971): 76–136; Hunter, *To 'Joy My Freedom*, 60–61.

75. FP, 7 July 1915.

76. FP, Report, 25 June 1915; FP, Report, 30 June 1915; FP, Report, 24 August 1915, all in HPCC.

77. FP, 30 June 1915.

78. HC, 18 August 1915; FP, Report, 24 June 1915, HPCC.

79. FP, Report, 26 July 1915, HPCC.

80. FP, Report, 25 July 1915, HPCC.

81. FP, 24 June 1915.

82. FP, Report, 14 July 1915, HPCC.

83. FP, 30 June 1915.

84. FP, Report, 2 July 1915, HPCC; FP, Report, 1 July 1915, HPCC.

85. FP, Report, 10 August 1915, HPCC. On smell and detection, though with a focus on white racism in the American South, see Mark M. Smith, *How Race Is Made: Slavery, Segregation, and the Senses* (Chapel Hill: University of North Carolina Press, 2006), 1–2, 35, 71–72. For helpful introductions to sensory history, see the engaging collection of essays by Mark M. Smith, Gerard J. Fitzgerald, Gabriella M. Petrick, Connie Y. Chiang, Richard Cullen Rath, James W. Cook, and David Howes in "The Senses in American History: A Round Table," *Journal of American History* 95:2 (2008): 378–451; as well as Mack, *Sensing Chicago*, 1–9.

86. FP, 7 July 1915.

87. FP, 22 July 1915.

88. FP, Report, 28 July 1915, HPCC.

89. FP, 28 July 1915.

90. FP, Report, 27 July 1915, HPCC.

91. FP, 27 July 1915.

92. FP, Report, 29 July 1915, HPCC.

93. FP, 29 July 1915.

94. FP, Report, 12 July 1915, HPCC.

95. FP, Report, 20 August 1915, HPCC.

96. On the social and political significance of everyday speech, see Jane Kamensky, *Governing the Tongue: The Politics of Speech in Early New England* (New York: Oxford University Press, 1997), esp. 5, 9–10, 15.

97. FP, Report, 6 September 1915, HPCC.

98. FP, Report, 16 September 1915, HPCC.

99. FP, Report, 17 September 1915, HPCC. No other documents in the Hammermill archive point to Mann as a company informant.

100. In addition to several key works cited above, see Brody, *Steelworkers in America*, 82–84; John A. Fitch, *The Steel Workers* (1910; repr., Pittsburgh: University of Pittsburgh Press, 1989), 214–15.

101. See "Paper Strike Spreads," *New York Times*, 21 March 1910, 3.

102. FP, Report, 5 August 1915, HPCC.

103. FP, 22 July 1915; FP, 29 July 1915.

104. FP, Report, 2 August 1915, HPCC.

105. FP, Report, 18 September 1915, HPCC.

106. "Teach, Don't Boss," *Hammermill Bond*, March 1918, 1.

107. Ernst Behrend to A. G. Becker, 28 June 1918, Folder: "Beater Room Strike, 1918," unprocessed box, HPCC; A. G. Becker to Ernst Behrend, 1 July 1918, Folder: "Beater Room Strike, 1918," unprocessed box, HPCC.

108. "Personnel Practices in Factory Administration," *Monthly Labor Review* (July 1937): 64, 66.

109. Paul S. Taylor, *Mexican Labor in the United States: Chicago and the Calumet Region* (Berkeley: University of California Press, 1932), 97.

110. Available at http://www.nlrb.gov/search/advanced, see Corinth Hosiery Mill, Inc. & American Federation of Hosiery Workers, 25 October 1939, 16 NLRB No. 43; Goshen Rubber and Manufacturing Company & United Rubber Workers of America, 28 March 1939, 11 NLRB No. 121; Continental Box Company & Federal Labor Union, 25 January 1940, 19 NLRB No. 92, all accessed 2 April 2014; see also *NLRB v. Bradford Dyeing Association*, 310 U.S. 318, 1940, https://bulk.resource.org/courts.gov/c/US/310/310. US.318.588.html, all accessed 2 April 2014.

3. WORKERS, MANAGEMENT, AND THE RIGHT TO SMOKE DURING WORLD WAR II

1. Local 600 Executive Board Minutes, June 5, 1945, in box 1, folder 11, UAW Local 600 Collection, Walter P. Reuther Library, Wayne State University (hereafter WPRL).

2. John Gunther, *Inside USA* (New York: Harper & Brothers, 1947), 398.

3. Allan M. Brandt, *The Cigarette Century: The Rise, Fall, and Deadly Persistence of the Product That Defined America* (New York: Basic Books, 2007), 97. Sociologists Robert S. Lynd and Helen Merrell Lynd argued that the Great Depression led men and women to smoke more as a "tension releaser." See Robert S. Lynd and Helen Merrell Lynd, *Middletown in Transition: A Study in Cultural Conflicts* (New York: Harcourt, Brace and Company, 1937), 280.

4. Gunther, *Inside USA*, 399.

5. See "Normandie's End," *Life*, 9 December 1946, 38; as well as United States Naval Institute, *The US Coast Guard in World War II* (Annapolis, Md.: United States Naval Institute, 1957), 66–67; Richard Goldstein, *Helluva Town: The Story of New York during World War II* (New York: Free Press, 2010), 78.

6. "Careless Workers Fined," *New York Times*, 12 February 1942, 13.

7. "12 Fined for Smoking in Aeronautical Plant," *New York Times*, 25 February 1942, 21.

8. "Jail Faces Smokers in War Factories," *New York Times*, 26 February 1942, 21.

9. "12 Fined for Smoking in Aeronautical Plant," 21.

10. "Jail Faces Smokers in War Factories," 21.

11. "Fined for Smoking on Pier," *New York Times*, 25 April 1942, 28. On the importance of New York's ports as employers of working men during the 1940s, see Joshua B. Freeman, *Working-Class New York: Life and Labor Since World War II* (New York: New Press, 2000), 18–19. During the 1940s and early 1950s, an estimated 400,000 workers labored in occupations that were dependent on the activities of the ports in New York.

12. "Curran Asks Mayor to Get Facts Straight Before Criticizing Pier Smoking Cases," *New York Times*, 13 May 1942, 21.

13. "Pier Smoking Brings Heavy Fines to 6 Men," *New York Times*, 24 October 1942, 16.

14. "Jail Faces Smokers in War Factories," 21.

15. Ibid.

16. Ibid.

17. "60 Days for Plant Smoker," *New York Times*, 11 March 1942, 21.

18. Ibid.

19. "'Shakedown' Attempt Laid to an Inspector," *New York Times*, 8 July 1943, 11.

20. "12 Fined for Smoking in Aeronautical Plant," 21.

21. "Curran Asks Mayor to Get Facts Straight," 21.

22. "Smoking Fine Protested," *New York Times*, 8 February 1944, 17.

23. On the importance of cigarettes in military life and wartime mobilization during World War I, see Tate, *Cigarette Wars*, 65–92.

24. "Here's the Cigarette *Reader's Digest* Didn't Know About," *Life*, 14 December 1942, 22; "All Right [*sic*] You Are Smoking More," *Life*, 18 January 1943, 58; "Go Modern—Smoke REGENT!" *Life*, 3 August 1942, 87. For a brief discussion of cigarette companies' efforts to connect their product to military service during World War II, see Brandt, *Cigarette Century*, 100.

25. John Bush Jones, *All-Out for Victory! Magazine Advertising and the World War II Homefront* (Waltham, Mass.: Brandeis University Press, 2009), 167, 166; John C. Burnham, *Bad Habits: Drinking, Smoking, Taking Drugs, Gambling, Sexual Misbehavior and Swearing in American History* (New York: New York University Press, 1994), 103.

26. See these and other wartime cigarette advertisements at the Stanford Research Into the Impact of Tobacco Advertising website, http://tobacco.stanford.edu. On women and smoking during World War II, see Kerry Segrave, *Women and Smoking in America, 1880–1950* (Jefferson, N.C.: McFarland & Company, Inc., 2005), 154–55, 196–97.

27. William H. Young and Nancy K. Young, *World War II and the Postwar Years in America: A Historical and Cultural Encyclopedia* (Santa Barbara, Calif.: ABC-CLIO, 2010), 12; Peter Collins, ed., *The Columbia Companion to American History on Film* (New York: Columbia University Press, 2003), 524. On Lucky Strikes marketing schemes during the war, see Richard Kluger, *Ashes to Ashes: America's Hundred-Year Cigarette War, the Public Health, and the Unabashed Triumph of Philip Morris* (New York: Vintage Books, 1997), 116–17; Brandt, *Cigarette Century*, 89.

28. *Casablanca*, dir. Michael Curtiz, Warner Bros., 1942; Kluger, *Ashes to Ashes*, 114–15. On images of smoking on screen during the 1930s, see Eric Burns, *The Smoke of the Gods: A Social History of Tobacco* (Philadelphia: Temple University Press, 2007), 187–88.

29. "Cigarettes Sent," *United Automobile Worker: Ford Facts*, 15 May 1944, 4A. On other efforts in the United States to organize cigarette donations for soldiers, see James C. Cooke, *Chewing Gum, Candy Bars, and Beer: The Army PX in World War II* (Columbia: University of Missouri Press, 2009), 65.

30. "Send 'Em Cigarets, Not Souvenirs," *United Automobile Worker: Tool Die & Engineering News Edition*, 1 August 1942, 3A.

31. Local 600 Executive Board Minutes, 21 December 1943, in box 1, folder 8, UAW Local 600 Collection, WPRL.

32. Local 600 Executive Board Minutes, 16 October 1945, in box 1, folder 9, UAW Local 600 Collection, WPRL.

33. "Factory No. 13—Dept. No. 81," *Local 599 Headlight*, 29 July 1942, 2.

34. B. H. Scott to E. L. Snyder, August 9, 1944, in box 7, Folder: "Correspondence from Briggs Personnel Director, 1943–1946," UAW Local 212 Collection, WPRL.

35. "Union Officer States Ford Strike Issues," *United Automobile Worker*, 15 April 1941, 2, in box 38, folder 4, UAW Local 3 Collection, WPRL; Louis Stark, "Ford Parley Today Expected by Dewey," *New York Times*, 7 April 1941, 11. The Ford Motor Company also maintained smoking bans at its operations in the Upper Peninsula of Michigan and in Brazil at the Fordlandia rubber plantation. See Greg Grandin, *Fordlandia: The Rise and Fall of Henry Ford's Forgotten Jungle City* (New York: Metropolitan Books, 2010), 63, 192.

36. "Unsettled Grievances," *United Automobile Worker: Local 212 Edition*, 1 August 1942, 3A.

37. Judith Stepan-Norris and Maurice Zeitlin, ed., *Talking Union* (Urbana: University of Illinois Press, 1996), 62. On the history of the Service Department at Ford, see Stephen H. Norwood, *Strikebreaking and Intimidation: Mercenaries and Masculinity in Twentieth-Century America* (Chapel Hill: University of North Carolina Press, 2002).

38. Ed Jennings, "Wildcat! The Wartime Strike Wave in the Auto Industry," *Radical America* 9 (1975): http://www.prole.info/texts/wartimestrikes.html, accessed 13 February 2012; Nelson Lichtenstein, *Labor's War at Home: The CIO in World War II* (New York: Cambridge University Press, 1982), 191.

39. "Walkout Ends at War Plant," *Detroit News*, 10 October 1942, 1, 2.

40. See "Big Finance Propaganda," *United Automobile Worker: Local 7 Edition*, 1 November 1942, 1. Nelson Lichtenstein points out that Chrysler managers used the company's "nuisance" no-smoking policies to harass autoworkers and unionists during the war years. See Lichtenstein, *Labor's War at Home*, 120.

41. "Walkout Ends at War Plant," 2; "Big Finance Propaganda," 1.

42. "Smoke-on-the-Job Strike," *Detroit News*, 10 October 1942, 6.

43. "Big Finance Propaganda," 1.

44. Steve Mysliwiec, "Supervisors Keep Home Fires Burning With Cigars and Cigarets," *United Automobile Worker: Dodge Main News Edition*, 15 October 1942, 4, in box 1, folder 12, Nick DiGaetano Collection, WPRL.

45. A. J. Cobb, "Burning Issues Vanish But This Reporter Is Ready if More Arise," *United Automobile Worker: Dodge Main News Edition*, 1 September 1942, 2A. For a similar observation made in a New York City factory, see Edward Pessen, "A Young Industrial Worker in Early World War II New York City," *Labor History* 22:2 (1981): 279.

46. Cobb, "Burning Issues Vanish," 2A.

47. "Walkout Ends at War Plant," *Detroit News*, 10 October 1942, 1.

48. "Smoke Ban Causes Chrysler Walkout," *New York Times*, 10 October 1942, 7.

49. "Factory No. 19—," *Local 599 Headlight*, 23 September 1942, 7.

50. Robert H. Zieger, *The CIO, 1935–1955* (Chapel Hill: University of North Carolina, 1995), 114.

51. Nelson Lichtenstein, *State of the Union: A Century of American Labor* (Princeton, N.J.: Princeton University Press, 2002), 44–45, 48–51, 60–61.

52. Numerous sit-down strikes occurred in numerous settings beyond basic industry during the early months of 1937 in the wake of the Flint sit-down strike. Small hotels, neighborhood bakeries, and the smallest tailoring shops with only one or two workers experienced strikes. In these strikes, demands for increased wages actually figured most prominently. See Gregory Wood, *Retiring Men: Manhood, Labor, and Growing Old in America, 1900–1960* (Lanham, Md.: University Press of America, 2012), 120.

53. Lichtenstein, *State of the Union*, 52; Zieger, *CIO*, 67, 94. The sit-down statistic for 1937 appears in James R. Green, *The World of the Worker: Labor in Twentieth-Century America* (New York: Hill and Wang, 1980), 157; see also Irving Bernstein, *The Turbulent Years: A History of the American Worker, 1933–1941* (Boston: Houghton Mifflin Company, 1969), 500.

54. Lichtenstein, *State of the Union*, 54.

55. For these statistics, see Lichtenstein, *Labor's War at Home*, 133, 134. On the sources of wartime strikes, in addition to Nelson Lichtenstein's *Labor's War at Home*, see Melvyn Dubofsky and Warren Van Tine, *John L. Lewis: A Biography* (Urbana: University of Illinois Press, 1986), 305; George Lipsitz, *Rainbow at Midnight: Labor and Culture in the 1940s* (Urbana: University of Illinois Press, 1994), 69–92.

56. John Anderson, "Questions and Answers on the Overtime Problem," 1–2, in box 7, folder 30, UAW Local 3 Collection, WPRL.

57. Joel Seidman, *American Labor from Defense to Reconversion* (Chicago: University of Chicago Press, 1953), 132.

58. F. H. Taylor to Walter Reuther, 23 March 1945, in box 7, folder: "Correspondence from Briggs Personnel Director, 1943–1946," UAW Local 212 Collection, WPRL.

59. See "Smith-Connally Act," in *The Home Front Encyclopedia: United States, Britain, and Canada in World Wars I and II*, ed. James Ciment and Thaddeus Russell (Santa Barbara, Calif.: ABC-CLIO, 2007), 1025; as well as Josiah Bartlett Lambert, *"If the Workers Took a Notion": The Right to Strike and American Political Development* (Ithaca, N.Y.: Cornell University Press, 2005), 115; Lichtenstein, *Labor's War at Home*, 153, 167–68.

60. "Let's Not Fall in the Company's Trap" (October 1944), in box 7, folder: "Correspondence from Briggs Personnel Director, 1943–1946," UAW Local 212 Collection, WPRL.

61. This chapter cautiously disagrees with the argument that union bureaucratization tempered or even undermined shop floor militancy during the war. On the institutionalization of CIO unions and its impact on the shop floor during World War II, see Lichtenstein, *Labor's War at Home*; Nelson Lichtenstein, "Ambiguous Legacy: The Union Security Problem during World War II," *Labor History* 18:2 (1977): 214–38; Zieger, *CIO*; Howard Kimeldorf, "World War II and the Deradicalization of American Labor: The ILWU as a Deviant Case," *Labor History* 33:2 (1992): esp. 248; Joshua Freeman, "Delivering the Goods: Industrial Unionism during World War II," *Labor History* (1978): 570–93; Seidman, *American Labor from Defense to Reconversion*, esp. 135–51. Nelson Lichtenstein, however, backs away from this argument in *State of the Union*. CIO institutionalization during World War II, however, furthered the cause of racial justice, as the federal government, civil rights activists, and progressive labor leaders pressed for more racial justice in defense industries. See, for example, August Meier and Elliott Rudwick, *Black Detroit and the Rise of the UAW* (New York: Oxford University Press, 1981); Lichtenstein, *State of the Union*, esp. 71–73, 76–88; Beth Tompkins Bates, *Pullman Porters and the Rise of Protest Politics in Black America* (Chapel Hill: University of North Carolina Press, 2001), esp. 178–83.

62. On the importance of skilled workers in the labor militancy of the 1930s, see Steve Babson, *Building the Union: Skilled Workers and Anglo-Gaelic Immigrants in the Rise of the UAW* (New Brunswick, N.J.: Rutgers University Press, 1991); Nelson Lichtenstein, *Walter Reuther: The Most Dangerous Man in Detroit* (New York: Basic Books, 1995).

63. "Unions Get Proposal in Flint Strike," *Detroit Free Press*, 18 July 1942, 5; "Pickets Line Tank Plant," *Detroit News*, 16 July 1942, 4.

64. "Smoke-Strikers Called a Disgrace to Nation," *Detroit News*, 19 July 1942, 1.

65. "State to Act in Tank Tie-Up," *Detroit News*, 21 July 1942, 1.

66. "Pickets Line Tank Plant," 4; "Unions Get Proposal in Flint Strike," 5.

67. "No Smoking Row Slows Tank Plant," *Detroit Free Press*, 16 July 1942, 13; "Strike Over 'No Smoking' Rule Cripples Tank Plant," *Chicago Daily Tribune*, 16 July 1942, 23.

68. "No Smoking Row Slows Tank Plant," 13.

69. "Pickets Line Tank Plant," 4.

70. Ibid.; "Unions Get Proposal in Flint Strike," 5.

71. "Unions Get Proposal in Flint Strike," 5.

72. "Pickets Line Tank Plant."

73. "Unions Get Proposal in Flint Strike," 5.

74. "Pickets Line Tank Plant," 4; "Unions Get Proposal in Flint Strike," 5.

75. "Appeal Made to Employees in Fisher Tank Plant Strike," *Los Angeles Times*, 19 July 1942, 10; "Fisher Assails Tank Strike," *New York Times*, 19 July 1942, 33.

76. "A Traitorous Strike," *Detroit Free Press*, 18 July 1942, 4.

77. "Factory No. 13—Dept. No. 81," *Local 599 Headlight*, 29 July 1942, 2.

78. "State To Act in Tank Tie-Up," 1.

79. Ibid.

80. "WLB Settles Tank Strike," *Detroit News*, 22 July 1942, 1; "Stoppages Gain in Production of War Goods," *Washington Post*, 23 July 1942, 2.

81. Melvyn Dubofsky, *The State and Labor in Modern America* (Chapel Hill: University of North Carolina Press, 1994), 190; Lichtenstein, *Labor's War at Home*, 167–68; Seidman, *American Labor from Defense to Reconversion*, 138.

82. James R. Green, *The World of the Worker: Labor in Twentieth-Century America* (New York: Hill and Wang, 1980), 183.

83. Jennings, "Wildcat!"

84. UAW veteran Henry Kraus recalled how Flint sit-down strikers sometimes fell asleep with lit cigarettes in the "dormitories" where they slept. See Henry Kraus, *The Many and the Few: A Chronicle of the Dynamic Auto Workers*, 2nd ed. (Urbana: University of Illinois Press, 1985), 96. For a description of the dormitories, see Robert Morss Lovett, "A GM Stockholder Visits Flint," *Nation*, 30 January 1937, 123.

85. "Strike Voted at Chevrolet War Plant," *Detroit News*, 2 November 1943, 1; "Workers Vote Strike, 4 to 1, at Chevrolet," *Washington Post*, 3 November 1943, 13.

86. "Free Mail to Soldiers," *United Automobile Worker*, 15 February 1944, 6.

87. "Strike Voted at Chevrolet War Plant," 1.

88. "4 Men Quit Again; 450 Idle at Rouge," *Detroit News*, 16 November 1943, 31; "Ford Walkout Proves Brief," *Detroit News*, 17 November 1943, 4; "WLB Blamed for Stoppage," *Detroit News*, 18 November 1943, 29; "400 Foundrymen Out at Saginaw," *Detroit News*, 21 November 1943, 8.

89. Jennings, "Wildcat!"

90. "Rest-Period Demand Costs Hours at Ford," *New York Times*, 31 December 1941, 9.

91. "Ford Workers Show Patriotism in Dispute over Rest Periods," *United Automobile Worker: Ford Facts*, n.d., n.p., in box 15, folder 13, UAW Unbound Newspaper Collection, WPRL.

92. "5,600 Are Out at Ford HP," *Detroit News*, 29 January 1944, 1; "A Ford Worker Is Reprimanded," *Chicago Daily Tribune*, 29 January 1944, 19.

93. Martin Glaberman, *Wartime Strikes: The Struggle Against the No-Strike Pledge in the UAW during World War II* (Detroit: Bewick Editions, 1980), 55.

94. Ben Garrison, "An Open Letter to Mr. Henry Ford," *United Automobile Worker: Ford Local 400 Highland Park Watchword Edition*, 15 February 1944, 1.

95. "No Wildcat Strikes," *United Automobile Worker: The Highland Park Local Watchword*, 15 August 1942, 4A.

96. Lichtenstein, *Labor's War at Home*, 191. Another account (though lacking in details) of the March 1944 incidents can be found in David E. Noble, *Forces of Production: A Social History of Industrial Automation* (New York: Oxford University Press, 1984), 23. For an extended discussion of a similar confrontation ("bloody riot") in 1943 at the River Rouge plant, see Steve Meyer, "Rough Manhood: The Aggressive and Confrontational Shop Culture of US Auto Workers during World War II," *Journal of Social History* 36:1 (2002): 139–42.

97. Lichtenstein, *Labor's War at Home*, 191–92.

98. Quoted in Ibid., 191.

99. Ibid., 192.

100. Ibid.

101. Glaberman, *Wartime Strikes*, 53. There were at least two more strikes against smoking bans in Michigan auto factories in 1944: "a dispute over smoking regulations" at the Chevrolet transmission plant in Saginaw (May 1944) and a "Mass smoking demonstration protesting shop-smoking regulations" at Cadillac in Detroit (December 1944). On the Chevrolet incident, see "New Tie-Ups Hit the Detroit Area," *New York Times*, 27 May 1944, 11; on the strike at Cadillac, see Glaberman, *Wartime Strikes*, 53.

102. "2,100 Walk Out on War Project in Front Royal," *Washington Post*, 18 June 1944, M3.

103. "Union Right in Walkout Is Upheld," *Baltimore Sun*, 25 November 1948, 1.

104. See "In the Matter of General Motors Corporation, Chevrolet Gear & Axle Division, Detroit, Michigan and International Union, United Automobile Aircraft and Agricultural Implement Workers of America, CIO—Local #235," in box 101, folder 29, UAW General Motors Department Collection, WPRL; as well as "Minutes of Shop Committee Meeting" (Chevrolet, St. Louis), 12 May 1945, 1, in box 101, folder 30, UAW General Motors Department Collection, WPRL; "Notice" (Chevrolet, Toledo), 1 May 1945, in box 101, folder 30, UAW General Motors Department Collection, WPRL.

105. "Ford Ends Founder's Ban on Smoking on the Job," *New York Times*, 30 October 1947, 13. Despite the end of the ban, women in offices were not allowed to smoke.

106. Ben Hamper, *Rivethead: Tales from the Assembly Line* (New York: Warner Books, 1986), 1.

107. For the quote and statistic, see Brandt, *Cigarette Century*, 97.

108. Emily Post, *Etiquette* (1927; repr., New York: Funk & Wagnalls Company, 1945), 444–47.

4. ANTISMOKING POLITICS IN POSTWAR WORKPLACES

1. Charles Seabrook, "Health Agency Called Soft on Smoking," no publication title, n.d., TI20221399, Legacy Tobacco Documents Library, University of California, San Francisco (hereafter LTDL); "Federal Agency Has New Smoking Woes," *Star-News* (Wilmington, N.C.), 11 May 1980, 6.

2. See Angel Kwolek-Folland, *Engendering Business: Men and Women in the Corporate Office, 1870–1930* (Baltimore: Johns Hopkins University Press, 1994); Sharon Hartman Strom, *Beyond the Typewriter: Gender, Class, and the Origins of American Office Work* (Urbana: University of Illinois Press, 1992); Jerome P. Bjelopera, *City of Clerks: Office and Sales Workers in Philadelphia, 1870–1920* (Urbana: University of Illinois Press, 2005). A key exception is Jill Andresky Fraser, *White-Collar Sweatshop: The Deterioration of Work and Its Rewards in Corporate America* (New York: W. W. Norton & Company, 2001). For a cultural history of the white-collar office that includes coverage of the later decades of the twentieth century, see Julie Berebitsky, *Sex and the Office: A History of Gender, Power, and Desire* (New Haven, Conn.: Yale University Press, 2012).

3. See Allan M. Brandt, *The Cigarette Century: The Rise, Fall, and Deadly Persistence of the Product That Defined America* (New York: Basic Books, 2007); Richard Kluger, *Ashes to Ashes: America's Hundred-Year Cigarette War, the Public Health, and the Unabashed Triumph of Philip Morris* (New York: Vintage Books, 1997).

4. "Non-Smokers Have Right to Breathe," *Guide* (Mechanicsburg, Pa.), 19 March 1980, 500027379, LTDL, emphasis in original. Gregory Wood conversation with Jason Thomas, 16 May 2012; follow-up e-mail from Jason Thomas, 15 June 2012. A former student of mine, Jason is the son of Lowell Thomas.

5. Brandt, *The Cigarette Century*, 2.

6. Michael B. Katz and Mark J. Stern, *One Nation Divisible: What America Was and What It Is Becoming* (New York: Russell Sage Foundation, 2006), 69.

7. William M. Blair, "Typical Smoker: Factory Man, 35," *New York Times*, 3 September 1971, 15. At the same time, an estimated 70 percent of blue-collar workers regularly smoked.

8. Gerhard Meerwein, Bettina Rodeck, and Frank Mahnke, *Color Communication in Architectural Space*, trans. Laura Bruce with Matthew Gaskins and Paul Cohen (Basel, Germany: Birkhauser Verlagi, AG, 2007), 103; Gavriel Salvendy, ed., *Handbook of Human Factors and Ergonomics* (Hoboken, N. J.: John Wiley & Sons, 2012), 609; Rita Gorarawa-Bhat, *The Social and Spatial Ecology of Work: The Case of a Survey Research Organization* (New York: Kluwer Academic, 2000), 117; see also Nikil Saval, *Cubed: A Secret History of the Workplace* (New York: Doubleday, 2014).

9. Meerwein et al., *Color Communication in Architectural Space*, 103; Salvendy, ed., *Handbook of Human Factors and Ergonomics*, 609; Michelle Murphy, "Toxicity in the Details: The History of the Women's Office Worker Movement and Occupational Health in the Late-Capitalist Office," *Labor History* 41:2 (2000): 193–94.

10. Salvendy, ed., *Handbook of Human Factors and Ergonomics*, 609; see also Saval, *Cubed*.

11. "Cigarettes' Evils Described," *Shrewsbury Register*, 11 March 1977, TI54520922, LTDL.

12. Geoffrey E. Greene, "Nonsmokers' Rights: A Public Health Issue," *Journal of the American Medical Association*, 239:20 (19 May 1978): 2126; Don C. Matchan, "The Case for the Nonsmoker, 1974," *Let's Live*, June 1975, 58–59, TITX0038656, LTDL.

13. "Cigarette Smoke," in *The Encyclopedia of Allergies*, 2nd ed., ed. Myron A. Lipkowitz and Tova Navarra (New York: Facts on File, 2001), 74; "Is Cigarette Smoke An Allergen?" www.sharecare.com/question/is-cigarette-smoke-an-allergen, accessed 13 June 2012; William J. Sayer, "Indoor Air Pollution: Effects on the Non-Smoker of Tobacco Smoke Indoors," no publication title, July 1974, 56, HKO0266092, LTDL. On allergy platforms, see Frank K. Kwong, with Bruce W. Cook, *The Complete Allergy Book* (Naperville, Ill.: Sourcebooks, 2002), 310.

14. "On the Job," *Smoking and Health Review*, November 1984, 2, TI19911212, LTDL.

15. Ruth Rosenbaum, "Skirmish Over Smokers' Rights," *New Times*, 10 December 1976, TI00961420, LTDL.

16. "Smoking and Tobacco Use," http://www.cdc.gov/tobacco/basic_information/health_effects/heart_disease/index.htm, accessed 16 June 2012; Environmental Protection Agency, "Indoor Air Facts, No. 5: Environmental Tobacco Smoke," in *BNA's Employee Relations Weekly*, 23 October 1989, 34, TI00582098, LTDL.

17. Environmental Protection Agency, "Indoor Air Facts," 33; Laura Kavesh, "Battle Lines Drawn: Nonsmokers on Offensive," *Orlando Sentinel-Star*, 21 July 1981, TITX0038698, LTDL.

18. Norman Conn, "Speak Up Against the Smokers," *New York Times*, 12 May 1985, CN26.

19. Toni Wood, "Rights of Nonsmokers Clouded by Puffs of Sidestream Smoke," *Olathe* (Kansas) *News*, 15 February 1981, TI12950822, LTDL. On the duration of a lit cigarette, see Greene, "Nonsmokers' Rights," 2125.

20. Conn, "Speak Up Against the Smokers," CN26; National Cancer Institute, "Secondhand Smoke and Cancer," http://www.cancer.gov/cancertopics/factsheet/Tobacco/ETS, accessed 16 June 2012.

21. Kluger, *Ashes to Ashes*, 200.

22. Ibid., 204.

23. Ibid., 226.

24. Surgeon General's Advisory Committee on Smoking and Health, *Smoking and Health: Report of the Advisory Committee to the Surgeon General of the Public Health Service* (Washington, D. C.: US Government Printing Office, 1964), esp. 141, 150, 155. For more on the production of the report, see Kluger, *Ashes to Ashes*, 242–62. By 1966, the number of cigarettes consumed in the United States had fallen by 7 percent. See Blair, "Typical Smoker," 15; Kluger, *Ashes to Ashes*, 326.

25. "Non-Smokers Have Right to Breathe," emphasis in original.

26. Kavesh, "Battle Lines Drawn."

27. For notable examples of this scholarship, see Heather Ann Thompson, *Whose Detroit? Politics, Labor, and Race in a Modern American City* (Ithaca, N.Y.: Cornell University Press, 2001); Robert O. Self, *American Babylon: Race and the Struggle for Postwar*

Oakland (Princeton, N.J.: Princeton University Press, 2003); Nancy Maclean, *Freedom Is Not Enough: The Opening of the American Workplace* (Cambridge, Mass.: Harvard University Press, 2006); Laurie B. Green, *Battling the Plantation Mentality: Memphis and the Black Freedom Struggle* (Chapel Hill: University of North Carolina Press, 2007); Julie Berebitsky, *Sex and the Office: A History of Gender, Power, and Desire* (New Haven, Conn.: Yale University Press, 2012).

28. Donna M. Shimp affidavit, in *Donna M. Shimp v. New Jersey Bell Telephone Company*, Superior Court of New Jersey, docket no. C-2904–75, 686007974, LTDL; "Nonsmoker's Order Is Made Permanent," *New York Times*, 22 December 1976, 63.

29. Andrew Froman, "Fired Worker Loses Anti-Smoking Fight," *Fort Lauderdale News*, 22 November 1978, TIFl0059362, LTDL.

30. Barbara Hanna, "Employers Find No Easy Answers," *Seattle Journal-American*, 21 May 1980, TI00151151, LTDL.

31. Maura Lerner, "Lawsuit Over Smoking Makes Tempers Smolder," *St. Louis Post-Dispatch*, 28 December 1980, TIMN270870, LTDL.

32. Kristen Iverson, *Full Body Burden: Growing Up in the Nuclear Shadow of Rocky Flats* (New York: Crown Publishers, 2012), 128, 130.

33. Steve Sink and Gayle Pollard, "Grocery Smoking Banned," *Miami Herald*, 19 June 1974, TIFL0059430, LTDL.

34. Rosenbaum, "Skirmish Over Smokers' Rights."

35. "Smoking and Health Don't Compute," *American Lung Association Bulletin*, July–August 1982, TI04490747, LTDL; *Lethal Weapon 2*, dir. Richard Donner, Warner Bros. Pictures, 1989; *9 to 5*, dir. Colin Higgins, 20th Century Fox, 1980.

36. "Would Rally Nonsmokers," *Milwaukee Journal*, 4 September 1973, TI53900191, LTDL; "Odor Only Warning," *San Diego Tribune*, 10 October 1975, TCAL0003500, LTDL; Mary Mancewicz, "Smoking Still Popular Vice Among Teens," *Grand Rapids* (Michigan) *Press*, 16 May 1981, TIMN290955, LTDL.

37. Ridgely Ochs, "Where Smoking Breaks the Law," *Newsday*, 8 April 1984, TI22110533, LTDL.

38. T. Berry to Bill Paschall, 4 April 1991, TI01351741, LTDL; Tommy Lake to Ron Cole, 8 January 1991, TI01351685, LTDL; Douglas Hammerick to Tobacco Institute, 30 April 1991, TI01352039, LTDL.

39. Ochs, "Where Smoking Breaks the Law," emphasis added.

40. "Nonsmokers Gain in War on Weed," *Los Angeles Times*, 20 February 1983, 17.

41. "Smoking and Health Don't Compute." Hewlett-Packard adopted a nearly identical policy. See Hewlett-Packard Smoking Policy, n.d., TI00440884, LTDL.

42. "Smoking and Health Don't Compute," n.p.

43. Bureau of National Affairs, *Where There's Smoke: Problems and Policies Concerning Smoking in the Workplace* (Rockville, Md.: BNA, 1987), 91, I29410299, LTDL.

44. "Smoking and Health Don't Compute," n.p.

45. Kavesh, "Battle Lines Drawn."

46. "Nonsmokers Gain in War on Weed," 17.

47. "Smoking Response," *Lewiston-Auburn* (Maine) *Sun*, n.d., TI26432478, LTDL.

48. Barbara Hanna, "Employers Find No Easy Answers," *Seattle Journal-American*, 21 May 1980, TI00151151, LTDL; see also Nancy Neff, "Tired of Smoke-Filled Rooms?" *American-Statesman* (Austin, Tex.), 12 September 1976, TITX0029365, LTDL.

49. Kavesh, "Battle Lines Drawn"; see also Annie-Laure Banon to Mel Hosanski, 21 December 1988, TI02551195, LTDL.

50. Hanna, "Employers Find No Easy Answers"; James L. Repace, "Effect of Ventilation on Passive Smoking Risk in a Model Workplace" (1984), TI04220152, LTDL.

51. Hanna, "Employers Find No Easy Answers."

52. Becky Smith to Susan M. Stuntz, 19 April 1989, TI01350588, LTDL. For a helpful introduction to the history of the Tobacco Institute, see "Tobacco Institute," in Howard Padwa and Jacob Cunningham, *Addiction: A Reference Encyclopedia* (Santa Barbara, Calif.: ABC-CLIO, 2010), 296–98.

53. Mrs. R. Faviano to Tobacco Institute, 10 October 1988, TI01352232, LTDL, emphasis added.

54. Joseph Guillemette to Susan M. Stuntz, n.d., TI01350664, LTDL.

55. Margaret E. Cook to Susan M. Stuntz, 20 October 1988, TI01352287, LTDL.

56. "Judge Studies Cigarette Smoke Suit," *Daily Town Talk* (Alexandria, La.), n.d. (1987), TI26432551, LTDL; "Suit Heard Over Cigarette Smoke," *State Times* (Baton Rouge, La.), 1 April 1987, TI26432543, LTDL.

57. "Secretary Asks Her Boss to Stop Smoking, Gets Fired," *Los Angeles Times*, 9 May 1984, A2.

58. Donna M. Shimp affidavit, in *Donna M. Shimp v. New Jersey Bell Telephone Company*, Superior Court of New Jersey, 1976, docket no. C-2904–75, 686007974, LTDL.

59. Mona Moore, "Smoking Foe Just Beginning," *Atlantic City Press*, 31 December 1976, TI45762849, LTDL; Rudy Johnson, "Nonsmoker Honored for Efforts," *New York Times*, 23 December 1976, 53.

60. "Summary of Decision Upholding Right of Nonsmoking Office Worker," in Environmental Improvement Associates, *Smoke-Free Work Areas: A Guide for Employees* (Salem, N.J.: Environmental Improvement Associates, 1976), 14–15, TI04490698, LTDL.

61. Quoted in "Hearts and Lungs First," *Sarasota Herald-Tribune*, 22 September 1978, n.p., TIFL0029757, LTDL.

62. Paul Knopick, "Tobacco and the Law," *Tobacco Observer*, n.d. (1978?), TI20221470, LTDL.

63. Ibid.

64. At the UCSF Legacy Tobacco Documents Library website, the search term "Donna Shimp" receives 685 hits in the Tobacco Institute collection. See http://legacy.library.ucsf.edu.

65. Quoted in Defendant's Motion to Dismiss, in *Paul Smith v. Western Electric Company*, Case No. 446121, Circuit Court of the County of St. Louis, Missouri, 1981, 18, 503812790, LTDL.

66. Defendant's Motion to Dismiss, in *Paul Smith v. Western Electric Company*, Case No. 446121, Circuit Court of the County of St. Louis, Missouri, 1981, 18, 503812790, LTDL.

67. Lerner, "Lawsuit Over Smoking Makes Tempers Smolder."

68. Joshua Marquis, "Health Issue Cited," *Los Angeles Daily Journal*, 22 September 1982, TI04841264, LTDL.

69. Alvan Brody, "Non-Smokers' Rights: Protection Against Involuntary Smoking in the Workplace," *Suffolk University Law School Journal* 13:2 (1982): 31, TITX0028068, LTDL.

70. "Secretary Asks Her Boss to Stop Smoking," A2.

71. Jefferson Cowie, *Staying Alive: The 1970s and the Last Days of the Working Class* (New York: New Press, 2010); Mike Davis, *Prisoners of the American Dream: Politics and Economy in the History of the US Working Class* (New York: Verso, 1986); Dana L. Cloud, *We Are the Union: Democratic Unionism and Dissent at Boeing* (Urbana: University of Illinois Press, 2011).

72. Brandt, *Cigarette Century*.

73. California Nonsmokers' Rights Foundation, "Clearing the Air at Work: Some Essential Background for Employees" (pamphlet), n.d., TI54500875, LTDL.

74. California Nonsmokers' Rights Foundation," Clearing the Air at Work."

75. Andrew H. Malcolm, "Mounting Drive on Smoking Stirs Tensions in Workplace," *New York Times*, 20 February 1987, A1.

76. Jim Wood, "GASP's Stand: No Butts About It," *San Francisco Examiner*, 29 January 1978, A6.

77. Donna M. Shimp, "Nonsmokers' Rights in the Workplace—A New Look," *American Lung Association Bulletin*, July–August 1978, TI04490741, LTDL.

78. Shimp, "Nonsmokers' Rights in the Workplace."

79. American Lung Association, "Second-Hand Smoke" (pamphlet), August 1986, 7, TI06220738, LTDL.

80. Smokers' use of "rights" rhetoric is detailed in chapter 6.

81. Ted Steinberg, *Down to Earth: Nature's Role in American History* (New York: Oxford University Press, 2009), 252–53; David Peterson del Mar, *Environmentalism* (Harlow, UK: Pearson Education Limited, 2006), 107; Gerald Markowitz and David Rosner, "From the Triangle Fire to the BP Explosion: A Short History of the Century-Long Movement for Safety and Health," *New Labor Forum* 20:1 (2011): 29 (quote).

82. Joan Sweeney, "Social Force Has Impact on Smokers," *Los Angeles Times*, 16 January 1984, TI27881190, LTDL.

83. Louise M. Mockaitis to Susan M. Stuntz, 10 June 1989, TI01350448, LTDL.

84. Kluger, *Ashes to Ashes*, 462.

5. "EXILED SMOKING" AND THE MAKING OF SMOKE-FREE WORKPLACES

1. John D. Barbour, "Edward Said and the Space of Exile," *Literature & Theology* 21:3 (2007): 293–95.

2. Edward W. Said, *Reflections on Exile: And Other Essays* (Cambridge, Mass.: Harvard University Press, 2000), 173. According to Said, exiles lose connections and community in their lonely wanderings, but they nonetheless gain the critical vantage point of the outsider in their considerations of culture and society.

3. Said, *Reflections on Exile*, 181.

4. On disruption, see Barbour, "Edward Said and the Space of Exile," 295.

5. Simon Chapman, Ron Borland, Michelle Scollo, Ross C. Brownson, Amanda Dominello, and Stephen Woodward, "The Impact of Smoke-Free Workplaces on Declining Cigarette Consumption in Australia and the United States," *American Journal of Public Health* 89:7 (1999): 1022; Said, *Reflections on Exile*, 173.

6. Quoted in Margie G. Quimpo, "Banished: Smokers Refraining Reluctantly," *Richmond News Leader*, 22 November 1990, 980051344, Legacy Tobacco Documents Library, University of California, San Francisco, http://legacy.library.ucsf.edu (hereafter LTDL); see also Colleen T. Moore to Tobacco Institute, 3 October 1991, TI01761985, LTDL.

7. "Businesses Increasingly Adopt Limits on Smoking," *Washington Post*, 18 June 1986, HE22.

8. Ibid.

9. Ibid.

10. Lawrence B. Richards, *Union-Free America: Workers and Antiunion Culture* (Urbana: University of Illinois Press, 2008); Jefferson Cowie, *Capital Moves: RCA's Seventy-Year Quest for Cheap Labor* (Ithaca, N.Y.: Cornell University Press, 1999); Joseph A. McCartin, *Collision Course: Ronald Reagan, the Air Traffic Controllers, and the Strike That Changed America* (New York: Oxford University Press, 2011); Elizabeth Fones-Wolf, *Selling Free Enterprise: The Business Assault on Labor and Liberalism, 1940–60* (Urbana: University of Illinois Press, 1994); Kim Phillips-Fein, "Business Conservatism on the Shop Floor: Anti-Union Campaigns in the 1950s," *Labor: Studies in Working-Class History of the Americas* 7:2 (2010): 9–26; Thomas J. Sugrue, *The Origins of the Urban Crisis: Race*

and Inequality in Postwar Detroit (Princeton, N.J.: Princeton University Press, 1996); Ruth Milkman, *Farewell to the Factory: Auto Workers in the Late Twentieth Century* (Berkeley: University of California Press, 1997), esp. 52, 80–83, 90–92; Nelson Lichtenstein, *State of the Union: A Century of American Labor* (Princeton, N.J.: Princeton University Press, 2002), esp. 212–18, 233–34; Michael Zweig, *The Working Class Majority: America's Best Kept Secret* (Ithaca, N.Y.: Cornell University Press, 2000).

11. For these aggregate statistics, see "US Cities Continued Drop in Union Membership," *New York Times*, 8 February 1985, B5; McCartin, *Collision Course*, 10; Steven K. Ashby and C. J. Hawking, *Staley: The Fight for a New American Labor Movement* (Urbana: University of Illinois Press, 2009), 34. The statistic for the overall number of organized US workers in 2009 is found in Dana L. Cloud, *We Are the Union: Democratic Unionism and Dissent at Boeing* (Urbana: University of Illinois Press, 2011), 184.

12. William Serrin, "Labor Unions Troubled by Drop in Members," *New York Times*, 31 May 1983, A16.

13. Robert H. Zieger and Gilbert J. Gall, *American Workers, American Unions: The Twentieth Century*, 3rd ed. (Baltimore: Johns Hopkins University Press, 2002), 258; Ashby and Hawking, *Staley*, 34; McCartin, *Collision Course*, 10.

14. Richards, *Union-Free America*, 2.

15. Melvyn Dubofsky, *The State and Labor in Modern America* (Chapel Hill: University of North Carolina Press, 1994), xii.

16. William L. Weis, "Curbs Give a Boost to Productivity," *Los Angeles Times*, 6 November 1983, G3.

17. American Lung Association, *More Facts & Features for Nonsmokers & Smokers: Smoking in the Workplace* (1981?), pamphlet, TI04490612, LTDL.

18. For the William Weis statistics, see Carol Kleiman, "Smoking Workers Costly," *Chicago Tribune*, 8 November 1981, M1; the final statistics are reported in Jack B. Johnston, "How Cigarets Send Money Up in Smoke," *Sacramento Bee*, 27 April 1981, C5, TI04490746, LTDL; Jane E. Brody, "Restricting Smoking in the Workplace," *New York Times*, 25 December 1985, 39.

19. Anthony P. St. John to all Chrysler employees, January 1989, TI07830297, LTDL; "Chrysler Corporation Smoking Policy Provisions," n.d., memo, TI50952392, LTDL.

20. Kentucky Utilities Company/Old Dominion Power Company Smoking Policy, 1 April 1992, memo, TI11460003, LTDL.

21. "Sample Smoking Policies," *Bulletin to Management*, 29 August 1991, 15, TI06550179, LTDL.

22. Alice Schultze, "An Office Casualty: My Right to Smoke," *New York Times*, 27 March 1988, LI28; Carole F. Erickson to Joseph E. Luecke, 3 June 1989, TI01350442, LTDL, emphasis in original.

23. Wanda Quesenberry to Tobacco Institute, 27 January 1991, TI01351667, LTDL; Douglas Hammerick to Tobacco Institute, 30 April 1991, 507671115, LTDL.

24. David Stacy to Tobacco Institute, 3 October 1991, TI01761984, LTDL.

25. Barry Storey to Tobacco Institute, 10 May 1991, TI01351925, LTDL.

26. Judy Meadows to Tobacco Institute, 24 January 1991, TI01351672, LTDL; Sharon Mitchell to Tobacco Institute, 10 January 1991, TI01351690, LTDL; Louise M. Mockaitis to Susan M. Stuntz, 10 June 1989, TI01350448, LTDL; see also Ashby and Hawking, 24.

27. Johnny Creech to Tobacco Institute, 10 May 1991, 507670932, LTDL; Charles Elmore to Tobacco Institute, 16 February 1991, TI01351646, LTDL; Cathy Hooper to Tobacco Institute, 4 April 1991, 507670637, LTDL.

28. Mrs. David Howard to Tobacco Institute, n.d., TI01351702, LTDL; Patricia Howlett to Tobacco Institute, 22 October 1991, TI01762158, LTDL. On fights over tobacco control

in Oklahoma during the 1990s, see Michael S. Givel and Andrew L. Spivak, *Heartland Tobacco War* (Lanham, Md.: Lexington Books, 2013), esp. 11–14.

29. Laurel Archer to Tobacco Institute, 27 January 1991, TI01351669, LTDL.

30. George Keenom to Matthew Dowd, 29 April 1991, TI01352065, LTDL; see also Rick Suryk to Tobacco Institute, 19 March 1991, TI01351698, LTDL.

31. On the signing of no-smoking pledges, see Beverly Sterling to Tom Ogburn et al., 23 January 1991, TI01351665, LTDL. For concerns about the use of names, see Margaret Louise Clark to Susan M. Stuntz, 4 October 1988, TI01352237, LTDL; as well as Connie Elliot to Ed Jenkins, summary of phone conversation, 13 January 1991, TI01351675, LTDL; Cindra O'Hara to Tobacco Institute, 16 March 1991, TI01351696, LTDL.

32. Jim Hope to Tobacco Institute, 16 February 1991, TI01351642, LTDL.

33. Kay Culiton to Tobacco Institute, 27 January 1991, TI01351668, LTDL.

34. Eve Nagler, "More Companies Order Less Smoking," *New York Times*, 23 August 1987, CN2.

35. Martha Nolan McKenzie, "So Don't Even Think About Smoking Here," *New York Times*, 29 December 1996, F13.

36. Gus Phillips to Sharon Stuntz, 9 May 1989, photostat image of handwritten message, TI01350645, LTDL.

37. Garolyn Buchanan to Tobacco Institute, 24 January 1991, TI01351666, LTDL.

38. "Smokers' Brains Change in Response to High Levels of Nicotine," *Chicago Tribune*, 23 February 2012, http://www.chicagotribune.com/health, accessed 18 February 2013.

39. Clarence Page, "Smokers Cry Foul, But We Only Have Ourselves to Blame," *Bangor Daily News*, 23 January 1988, 1.

40. Karen Casey, *If Only I Could Quit: Recovering from Nicotine Addiction* (Center City, Minn.: Hazelden Foundation, 1987), 91–92.

41. Ashby and Hawking, *Staley*, 230.

42. Mrs. Elaine Saunders to Tobacco Institute, 8 January 1991, TI01351685, LTDL; Deanna Thompson to Tobacco Institute, 8 January 1991, TI01351685, LTDL. See also unnamed writer to Tobacco Institute, 23 January 1991, TI01351664, LTDL.

43. "Scott Paper Bans Smoking at Kentucky Plant," *Beaver County* (Pennsylvania) *Times*, 21 August 1995, A5.

44. Betty Frankenfield to Tobacco Institute, 1 May 1991, TI01352020, LTDL; see also Mikey Maslankowski to Susan Stuntz, 11 October 1988, TI01352230, LTDL; Brad Gunder to Tobacco Institute, 10 January 1991, TI01351690, LTDL.

45. Jennifer Riddle, "Company Tells Workers: Quit Smoking," *Wisconsin State Journal*, n.d., TI09581174, LTDL.

46. Reprinted in Tobacco Institute, "What Other Organizations Have Done," n.d., TI0212–2196, LTDL. On the number of smokers at USG, see "No Smoking or No Work," *New York Times*, 28 February 1988, 48.

47. US Geological Survey, "Some Facts About Asbestos," http://webharvest.gov/peth04/20041106200326/http://pubs.usgs.gov/fs/fs012–01/fs012–01.pdf, accessed 16 June 2011.

48. For a helpful overview of asbestos use in US history, see Rachel Maines, *Asbestos and Fire: Technological Trade-Offs and the Body at Risk* (New Brunswick, N.J.: Rutgers University Press, 2005), esp. 7–11.

49. "US Gypsum Company," http://www.mesothelioma.com/asbestos-exposure/companies/united-states-gypsum.htm, accessed 13 June 2011.

50. On mineral wool as a "suspected health hazard," see Maines, *Asbestos and Fire*, 13. On the limited correlation between cancer risks and mineral wool, see L. Lipworth et al., "Occupational Exposure to Rock Wool and Glass Wool and Risk of Cancers of the Lung

and the Head and Neck: A Systematic Review and Meta-Analysis," *Journal of Occupational and Environmental Medicine* 51:9 (2009): 1075–87; H. Pohlabeln et al., "Lung Cancer and Exposure to Man-Made Vitreous Fibers: Results from a Pooled Case-Control Study in Germany," *American Journal of Industrial Medicine* 37:5 (2000): 469–77.

51. "The Great Energy Cavity," *The New Scientist*, 12 August 1982, 446.

52. On the number of pending suits from USG workers, see "Big Brother Says Stop Smoking," *The Tennessean*, 7 February 1987, TI26461411, LTDL. The statistic of forty thousand pending court cases filed by asbestos installers and the Charles Patrick remarks are quoted in Joseph R. Tybor and Sallie Gaines, "No Smoking!" *Chicago Tribune*, 25 January 1987, C1.

53. Tobacco Institute, "What Other Organizations Have Done"; and "No Smoking!" *Chicago Daily Tribune*, 25 January 1987, 4. On the inapplicability of the ban at the company headquarters in Chicago, see "Firm Bans Smoking at Work or Home," *Washington Post*, 21 January 1987, A7.

54. Tobacco Institute, "What Other Organizations Have Done."

55. Patrick J. Traub, "Bayh Signs Bill Supporting Smokers' Rights," *Indianapolis Star*, 9 May 1991, TI28520104, LTDL; "'Smokers' Rights' Laws Ignite Battles," news clipping, no title of periodical, 23 May 1991, TIMS00027420, LTDL.

56. "None of an Employer's Business," *New York Times*, 7 July 1991.

57. Traub, "Bayh Signs Bill Supporting Smokers' Rights."

58. Tobacco Institute (?), *Smokers' Rights Action Guide* (1993), 17, booklet, TI35962624, LTDL; see also Stephen D. Sugarman, "Disparate Treatment of Smokers in Employment and Insurance," in *Smoking Policy: Law, Politics, and Culture*, ed. Robert L. Rabin and Stephen D. Sugarman (New York: Oxford University Press, 1993), 178.

59. "If You Light Up on Sunday, Don't Come in on Monday," *Business Week*, 25 August 1991, http://www.businessweek.com/printer/articles, accessed 19 February 2013; Janny Scott, "'Smokers' Rights' Asserted Under New Job Bias Laws," *Los Angeles Times*, 23 July 1991, http://articles.latimes.com/print/1991–07–23/news, accessed 19 February 2013.

60. Quoted in Washington, Perito, and Dubuc, "Memorandum," 12 November 1990, TI02091277, LTDL. This is a letter from a law firm on behalf of the Tobacco Institute to a city council member in Washington, DC, which argued against proposed legislation in the capital that would allow to employers to turn away smokers when they applied for work.

61. Washington, Perito, and Dubuc, "Memorandum."

62. Tobacco Institute, "Protecting Individual Privacy," n.d., TI28590168, LTDL.

63. Maria Fedele and Ron Borland, "Characteristics of Exiled Smoking from Workplaces," *Psychology & Health* 13:3 (1998): 545; Ron Borland and Claire Davey, "Impact of Smoking Bans and Restrictions," in *Tobacco: Science, Policy, and Public Health*, ed. Peter Boyle, Nigel Gray, Jack Henningfield, John Seffrin, and Witold Zatonski (Oxford, UK: Oxford University Press, 2004), 717. Other scholars use the term "doorstop smoking." See Odette Parry, Stephen Platt, and Carolyn Thomson, "Out of Sight, Out of Mind: Workplace Smoking Bans and the Relocation of Smoking at Work," *Health Promotion International* 15:2 (2000): 129.

64. Laura Blumenfeld, "What a Drag! Smokers Huff and Puff on the Street," *Washington Post*, 26 June 1991, C1. On exile as a "signature of displacement," see Peter Fritzsche, "Spectors of History: On Nostalgia, Exile, and Modernity," *American Historical Review* 106:5 (2001): 1588.

65. Blumenfeld, "What a Drag!" C1.

66. Ron Borland and N. Owen, "Need to Smoke in the Context of Workplace Smoking Bans," *Preventive Medicine* 24:1 (1995): 56–60. On the need of smokers to maintain blood nicotine levels to avoid withdrawal symptoms, see Ron Borland, M. Cappiello, and N. Owen, "Leaving Work to Smoke," *Addiction* 92:10 (1997): 1361.

67. Fedele and Borland, "Characteristics of Exiled Smoking from Workplaces," 545.

68. Borland, Cappiello, and Owen, "Leaving Work to Smoke," 1361; W. Kip Viscusi, *Smoke-Filled Rooms: A Postmortem on the Tobacco Deal* (Chicago: University of Chicago Press, 2002), 101; George F. Will, "War Against Smoking Filled with Ironies and Paradoxes," *Deseret News*, 21 March 1996, A24.

69. George Keenom to Tobacco Institute, 29 April 1991, TI01352065, LTDL; Carolyn Frazier to Tobacco Institute, 29 September 1991, TI01762017, LTDL; see also Rick Wolfe to Tobacco Institute, 29 October 1991, TI01762236, LTDL.

70. Glenda Hooks to Tobacco Institute, 10 January 1991, TI01351690, LTDL.

71. Mildred Le Masters to Tobacco Institute, 14 September 1991, TI01762116, LTDL; Marilyn Evans to Tobacco Institute, 2 November 1991, TI01762222, LTDL.

72. Philip S. Gutis, "LI Workers Brave Elements to Get in a Smoke," *New York Times*, 20 February 1987, A16.

73. Pam Massingill to Tobacco Institute, 16 October 1991, TI01762178, LTDL; Marilyn Evans to Tobacco Institute, 2 November 1991, TI01762222, LTDL.

74. Frank J. Siverhus to Susan M. Stuntz, 6 November 1988, TI01352208, LTDL; Colline Steede to Tobacco Institute, 6 December 1990, TI01351676, LTDL; see also Blumenfeld, "What a Drag!" C4.

75. Sharon Epperson, "More Employers Making Smokers Take It Outside," *Washington Post*, 11 September 1990, D1; "Jim Brent to Tobacco Institute, 6 December 1990, TI01351676, LTDL. For additional references along these lines, see Julia Miller to Tobacco Institute, 24 January 1991, TI01351671, LTDL; "State Agency's Smoking Ban Is Upheld by Hearing Officer," *St. Petersburg Times*, 2 January 1991, TIFL0011332, LTDL.

76. "State Agency's Smoking Ban Is Upheld by Hearing Officer."

77. Sandy Strzyzykowski to Tobacco Institute, 17 March 1991, TI01351582, LTDL.

78. "Smoking Ban at Work Place a Fiery Issue," *Los Angeles Times*, 1 September 1978, TI04380194, LTDL.

79. Sharon Epperson, "More Employers Making Smokers Take It Outside," *Washington Post*, 11 September 1990, D2; Diane Ketcham, "Widespread Compliance in Suffolk," *New York Times*, 16 March 1986, LI1.

80. S. Chapman, S. Haddad, and D. Sindhusake, "Do Work-Place Smoking Bans Cause Smokers to Smoke 'Harder?' Results from a Naturalistic Observational Study," *Addiction* 92:5 (1997): 607–10.

81. Sue Farmer to Tobacco Institute, 4 November 1991, TI01762217, LTDL.

82. Ann Doyle, "Newsroom Begins Ban on Smoking," *Tallahassee Democrat*, 14 June 1984, 0033156, LTDL.

83. Epperson, "More Employers Making Smokers Take It Outside," D2.

84. Amy Zuckerman, "City Smokers Less Than Militant About Not Lighting Up on the Job," *Worcester Evening Gazette*, 20 January 1983, TI03870462, LTDL.

85. Said, *Reflections on Exile*, 186.

6. ORGANIZED LABOR AND THE PROBLEM OF "SMOKERS' RIGHTS"

1. Joe F. McNeely to Aluminum Company of America, Warrick Operations, 17 May 1989, TI01350031, Legacy Tobacco Documents Library, University of California, San Francisco, http://legacy.library.ucsf.edu (hereafter LTDL).

2. Stephen K. Ashby and C. J. Hawking, *Staley: The Fight for a New American Labor Movement* (Urbana: University of Illinois Press, 2009); Dana L. Cloud, *We Are the Union: Democratic Unionism and Dissent at Boeing* (Urbana: University of Illinois Press, 2011).

3. Tip O'Neill with Gary Heymel, *All Politics Is Local and Other Rules of the Game* (Holbrook, Mass.: Bob Adams, Inc., 1994), xv.

4. *Roger & Me*, dir. Michael Moore, Warner Home Video, 1989. The term "sit-down fever" appears in Michael Denning, *The Cultural Front: The Laboring of American Culture*

during the Twentieth Century (New York: Verso, 1997). On the history of the UAW during the era of the Flint sit-down strike in 1936–1937, see Sidney Fine, *Sit-Down: The General Motors Strike of 1936–1937* (Ann Arbor: University of Michigan Press, 1969); Irving Bernstein, *The Turbulent Years: A History of the American Worker, 1933–1941* (Boston: Houghton Mifflin Company, 1969); Nelson Lichtenstein, *State of the Union: A Century of American Labor* (Princeton, N.J.: Princeton University Press, 2002). On the history of cannery unionism, see Vicki L. Ruiz, *Cannery Women, Cannery Lives: Mexican Women, Unionization, and the California Food Processing Industry, 1930–1950* (Albuquerque: University of New Mexico Press, 1987). On labor militancy in West Virginia in the early twentieth century, see David Allen Corbin, *Life, Work, and Rebellion in the Coal Fields: The Southern West Virginia Miners, 1880–1922* (Urbana: University of Illinois Press, 1981).

5. Mark Finston, "Union Officials Boycott Rutgers Anti-Smoking Conference," *Newark Star-Ledger*, 28 February 1979, TI47271975, LTDL.

6. US Department of Health and Human Services, *The Health Consequences of Involuntary Smoking: A Report of the Surgeon General* (Rockville, Md.: Office on Smoking and Health, 1986), http://profiles.nlm.nih.gov/ps/access/NNBCPM.pdf, accessed 17 June 2013.

7. Patrick J. Campbell, James L. Walker, Edward J. Carlough, John DeConcini, and William W. Winpisinger to Lane Kirkland, 15 December 1986, TI29811705, LTDL; "Union Statement in Response to the 1986 Surgeon General's Report," TI29811706, LTDL. Lane Kirkland was then president of the AFL-CIO.

8. "Statement by the AFL-CIO Executive Council on Smoking in the Workplace," 19 February 1986, TI29811708, LTDL.

9. On voluntarism, see Leon Fink, *In Search of the Working Class: Essays in American Labor History and Political Culture* (Urbana: University of Illinois Press, 1994), 156.

10. "UAW Files Unfair Labor Practice Against Caterpillar Over Smoking Ban," http://www.metrowestdailynews.com/article/20080530/NEWS/305309996, accessed 27 March 2014; "UAW Members Win Smoking Ban in Atlantic City Casinos," http://www.uaw.org/articles/uaw-members-win-smoking-ban-atlantic-city-casinos, accessed 27 March 2014.

11. See "American Smoker-Nonsmoker Consensus," *New York Times*, 13 May 1984, D22.

12. Joe McCullough to Ron Cole, Tim Hyde, and Tom Ogburn, 28 January 1991, TI01351660, LTDL; Tobacco Institute, Region IX Report (Arizona, California, Nevada, Utah), n.d. (1991?), TI07640159, LTDL. On the history of trucker unionism and the Teamsters, see Shane Hamilton, *Trucking Country: The Road to America's Wal-Mart Economy* (Princeton, N.J.: Princeton University Press, 2008); David Witwer, *Corruption and Reform in the Teamsters Union* (Urbana: University of Illinois Press, 2003).

13. "New Smoking Ban Ended By Factory," *New York Times*, 30 November 1965, 29.

14. For similar points, see Ashby and Hawking, *Staley*.

15. Fred Rahning to Tobacco Institute, 8 May 1991, TI01351834, LTDL.

16. Paul Hays to Tobacco Institute, 8 May 1991, TI01351833, LTDL.

17. Donna M. Shimp affidavit, in *Donna M. Shimp v. New Jersey Bell Telephone Company*, Superior Court of New Jersey, docket no. C-2904-75, 686007974, LTDL.

18. Ibid.

19. Ibid.

20. Jefferson Cowie, *Stayin' Alive: The 1970s and the Last Days of the Working Class* (New York: New Press, 2010), 29.

21. Donna M. Shimp affidavit.

22. Cowie, *Stayin' Alive*, 215, 219, 222, 224–25.

23. Margaret Brennan, quoted in "Statement of the Joint Council of Flight Attendants Unions, Presented to the Committee on Airliner Cabin Air Quality," National Academy

of Sciences, Washington, DC, 14 June 1985, TI13141144, LTDL; see also Kathleen Barry, *Femininity in Flight: A History of Flight Attendants* (Durham, N.C.: Duke University Press, 2007), 214; Jennifer Zelnick, Richard Campbell, Charles Levenstein, and Edith Balbach, "Clearing the Air: The Evolution of Organized Labor's Role in Tobacco Control in the United States," *International Journal of Health Services* 38:2 (2008): 322.

24. Zelnick et al., "Clearing the Air," 323–24. On the history of 1199SEIU under Dennis Rivera's leadership, see the updates to Leon Fink and Brian Greenberg, *Upheaval in the Quiet Zone: 1199SEIU and the Politics of Health Care Unionism*, 2nd ed. (Urbana: University of Illinois Press, 2009); William W. Sales Jr. and Roderick Bush, "Black and Latino Coalitions: Prospects for New Social Movements in New York City," in *Race and Politics: New Challenges and Responses for Black Activism*, ed. James Jennings (New York: Verso, 1997), 144.

25. Robert Storch to Tobacco Institute, 30 April 1991, TI01352049, LTDL; "Faculty, Employees Fight Smoking Ban," *Pittsburgh Post-Gazette*, 24 December 2008, http://www.post-gazette.com, accessed 8 June 2013.

26. Peter Lewandowski to Tobacco Institute, 11 October 1991, TI01762188, LTDL.

27. Saul A. Rubinstein and Thomas A. Kochan, *Learning from Saturn: A Look at the Boldest Experiment in Corporate Governance and Employee Relations* (Ithaca, N.Y.: Cornell University Press, 2001); Norman Caulfield, *NAFTA and Labor in North America* (Urbana: University of Illinois Press, 2010), esp. 121–22; Michael Schiavone, *Unions in Crisis? The Future of Organized Labor in America* (Westport, Conn.: Praeger, 2008), 73.

28. See Gary Givliano to Tobacco Institute, 6 May 1991, TI01351855, LTDL; Dale Haught to Tobacco Institute, 6 May 1991, TI01351855, LTDL; Stan Bodzman to Tobacco Institute, 2 October 1991, TI01761993, LTDL; David Solomini to Tobacco Institute, 12 December 1990, TI01351679, LTDL. On the history of United Electrical Workers, see Ronald W. Schatz, *The Electrical Workers: A History of Labor at General Electric and Westinghouse, 1923–60* (Urbana: University of Illinois Press, 1983); for the later years, see Ronald L. Filippelli and Mark D. McColloch, *Cold War in the Working Class: The Rise and Decline of the United Electrical Workers* (Albany: State University of New York Press, 1995). On management changes at Champion Sparkplug in the early 1990s, see Larry P. Vellequette, "Champion Moving Last Work from City," *Toledo Blade*, 18 May 2010, http://www.toledoblade.com/local/2010/05/18/Champion-moving-last-work-from-city-firm-helped-to-put-Toledo-on-map.html, accessed 14 June 2013.

29. Josephine Fidda to Tobacco Institute, 30 April 1991, TI01352051, LTDL.

30. Maurice Edwards to Tobacco Institute, 6 May 1991, TI01351855, LTDL.

31. Omuwunmi Y. O. Osinubi, Elizabeth Barbeau, Jill M. Williams, and Glorian Sorensen, *Tobacco Control in the Workplace* (New York: Nora Science Publishers, Inc., 2005), 41.

32. "Cold Turkey," *Time*, 2 February 1987, 2024271409, LTDL; "Firm Bans After-Hours Smoking," *Fargo Forum*, n.d., TI20120060, LTDL.

33. "Ban on Smoking On/Off Job Evokes Widespread Criticism," *Tobacco Observer*, n.d., TI53360972, LTDL.

34. "Smoking Ban," Associated Press press release (Gypsum, Ohio), 26 January 1987, 2024271407, LTDL.

35. Jennifer Riddle, "Company Tells Workers: Quit," *Wisconsin State Journal*, n.d., TI09581174, LTDL." US Gypsum, the parent company of USG Acoustical Products, had long fought to keep unions and the state out of its factories, suing the War Labor Board (WLB) during World War II to preclude a 1943 order to sign a contract with the United Steel Workers of America (USWA) at one of its factories in Ohio and fighting off a ten-week multiplant strike in the summer of 1942. On the anti-union moves at USG during World War II, see "Strikes, Taxes, and Federal Suits Cut US Gypsum Profit,"

Chicago Daily Tribune, 14 February 1942, 25; "US Gypsum Again Refuses the Order of WLB," *Chicago Daily Tribune*, 25 June 1943, 25; "Sues WLB to Bar FDR Dictating Labor Pacts," *Chicago Daily Tribune*, 24 September 1943, 18.

36. "Corsicana Mayor Says Firm Faces Test on Smoking Ban," *Houston Post*, 22 January 1987, TI26460244, LTDL.

37. "Concern Warns It Will Dismiss All Who Smoke," *New York Times*, 21 January 1987, A16.

38. Gil Belles, Letter to the Editor, *Chicago Tribune*, 17 February 1987, 16.

39. George Orwell, *1984* (1949; repr., New York: Signet, 1977), 297 (quote). For the film version during this period, see *1984*, dir. Michael Radford, 20th Century Fox, 1984.

40. Editorial, *Chicago Sun-Times*, 22 January 1987, 38, TI07202034, LTDL.

41. "Big Brother Says Stop Smoking."

42. "Big Brother vs. Weed," *Roanoke Times & World*, 22 January 1987, TI26462753, LTDL.

43. "Ban on Smoking On/Off Job Evokes Widespread Criticism," *Tobacco Observer*, n.d., TI53360972, LTDL.

44. See *Tobacco Observer*, March 1987, 506647777, LTDL.

45. On American society during the 1970s, see Bruce J. Schulman, *The Seventies: The Great Shift in American Culture, Society, and Politics* (New York: Da Capo Press, 2002); David Farber, *Taken Hostage: The Iran Hostage Crisis and America's First Encounter with Radical Islam* (Princeton, N.J.: Princeton University Press, 2005), esp. 10–34; Thomas Borstelmann, *The 1970s: A New Global History from Civil Rights to Economic Inequality* (Princeton, N.J.: Princeton University Press, 2012); Cowie, *Stayin' Alive*.

46. Gil Troy, *Morning in America: How Ronald Reagan Invented the 1980s* (Princeton, N.J.: Princeton University Press, 2005), 241.

47. "The Fanatic Approach," *Newport News Press*, 24 January 1987, TI26462494, LTDL; "Ban on Smoking On/Off Job Evokes Widespread Criticism."

48. "Firm Bans Smoking at Work or Home," *Washington Post*, 21 January 1987, A7.

49. "Smoking Rule Is Un-American," *Fort Wayne Journal Gazette*, 27 January 1987, TI26430057, LTDL.

50. "Ban on Smoking On/Off Job Evokes Widespread Criticism."

51. Statistic cited in Steven F. Hayward, *The Age of Reagan: The Conservative Counterrevolution, 1980–1989* (New York: Crown Forum, 2009), 173.

52. On the PATCO strike, see Joseph A. McCartin, *Collision Course: Ronald Reagan, the Air Traffic Controllers, and the Strike That Changed America* (New York: Oxford University Press, 2011); Joseph A. McCartin, "'Fire the Hell Out of Them': Sanitation Workers' Struggles and the Normalization of the Striker Replacement Strategy in the 1970s," *Labor: Studies in Working-Class History of the Americas* 2:3 (2005): 68–71, 91–92; Lichtenstein, *State of the Union*, 234–35. On Reagan's faith in free markets and anti-union measures, see Robert H. Zieger and Gilbert J. Gall, *American Workers, American Unions: The Twentieth Century*, 3rd ed. (Baltimore: Johns Hopkins University Press, 2002), 248, 256; Kim Phillips-Fein, *Invisible Hands: The Businessmen's Crusade Against the New Deal* (New York: W. W. Norton & Company, 2010).

53. "Labor Secretary Shunned at AFL-CIO Parley," *New York Times*, 24 February 1983, A18.

54. For an introduction to "employment-at-will," see Robert W. Emerson, *Barron's Business Law*, 5th ed. (New York: Barron's Educational Services, Inc., 2009), 556–57; Bruce Barry, *Speechless: The Erosion of Free Expression in the American Workplace* (San Francisco: Berrett-Koehler Publishers, Inc., 2007), esp. 42–62. Laws that preclude racial and gender discrimination (such as the Civil Rights Act of 1964), for instance, or those laws that protect the right to organize unions (the 1935 National Labor Relations Act), are examples of limitations to employment-at-will doctrine.

55. "Statement by Christopher Scott," North Carolina State AFL-CIO, n.d., TI09711103, LTDL.

56. Vivid illustrations of this point are found in Allan M. Brandt, *The Cigarette Century: The Rise, Fall, and Deadly Persistence of the Product That Defined America* (New York: Basic Books, 2007).

57. "Smoking Ban," Associated Press press release (Gypsum, Ohio), 26 January 1987, 2024271407, LTDL.

58. "Corsicana Mayor Says Firm Faces Test on Smoking Ban," *Houston Post*, 22 January 1987, TI26460244, LTDL; "Smoking Ban," Associated Press press release (Greenville, Miss.), 26 January 1987, 2024271408, LTDL.

59. "Smoking Ban," Associated Press press release (Gypsum, Ohio), 26 January 1987, 2024271407, LTDL.

60. "Smoking Ban," Associated Press press release (Greenville, Miss.), 26 January 1987, 2024271408, LTDL.

61. Hayward, *Age of Reagan*, 231–232.

62. "PHOTOPINION," *Chicago Tribune*, 30 January 1987, TI26430041, LTDL.

63. Michael Abromowitz, "Smoking Rules Spread Like Wildfire," *Washington Post*, 9 December 1987, F1.

64. Abromowitz, "Smoking Rules Spread Like Wildfire," F1.

65. Robert D. McFadden, "Smoking Restrictions Increased," *New York Times*, 15 September 1989, A20.

66. "USG Smoking Rule Is Blackmail," *Herald* (Everett, Wash.), 5 May 1987, TI26461870, LTDL.

67. "USG Smoking Rule Is Blackmail."

68. Highland Yarn Mills, Inc. & Amalgamated Clothing and Textile Workers Union, AFL-CIO, 313 NLRB No. 31, 23 November 1993, 203, http://www.nlrb.gov/search/advanced (hereafter NLRB website), accessed 15 April 2013. The URLs for board decisions that are provided online are too long to provide in the notes.

69. Barry, *Speechless*, 59.

70. Historians and labor educators find fault with conservatives' frequent abilities to shape the politics and rulings of the National Labor Relations Board, a problem that undercut the social justice principles at the core of the Wagner Act and the purpose of the NLRB. The cases discussed in this chapter, however, suggest that the board could be pragmatic, regardless of partisan influence. Helpful considerations of partisan influence on the NLRB include James A. Gross, *A Shameful Business: The Case for Human Rights in the American Workplace* (Ithaca, N.Y.: Cornell University Press, 2010), esp. 84, 88, 93, 95, 102; James A. Gross, *Broken Promise: The Subversion of U.S. Labor Relations* (Philadelphia: Temple University Press, 1995); Jean-Christian Vinel, *The Employee: A Political History* (Philadelphia: University of Pennsylvania Press, 2013); Donna T. Haverty-Stacke and Daniel Walkowitz, "Introduction," in *Rethinking US Labor History: Essays on the Working-Class Experience, 1756–2009*, ed. Donna T. Haverty-Stacke and Daniel Walkowitz (New York: Continuum Books, 2010), 1 (quotes); Lane Windham, "Signing Up the Shipyard: Organizing Newport News and Reinterpreting the 1970s," *Labor: Studies in Working-Class History of the Americas* 10:2 (2013): esp. 48. The complete text of the National Labor Relations Act (Wagner Act) can be found at http://www.nlrb.gov/national-labor-relations-act, accessed 14 August 2013.

71. Richard Kluger, *Ashes to Ashes: America's Hundred Year Cigarette War, the Public Health, and the Unabashed Triumph of Philip Morris* (New York: Vintage, 1997), 698–99. On smokers' denials and industry efforts to obscure the dangers of cigarettes, see Robert N. Proctor, *Golden Holocaust: Origins of the Cigarette Catastrophe and the Case for Abolition* (Berkeley: University of California Press, 2011), esp. 205–339; and Brandt, *Cigarette Century*.

72. Allied-Signal, Inc., Kansas City Division & District 71, International Association of Machinists and Aerospace Workers, AFL-CIO, 307 NLRB No. 118, 29 May 1992, 752–63, NLRB website, accessed 16 April 2013; Danny Daniels, quoted in "More Companies Banning Smoking," 6 February 1990, TI29840878, LTDL.

73. Allied-Signal, Inc., Kansas City Division & District 71, International Association of Machinists and Aerospace Workers, AFL-CIO, 307 NLRB No. 118, emphases in original. On the maintenance of secrecy as a managerial tool, see David Shulman, *From Hire to Liar: The Role of Deception in the Workplace* (Ithaca, N.Y.: ILR Press, 2007), 95–96.

74. YHA, Inc. & Service Employees International Union Local 627, AFL-CIO, 307 NLRB No. 123, 29 May 1992, 782–86, NLRB website, accessed 14 April 2013, emphases in original.

75. Frank Leta Honda & District 9, International Association of Machinists and Aerospace Workers, AFL-CIO, 321 NLRB No. 69, 17 June 1996, 482–97 ("egregious and widespread" quoted on p. 484), NLRB website, accessed 10 April 2013.

76. Mullican Lumber Company & International Brotherhood of Teamsters, Local Union No. 175, AFL-CIO, 310 NLRB No. 140, 25 March 1993, esp. 839 (quote), NLRB website, accessed 10 April 2013.

77. Ibid., esp. 839.

78. Howe K. Sipes Company & Furniture Workers' Division, International Union of Electronic, Electrical, Salaried, Machine and Furniture Workers, AFL-CIO, Local 282, 319 NLRB No. 6, 21 September 1995, 32, NLRB website, accessed 12 April 2013.

79. Ibid., 34.

80. Ibid., 32.

81. For James McDonald's threatening statements, see USA McDonald Corporation d/b/a Norco Products & International Brotherhood of Teamsters, Chauffeurs, Warehousemen and Helpers of America, Local Union No. 2, AFL-CIO, 288 NLRB No. 151, 31 May 1988, 1418, NLRB website, accessed 8 April 2013.

82. Ibid., 1422–23.

83. Ibid., 1421–24. Pollack's remarks are referenced on p. 1422.

84. Nyari Odette, Inc. & Local 274, Hotel & Restaurant Employees & Bartenders International Union 229 NLRB No. 4, 21 April 1977, 141, NLRB website, accessed 8 April 2013.

85. On work cultures in restaurants during the late twentieth century, see Anthony Bourdain, *Kitchen Confidential: Adventures in the Culinary Underbelly* (New York: HarperCollins, 2000); Steve Dublanica, *Waiter Rant: Thanks for the Tip—Confessions of a Cynical Waiter* (New York: HarperCollins, 2008).

86. Nyari Odette, Inc., 229 NLRB No. 4, 143.

87. Ibid., 138.

88. Thomas L. Haskell, "The Curious Persistence of Rights Talk in the 'Age of Interpretation,'" *Journal of American History* 74:3 (1987): 988. For helpful examples of the persistence of civil rights era language and politics in the 1970s and the 1980s, see William H. Chafe, *The Unfinished Journey: America Since World War II*, 6th ed. (New York: Oxford University Press, 2007), 412, 413, 414–21; Troy, *Morning in America*, 266, 269–70; Borstelmann, *The 1970s*, esp. 73–108; Joe W. Trotter and Jared N. Day, *Race and Renaissance: African Americans in Pittsburgh Since World War II* (Pittsburgh: University of Pittsburgh Press, 2010); Windham, "Signing Up the Shipyard," 37–38.

89. *Chicago Tribune*, 30 January 1987, TI26430041, LTDL. On human rights discourses during the 1970s, see Barbara Keys, *Reclaiming American Virtue: The Human Rights Revolution of the 1970s* (Cambridge, Mass.: Harvard University Press, 2014).

90. Curt Suplee, "Walls of Opinion Close In On Smokers," *Orlando Sentinel*, 16 April 1987, http://articles.orlandosentinel.com/1987–04–16/lifestyle/0120260196_1_smoking-quit-non-smokers, accessed 20 June 2011.

91. "A Precious Freedom: The Right to Be Stupid," *Seattle Times*, 23 January 1987, TI26462055, LTDL.

92. Andrew Ross, *No-Collar: The Humane Workplace and Its Hidden Costs* (Philadelphia: Temple University Press, 2003), 216; Jill Andresky Fraser, *The White-Collar Sweatshop: The Deterioration of Work and Its Rewards in Corporate America* (New York: W. W. Norton & Company, 2002).

93. I am reminded of historian Sara Evans' insights about how the experience of conflict at the "juncture of public and private" can give rise to resistance politics and social movements in my considerations of worker-smokers' personal experiences with addiction to nicotine and their frustrations with no-smoking policies. Evans' examinations of women's engagement with the politics of sexism in social movements certainly gave rise to significantly more prominent and more broadly based forms of organizing and political activism. See Sara Evans, *Personal Politics: The Roots of Women's Liberation in the Civil Rights Movement & the New Left* (New York: Vintage Books, 1980), 21.

94. Nancy Skelton, "No More Ifs, Ands, Butts—It's Law," *Los Angeles Times*, 14 April 1985, A30.

95. Mary Ann Glendon, *Rights Talk: The Impoverishment of Political Discourse* (New York: Free Press, 1991), x, xi; see also Melvyn Dubofsky, *The State and Labor in Modern America* (Chapel Hill: University of North Carolina Press, 1994), 235. On the themes of backlash politics and conservatism since the era of the 1960s, see Jeffrey R. Dudas, "In the Name of Equal Rights: 'Special' Rights and the Politics of Resentment in Post–Civil Rights America," *Law & Society Review* 39:4 (2005): 723–57; Michael J. Klarman, "How *Brown* Changed Race Relations: The Backlash Thesis," *Journal of American History* 81:1 (1994): 81–118; Lisa McGirr, *Suburban Warriors: The Origins of the New American Right* (Princeton, N.J.: Princeton University Press, 2002); Joseph Crespino, *In Search of Another Country: Mississippi and the Conservative Counterrevolution* (Princeton, N.J.: Princeton University Press, 2007); Susan Faludi, *Backlash: The Undeclared War Against American Women* (New York: Anchor Books, 1992); Phillips-Fein, *Invisible Hands*; Borstelmann, *The 1970s*, 45–53.

96. George I. Lovell, *This Is Not Civil Rights: Discovering Rights Talk in 1939 America* (Chicago: University of Chicago Press, 2012), xi.

97. Dudas, "In the Name of Equal Rights," 732.

98. Leah R. Ware to Susan M. Stuntz, 7 June 1989, TI01350447, LTDL, emphasis in original.

99. Barbara Klismick to Susan M. Stuntz, 10 October 1988, TI01352231, LTDL; Sharon Lang to Susan M. Stuntz, 2 April 1989, TI01350711, LTDL; Edward F. Beckham to Susan M. Stuntz, n.d. (1989?), TI01352245, LTDL; Mary B. Deuby to Susan M. Stuntz, 19 October 1988, TI01350176, LTDL; Howard Alferd to Sharon ——, 10 May 1989, TI01350499, LTDL.

100. Tobacco Institute, *Smoking in the Workplace: Some Considerations* (1991), pamphlet, TI46660977, LTDL.

101. Orange County Chamber of Commerce, "Responses from Questionnaires RE: Business Smoking Policies" (1991), 3, TCAL0247088, LTDL.

102. Ibid., 1.

103. McGirr, *Suburban Warriors*; Eric Foner, *The Story of American Freedom* (New York: W. W. Norton & Company, 1998), 312–13, 315.

104. Orange County Chamber of Commerce, "Responses from Questionnaires," p. 3, 6, 8, 10, emphases in original.

105. Ibid., p. 10, 12, emphases in original.

CONCLUSION

1. John Fred Cirillo to R. J. Reynolds Tobacco Company et al., 22 September 1998, 520760899, Legacy Tobacco Documents Library, University of California, San Francisco, http://legacy.library.ucsf.edu (hereafter LTDL).

2. "Nicotine and Tobacco In-Depth Report," *New York Times*, n.d., http://www.nytimes.com/health/guides/disease/nicotine-withdrawal/print.html, accessed 30 November 2013.

3. "Gallup Survey Results," PR Newswire Association, 1 August 1994, TIMN 327242, LTDL. For a different estimate, see Stanton A. Glantz, John Slade, Lisa A. Bero, Peter Hanauer, and Deborah E. Barnes, *The Cigarette Papers*, foreword by C. Everett Koop (Berkeley: University of California Press, 1996), 59. In this overview of tobacco industry practices during the second half of the twentieth century, the authors estimate that 90 percent of smokers' quit attempts fail.

4. On the argument for abolition, see Robert N. Proctor, *Golden Holocaust: Origins of the Cigarette Catastrophe and the Case for Abolition* (Berkeley: University of California Press, 2011).

5. David M. Daughton, DeWolf Roberts, Kashinath D. Patil, and Stephen I. Rennard, "Smoking Cessation in the Workplace: Evaluation of Relapse Factors," *Preventive Medicine* 19 (1990): 227–30.

6. See Frederick Winslow Taylor, *The Principles of Scientific Management* (New York: Harper & Brothers Publishers, 1913); along with Joanne B. Ciulla, *The Working Life: The Promise and Betrayal of Modern Work* (New York: Three Rivers Press, 2000), 93–95; David Montgomery, *The Fall of the House of Labor: The Workplace, the State, and American Labor Activism, 1865–1925* (Cambridge, UK: Cambridge University Press, 1989), esp. 178–79. On "incentive theory," see Douglas Mitchell, Flora Ida Ortiz, and Tedi K. Mitchell, *Work Orientation and Job Performance: The Cultural Basis of Teaching Rewards and Incentives* (Albany: State University of New York Press, 1987), 32.

7. Mitchell, Ortiz, and Mitchell, *Work Orientation and Job Performance*, 32.

8. NBC Nightly News transcript, 11 November 1975, Radio TV Reports, Inc., TIMN275779, LTDL. On the long history of employer paternalism in the context of twentieth-century wage labor, see David L. Carlton, "Paternalism and Southern Textile Labor: A Historiographical Review," in *Race, Class, and Community in Southern Labor History*, ed. Gary M. Fink and Merl E. Reed (Tuscaloosa: University of Alabama Press, 1994), 17–26; David Leverenz, *Paternalism Incorporated: Fables of American Fatherhood, 1865–1940* (Ithaca, N.Y.: Cornell University Press, 2003); Ciulla, *Working Life*, 96–97.

9. Lindsey Gruson, "Employers Get Tough on Smoking at Work," *New York Times*, 14 March 1985, B1.

10. "Workplace Smoking: Corporate Practices and Developments," *BNA's Employee Relations Weekly*, 23 October 1989, 22, TIMN303800, LTDL.

11. Diane Faught to Tobacco Institute, 23 March 1991, TIO1351713, LTDL.

12. Jack Healy, "Legal Use of Marijuana Clashes With Job Rules," *New York Times*, 7 September 2014, http://www.nytimes.com/2014/09/08/us/legal-use-of-marijuana-clashes-with-workplace-drug-testing.html, accessed 22 September 2015; Harriet Brown, "For Obese People, Prejudice in Plain Sight," *New York Times*, 15 March 2010, http://www.nytimes.com/2010/03/16/health/16essa.html, accessed 21 September 2015; Damon Darlin, "Extra Weight, Higher Costs," *New York Times*, 2 December 2006, http://www.nytimes.com/2006/12/02/business/02money.html, accessed 21 September 2015; Gary Rivlin, "The Long Shadow of Bad Credit in a Job Search," *New York Times*, 11 May 2013, http://www.nytimes.com/2013/05/12/business/employers-pull-applicants-credit-reports.html, accessed 18 September 2015.

13. "Gallup Survey Results"; John R. Hughes, "Motivating and Helping Smokers to Stop Smoking," *Journal of General Internal Medicine* 18:12 (December 2003): 1053–1057; Glantz et al., *Cigarette Papers*, 59.

14. Tamar Nordenberg, "It's Quittin' Time: Smokers Need Not Rely on Willpower Alone," http:www.fda.gov/fdac/features/1997/797_smoke.html, accessed 12 August 2014.

15. "Gallup Survey Results"; "Plan to Become an Ex-Smoker for Good," *New York Times*, 12 November 2012, http://well.blogs.nytimes.com/2012/11/12/plan-to-become-an-ex-smoker-for-good, accessed 30 November 2013.

16. "Gallup Survey Results."

17. The Gallup Poll, "Tobacco and Smoking" (2013), http://www.gallup.com/poll/1717/tobacco-smoking, accessed 2 December 2013.

18. The Gallup Poll, "Tobacco and Smoking"; "Nicotine and Tobacco In-Depth Report."

19. "Nicotine and Tobacco In-Depth Report."

20. "Nicotine and Tobacco In-Depth Report."

21. "Nicotine and Tobacco In-Depth Report"; The Gallup Poll, "Tobacco and Smoking."

22. Robert Pear, "Percentage of Americans Lacking Health Coverage Falls Again," *New York Times*, 17 September 2013, http://www.nytimes.com/2013/09/18/us/percentage-of-americans-lacking-health-coverage-falls-again.html, accessed 9 December 2013.

23. On the Glenbeigh Hospital program, see Jon Nordheimer, "Hard-Core Smokers Face Their Addiction," *New York Times*, 3 August 1988, http://www.nytimes.com/1988/08/03/garden/hard-core-smokers-face-their-addiction.html, accessed 9 December 2013; on the Mayo Clinic program, see Gina Kolkata, "Hard-Core Smokers, Last Ditch Remedies," *New York Times*, 29 July 1997, http://www.nytimes.com/1997/07/29/science/hard-core-smokers-last-ditch-remedies.html, accessed 9 December 2013.

24. "Nicotine and Tobacco In-Depth Report"; Jeffrey M. Jones, "Smoking Habits Stable; Most Would Like to Quit," 18 July 2006, http://www.gallup.com/poll/23791/smoking-habits-stable-most-would, accessed 30 November 2013.

25. The Gallup Poll, "Tobacco and Smoking"; Lizette Alvarez, "The Holdouts," *New York Times*, 27 August 2010, www.nytimes.com/2010/08/29/nyregion/29smokers.html, accessed 13 August 2013.

26. Alvarez, "Holdouts."

27. The Gallup Poll, "Tobacco and Smoking."

28. Sabrina Tavernise and Robert Gebeloff, "Smoking Proves Hard to Shake Among the Poor," *New York Times*, 24 March 2014, http://www.nytimes.com/2014/03/25/health/smoking-stays-stubbornly-high-among-the-poor.html, accessed 3 April 2014. On social and cultural obstacles to smoking cessation in rural areas, see Karen M. Butler et al., "Culturally-Specific Smoking Cessation Outreach in a Rural Community," *Public Health Nursing* 30:1 (2013): 44–54; T. D. Hutcheson et al., "Understanding Smoking Cessation in Rural Communities," *Journal of Rural Health* 24:2 (2008): 116–24; American Lung Association, *Cutting Tobacco's Roots: Tobacco Use in Rural Communities* (2012), http://www.lung.org/assets/documents/publications/lung-disease-data/cutting-tobaccos-rural-roots.pdf, accessed 30 March 2014.

29. Alvarez, "Holdouts"; Tavernise and Gebelof, "Smoking Proves Hard to Shake Among the Poor." On "denormalization," see Ronald Bayer and Kathleen E. Bachynski, "Banning Smoking in Parks and on Beaches: Science, Policy, and the Politics of Denormalization," *Health Affairs* 32:7 (2013): 1291–92.

30. Tavernise and Gebeloff, "Smoking Proves Hard to Shake Among the Poor"; Matt Richtel, "The E-Cigarette Industry, Waiting to Exhale," *New York Times*, 26 October 2013,

http://www.nytimes.com/2013/10/27/business/the-e-cigarette-industry-waiting-to-exhale.html, accessed 10 January 2014.

31. Alvarez, "The Holdouts."

32. "E-Cigarettes: Questions and Answers," http://www.fda.gov/ForConsumers/ConsumerUpdates/ucm225210.htm, accessed 31 December 2013.

33. Sabrina Tavernise, "Use of Electronic Cigarettes Grows," New York Times, 28 February 2013, http://www.nytimes.com/2013/03/01/health/use-of-electronic-cigarettes-grows.html, accessed 8 June 2013.

34. Liz Alderman, "E-Cigarettes Are in Vogue and At a Crossroads," New York Times, 12 June 2013, http://www.nytimes.com/2013/06/13/business/e-cigarettes-are-in-vogue-and-at-a-crossroads.html, accessed 18 June 2013; Sabrina Tavernise and Robert Gebeloff, "In a New Divide, Smoking Is Becoming a Habit of the Poor," New York Times, 25 March 2014, A17.

35. Tavernise, "Use of Electronic Cigarettes Grows." The statistic for e-cigarette sales is for 2012.

36. Alderman, "E-Cigarettes Are in Vogue and At a Crossroads."

37. "Electronic Cigarettes (E-Cigarettes)," http://www.fda.gov/newssevents/public healthfocus/ucm172906.htm, accessed 2 December 2013.

38. Jen Christensen, "E-Cigarettes: Healthy Tool or Gateway Device?" CNN Health, 13 September 2013, http://www.cnn.com/2013/09/12/health/e-cigarettes-debate, accessed 2 December 2013.

39. Christensen, "E-Cigarettes"; Sabrina Tavernise and Barry Meier, "For E-Cigarettes, the Regulatory Battle Now Begins," New York Times, 24 April 2014, http://www.nytimes.com/2014/04/25/business/for-e-cigarettes-the-regulatory-battle-now-begins.html, accessed 27 April 2014. Diethylene glycol is a toxic chemical that is used frequently in the manufacturing of numerous "industrial products," including antifreeze. See Leo J. Schep, Robin J. Slaughter, Wayne A. Temple, and D. Michael G. Beasley, "Diethylene Glycol Poisoning," Clinical Toxicology 47:6 (2009): 525.

40. Glantz et al., Cigarette Papers, 74–76.

41. Allan M. Brandt, The Cigarette Century: The Rise, Fall, and Deadly Persistence of the Product That Defined America (New York: Basic Books, 2009), 364; Glantz et al., Cigarette Papers, 77; Richard Kluger, Ashes to Ashes: America's Hundred-Year Cigarette War, the Public Health, and the Unabashed Triumph of Philip Morris (New York: Vintage, 1997), 599–603.

42. "Tobacco Companies Bet on Electronic Cigarettes," CBS News, http://www.cbsnews.com/news/tobacco-companies-bet-on-electronic-cigarettes, accessed 9 January 2013.

43. Stuart Elliot, "Campaigns for E-Cigarettes Borrow from Tobacco's Heyday," New York Times, 5 December 2012, http://www.nytimes.com/2012/12/06/business/media/campaigns-for-electronic-cigarettes-borrow.html, accessed 12 December 2013. For examples of Blu e-cigarette commercials, see "'Freedom' Featuring Jenny McCarthy," http://www.youtube.com/watch?v=mUJ5W2pz1XI, accessed 13 January 2014; "Stephen Dorff Rises from the Ashes," http://www.youtube.com/watch?v=VZishwAt_RM, accessed 13 January 2014.

44. Kia Gregory, "New York Council Votes to Ban Foam Food Containers and to Curb E-Cigarette Smoking," New York Times, 19 December 2013, http://www.nytimes.com/2013/12/20/nyregion/new-york-council-votes-to-ban-foam-food-containers-and-to-curb-e-cigarette-smoking.html, accessed 9 January 2014.

45. Lindsay Fox, "Looser Rules for Life-Saving E-Cigs," New York Times, 20 August 2013, http://www.nytimes.com/roomfordebate/2013/08/20/the-ambiguous-allure-of-the-e-cig/looser-rules-for-life-saving-e-cigs, accessed 9 January 2014.

46. Amy L. Fairchild and James Colgrove, "The Case for Tolerating E-Cigarettes," *New York Times*, 8 December 2013, http://www.nytimes.com/2013/12/09/opinion/the-case-for-tolerating-e-cigarettes.html, accessed 9 January 2014. On harm reduction, see the helpful overview in Canadian Paediatric Society, "Harm Reduction: An Approach To Reducing Risky Health Behaviours in Adolescents," *Pediatric Child Health* 13:1 (2008): 53–56.

47. Iain Gately, *Tobacco: A Cultural History of How an Exotic Plant Seduced a Civilization* (New York: Grove Press, 2001), 66.

Index

Page numbers in italics refer to illustrations.